TEACHING ALL NATIONS

TEACHING ALL NATIONS

INTERROGATING THE MATTHEAN GREAT COMMISSION

MITZI J. SMITH AND JAYACHITRA LALITHA, EDITORS

Fortress Press
Minneapolis

TEACHING ALL NATIONS

Interrogating the Matthean Great Commission

Cover design: Tory Herman

Cover image: Gianni Dagli Orti / The Art Archive at Art Resource, NY

Library of Congress Cataloging-in-Publication Data is available

Print ISBN: 978-1-4514-7049-9

eBook ISBN: 978-1-4514-7989-8

The paper used in this publication meets the minimum requirements of American National Standard for Information Sciences — Permanence of Paper for Printed Library Materials, ANSI Z329.48-1984.

Manufactured in the U.S.A.

This book was produced using PressBooks.com, and PDF rendering was done by PrinceXML.

CONTENTS

Part I. Colonial Missions and the Great Commission: Re-Membering the Past

Part II. Womanist, Feminist, and Postcolonial Criticisms and the Great Commission

Contributors

Karen D. Crozier (PhD, Claremont School of Theology) holds a joint appointment as Assistant Professor of Practical Theology at Fresno Pacific Biblical Seminary and Director of Faculty Development (Diversity, Peace and Justice) at Fresno Pacific University. She is currently working on a book entitled *Redeeming Racism and Other Isms: A Practical Theology of Healing and Hope.*

Lynne St. Clair Darden (PhD, Drew University) is Assistant Professor of New Testament at the Interdenominational Theological Center in Atlanta, Georgia.

Lord Elorm-Donkor (PhD, University of Manchester) is the District Pastor of the Church of Pentecost in Birmingham, UK, and was recently been appointed the Principal of the new Birmingham Christian College. He received his BA in Theology from the Cornerstone Christian College and the University of Stellenbosch in South Africa; MA in Theology (Missions Studies) from the University of Manchester; MPhil in Pentecostal and Charismatic Studies from the University of Birmingham. His areas of research include the interaction between the gospel and African culture and philosophy, theological ethics in the virtue framework, and Wesleyan studies.

Rohan P. Gideon is a Doctoral Research Student in the University of Manchester. He has taught Christian Theology at the Tamilnadu Theological Seminary, Madurai, India. He is author of *Child Labour in India: Challenges for Theological Thinking and Christian Ministry in India* and has written articles concerning children's agency in Indian liberation theology and missions.

Dave Gosse (PhD, Howard University) is a lecturer in the Department of History, University of West Indies Mona. His doctorate is in Caribbean/Latin American History, and he teaches several courses in African, Latin American, Caribbean, and North American History. He specializes in nineteenth- and twentieth-century Jamaican history. He is the author of *Abolition and Plantation Management in Nineteenth Century Jamaica.*

Jayachitra Lalitha (PhD, Serampore University, India) is Associate Professor of New Testament and Greek, Dean of Women's Studies, and Coordinator of Church Women Centre at the Tamilnadu Theological Seminary, Madurai, Tamilnadu, India. Her research interests include post-Pauline literature, postcolonial biblical hermeneutics, and feminism. She co-chairs the World Christianity Group of the American Academy of Religion.

MarShondra Scott Lawrence, LLPC (MDiv, Ashland Theological Seminary/Detroit) is a chaplain, counselor, adjunct professor, and community developer. Lawrence works with people who are homeless and/or are in substance abuse recovery. She also works with urban organizations committed to the well-being of residents and neighborhoods.

Michelle Sungshin Lim (PhD, Drew University) is Executive Director of the Institute of Education and Transformation. She is an activist, teacher/scholar/feminist theologian, an avid world traveler, and painter of theological themes. Formerly, Dr. Lim was Assistant Professor of Constructive Theology and Culture and Associate Director of the Korean DMin Program at New York Theological Seminary.

Beatrice Okyere-Manu (PhD, University of KwaZulu Natal Pietermaritzburg, South Africa) is a Lecturer in Ethics Studies, School of Religion, Philosophy and Classics (SRPC) at the University of KwaZulu-Natal South Africa. Her research interests are in HIV and AIDS, ethical issues in gender and sexuality, and African Women's Social and Economic Developmental Issues.

Anthony G. Reddie (PhD, University of Birmingham) is the editor of *Black Theology: An International Journal.* His doctorate is in Education (with Theology). Reddie also earned a BA in History from the University of Birmingham. He has written over fifty essays and articles on Christian education and black theology. He is the author and editor of fourteen books. His latest book is *SCM Core Text: Black Theology* (2012).

June C. Rivers (PhD, Michigan State University) has been a Youth on a Mission (YOAM) Coordinator since 1989 for the Church of God in Christ. In this capacity, she leads teams of youths and adults to engage in short-term missionary work for two weeks in an international country. June is also a retired educator with a BA and MA from Wayne State University and an MDiv in Counseling from Ashland Theological Seminary/Detroit. Her doctorate is in Elementary Education.

Mitzi J. Smith (PhD, Harvard University) is Associate Professor of New Testament and Early Christian Studies at Ashland Theological Seminary in Detroit. She holds an MA degree in Black Studies from The Ohio State University and an MDiv from Howard University School of Divinity. She is the author of *The Literary Construction of the Other in the Acts of the Apostles: Charismatics, the Jews, and Women* (Eugene, OR: Pickwick, 2011) and is editing *I Found God in Me: A Womanist Biblical Hermeneutics Reader* (Eugene, OR: Cascade Books).

Sheila F. Winborne (PhD, Harvard University) is Visiting Lecturer in Religious Studies, Department of Philosophy and Religion, at Northeastern University with a specialization Religion and Visual Culture.

Gosnell L. Yorke (PhD, McGill University, Canada) is of Caribbean origin and currently is Professor of Biblical Studies and Bible Translation in the School of Religion and Theology at Northern Caribbean University, Jamaica. Formerly, he taught in the School of Religion, Philosophy, and Classics at the University of KwaZulu-Natal, South Africa; served as Professor *Extraordinarius* in the College of Human Sciences, University of South Africa; and as a Translation Consultant for the United Bible Societies (Africa Area). He has published in the areas of biblical studies, the Bible in Africa and its Diaspora, and Bible translation. He contributed to *The Africana Bible: Reading Israel's Scriptures from Africa and Its Diaspora* (Fortress Press, 2009); *Handbook of Theological Education in Africa* (World Council of Churches, 2012); and the *Encyclopedia of Caribbean Religions* (Illinois University Press, 2013).

Foreword

Gosnell L. Yorke

In recent years and in academic circles including biblical studies, there has been a steady increase and crescendo in the volume of postcolonial voices emanating from the "Global South"; from those who, historically, have been rendered voiceless and considered practically of little or no value. And perhaps this increase in both voices and volume, in terms of both quantity and intensity, is best exemplified in the ever-growing corpus of scholarship that seeks to interrogate the dominant and dominating paradigms that have marked and marred academic, ecclesiastical, and other forms of discourse.

Those paradigms have been creatively collocated over the years in three alliterative phrases: "Christianity, Commerce, and Civilization"; "Missionaries, Merchants, and Mercenaries"; and "God, Gold, and Glory." The present point, essentially, is this: the Bible, the Book of the Church, has sometimes found itself in bad company. It has had a rather ambivalent impact on those who have been brought within its sphere of influence in that it has not only served as a liberating and humanizing agent in some cases, but as a blunt and brutal instrument of economic, academic, gender-based, and other forms of oppression in other cases as well.

This volume comes as a timely demonstration of precisely that. It presents us with a multidisciplinary onslaught on, and a sustained critique of, what has long been a focus text in ecclesiastical and now especially in missiological circles, to wit, the so-called Great Commission, Matt. 28:16-20. This volume takes part in the on-going postcolonial push to problematize, to prod, and to provide us with new and exciting ways of seeing and saying things, but from the "underside"—from those who have been pushed aside to the periphery. Such pushed-aside people include women of all colors and men of color—be they Africans or others who share similar existential locations. The volume points to those "others" who usually are not numbered among the privileged and the powerful but instead find themselves among the despised and the rejected. In short, the volume is really about the demographic bifurcation that exists between "the West and the Rest," as ideologically understood—a bifurcation that the traditional execution of the Great Commission, as is shown over and over again here, has played no small part in reinscribing.

If anything, then, this volume, which is wide-ranging in its reach in terms of both geography and culture, is a clarion call for a more authentic and humanizing mission as God in Christ would wish; a mission that is to be distinguished from the sometimes dehumanizing effects that, wittingly or unwittingly, the Matthean Great Commission has had and continues to have on those who, ostensibly, are meant to be its beneficiaries. It is a volume that I would therefore commit to the reader's careful attention with the hope, in the words of the late great British New Testament scholar C. H. Dodd, that it would "tease our minds into active thought."

Introduction

Mitzi J. Smith and Jayachitra Lalitha

"The Spirit of the Lord is upon me because he has anointed me to bring good news to the poor. He has sent me to proclaim release to the captives and recovery of sight to the blind, to let the oppressed go free, to proclaim the year of the Lord's favor."
(Luke 4:18-19 NRSV)

"We trust that during the entire time you are on earth, you will compel and use your zeal in making the barbarian nations come to know God...not only through edicts and admonitions, but also through force and arms if necessary so that their souls may share in the kingdom of heaven."
—Pope Clement VII[1]

And Jesus came and said to them, "All authority in heaven and earth has been given to me. Go therefore and make disciples of all nations, baptizing them in the name of the Father and of the Son and of the Holy Spirit, and teaching them to obey everything I have commanded you. And remember, I am with you always, to the end of the age."
(Matt. 28:18-20 NRSV)

Throughout the history of European Christian imperialism's global conquest and seizure of lands, wealth, and peoples and the concomitant Christian evangelization of the colonized, including in the Americas, the *evangelizing conquest* method prevailed over the *missionary action* approach.[2] The missionary action approach hoped to appeal to the reason of the natives through convincing arguments so that they would voluntarily become Christians. The violent evangelizing conquest method that dominated foreign missions proposed to gain control over native populations by any means necessary in

---

1. Luis N. Rivera, *A Violent Evangelism: The Political and Religious Conquest of the Americas* (Louisville: Westminster John Knox, 1992), 218.

2. Ibid., 229.

1

order to facilitate their conversion to Christianity, and, by extension, the speedy and less complicated dominance and enculturation of colonized lands and peoples.[3] Consequently, peoples who refused evangelistic strategies were forced under threat of death to convert to Christianity. European imperialism (and later American colonialism) in partnership with Christian evangelism spread their own tables with the resources of foreign lands, rendering the native people oppressed and impoverished. As Bishop Desmond Tutu has asserted, "They [the missionaries] said 'let us close our eyes and pray.' When we opened them, we had the bible, and they had the land." [4]

Katie Cannon argues in her article "Christian Imperialism and the Transatlantic Slave Trade" that Christian imperialism and the Matthean Great Commission as the biblical mandate for European missionaries to take the gospel to foreign lands were two sides of the same coin.[5] Cannon coined two terms that name and describe the partnership between imperialism and Christian missions. The first term, a *missiologic of imminent parousia*, refers to the connection created between the imminence of the *parousia* (or the Second Coming of Christ) as understood in the Bible and cultural rationale legitimating particular mission strategies of Christian imperialists.[6] The second term Cannon coined is *theologic of racialized normativity*, which refers to white supremist ideologies that declared that God ordained Africans and other foreigners as "natural slaves" and whites or Europeans as their "natural masters."[7] Based upon this type of ideology, white supremacists declared that true obedience to God or Jesus Christ was demonstrated when Africans submitted to and worked diligently for their masters.

We would also conceptualize a *theologic of normalized othering* and *missiologic pedagogy of perpetual submission* operative more recently in missional activities of fundamentalists and some evangelical Christians with their renewed urgency to fulfill the so-called Great Commission to the untaught (or insufficiently taught) and unsubdued *others*— an urgency that subordinates and ignores real social justice needs but continues to call for pedagogical submission to white Christian norms and ideas. Gospel and evangelization have been essentialized among too many as only or primarily preaching and teaching *the other*. Thus, the Gospel witness as the embodiment or incarnation (the

---

3. Ibid., 226–28.

4. Steven D. Gish, *Desmond Tutu: A Biography* (Westport, CT: Greenwood, 2004), 101.

5. Katie Cannon, "Christian Imperialism and the Transatlantic Slave Trade," *Journal of Feminist Studies in Religion* 24, no.1 (2008): 127–34.

6. Ibid., 128.

7. Ibid., 130–32.

praxis) of love and social justice is marginalized or ignored. But as Paulo Freire asserts, "There is no true word that is not at the same time a praxis."[8] Human existence is nourished with "true words" emerging from human dialogue, and true dialogue "cannot exist, however, in the absence of a profound love for the world and for people."[9]

This project explores the history, use, and interpretation of the so-called Great Commission (Matt. 28:18-20; cf. Mark 16:14-18; Luke 24:44-49; John 20:19-23; *Didache* 7:1) and its impact as the metanarrative for foreign and domestic missions. In Matt. 28:18-20, Jesus, with the authority of heaven and earth, sent his disciples to teach all nations baptizing them in the name of the Father, the Son, and the Holy Spirit. *All nations*, as the object of teaching, are historically and traditionally the subordinated *other*. Integral to the project of empire building is the colonizing, marginalizing, and othering of conquered nations and peoples. Historically, missionaries in partnership with European colonizers (or vice versa) in the quest to expand their territories, wealth, and power have colonized indigenous peoples, enslaved and shipped them off to foreign shores, demonized their culture, especially their religious beliefs and practices, constructed them as *other* over against their white Christian selves, and imposed upon them white Christian behavioral norms. As we interrogate the Great Commission, we do so recognizing the historical and contemporary presence and vestiges of the empire's shadows that must be underscored in biblical criticism,[10] and in other critical disciplines. We must ask how the other is viewed and represented.[11] We must also ask what is the impact of this gaze and representation on the other, and how is it manifested?

What happens when we read differently, rejecting the dominant culture's rendering of Matt. 28:18-20 as the guiding hermeneutical lens for understanding and doing missions and missional pedagogy? The Great Commission demands or encourages a passive, banking model of education that does not value dialogue. Certain people, historically white Christians, have been (and in some places and spaces still are) considered the primary and most competent teachers of all others; and many marginalized peoples have been so convinced, worshipping at the altar of white superiority and sacrificing their own agency of critical engagement, self-definition, and cultural identity. Dialogue is deterred and proscribed by persons who consider themselves "the

---

8. Paulo Freire, *Pedagogy of the Oppressed* (New York: Continuum, 1997), 68.

9. Ibid., 69–70.

10. Fernando Segovia, *Decolonizing Biblical Studies: A View from the Margins* (Maryknoll, NY: Orbis Books), 130.

11. Ibid., 126.

owners of truth and knowledge, for whom all non-members" are other.[12] When one group reserves for themselves the sole authority to define, name, and order the world, dialogue cannot occur.[13]

The iconic labeling of Matt. 28:18-20 as the Great Commission provided scriptural rationale for the invasion, colonization, and biased teaching of others while compartmentalizing, totally ignoring, or devaluing the humanity and justice rights of others. The Great Commission elevates teaching above alleviating poverty, healing the diseased, sheltering and clothing the poor with dignity, a living wage and affordable decent housing, and being compassionately present for the imprisoned. In fact, some contemporary ministries have and continue to withhold food and clothing from desperate people unless they listen to a sermon.[14] After the Haitian earthquake in 2010, some Christian groups scrambled to reach Haiti to teach Haitians the gospel, even while many crawled from under the rubble praising God.[15] The elevation of the Great Commission above social justice and love might largely explain the plethora or multiplicity of urban churches that fail to address the suffering and poverty around them. Education, especially religious education and evangelization, should be "the practice of freedom,"[16] of social *and* spiritual liberty.

By focusing primarily on teaching and preaching as the realization of the gospel, we create a hierarchical and dualistic class system of teachers and non-teachers; privileged, elite, properly educated white males are anointed/commissioned by the dominant class of privileged, elite, educated white males to go and to mentor and send others, others predominantly like themselves. And the command to love one's neighbor is only possible if it does not interfere with the Great Commission or loving one's neighbor is redefined and reconfigured to align with the priority of the Great Commission. The priority Jesus gave

12. Freire, *Pedagogy of the Oppressed*, 71.

13. Ibid., 69–70.

14. I have known and know of churches and ministries that insist that the homeless and poor sit through an hour-long sermon as a prerequisite for receiving a free meal.

15. Cathy Lynn Grossman, "Haiti earthquake blame game: God or the devil?" January 17, 2010. Online: http://content.usatoday.com/communities/Religion/post/2010/01/haiti-earthquake-blame-game-god-or-the-devil/1#.Uvqlxu8XfW4;. Arthur Brice, "Many Haitians' religious faith unshaken by earthquake." January 19, 2010. Online: http://www.cnn.com/2010/WORLD/americas/01/18/haiti.earthquake.faith/index.html. In my Facebook newsfeed I read posts by some evangelical Christians in which they were recruiting volunteers to go and evangelize Haitians while many were still lying under the rubble.

16. bell hooks, *Talking Back: Thinking Feminist. Thinking Black* (Boston: South End Press, 1989), 72. See also Freire, *Pedagogy of the Oppressed*, 74.

to the proactive moral behaviors or acts of justice listed at Matt. 25:35-45 is subordinated to the Great Commission. The Great Commission and its emphasis on teaching draws us away from or blinds us to the importance of contexts, social justice, and the significant and diverse ways that other persons, including children, can contribute to the task of spreading the gospel and of being the presence of God in the world. The particular contexts and needs of different peoples are sacrificed in favor of a universal canopy under which an uncritical idolatry of the Great Commission has summoned and hypnotized us.

In this volume, we attempt to critique and raise contextually relevant questions about the Great Commission. What impact does the very conceptualization of the Great Commission have upon those who see themselves as the commissioned and those to whom they are commissioned? Does it promote a mutual humanity or an inhumanity of one toward the other and thus the dehumanization of both the commissioned and his *others*? How does the identification of Matt. 28:18-20 as the Great Commission support the subordination of non-literate peoples to literate peoples, of women to men, of one ethnic people or social class to another ethnic group or socially constructed class, and social justice to teaching? How has the Great Commission (its construction and deployment) emerged from and colluded with imperialism, racism, sexism, classism, casteism, heterosexism, and ageism? What voices are misrepresented or muted and what voices are privileged? Is it possible to discuss and engage in missions in non-oppressive and non-patronizing ways, particularly if we have consented to be wed to a text like Matt. 28:18-20 as a universal metanarrative? Is it even necessary to have such a metanarrative? How has and does the Great Commission limit our geographic or spatial understanding of where or among whom we should do missions? How might contemporary missions be more liberating and reflect the love of God for all God's creation, and what Scriptures might inform and help us accomplish this task? And as Musa Dube asks, "How can postcolonial [or neo-colonial] subjects read the bible without perpetuating . . . a self-serving paradigm of constructing one group as superior to another?" What is our ethical duty?[17]

This project is also about uncritical loyalty to religious terms and phrases that we allow to circumscribe our own agency and analytical thinking. We sometimes permit titles/headings, nomenclature, and religious jargon to usurp our privilege, and the necessity, of reading, rereading, and reading again Scripture, listening for God's voice anew. Because they are codified in Bible translations and commentaries, we trust the titles/headings, names, religious

---

17. Musa W. Dube, *Postcolonial Feminist Interpretation of the Bible* (St. Louis: Chalice, 2000), 15.

jargon, and labels constructed by scholars to be our theological and interpretive guides or to constitute, *in nuce*, definitive interpretations that we dare not question or transgress. The codified nomenclature, titles, and religious jargon, stymie any further need of reflection, revision, rereading, or interpretation. We no longer need to think seriously, extensively, or differently about the subject or the text subsumed under the heading or nomenclature, except maybe to reinforce the tradition. The nomenclature, heading, or jargon predominates.

It is difficult to get Bible students to transcend the titles, jargon, or headings that precede and are meant to summarize blocks of texts in their Bibles. They cannot think creatively because they consider the title to be sacred, pure, objective truth that describes how they should read the text. To interrogate the interpretative inscriptions is considered disrespectful to the text or a mark of arrogance; as Christians and students of scripture, they are hermeneutically constrained by embedded titles and nomenclature. Traditional Christian nomenclature becomes sacralized, iconized, and untouchable, except by an authorized few. The hermeneutical dust has settled and students are convinced that we know all we need to know about a story, text, phrase, or idea. A lot of dust has settled on the Great Commission.

In this volume scholars (and nonscholars) in various disciplines, including biblical studies, history, postcolonial criticism, womanist and feminist criticism, art history, missions, and theology, explore some of these issues, questions, and more about the Great Commission. The contributors to this volume are women and men situated geographically, culturally, and intellectually, in Africa, the Caribbean, the United States, and Asia. We are teachers and students of religion, pastors, preachers, and missionaries. Our questions, perspectives, and methodologies sometimes overlap, coincide, and/or differ, to varying degrees; all are contextual. The positions we express with respect to the Great Commission differ in some respects, but we agree on the need for critical reflection or interrogation.

Part 1: Colonial Missions and the Great Commission: Re-Membering the Past

This volume begins with a group of articles that unearth the much-undisclosed nexus between colonialism and Europe and North American mission projects. Dr. Beatrice Okyere-Manu's essay, "Colonial Mission and the Great Commission in Africa," takes us to the continent of Africa through pre-colonial, colonial, and postcolonial times to reflect upon the activities of the missionaries in Africa driven by the Great Commission. She acknowledges the positive impact of the missionaries' contribution along with their failures regarding their inability to confront human suffering, abuse, and inequalities against the indigenous Africans. Her suggestions for a postcolonial mission are quite challenging to the extent of embracing a liberating message that will address issues of social justice. She is clear in affirming that "not until our message addresses contemporary social injustices," such as systemic inequalities, poverty, HIV/AIDS, as well as violence against women and children, can we hope to achieve a holistic commission.

Dr. Dave Gosse's essay, "Examining the Promulgation and Impact of the Great Commission in the Caribbean, 1492–1970: A Historical Analysis," delves into the cultural domination of European and later North American missionaries in the process of evangelizing the Caribbean. Gosse unfolds the painful history of how the church in both the British and French colonial Caribbean served the needs of white people without considering the agency of enslaved African people. After the abolition of the slave trade in the nineteenth century (post-emancipation period), the Caribbean church of Africans began to gain autonomy; however, they continued to remain under colonial state. While Protestant missionaries from North America gradually gained popularity over Catholic missions in the twentieth century, race and class stratification became more visible. Pentecostalism and Rastafarianism (in Jamaica) along with Caribbean theology developed as a counterculture of the Protestant missionary agenda. However, Gosse argues that the racial residues of social damage done to the psyche of the people still remain institutionalized. The Caribbean church can become independent of its colonial roots only if "the psyche of its predominantly black and Indian populations is repaired and empowered to truly fulfill the mandate and mission of the Lord Jesus Christ."

Dr. Mitzi J. Smith, in her essay, "US Colonial Missions to African Slaves: Catechizing Black Souls, Traumatizing the Black *Psychē*," discusses how colonial missions propagated a strange coexistence of plantation missions dedicated to evangelizing black Africans and creating submissive slaves. This created a dichotomous African self with a soul to be saved and a body to be enslaved, thereby inflicting trauma on the black *psyche*. She examines slave catechisms exposing how "the Christianizing and/or catechizing of the slaves functioned both as a salve to relieve the Christian conscience sometimes harassed by the evil nature of slavery and as a justification for slavery."

PART 2: WOMANIST, FEMINIST, AND POSTCOLONIAL CRITICISMS AND THE GREAT COMMISSION

This section consists of essays that employ the hermeneutical lenses of womanist, dalit feminist, and postcolonial methodologies for reading and critiquing the Great Commission.

Dr. Jayachitra Lalitha's essay, "The Great Commission: A Postcolonial Dalit Feminist Inquiry," problematizes the absence of women disciples among the recipients of the Great Commission, as well as the vernacular translation of *nations* as *jaathigal*, which means caste groups in the Indian subcontinent. Thus, this Matthean pericope has deepened caste divisions in India, and strengthened an already existing bias against women in the society. Empire and imperialism collaborated with male authority both in colonizing and colonized lands. Colonial missions also ignored the gender dynamic. Lalitha attributes both Jewish particularism and a universalist Great Commission in Matthew as postcolonial. Jesus' confrontation of Jewish authorities who collaborate with Roman imperial powers, along with his insistence of Jewish priority in God's mission, clearly set him against Roman imperial agenda. Further, the narrative of the Great Commission that extends beyond Jews to all nations is yet another postcolonial act. She shows how Brahmanism and patriarchy collaborated with colonialism to push dalit women to the periphery of knowledge production. A postcolonial dalit feminist reading of the Great Commission continues to decolonize the minds of dalit women from the clutches of Brahmanism and patriarchy.

In "Privilege but No Power: Women in the Gospel of Matthew and Nineteenth-Century African American Women Missionaries through a Postcolonial Lens," Dr. Lynne St. Clair Darden attempts to demonstrate, through a "Christian hybrid identity construction," the complexity of cultural negotiations for nineteenth and early twentieth-century African American women missionaries to Africa. Through that cultural framework she critically examines the role of women in the Matthean prologue and epilogue in the context of mission. She powerfully exposes the paradox of African American women missionaries converting the Africans in their homeland to Christian civilization, "a culture that denied, deprived, and disenfranchised the African American." Thus she reveals the complex "identity construct in that the marginalized often mimic the imperial ideological processes and practices of the dominant society." The women fall in line with the imperial ideology of the text so that the exploitative sociopolitical tactics of empire are transferred into the "Christian mission of negating gender egalitarianism."

Dr. Mitzi J. Smith in her essay, "'Knowing More than is Good for One': A Womanist Interrogation of the Matthean Great Commission," challenges the dominant perspective for reading Matthew and Mathew's Jesus through the lens of teaching. She interrogates how the exaltation of teaching has subordinated acts of social justice in Matthew. As a womanist iconoclast, Smith interrogates the Great Commission as "constructed, oppressive epistemic iconography." Her use of a womanist lens privileges black women's experiences and ways of knowing or epistemologies. Smith shifts attention from Jesus as paradigmatic teacher of passive recipient nations to Jesus as *God with us*. "As God with us, in Jesus social justice and teaching do not strive for mastery over each other and are not at war in his incarnate body. But Jesus' practice of social justice and teaching organically constitute the interactive presence of God with us."

PART 3: THEOLOGY, ART HISTORY, AND THE GREAT COMMISSION

Dr. Sheila F. Winborne in her essay, "Images of the Jesus in Advancing the Great Commission," moves beyond the traditional claims of Christian colonial art as visually portraying the Sacred to how such images have manifested power and political control within and outside of the church. Winborne argues that the visual arts, specifically renderings of a white Christ, have played a significant role in impacting and imaging Christian beliefs and practices. The projection of the White Jesus ought to be understood through western cultures and concepts of "chosen" versus "Other." The most effective presentations of the white Christ are those "rendered in realistic style." Calling for a "deconstructive analysis of Christian art," Winborne argues that we must understand the ways in which visual art advances oppressive mythical narratives, critically observing the "interrelatedness of our faith and art histories," in order to stop reinscribing some of the same oppressive myths.

"The Great Commission in the Face of Suffering as *Minjung*" by Dr. Michelle Sungshin Lim deals with the role of North American and European missions in creating the structure and system that favors the "white-supremacist-capitalist-patriarchy." While missionaries failed to recognize other religious practices in the native lands, they also upheld a superior mindset that objectified the natives. As a means to rectify the damage done in the past, she suggests a "Christ-praxis" by revisiting Ahn Byung Mu's claim that *minjung* is *ochlos*. By identifying *ochlos* as *minjung*, a theology of "God-walk" (versus "God-talk") enhances liberation from oppression. She identifies the danger in the current South Korean churches that follow the model of "white-supremacist-capitalist-patriarchy" of North America and suggests that their missionary strategy should empower the poor in the Global South.

Rohan P. Gideon in his essay, "Children's Agency and Edinburgh 2010: The Great Commission or a Greater Omission?", attempts to explain why the agency of children is significant in understanding Christian missions. He shows "how the whole Christian mission motif to preach and to lead also translates in adult-children relationships as adults' prerogative to prescribe and control, especially in understanding the place and role of children in mission." He employs agency as prescribed in postcolonial criticism along with the theological significance of the agency of the marginalized as explained in the doctrine of the Trinity. "Child in the midst," a theme from the Child Theology movement, is suggested as a means to enhance the agency of children in theological discussions.

Part 4: The Great Commission and Christian Education: Rethinking Our Pedagogy

Drs. Karen D. Crozier, Anthony G. Reddie, and Lord Elorm-Donkor deal with the nexus between the Great Commission and Christian education and the psychological and moral damage inflicted on black peoples. They are convinced that missionary strategies of white supremacy failed to recognize God's image in those they missionized and the efficacy of indigenous religious beliefs. The European colonizing elements in the teachings of the Great Commission failed to incorporate a radical, new way of being human, and thus distorted the humanness of all, inflicting damage on black peoples and their communities.

In her essay, "Interrogating the Matthean Great Commission for US Christian Education: Reclaiming Jesus' Kingdom of God Message for the Church," Dr. Karen D. Crozier draws insights from Howard Thurman to develop Christian education as a means to demonstrate that "our identity, as humans, lies beyond the non-ontological particulars such as religion, race, color, creed, gender, class, sexuality, denominations, and national origin that alienate us from self, others, the world, and the divine." Crozier questions the very use of the term the Great Commission and reclaims the significance of Jesus' message for social, political, economic, and religious emancipation.

Dr. Anthony G. Reddie's essay, "Beginning Again: Rethinking Christian Education in Light of the Great Commission," highlights the importance of identity and self-esteem in Christian education and argues that Christian education should be concerned about wider questions of human growth and development. As mission aims at God's saving activity in the world informing people about Christian faith, the role of the Christian educator is also linked to affirming self-esteem in people. Reddie challenges us to rethink Christian education in light of black theology and transformative learning in order to reformulate the Christian identity of Africans over against hierarchical white supremacy.

In his article, "Christian Moral Education and the Great Commission in an African Context," Dr. Lord Elorm-Donkor addresses the absurdity of the dual reality of so-called successful Christian missions in Africa alongside obvious sociopolitical and economic degeneration. He asks whether Christian missions were as successful as purported in making disciples in Africa. Elorm-Donkor discusses the collateral sociopolitical and economic damage inflicted upon Africa's "moral conceptual scheme" and argues for an integration of African traditional religion and Christian moral education that can complement each other.

Part 5: The Great Commission's Impact on/in the Church: Voices from Beyond the Academy

MarShondra Scott Lawrence in her essay, "A United States Inner-city Oriented Great Commission," writes as a Christian who grew up in and loves the people of the inner cities. She sheds light on how inner cities in the United States exist more or less as invisible *glocal ghettos*. Lawrence argues that the Great Commission must be understood as a challenge to engender social justice and love in the inner cities in order to improve the living conditions and realities of their residents who have been rendered invisible.

In her essay, "The Great Commission's Impact on a Short-term Missionary and Lay Leader in the Church of God in Christ," Dr. June C. Rivers shares the story of her grandmother who was revolutionary in her own right in embodying the Great Commission with love and social justice. Her father Rev. Havious Green and Bishop Charles Harrison Mason, the founder of the Church of God in Christ, also influenced her with their insistence on social justice and African cultural identity. They relied not on one biblical text as a paradigm for doing missions, but on several. From her own experience as a short term missionary coordinator for Youth on a Mission (YOAM) to Africa, South America, Caribbean islands, and Asia, Rivers believes that the "role of the church is . . . to embody the love of Jesus Christ by exemplifying acts of charity."

PART I

Colonial Missions and the Great Commission: Re-Membering the Past

1

Colonial Mission and the Great Commission in Africa

Beatrice Okyere-Manu

INTRODUCTION

Several studies that have been carried out on the Great Commission argue that the call of Christ in Matt. 28:18-20 was not only for the early disciples but rather for all followers to come, to extend the gospel to all nations, thus the command: "Go therefore and make disciples of all nations, baptizing them in the name of the Father and of the Son and of the Holy Spirit, and teaching them to obey everything that I have commanded you." The Great Commission according to Joe Kapolyo "is given by the highest authority in the Universe, and it is binding on all disciples for all times. No other task comes with the same authority, the same universal scope or the same eternal consequence."[1] This universal mandate given by Jesus prompted the early Christians long before the nineteenth century to embark on mission. This mission was intended to extend the gospel to all nations, including Africa, in order to make more converts, expand the church, and thus hasten the coming of Jesus Christ. Although the command of Jesus is clear, it has been argued that the same command was misinterpreted and used as the explanation for opening the way and instigating imperialism in most foreign lands.[2] Specifically to Africa, the command motivated missionaries such as David Livingstone (1813–73), "to 'open up' the continent for Western Christianity, commerce and civilization."[3] The period following Livingstone's expedition saw many missionaries and traders continue on the road he paved

---

1. Joe Kapolyo, "Matthew," *Africa Bible Commentary*, ed. Tokunboh Adeyemo (Nairobi: World Alive Publishers, 2006), 1170.

2. Greg Cuthbertson, "The English-speaking Churches and Colonialism," in *Theology & Violence: The South African Debate,* ed. Charles Villa-Vicencio (Johannesburg: Skotaville, 1987), 16–17.

into the continent, and this eventually led to the colonization of Africa. This raises a number of questions such as:

- What did the missionaries who came to Africa inevitably overlook that resulted in the exacerbating of inequality, injustice, and human suffering?
- What prompted them to choose a focus on teaching over addressing human suffering?
- Was this the intention of Jesus when he mandated his disciples to go?

These are a few of the questions that this chapter seeks to answer. I intend to do a reflection on the activities of the missionaries in Africa driven by the Great Commission. While accepting their contributions as necessary and in some ways appropriate, I intend to explore the missionaries' role of silence in influencing the injustices and inhumane activities exacted against the indigenous Africans. This contribution, therefore, is a critique of missionary activities under the guise of the Great Commission. It is divided into four sections: first, it shows that colonial missions to Africa were intertwined with the Great Commission. Second, it looks at the activities of the missionaries in particular and the positive impact of their activities on the indigenous people and on the continent as a whole. Third, this chapter will critically assess the negative impact of the role played by the missionaries contributing to issues of inequality, traumatic experience, and injustice as well as the influence of these factors on the indigenous African people. Finally, the chapter discusses the ethical implication of the Great Commission for postcolonial mission in Africa.

The Relationship between Colonial Missions and the Great Commission

It is not the intention of this section of the chapter to give a comprehensive history of colonial missions in Africa; this has been done by a number of scholars. Rather, it seeks to explain the existence of a relationship between the missionaries and European colonists and the impact of said relationship on the missionaries' agenda. It must be noted that the actual date when Christianity came to Africa has been contested by a number of scholars. Edwin Smith believes that in "the early period of her [African] history, the church has never been absent from Africa. Christian communities existed in Africa long before

3. Musa Dube, "The Scramble for Africa as the Biblical Scramble for Africa: Postcolonial Perspectives," in *Postcolonial Perspectives in African Biblical Interpretations*, ed. Musa Dube, Andrew Mbuvi, and Dora Mbuwayesango (Atlanta: Society of Biblical Literature, 2012), 1–26 (2).

they were found in the British Isles and Northern Europe."[4] In the same vein, Labode Modupe has also argued that Christianity already existed in Egypt as far back as the third century.[5] However, most historians attribute the introduction of Christianity in Africa to the Portuguese expedition around the fifteenth century.[6] During this time, Islamic activity on the west coast of Africa was expanding. In order to explore the extent of this activity (with the aim of bringing it to an end) and at the same time to fulfill the Great Commission, Prince Henry of Portugal trained men and sent them to Africa.[7] It was through that expedition that most cities in the coastal region of Africa, such as Cape Verde, Elmina, Sao Tome and Mombasa, came under Catholicism, which was then the state religion in Portugal. Commenting on the Portuguese activities in the early history Modupe argues that

> The case of the Portuguese exemplifies the close relationship between Crown and Church. In the treaty of Tordesillas (1494), the pope recognized Portuguese claims to Africa. The crown was also responsible for attempting to convert the indigenous people to Christianity. Much of the missionary effort over the next two and half centuries was conducted under Portuguese authority.[8]

The Spanish, German, and Dutch nations were also exploring the continent around the same period. It was believed that their attempts were unsuccessful. Charles Grooves attributes their unsuccessful attempts to the following reasons:

- The missionaries only concentrated on the coastal populations especially the ruling elites;
- They were a few in number with limited financial resources; most of them could not cope with the harsh local weather and politics;
- There was the belief in some quarters in Europe that it was not necessary to convert Africans;
- and most importantly economic interest was more prominent.[9]

4. Edwin Smith, *The Christian Mission in Africa* (London: International Missionary Council, 1926), 8.

5. Labode Modupe, "Christianity: Missionaries in Africa," in *Encyclopaedia of Africa*, ed. Kwame Anthony Appiah and Henry Louis Gates, Jr. (New York: Basic Civitas Books, 1999) 270–77 (274).

6. Olayemi Akinwumi, "Political and Spiritual Partition: The impact of the 1884/85 Berlin Conference on Christian Mission in Africa," in *Christianity in Africa and the African Diaspora*, ed. AfeAdogame, Roswith Gerloff, and Klaus Hock (London: Continuum, 2008), 9–19(10).

7. Katie Geneva Cannon, "Christian Imperialism and the Transatlantic Slave Trade," *Journal of Feminist Studies in Religion* 24, no. 1 (2008): 127–134.

8. Modupe, "Christianity: Missionaries in Africa," 274.

9. Charles P. Groves, *The Planting of Christianity in Africa* (London: Lutterworth, 1948), 11.

Eventually with the abolition of the slave trade and the revival of missionary work in Europe, there was a renewal of missionary work on the African continent.[10]Musa Dube is of the opinion that "it was not until the modern European imperial movements of the eighteenth to nineteenth century that a more forceful agenda was undertaken to Christianize sub-Saharan Africa."[11] The success of the missionaries this time was attributed to the new strategies they employed, which include strategies such as changes in the evangelization method, employment of more missionaries and indigenous people to preach the gospel, availability of funds, and cooperation between the different denominations in the continent.[12] In the past, scholars of African Christianity separated church from mission and mission from empire. But nowadays various scholars are arguing for the interconnectedness of these three entities.[13]It is for this reason that scholars of history have argued that colonial mission was intertwined with the Great Commission. While the spread of the gospel ensued, the colonial mission had another agenda that in several ways impacted on missionary work in Africa. For example, Robert Woodberry posits that "the British were the most powerful Colonizers in the nineteenth and the twentieth century and thus were presumably able to impose their will and extract resources from colonial subjects."[14] It is believed that most of the missionaries in the colonies, especially the British colonies, could not challenge colonial leaders because they lacked the necessary power to do so; therefore, they had to compromise with the whims and caprices of the colonial leaders.[15]For example, the missionaries had to travel with the European merchants to the mission field in order to enjoy the protection of the colonial official on their journey. Even in the mission field, the European merchants and the colonial officials were the only people the missionaries could associate with.[16] Hence their relationship was cemented to the point that in most cases the "missionaries acted

10. E. Bolaji Idowu, "The Predicament of the Church in Africa," in *Christianity in Tropical Africa*, ed. Christian Baëta (Oxford: Oxford University Press, 1968), 417–40 (417).

11. Dube, "The Scramble for Africa," 2.

12. Akinwumi, "Political and Spiritual Partition," 11.

13. David Maxwell, "Writing the History of African Christianity: Reflections of an Editor," *Journal of Religion in Africa*, 36, no. 3 (2006): 379–99 (395).

14. Robert D. Woodberry, "The Shadow of Empire: Christian Missions, Colonial Policy and Democracy in Post-Colonial societies," (PhD diss., University of North Carolina, 2004), 3.

15. Abbe Livingstone Warnshuis, *The Relations of Missions and Government in Belgian, French, and Portuguese Colonies* (London: International Missionary Council, 1923), 13.

16. Dana Robert, "The Great Commission in an Age of Globalization," in*Antioch Agenda: Essays on the Restorative Church in Honor of Orlando E. Costas*, ed. Daniel Jeyaraj, Robert W. Pazmiño and Rodney L. Petersen (New Delhi: Indian Society for the Promotion of Christian Knowledge, 2007), 1–22 (10).

as intermediaries in the early years of colonial rule between Africans and the Europeans for they served as advisors to the indigenous rulers. In this role, their influence was usually biased towards colonial government and the rapid cultural 'Europeanisation' of the African population."[17] Thus, the closed nature of their relationship influenced the missionaries' activity on the continent. Modupe has observed that "a few missionaries actively helped European government defeat African states, and other missionaries protested against abuses associated with colonial government but did not question the authority of these governments to colonize Africa."[18] It is with this background that Norman Etherington writes,

> ... secular historians have reached a virtual consensus on the question of Christianity and colonialism. Phrased in different ways by different authors, it is that the missionaries, who aimed to replace African cultures with European 'civilisation' and who frequently allied themselves with colonial governments, nevertheless transmitted a religion which Africa turned to suit their own purposes: spiritual, economic and political.[19]

Modupe continues to assert that "it appeared that most missionaries accepted colonialism and worked within the system. Some governments attempted to forge links with missionaries: both the Portuguese and Belgian government privileged missionaries from nations working in the colonies. Most of the missionaries and colonial government worked closely together, although they did not have the same goals and were often in conflict."[20] It must be noted that those missionaries who stood up against colonial interests were sometimes sued or sent back to their country of origin.[21] Such acts affected the missionaries' work greatly: it silenced them and as has been noted above, influenced their initial agenda of spreading the gospel. As a result of the intimate relationship between colonizers and missionaries, colonial officials and the European merchants played significant roles in directing and facilitating the missionary project to their own advantage.[22] So far we have argued that even though the Great Commission prompted missionary work into Africa, it was entangled with colonial mission by Europeans in Africa. This relationship impacted both

17. John Anthony Christopher, *Colonial Africa* (Totowa, NJ: Barnes and Noble, 1984).

18. Modupe, "Christianity: Missionaries in Africa," 276.

19. Norman Etherington, "Recent Trends in the Historiography of Christianity in Southern Africa," *Journal of Southern Studies* 22, no. 2 (1996): 201–19 (209).

20. Modupe, "Christianity: Missionaries in Africa," 276.

21. Harry Langworthy, *Africa for Africans: The Life of Joseph Booth* (Bonn: Verlang für Kultur und Wissenschaft, 1996).

positively and negatively on their activities. It is with this background that the next section critiques the missionary activities in Africa. In my critique, I will resist the temptation of critiquing missionary activities in every country on the continent, though that would have given a complete overview of their activities in Africa. Due to space limitations, I will give a generalized critique of missionary work on the continent as a whole.

CRITIQUE OF MISSIONARY ACTIVITIES IN AFRICA

Although there were positive results as a consequence of the missionaries' teaching motivated by the Great Commission on the continent, there were important aspects they omitted that had negative impacts on their work. For the sake of this chapter, the activity of the colonial missionary will be divided into two areas: positive and negative.

POSITIVE ACTIVITIES

Missionaries and colonial mission made a great impact on the continent of Africa. The major impact includes general literacy in health, teaching and conversion into Christianity, education with the view of expanding the size of elite and middle class, and exposure of and rallying against abuse in the indigenous cultures. This section explores the positive impact of the missionary work under the theme of teaching driven by the Great Commission.

TEACHING INSPIRED BY THE GREAT COMMISSION

The missionaries who came to Africa, particularly the Protestant missionaries, were interested in converting the indigenous people of Africa to Christianity as mandated by the Great Commission. With this in mind, in every territory they entered, they tried to develop a written form of the oral language of that territory. They also translated the Bible into these languages and then taught the indigenous people how to read and write.[23] Consequently, their motivation for the education they provided for the indigenous people in Africa was to create a basis for the gospel with the intention of converting the colonies to Christianity.[24] Through this strategy, a number of educated indigenous lay leaders and clergy were trained to help spread the word among their own

22. Michael D. McGinnis, "From Self-reliant Churches to Self-governing Communities: Comparing the Indigenization of Christianity and Democracy in Sub-Saharan Africa," *Cambridge Review of International Affairs* 20, no. 3 (2007): 401–16 (404).

23. Kenneth Ingham, *Reformers in India, 1793–1833: An Account of the Work of Christian Missionaries on Behalf of Social Reform* (Cambridge: Cambridge University Press, 1956), 96–109.

people.[25]The strategy of teaching the indigenous people to read and write occurred within the context of the conviction of the missionaries that all people are created in the image of God and are redeemable. This strategy ran counter to the popular anthropological ideology during the nineteenth century that "dark skinned people are incapable of abstract thought and cannot be civilized through education."[26] In his writing about the activities of the missionaries around the mid-nineteenth century, William Brown mentions that "the success of the mission was, on the whole, highly pleasing. The congregations were considerable; numbers of the natives baptized, many of whom were also admitted as communicants. The influence of the mission extended far beyond the stations; it was felt in a great part of the surrounding country."[27] Education, therefore, became an enticement for conversion. Although many missionaries viewed the delivery of social services as a practical application of their faith, their primary purpose was to spread the gospel to unbelievers.[28] Therefore, they did not concern themselves very much with what the indigenous people were going through socially but pursued their goal of sharing the gospel and consequently the elevation of education (as a basis for conversion) over social justice at the time. As a result, by the 1940s about ninety-seven percent of the population of students in Ghana and Nigeria were believed to have been educated by missionary schools. In South Africa, there were an estimated 5,360 mission-sponsored schools as opposed to 230 state-sponsored schools.[29]Subsequently, as Horton Robin asserts:

> With the advent of the twentieth century . . . Europeans came to be seen as symbols of power, and Christianity itself came to be seen as part of a larger order, comprising Western education, colonial administration, commerce and industry, with which everyone had henceforth to reckon. These changes created a much more favorable climate for conversion.[30]

24. Dick Kooiman, "Who is to Benefit from Missionary Education? Travancore in the 1930s," in *Missionary Encounters: Sources and Issues*, ed. Robert A. Bickers and Rosemary Seton (Surry: Curzon, 1996), 153–73 (158–59).

25. W.H. Taylor, "Missionary Education in Africa Reconsidered: The Presbyterian Educational Impact in Eastern Nigeria 1846–1974," *African Affairs* 83(1984): 189–205(196).

26. Brian Stanley, *The Bible and the Flag: Protestant Missions and British Imperialism in the Nineteenth and Twentieth Centuries* (Leicester: Apollos, 1990), 162.

27. William Brown, *The History of Christian Missions*, vol. 2(London: Thomas Baker, 1864), 532.

28. Ibid.

29. Edward H. Berman, "African Responses to Christian Mission Education," *Africa Studies Review* 17 (1974): 527–40(527).

One major success of the missionaries' educational activity was that it produced more indigenous people with skills for "running western style bureaucratic organizations."[31] Besides the training of the indigenous people, the missionaries managed to carry out their core agenda of spiritual transformation as prescribed by the Great Commission.

GENERAL HEALTH CARE

In addition to evangelization and education, colonial leaders opened opportunities for missionaries to build hospitals and other institutions to help the indigenous people with their numerous ailments. For example, C. J. Zvobgo says that "Christian missionaries established medical missions both because they regarded the ministry of healing as an integral part of the Christian witness and because they viewed medical missions as an important evangelistic agency."[32] Therefore, indigenous people seeking medical care became potential Christian converts. Writing about missionary work in northern Nigeria, Andrew Barnes quoted Akiga the Tiv who observed that "there was medicine at every mission station and treatment was given to the sick. Of all the work that the mission does, this pleases the people most."[33] Missionary Clara Bridgman founded the Bridgman Memorial Hospital in Johannesburg in 1928, which focused on improving childcare.[34] Thomas Hakansson narrates the story of Jackob Janssen Dannholz, an Evangelical Lutheran and a trained nurse who established a mission station in South Pare in Tanzania, whose goal was to show the destructiveness of deleterious practices on children. These practices include polygyny, female circumcision, premarital sex, and beliefs in ancestral and all other forms of spirits. Dannholz believed these practices produced a dangerous environment for children and called them "animistic beliefs." He therefore "used preaching and demonstration to spread his message."[35] He would demonstratively deliver children slowly in order to show that a clean and

30. Robin Horton, "African Conversion," *Journal of the International African Institute* 41 (1971): 85–108 (86).

31. Woodberry, "The Shadow of Empire,"28.

32. C. J. Zvobgo, "Aspects of Interaction between Christianity and African Culture in Colonial Zimbabwe, 1893–1934," *Zambezia* 13 (1986): 43–57 (54).

33. E. Andrew Barnes, *Making Headway: The Introduction of Western Civilization in Colonial Northern Nigeria* (Rochester, NY: University of Rochester Press, 2009), 145.

34. David Hardiman, *Healing Bodies, Saving Souls: Medical Mission in Asia and Africa* (New York: Rodopi, 2006), 40.

35. Thomas Hakansson, "Pagan Practices and the Death of Children: German Colonial Missionaries and Child Health Care in South Pare, Tanzania," *World Development* 26, no. 9 (1998): 1763–772 (1768).

properly conducted birth would produce healthy children.[36] Through this strategy he managed to attract a number of converts. Many other mission hospitals were opened in various parts of the continent to treat the indigenous people, and also functioned as a strategy for spreading the gospel and making converts. William Brown, writing on the positive impact of colonial mission prompted by the Great Commission in Africa, adds the following:

> The people under the care of the missionaries made considerable advances in some of the more common and necessary arts of civilized life. Many of them built themselves convenient houses, some of them of stone, instead of their old smoky unhealthy huts. In place of the skins of animals which they used to throw over their bodies, the men adopted in part the European dress, while the women who had learned to sew made decent clothes for themselves and their daughters. Though they were previously not simply a pastoral people, but cultivated millet and other produce, yet now their husbandry was considerably extended. They obtained ploughs and other agricultural implements, and many of them occupied themselves in the culture of corn, which they sold to the Dutch farmers for cattle, clothing, soap, salt, and other useful articles. Vaccination also was introduced among them, and we trust that it may check in future the frightful ravages which small-pox was accustomed to make among them.[37]

From the above quotation, there is no doubt that healthcare became one of the major concerns of the missionaries, and this resulted in the building of mission hospitals and the provision of western medicine, which improved the survival rate of the indigenous people on the continent. It also helped to increase the number of converts into the Christian faith.

THE NEGATIVE ROLE PLAYED BY THE MISSIONARIES IN AFRICA

Despite all the positive impacts of colonial mission prompted by the universal mandate of the Great Commission, most African scholars have argued that the same biblical text was used to abuse Africans through the missionaries' relationship with the imperialist programs. It is with this background that this section explores the activities of the missionaries that negatively impacted the indigenous people on the continent. I will specifically explore what the

36. Ibid.
37. Brown, *The History of Christian Missions,* 534.

missionaries disregarded that exacerbated the trading in human beings, as well as the various abuses committed against the indigenous Africans.

INDIGENOUS ABUSES AND THE MISSIONARIES

The missionaries viewed the Great Commission as the mandate to convert the indigenous people to Christianity, and they dedicated all their efforts and the means at their disposal, including coercion, to make this happen. For instance, Alan Rider tells of how the Portuguese influenced King of Benin and his subjects with economic incentives for conversion. The Portuguese missionaries promised the king that submission to baptism "would bring guns as well as grace."[38] Accordingly, the King of Benin and his subjects were enticed into Christianity. The number of schools, as well as hospitals, that were opened was used as a tool to lure many into the Christian faith. Yet the irony of the missionaries' activities was that the relationship formed with the colonial mission affected their activities on the continent. For example, in the British colonies, the state was against mass education while the missionaries preferred it. As a result, the missionaries were influenced by the colonial leaders to structure the content of their education to suit the interests of the colonial leaders, business elites, and the European settlers. This eventually led to many forms of inhumane treatment. As noted above, it is clear that the colonial leaders influenced the missionaries' education to their own advantage. For example, the European merchants wanted clerks and translators to work in their companies. Therefore, the missionaries were mandated to focus their education on practical skills such as carpentry and masonry that were needed to suit their own interests.[39] The European settlers, on the other hand, needed farmers and construction workers, and thus they opposed the post–elementary education of the indigenous people in the field of academic and administrative skills.[40] Other groups of people who prevented the education of indigenous people of Africa were the slave owners (particularly those who used unskilled laborers). Slave owners opposed the teaching of slaves. As a result of the relationship between the colonial leaders and the missionaries, the latter could not resist but had to comply with the colonial leaders' program. So even though they provided education for the indigenous Africans, the education was geared to serve the agenda of the colonial leaders. Speaking of colonial influences

---

38. Akinwumi, "Political and Spiritual Partition," 11.

39. Ingham, *Reformers in India*, 56–61.

40. O. W. Furley and T. Watson, *A History of Education in East Africa* (New York: NOK, 1976), 87–88.

and discrimination of Africans from higher education in Lusophone, Africa (specifically Mozambique), Renato Matusse (1997) gave an example:

> Liceu 5 de Outubro (now Josina Machel Secondary school) opened in 1910 in Maputo, the nation's capital, with no Afro-Mozambicans enrolled. In 1960 the same institution had only 30 Afro-Mozambicans out of the total of some 1000 students. When the national university, the University of Lourenco Marques (now the University of Eduardo Mondlane), was opened in 1963, only five of the 300 students were African origin and who had one of the indigenous Mozambican languages such as Cicopi, Gitonga or Xirhonga as a mother-tongue.[41]

It must be noted that the scenario in Mozambique was similar to what was happening in Angola and Guinea Bissau.[42] Only a few Africans benefitted from the university education provided. Most Africans were only given basic education to enable them to serve the colonial leaders. Another negative impact of the teachings brought forth by missionaries was that in their attempt to spread the gospel, they often had an ethnocentric attitude. With the belief of the superiority of their own culture in mind, the missionaries fought against practices in the cultures belonging to the indigenous people of Africa.[43] They, therefore, imposed their own culture and worldview on the natives deeming all their practices demonic, particularly African traditional religion. With regard to this, Kwame Bediako says that "in failing correctly to apprehend and follow the apostolic precedent in their understanding of African 'heathenism', our modern missionaries, by the same token, deprived themselves of the means of recognizing and articulating the universal nature and activity of Christ among the 'heathen' they encountered."[44] It is with this background that Dube argues that "the imperialist ideology of expansion uses the promotion of its own cultural values to devalue, replace and suppress diversity. Its strategy is characterized by massive inclusivity but not equality."[45] Another negative role the missionaries played on the continent is that although most of them saw

---

41. Gosnell Yorke and Edouard Kitoto Nsiku, "Bible Translation and Theological Education in Lusophone and Spanish Speaking Africa," in *Handbook of Theological Education in Africa*, ed. Isabel Apawo Phiri and Dietrich Werner (Oxford: Regnum Books International, 2013), 500–507 (503).

42. Ibid.

43. Woodberry, "The Shadow of Empire," 15.

44. Kwame Bediako, *Theology and Identity: The Impact of Culture upon Christian Thought in the Second Century and in Modern Africa* (Oxford: Regnum Books, 1999), 245.

45. Dube, "The Scramble for Africa," 34.

the delivery of social services as a practical application of their faith, they ignored it and concentrated on their primary purpose to spread the gospel to native unbelievers.[46] As a result, they employed all means, whether positive or negative, to make sure their agenda was fulfilled, even to the point of using the Bible to validate the suppression and subjugation of the indigenous African. For example, "the white Christians who came to South Africa saw themselves as God's chosen people on divine mission like the Israelites."[47] This misinterpretation of the Bible eventually led to the idea of apartheid and the inhumane suffering of Africans in South Africa. It is such practices that resulted in the popular African story that when the white missionaries came to the continent our country, he had the Bible and we had the land. They asked us to close our eyes and pray and on opening our eyes after the prayer, the white man had the land and we had the Bible.[48] This story suggests that missionary activities in Africa were hugely caught up by colonial subjugation of Africans.[49]

THE MISSIONARIES' RESPONSE TO THE TRADING IN HUMAN BEINGS

Another negative impact of the missionaries' stance of elevating their agenda of teaching and making disciples and ignoring issues of social justice was that it encouraged the inhumane trading in indigenous men and women which lasted "for a period of nearly 500 years, from 1400 to 1900."[50] This is perceived as one of the greatest tragedies the continent has witnessed, and it is with this background that David Brion Davies described the nature of the slave trade in his book as inhumane bondage.[51] Lamenting the impact of the evils of the slave trade, Patrick Manning reiterated Paul Bairoch, stating that "Slavery was corruption: it involved theft, bribery, and exercise of brute force as well as ruses. Slavery thus may be seen as one source of pre-colonial origins for modern corruption."[52] It must be noted that not only was the slave trade seen as the pre-colonial origin of modern-day corruption as Manning posits, but

46. Woodberry, "The Shadow of Empire,"403.

47. Albert Grundlingh and Hilary Sapire, "From Feverish Festival to Repetitive Ritual?: The Changing Fortunes of the Great Trek Mythology in an Industrializing South Africa, 1938–1988," *South Africa Historical Journal* 21 (1989): 18–38.

48. Steed Vernyl Davidson, Justin Ukpong, and Gosnell Yorke, "The Bible and Africana Life: A Problematic Relationship," in *The Africana Bible: Reading Israel's Scriptures from Africa and the African Diaspora*, ed. Hugh R. Page, Jr. (Minneapolis: Fortress Press, 2010), 39–44 (39–40).

49. Ibid. 40.

50. Nathan Nunn, "The Long-term Effects of Africa's Slave Trades," *Quarterly Journal of Economics* 123, no.1 (2008): 139–76 (142).

51. David Brion Davis, *Inhuman Bondage: The Rise and Fall of Slavery in the New World* (New York: Oxford University Press, 2006).

also it took away able men and women from the continent. Nathan Nunn believes that during the period of the transatlantic slave trade approximately twelve million Africans were sold and sent out of Africa.[53] To him, this figure does not even include those who were intentionally killed during the raids to capture slaves, as well as those who died on the voyage and were thrown into the sea. As a result, it has been argued that trading in human beings diminished the population of the continent by half by the year 1850.[54] The nature of the human trade was such that the slaves were abused and starved en route to the new World. As such, many lost their lives due to diseases and unhygienic conditions. It is estimated that the death toll of slaves from their original home to the coast alone ranged between 10 and 50 percent, depending on where the slaves came from. For those from inland villages, the journey took longer than those from the coastal areas. In the same way, depending on the time stretch of the voyage from Africa, the estimated death toll for cross-Atlantic deaths ranged from 7 to 20 percent.[55] Even before they were transported, they were chained and put in dungeons awaiting the slave ship. While all these inhuman activities were being perpetrated, the missionaries continued teaching and making disciples. Even though some were not happy with the inhuman trade, they were afraid of the Colonial administrators. No wonder it took nearly five hundred years, as indicated above, for slavery to be abolished. Narrating her experience of how the missionaries used biblical texts to justify their actions to inflict suffering at the Elmina castle in Ghana, Nienke Pruiksma mentions how a chapel was built directly on top of the dungeon where millions of slaves were kept before their journey to the New World. This chapel contained an inscription from Ps. 132:13-14 ("For the Lord has chosen Zion; he has desired it for his habitation: 'This is my resting place forever; here I will reside, for I have desired it.'" NRSV).[56] I vividly recall my own emotional experience visiting the castle and being told by the tour guide that while dozens were in chains suffering crying and dying of hunger, torture, flogging, pain, and diseases as they waited to be transported, the Dutch missionaries would be praying and worshipping God regularly in the chapel

52. Patrick Manning, *Slavery and African Life: Occidental, Oriental, and African Slave Trades* (Cambridge: Cambridge University Press 1990),124.

53. Nunn, "The Long-term Effects of Africa's Slave Trades," 142.

54. Manning, *Slavery and African Life,* 171.

55. Paul E. Lovejoy, *Transformation of Slavery: A History of Slavery in Africa.* Second Edition (Cambridge: Cambridge University Press, 2000), 63–64.

56. Nienke Pruiksma, "Liberating Interdependence and a People-Centered Mission" (paper presented at *The Society of Biblical Literature Annual Meeting 2005,* Philadelphia, PA, November 2005), 2.

above the dark dungeon. Such situations raise a number of ethical questions, such as which God was the missionaries worshipping above the dungeon? Was it the same God who mandated them to go and make disciples of all nations? Why were the missionaries not concerned with the human suffering going on in the castle? Was it right for them to ignore human suffering over worship and teaching? One of the effects of the slave trade on the indigenous African was that villages rose up against villages through warfare, raids as well as kidnapping as the demands for slaves increased. In addition, there was increase of internal fighting among the different ethnic groups "insecurity confined people within ethnic boundaries constructing spheres of interaction"[57].This resulted in indigenous people protecting themselves through various means and the slave traders took advantage of the situation, trading knives, swords, and other weapons to the indigenous people in exchange for slaves.[58] Martin Klein has observed that "communities began enslaving their own. Judicial penalties that formerly had taken the form of beatings, payment of compensation or exile, for example, were now converted to enslavement."[59] It must be noted that "in many areas, the slave trade pitted neighbor against neighbor,"[60] and destroyed the communitarian spirit that existed in pre-colonial Africa and brought about insecurities and mistrust. Nunn believes that the high level of ethnic fractionality that we are experiencing in Africa today may be due to the impact of the slave trade where fear of being raided prevented the formation of large communities and gave way to smaller ethnic fractionality.[61] Emmanuel Akyeampong narrates a story of how a chief of Whuti, jealous of a leader of a drumming group, tricked the whole group of drummers of Atorkor in modern-day Ghana and sold them to the European slave traders.[62] Another story is told of how a common practice "the red water ordeal" that existed whereby the chief of Cassanga modern day Guinea Bissau will force people accused of crime to drink a poisonous red liquid. If the accused vomits, then he will be considered guilty sold into slavery and his possessions confiscated. On the other hand if the accused does not vomit, he will be declared not guilty but since

57. Kusimba, Chapurukha M. "Archaeology of Slavery in East Africa," African ArchaeologicalReview, 21 (2004), 59–88 (66).

58. Walter Hawthorne, "The Production of Slaves Where There was No State: The Guinea-Bissau Region, 1450–1815," *Slavery & Abolition* 20 (1999): 97–124 (109–108).

59. Martin Klein, "The Slave Trade and Decentralized Societies," *Journal of African History* 42 (2001): 49–65 (59).

60. Hawthorne, "The Production of Slaves," 106–107.

61. Nunn, "The Long term effect of Africa's Slave Trades" 5.

62. Emmanuel Akyeampong, "History, Memory, Slave-Trade and Slavery in Anglo (Ghana)," *Slavery & Abolition* 22 (2001): 1–24 (8–9).

the liquid was poisonous, the accused would automatically die with time. His possessions would be confiscated by the king and his family would be sold into slavery. The chief did this to acquire possession from his subjects as well as to acquire slaves for sale. "Slavery was a form of judicial punishment particularly for such crimes as murder, theft and sorcery." As noted above, in the midst of these insecurities, mistrust, and injustices the missionaries took a silent stance and concentrated on spreading the gospel and planting new churches without interfering with the agenda of the colonial leaders, even though most of the people they evangelized were being sold into slavery. To them, the future of the soul was more important than the earthly sufferings of their converts. It was not surprising that among other things, most of the slaves were given Christian names for identification.[63]Katie Cannon has argued that the transatlantic slave trade was founded on Christianity with its interpretation and application of the Matthean Great Commission.[64] In addition to the trading of human beings, there were a number of abuses meted out against the indigenous African people by the colonial leaders of which the missionaries had little or no say. Describing the nature of the some of the abuse, Niall Ferguson says that "native peoples were taxed, robbed or wiped out,"[65]and the missionaries could not do much about it but assumed a silent stance for fear of deportation, as indicated above.

ETHICAL IMPLICATIONS OF POSTCOLONIAL MISSION IN AFRICA

So far this chapter has discussed a number of activities that missionaries, inspired by the Great Commission, performed in Africa. It has noted the positive impact of their activities and also brought to the fore some of their failures regarding their inability to confront human suffering, abuse, and inequalities against the indigenous Africans, as the missionaries rather concentrated mostly on teaching. As noted, the role played by the colonial missionaries in Africa poses a number of ethical questions: Was it right that the missionaries should elevate teaching over social justice? Why did they overlook the suffering and inhumane treatment of the people to whom they were proclaiming the gospel? Was that the mandate Jesus gave to his disciples? It must be noted that the many unresolved moral questions call for ethical theories to understand the role played by the missionaries. One such theory is the consequentialist approach

63. Mary C. Karasch, *Slave Life in Rio de Janeiro* (Princeton, NJ: Princeton University Press, 1987), 4–9.

64. Cannon, "Christian Imperialism," 1.

65. Niall Ferguson, *Empire: The Rise and Demise of the British World Order and the Lessons for Global Power*, (New York: Basic Books, 2002), 116.

to ethics. Consequentialism affirms that the moral reasoning of any action is to be found in its consequences. In other words, actions are considered right and wrong depending on the consequences they produce. The right act—in any circumstance—is the act that produces the best overall result as determined by the relevant theory of value.[66] This approach suggests that the consequences of an action, rather than the action itself, determine what is right or wrong in ethical matters; thus, the end justifies the means. A document from the World Council of Churches (WCC) has noted that in ethical matters the actions that "achieve the greatest happiness for the greatest number of people" are what determine whether an action is right or wrong.[67] Using this theory as a lens, therefore, to view the missionaries' activities of elevating teaching over social justice is as much a moral issue as the structures that were put in place by the colonial leaders. This is because the greatest numbers of the indigenous people were not happy with the consequences of Missionaries silence to issues of social injustice imposed on them by the Colonial Administration. The whole experience of the transatlantic slave trade was an example of actions full of unhappiness for the greatest number of Africans, actions that led to their pain, suffering, and death. Another ethical theory that will help us answer the above questions is Emmanuel Kant's ethics of duty or what is commonly referred to as deontology. This approach to ethical matters, argues that an action is morally right only if it is done out of a sense of duty.[68] This implies that "some actions are right or obligatory, irrespective of their consequences, while other actions are wrong, irrespective of their consequences."[69] Relating this theory to the part the missionaries played, it is evident that even though they had the duty to preach a holistic message, they chose to elevate teaching over social justice issues and remained silent to the numerous inhuman practices against the indigenous Africans which made their actions problematic. It must be noted that the missionaries' message in its totality was to be a message of liberation from sin as well as social injustices and inequalities.

66. Tom L. Beauchamp and James F. Childress, *Principles of Biomedical Ethics*, 6th ed. (New York: Oxford University Press, 2009), 337.

67. World Council of Churches, *Facing AIDS: The Challenges, the Church's Response* (Geneva: World Council of Churches, 1997), 52.

68. George Chryssides and John Kaler, *An introduction to Business Ethics*. (London: Chapman and Hall 1993) 97.

69. Torbjörn Tännsjö. *Understanding Ethics: An introduction to Moral Theory*. (Edinburgh: Edinburgh University Press, 2002). (54)

What Ought We to Do?

In practical terms, what ought postcolonial African missions entail? What ought those who carry the great commission do? As has been noted, the message of the Great Commission is not about elevating teaching but also about restoring justice and equality.[70] We are being challenged to understand how our interpretation and responses to the Great Commission are to be redeemed and appropriated in postcolonial Africa in a way that presents a holistic ministry to all. Andrew Porter has argued that "missionary work and education, despite their manifest limit, often had an important liberating impact and were welcomed for that."[71] This liberating impact is what colonial mission overlooked resulting in a number of injustices. Postcolonial missions must be challenged to embrace a liberating message that will address issues of social injustices and not elevate teaching at the expense of justice. It must not be contaminated or influenced by any oppressive agenda, but it must present the message as it is. Kapolyo adds that "as the number of Christians grows in Africa, let the church on the continent be found faithful in advancing the frontiers of mission for the honor and glory of Jesus our Lord."[72] Not until our message addresses contemporary social injustices and issues of inequalities such as HIV and AIDS, modern-day human trafficking, crime, poverty, hunger, ecological crisis, violence against women and children, and in recent times violence against men and people of different sexual orientation, a holistic commission cannot be achieved. Postcolonial missions cannot condone abuse and human suffering. Therefore, responding to these challenges requires re-contextualizing the Great Commission with prophetic focus that fearlessly affirms God as a compassionate God who is interested in liberating all people, women and men alike.

70. See Mitzi J. Smith's essay, "'Knowing More than is Good for One': A Womanist Interrogation of the Matthean Great Commission," in this volume.

71. Andrew Porter, "'Cultural Imperialism' and the Protestant Missionary Enterprise, 1780–1914," *Journal of Imperial and Commonwealth History* 25 (1997): 367–91 (333).

72. Kapolyo, "Matthew," 1170.

2

Examining the Promulgation and Impact of the Great Commission in the Caribbean, 1492–1970: A Historical Analysis

Dave Gosse

INTRODUCTION

Yale University church historian Lamin Sanneh in his book, *Translating the Message: The Missionary Impact,* highlights the fundamental principle of translatability in the growth of Christianity from a small first-century Jewish sect to a global religious power. Sanneh writes,

> . . . from its origins, Christianity identified itself with the need to translate out of Aramaic and Hebrew, and from that position came to exert a dual force in its historical development. One part of that was the resolve to relativize its Judaic roots, with the consequence that it promoted significant aspects of those roots. The other part was the destigmatization of Gentile culture by adopting that culture as a natural extension of the life of the new religion. . . . Thus it was that the two subjects, the Judaic and Gentile, became closely intertwined in the Christian dispensation, both crucial to the formative image of the new religion.[1]

---

1. Lamin Sanneh, *Translating the Message: The Missionary Impact on Culture,* 2nd ed. (Maryknoll, NY: Orbis Books, 2009), 1.

Kenneth Scott Latourette concurs with Sanneh and argues that one of the reasons for the growth of Christianity by the sixth century was that the nature of Christianity had been greatly changed from that of its New Testament origins to fit the various environments it had penetrated. Thus, Christianity was a potent force in the various gentile territories as its belief in the miraculous power of the cross and the rites of the church to expel demons, to cure diseases in humans and beast, and to fend off physical disaster had tremendous appeal to the various minds of the respective cultures.[2]

This missiological imperative of translatability into the various cultures that the Christian church has sought to convert unfortunately has not remained the driving philosophy during the long history of the Christian church. As such, the gospel of the Christian church has been oftentimes hijacked by powerful invading Christian societies resulting in a Christian culture being foisted on other subjugated cultures.

One such example is the case of the Niger Delta Missions in Nigeria of the nineteenth century. Henry Venn, the secretary of the Church Missionary Society (CMS) in London, sought to emphasize the concept of the indigenous church as the central construct of mission theory. A church was judged to be indigenous when it was self-propagating, self-financing, and self-governing. Venn developed his theory of mission in a series of pamphlets and policy statements written in the years 1846–65.[3] Venn was convinced that in their missions to Africa, Africans were capable of leading missionary enterprises and as such had given African Anglican Bishop S. A. Crowther full control of the Niger Delta Mission. Venn believed that it was the European missionaries' job to train black clergymen and to organize the church until it was financially self-supporting, self-propagating, and self-governing (*native agency*). As soon as these aims were achieved the church should become independent of its parent body. At this stage the European missionary was expected to move on and repeat the same process elsewhere. It was in such a context that Venn in 1864 persuaded the Archbishop of Canterbury to appoint Crowther as the first African Bishop of the CMS Niger Mission.[4]

However, as soon as Venn died in 1872, this philosophy of native agency died with him as the policy came to be questioned. The questioning coincided

2. Kenneth Scott Latourette, *The Thousand Years of Uncertainty: A.D. 500–1500* (New York: Harper & Brothers, 1938), 7.

3. Wilbert R. Shenk, "Venn, Henry," *Biographical Dictionary of Christian Missions*, ed. Gerald H. Anderson (New York: Macmillan, 1998), 698.

4. Waibinte Wariboko, *Planting Church Culture at New Calabar* (San Francisco: International Scholars, 1998), 128.

with the growing desire of British officialdom directly to govern the now successful Niger Delta mission that Crowder had successfully led. Within the hierarchy of the CMS, the powers of Bishop Crowther were gradually taken from him and restored to Europeans. Europeans were appointed to manage all administrative matters pertaining to the Niger Mission.[5] More important was the campaign to cast doubt on the leadership ability of West Africa's first native Bishop, as the CMS later announced at the death of Bishop Crowther in 1891 that no other African would be appointed to succeed him as Bishop of the Niger.[6]

Given the colonial context, the African leaders who were partners with Crowther interpreted the CMS's actions as racist and a deliberate move to deny the Africans any rights in the leadership of their church or to play any part in determining their own spiritual development. Thus, in 1892, a number of these African leaders seceded from the Church of England and formed their own indigenous church entitled "The Niger Delta Pastorate Church."[7] Although the initiative by these African leaders was not successful in that they later rejoined the Church of England, numerous African scholars argue that the racial stereotyping of Africans as inferior and incapable of leading a successful church was the main reason for humiliating Bishop Crowther. This was especially so since Western Europe was in the midst of colonizing the Africans and justifying their colonization on the basis of the weaknesses of the Africans, their culture, and civilizations. Christian principles and values had become subservient to politics.

It is not surprising that missionary outreach by Europeans since the fifteenth century (expansion into the Americas) and later by North Americans in the nineteenth and twentieth centuries and following has displayed this tendency to subjugate native societies, since these Euro-Americas have been wedded to European colonialism. As such, the translatability of European and North American Christianity into the contemporary dress of Caribbean culture, in particular, has been ignored. In fact, a reversal has been in effect as European and later American missionaries have been most critical of Caribbean culture, viewing it as "inferior" and deliberately seeking to replace it with their respective cultures as the norm. The gospel of Jesus, the Christ, as a neutral gospel for all humankind of all nations, in which all persons can hear the gospel in their language, has been replaced since the fifteenth century with a primarily Euro-North American gospel. This distortion of the gospel is primarily because

5. Ibid., 128–29.

6. Ibid., 129.

7. Ibid.

of the colonial expansion of Europe into the Americas and the nature of European Christianity that had become subservient to the colonizing mission and its goals.

PART ONE: THE EUROPEAN CHURCH IN THE CARIBBEAN

THE SPANISH PARADIGM IN THE CARIBBEAN

When Columbus reached the American continent in 1492, it was inhabited by fifty-seven million people, one-eighth of the world's population at that time. The indigenous people belonged to different nations and had achieved different levels of civilizations.[8] At the end of the fifteenth century when the Spaniards invaded the Caribbean region, they found the Ciboneys, the first inhabitants of these islands, living on the western coast of Cuba and in the remote areas of Haiti. They lived in caves and fed on fish, oysters, and other types of seafood. The Tainos, a branch of the great Arawak population, inhabited the center and east of Cuba, Jamaica, Haiti, and Puerto Rico. The Caribs lived in the east and south of Puerto Rico in the Lesser Antilles.[9]

Towards the end of 1493, Columbus landed for a second time, in Hispaniola, this time with seventeen ships and approximately 1,500 people. Among them were members of the clergy such as the Reverend Bernardo Boyl, Apostolic vicar of the newly discovered region. Twelve other members of the clergy accompanied the Reverend Boyl. Although some of these clergymen returned home between 1494 and 1495, the remaining clergymen watched powerlessly as the Spanish conquest transformed what was once a peaceful region into a violent colony. Thousands of Tainos were enslaved and forced to work by men who had come to the region for quick economic gains.[10]

Despite the initiative of Queen Isabella of Spain who attempted to regulate the affairs in the Caribbean by insisting that the Indians were to pay low taxes (a tax similar to that paid by servants in Spain) and receive protection from the authorities, the Indians were still exploited. Thus, on March 20, 1503, Governor Ovando received an order from the Queen reminding him to treat the Indians well and to let them live in their own communities, ruled by a state governor who was to defend their rights and give them protection. Each community was also to receive a church with a priest to educate the inhabitants in the Catholic faith and allegiance to the Castilian Crown.[11] Moreover, a school was to be built

8. Armando Lampe, *Christianity in the Caribbean* (Kingston: University of the West Indies Press, 2001), 2.

9. Ibid., 2–3.

10. Ibid., 3.

next to the church where the children would assemble twice daily so that the priest could teach them reading and writing and basic Christian prayers.[12]

However, the Queen's idea was totally contrary to the colonists' interests, since the lucrative Spanish domination over the island was based on land distribution among the colonists as well as on Indian enslavement. The colonists got their wish and, as mandated on the royal decree of December 20, 1503, the taxes paid by the Indians were given to the colonists instead of to the Crown. In return, the colonists were to give protection to the Indians and educate them in the Catholic faith with the help of priests. This was the beginning of the Encomienda system (under which land and inhabitants were granted to colonists). In this way the Crown achieved high economic growth but at a high cost. Forced labor resulted in the suicide of thousands of Indians who drank cassava juice; many women aborted or killed their offspring, while others were victims of hunger, or of the newly acquired diseases introduced by the Europeans against which they had no defense. A survey of 1508 indicated that in that year, there were only 60,000 Indians remaining on the island. It is estimated that in 1492 the population had been five or six times greater.[13]

From the very outset of initial contact of European Christianity (Catholicism) in the Caribbean, Christianity was fraught with various inconsistencies and difficulties due to the merger of church and state (*Patrona Real*) as being central to the Spanish colonial apparatus and to the over-exploitation and genocide by the Spanish conquistadors, which merely resulted in the laws (*Burgos Laws*) of December 27, 1512.[14] Armando Lampe argues that the new laws were useless to protect the Indians as once again the legal status of the natives of America was redefined as "free vassals of the Spanish Crown," free people with the right to their own homeland and their own economy. But as vassals, they were also obliged to serve the Crown with their labor, provided that this included regular time off and payment in kind of clothes and furniture. At the same time, these laws reconfirmed the conditions imposed by the Pope to convert the Indians to the Christian faith. These laws also perpetuated a false impression of an interrelated community life between the newcomers and

11. The Kingdom of Castile was one of the powerful political provinces in Spain responsible for the unification of Spain as a modern state. Between the twelfth and the sixteenth centuries, the Kingdom of Castile formed political alliances with the provinces of Leon, Navarre, and Aragon and was by default the Spanish government of the period.

12. Ibid., 5.

13. Ibid.

14. These are the first codified laws drafted by the Castilian crown with reference to the governing of the indigenous peoples of the Caribbean.

the natives, including the Encomienda system, by assuming that the Europeans would, by example, promote a fraternal reorientation of the Indians to Christian life. It was evident that the Burgos Laws did not take into account the proven selfishness of the colonists and their desire for power and riches, which was contrary to the Christian faith.[15]

Although the advocacy for the Indians intensified under Bartholemeu Las Casas,[16] the majority of the Indian communities established in Hispaniola had disappeared. By 1520 those who had not been killed by disease had fled to the mountains to escape the encomenderos who remained in need of slaves, not so much for work in the mines but for their booming plantations.[17] Spanish colonialism had developed a paradigm of exploiting the inhabitants of the Caribbean through forced and slave labor along with the environmental and ecological destruction of the natural habitat of the Caribbean. They had benefitted economically as a result, and it was only a matter of time before other European powers would replicate and enhance the development model pursued by the Spanish colonialists.

OTHER EUROPEANS IN THE CARIBBEAN

The economic success of Spain brought an almost immediate response from Northern European countries led primarily by the Dutch, who were eager and able to fill the breach caused by Spain. Spain was unable to build merchant marine capacity fast enough to supply the needs of its rapidly expanding and far-flung American empire. Much of the sixteenth and seventeenth centuries in the Caribbean, therefore, resolved itself into a kind of undeclared war among Holland, England, France, and Spain for Caribbean commerce.[18]

The English first established colonies in the eastern islands of the Caribbean between 1623 and 1635, and later in the western Caribbean, such as Jamaica, in 1655.[19] The French followed a similar pattern starting from the eastern Caribbean island of St. Kitts in 1625, along with Martinique, Guadeloupe,

15. Ibid., 7–8.

16. Las Casas was a Dominican priest from Seville, Spain who was originally an explorer but became a devoted advocate on behalf of the Indians in the Caribbean. He was the first residential bishop of Chiapas, Mexico, and had become so influential as a priest in the Caribbean that he was given a formal title of "Protector of the Indians" in the Caribbean.

17. Ibid., 14.

18. Tony Martin, *Caribbean History from Pre-Colonial Origins to the Present* (NJ: Prentice Hall, 2011), 40.

19. Lampe, *Christianity in the Caribbean,* 84.

Grenada, St. Lucia and moving westwards to capture the important island of St. Dominque (Haiti) in 1697.[20]

Ministers of the Church of England (Anglicans) were at work from the early days of settlement in the British Caribbean; meanwhile, the Jesuits (Catholics) were the first missionaries to work with the French colonists as early as the 1640s.

In each British colony, the small and highly organized parish church became the center both of ecclesiastical life and of civil administration. The parish became the basic unit of ecclesiastical and civil administration in the West Indies. Each parish had a vestry (or governing body) elected annually by the freeholders of property within the boundaries of the parish. The vestry was required by law to make provision for the maintenance of the church. This included the responsibility of providing a church building as well as a salary and suitable accommodation for the incumbent minister. The rector of the parish was an ex officio member of the vestry. The ability of the vestry to discharge these obligations depended on the size and economic circumstances of the parochial community of freeholders. The function of the parish as the basic unit of civil administration, and especially as the basic unit of local government, took precedence over its function as an ecclesiastical district. As such, the ecclesiastical authority was not an independent institution of the civil authority and was largely subjected to the state. The recruitment of the clergy was conducted through initiatives of the local vestry and the colonial governor, although the bishop of London was responsible for issuing a license to clergy intending to hold ecclesiastical office in the colonies. Upon arrival in the colonies, however, the clergy was subject to the supervision of the civil authorities.[21]

The church in both the British and French colonial Caribbean, therefore, was a part of the colonial ruling class that had two distinct societies in each colony: these could be defined as (1) the society of free persons and (2) of the enslaved Africans. As far as the colonial legislators were concerned, the established church was to serve the needs of a white society.

Early attempts to extend the church's mission toward the blacks (slaves and free) were met with widespread resistance in the Caribbean. The colonial legislatures were able to define the scope of the church's mission as they saw fit. In Barbados, legislation was enacted to prevent the Quakers from admitting slaves to their meetings. In Jamaica, despite the pious injunction inserted in the

20. James Ferguson. *The Story of the Caribbean People* (Kingston, Jamaica: Ian Randle Publishers), 1990, 68.

21. Lampe, *Christianity in the Caribbean,* 87.

slave code of 1696 requesting "all masters, mistresses, owners, and employers" to make provision for the religious instruction and conversion of their slaves, little action was taken to give effect to it. The real intention of the Jamaican legislators in this regard seemed to have been more accurately expressed in the text of the law in which that legislature fixed the fee for administering the sacrament of Holy Baptism to a slave at £1 3s. 9d.,[22] "a sum large enough to be prohibitory." Generally, the church's mission to the enslaved Africans was discouraged in all the territories of the Caribbean—whether British, French, Dutch, or Danish.[23]

For all persons attending public worship in any of the European-led churches, the seating arrangements emphasized the distinctions based on class and race, which the local magnates considered necessary for the preservation of a slave society. There was limited seating accommodation in most church buildings. In fact, few buildings provided seating accommodation for a congregation of more than 150. In addition, the system of renting pews, which was managed by the vestry, operated in such a way as to ensure that the correct social order was observed in church. And as the number of coloreds and blacks attending church services increased towards the end of the eighteenth century, they were forced to take their places at the back of the church and in the gallery.[24]

There were, however, exceptions. Influenced by the work of the regular clergy of the Roman Catholic Church in the French West Indies, Christopher Codrington, governor of the Leeward Islands and owner of several plantations there and in Barbados, believed that it was unlikely that the secular clergy of the Church of England would extend the church's mission to the slaves. Codrington, anxious as he was to appoint those who possessed the training and discipline that would qualify them for missionary work among the slaves, was unable to recruit anyone. In his last will and testament, he sought to remove the deficiency. He bequeathed his estates in Barbados to the recently formed Society for the Propagation of the Gospel (SPG) into foreign parts for the

22. 1£ is a British pound; 3s is three shillings and 9d is nine pence. In the 1800s in the British Caribbean, 1£ was equivalent to about $4–5 US, and a shilling, about $0.30–0.40 US. Enslaved Africans were not paid for their services, and the few skilled slaves that were paid for jobs on or off the plantation would earn from one to two shillings at most. For enslaved Africans earning as much as one shilling per day, they would have to save twenty-three shillings in no less than twenty-three days to pay for baptism, so all their savings would be paid to the church. It was clear that the average enslaved African who was not paid at all could not afford such a luxury. The few enslaved Africans who might have been able to save money might not have chosen to use it for baptism.

23. Ibid., 91–92.

24. Ibid., 99.

purpose of establishing a college in Barbados to train ministers for missionary work in the colonies. He directed that the estates should be kept intact, and that the slave population should be maintained and provided with the means for conversion.[25]

The need to encourage colonists to settle in the British colonies in order to ensure the military and economic security of the colonies led to the application of a higher level of religious tolerance than that of seventeenth-century England.[26] Thus, Roman Catholics, Methodists, Moravians, Jews, Quakers, and other nonconformist churches such as Baptists and Wesleyans became part of the religious establishment of the colonies in the British Caribbean.

The colonial state's control of the church did not change until 1824 when Jamaica and Barbados were given their own bishops with the resources to serve in areas the church had forgotten. Secondly, with the abolition of the slave trade in the British Caribbean in 1834 and the abandonment of apprenticeship[27] in 1838, full freedom was now extended to the former slaves in the British colonies, 1848 in the French and Danish colonies, and 1886 in the Spanish colonies.

Missionary Activity in the Post-emancipation Period

The post-emancipation period in the Caribbean provided a golden opportunity for both Catholic and Protestant missionaries to finally position the Caribbean church to become self-autonomous, self-financing, and self-propagating. The majority black population that constituted the Caribbean was now free and could now be more mobilized and empowered by their missionaries. Unfortunately, the Caribbean people entered a new round of colonialism as missionary ideology generally remained in line with that of the colonial state, therefore limiting the spiritual, social, economic, and political growth of the Caribbean peoples.

By the later nineteenth and twentieth centuries, Protestantism overtook Catholicism as the major religious expression and played a major role in the spiritual formation of the Caribbean as most of these missionaries came from the United States, especially in the twentieth century. As such, the religious

25. Ibid., 95–96.

26. Ibid., 89.

27. Apprenticeship was the "preparatory" period from the end of formal slavery in 1834 to full freedom in 1838 in the British territories. During this period, former slaves were called "apprentices" and were compelled to work for forty and a half hours per week for their former masters for no charge. Work done outside of the compulsory hours by the apprentices attracted a charge that would be negotiated between apprentices and planters.

landscape became more complex and competitive. These Protestant churches that populated the Caribbean landscape encompassed the Pentecostals, Seventh-day Adventists, Jehovah's Witnesses, and more recently the Church of the Latter-day Saints (Mormons). We must also include the Holiness movements encompassing the various Church of God movements, in addition to the Revivalist movements such as the Shouters in Trinidad and Tobago, St. Vincent, Grenada, and Guyana; the Shakers and Streams of Power in St. Vincent; the Tie Heads (members of the Jerusalem Apostolic Spiritual Baptist Church) in Barbados and St. Lucia; and the Jordanites of Guyana.[28]

Race and class stratification is a most important feature of missionary activity in the post-emancipation period and significantly shaped the Caribbean church in the nineteenth and twentieth centuries. From around 1840 to the 1900s, race and class have been significant in also impacting church membership. The colonial state and its ideology of stratifying persons into groups have been significant in determining church affiliation. Such a religious alignment was to continue up to the present period and had a profound effect on the churches' ministry to the large society.[29]

For example, in the early 1800s, the Native Baptist Church attracted the largest following among the ex-field slaves, and later among the working class. While the Methodist and Anglican churches were popular among the mulattoes and free blacks, and later among the middle class. The Moravian Church, because of its endorsement of and participation in the institution of slavery, became and remained a marginal denomination among working-class Africans. Most of the Europeans in the colonies retained membership in the established churches such as the Anglicans, Presbyterians, Congregationalists, and the Roman Catholics.[30]

The Roman Catholic, Anglican, Presbyterian, Lutheran, and Dutch Reformed Churches were principal subscribers to the institution of slavery. After emancipation, these churches remained the traditional and recognized groups in the colonial Caribbean, and membership in those churches was extremely important as they became vehicles for social and economic mobility. Within the first decade after emancipation, membership in the Baptist Church multiplied a hundredfold as it was the church of the ordinary working-class

---

28. Richard S. Hillman and Thomas J. D'Agostino, eds., *Understanding the Contemporary Caribbean* (Kingston: University of West Indies Press, 2009), 291.

29. Robert J. Stewart, "Religion, Myths and Beliefs: Their Socio-Political Roles," in *General History of the Caribbean,* ed. P. C. Emmer, Bridget Bereton, B. W. Higman (London: Unesco, 2004), 4:62–63, 65–66.

30. Patrick Hylton, *The Role of Religion in Caribbean History* (Washington, DC: Billpops, 2002), 62.

blacks. It had become the fourth largest denomination in the Caribbean, preceded only by Roman Catholicism, Anglicanism, and Methodism. [31]

The class and color contradictions that were features of colonial life in the respective territories were also manifest in the Christian Churches and continue even until today. These cleavages are present even in small colonies like the Cayman Islands where most of the inhabitants are Africans. The overwhelming majority of the 7,000 people in the Turks and Caicos Islands are also Africans, but the economic and social life of the colony was and continues to be controlled by Europeans who constitute less than one percent of the population. Most Europeans live on the island of Grand Turk, and the Church of England is the strongest there. Most Africans live in the Caicos Islands, and the Baptist and Wesleyan (Methodist) churches are strongest there.[32]

Using Jamaica as an example of the British West Indies can further explain how the social construct of race and class became critical features in not only the social construction of the society but also in its religious expression. Entering the twentieth century, at the base of the society were the ex-slaves and their descendants. Separating the base from the white elites, who were at the apex, were the children of miscegenation—the offspring of members of the white managerial class and black slave and ex-slave women. The most important criterion of social worth and status was skin color. In a real sense, therefore, despite the fact that slavery had been dismantled, the social stratification of the colony remained much the same as it had been in pre-emancipation Jamaica. The difference was that the slaves were now free. Given time, education, and the attainment of some of the status symbols, among which was religious affiliation prized by the society, a few might reach the lower rungs of the middle class ladder or, at least, the upper levels of the lower class gradations. Beyond that, social mobility was impossible since elitism was associated with white skin pigmentation.[33]

The distribution of church membership in Jamaica showed a race and color bias as well. Whites were Anglicans, although Scotsmen, not surprisingly, showed a preference for the Presbyterian Kirk.[34] As the established churches of the British realm, the Anglican and Presbyterian churches enjoyed great prestige. The urban membership of the Methodist church in the island was almost exclusively colored. This may be explained by the fact that the early Methodist missionaries concentrated their efforts in and about Kingston where

31. Ibid.

32. Ibid.

33. Dale Bisnauth, *History of Religions in the Caribbean* (Kingston: Kingston Publishers, 1989), 196.

34. The Presbyterian Church in Scotland is known informally by its Scots language as "the Kirk."

there was a heavy concentration of free colored people. Nevertheless, the colored nature of the Methodist congregations contrasted sharply with the urban membership of the Baptist church that was almost exclusively black. The membership of the Baptist church was responsible for its reputation that it was a "poor man's" church. The reputation, in turn, might have helped to make the Baptist church attractive to the blacks who lived in poverty.[35]

The race and color pattern of church membership seen in Jamaica might not have been as neatly drawn in all the British colonies, but the pattern itself was repeated from colony to colony. It was the peculiar missionary thrusts and emphases of the several churches in the pre-emancipation period that were responsible for the development of the pattern. Those emphases themselves were, in the first place, determined by the very nature of the plantation society.[36]

In places such as Bermuda, the Bahamas, and the Cayman Islands where the sugar plantation did not develop and where there was no white plantocracy to serve, the Anglican Church was tardy in establishing a footing. Meanwhile, the substantial numbers of whites there joined the Presbyterian, Independent (Congregational), and Methodist churches. Even so, the race and color bias in church membership developed. Thus, in New Providence, the Methodist church became the church of the whites and coloreds, while the Baptist membership was almost exclusively black. In Bermuda, the Presbyterian, Independent, and (later) the Anglican churches served the white islanders, while the Methodist church served the blacks.[37]

Even the Baptist church in Jamaica was affected by racial and class distinctions as the Native Baptists, which had predominantly black leadership separated from the other Baptists connected to the worldwide Baptist movement, since they now had white leadership. These racist attitudes and prejudices were evident even among the most eminent and distinguished Baptist and Methodist clergymen of the period. In his commentary on the class and color contradictions in Haiti, the Reverend Edward B. Underhill, secretary of the Baptist movement, wrote,

> The long existing feud between the brown and the black in Hayti, unchecked by the energy and superior will of the white, has been the fruitful source of its anarchy and decrepitude. It is incumbent on every friend of the negro race to discourage, and in every proper

35. Ibid.
36. Ibid., 197.
37. Ibid.

way to repress, a similar strife in Jamaica. For years to come the predominance of the European will be necessary for this purpose – to harmonize, by impartial and just regard to the rights of all, the conflicting social elements which differing color and race produce.[38]

Reverend Underhill identified color differences as the basis of the social contradictions in Haiti. According to him, the resolution of these social conflicts could only be provided by white leadership. Haiti, the only country in the Western Hemisphere at the time that was not ruled by Europeans, was condemned by the good Reverend for its state of "anarchy and decrepitude." Not one single word was mentioned by him about the intrigues, conspiracies, and unrelenting economic and political siege of Haiti by the Western powers that kept the country in a state of instability and zero-growth. His deep-seated bigotry is laid bare by his appeal to those who were concerned about the welfare of the African people to "discourage and even repress any striving on the part of Africans to create another Haiti"—that is, to rule themselves.[39]

The eminent theologian and church administrator made it clear that without European leadership Africans would become victims of their own savagery and ineptitude and degenerate into a state of anarchy. These views, incidentally, were similar to those of the philosopher David Hume and President Jefferson of the United States, among others. Jefferson the distinguished third President of the United States and the author of the famous phrase "all men are created equal," nevertheless stated in 1781 that "blacks were inferior to the whites in the endowments both of body and mind."[40] Hume, on the other hand, an outstanding British enlightenment philosopher, categorically stated his views on Africans as follows:

I am apt to suspect the Negroes to be naturally inferior to the whites. These scarcely ever was a civilized nation of that complexion, or even any individual eminent in action or speculation. No indigenous manufacturers amongst them, no arts, no sciences. On the other hand, the most rude and barbarous of the whites, such as the ancient Germans, the present Tartars, have still something eminent about them . . . Such a uniform and constant difference could not happen .

38. Hylton, *The Role of Religion in Caribbean History*, 67.

39. Ibid., 68.

40. Mary B. Norton et al., eds. *A People and a Nation,* 5th ed. (Boston: Houghton Mifflin Co., 1998), 180.

. . if nature had not made original distinction betwixt these breeds of men.[41]

Reverend Underhill's commentaries about Africans in Jamaica were equally reprehensible. He stated that the "people of Jamaica are great deceivers and liars," adding that it might be a remnant of slavery influences, but that it seemed in most cases "inherent in their character, almost a natural peculiarity." [42] This opinion regarding the relationship between Africans and Europeans was universal among Europeans, secular and clerical, in Europe and in the colonies.

PART TWO: THE AFRO-CHRISTIAN RESPONSE

An African or an indigenous form of religious expression, which took different forms, also developed in tandem with the traditional European church in the Caribbean. This African or indigenous religious expression was further fueled by the colonial realities, particularly the impact of race and class stratification both in the Caribbean and in the Caribbean church.

The foreign missionaries had a most difficult time eliminating the desire of the majority black population for greater forms of African derived religious expression. To be fair to these missionaries, this was not a new problem but one that earlier missionaries grappled with during the period of slavery. With emancipation however the dynamics had changed as they had to now compete to gain the loyalty of the black population. This was even more pronounced in British colonies like Jamaica after the 1860s, when there were thousands of new arrivals of African indentured servants into the colonies.

Thus by the middle of the twentieth century there were a plethora of African derived religions throughout the British, French, Spanish and Dutch Caribbean. What was distinguishable about these religions was the extent to which Christian doctrines, practices, rituals, and symbols were important features. Such religious expressions include Afro-Catholic ones such as Vodou in Haiti, Santeria in Cuba, the Dominican Republic, and Puerto Rico. The Afro-Protestant ones include the Spiritual Baptists in Trinidad and Tobago, Revivalism, Kumina and Convince in Jamaica, the Big Drum in Grenada and Carricou and the Kele in St. Lucia.[43]

By the earliest twentieth century, the two more powerful responses to the mainline Christian churches have been Pentecostalism and Rastafarianism.

41. Emmanuel Chukwudi Eze, ed., *African Philosophy* (Oxford: Blackwell Publishers, 1998), 214.

42. Hylton, *The Role of Religion in Caribbean History*, 67.

43. Hillman and D'Agostino, eds., *Understanding the Contemporary Caribbean*, 290.

PENTECOSTALISM

By the 1930s, Pentecostal churches had become firmly rooted in Caribbean religious life. They continued to grow vigorously for the rest of the century. The mere fact that it began to grow significantly in the final decades of British colonialism in the West Indies is seen by some scholars as a desire for democratic expression among subject peoples. More important it has become a form of resistance against British colonial society and a rejection of the traditional churches with their British connections. The participatory nature of its worship and its simplicity with respect to church symbols and paraphernalia is symbolic of earlier forms of Afro-Christian expressions that were always in tension with the traditional Christianity.[44]

Caribbean scholars have been ambivalent in critiquing the value of Pentecostalism and its impact on Jamaica. On a positive note, the adherents have been largely from the poor working class in society. As such, it has provided for many of its poorly formally educated leaders and followers a sense of empowerment that would have otherwise left them powerless.[45] Secondly, their mode of communication in their country's Creole language provides a form of affirmation to many working-class persons who are still primarily discriminated against for not being able to express themselves fluently in the European tongue of their respective colonizers. Thus, their working class audience can easily identify with the Pentecostals, as they share similar socioeconomic struggles.[46]

On a negative note, however, scholars argue that Pentecostals have failed to understand and discuss the sinful fundamental social and political structures of the Caribbean and have promoted more the role of individual sin and individual salvation. As such they are weak in critically challenging the status quo and in helping to challenge their large following into bringing about critical social and political change for the many Caribbean people. They are also seen as maintaining a neocolonial dependency on the United States in terms of their theology, funding, and in the type of programs that they execute.[47]

RASTAFARIANISM

Rastafarianism developed in Jamaica in the 1930s as an indigenous religious expression of poor working class blacks, and it has also become a popular phenomenon throughout the Caribbean and the world. Its worldview has been

---

44. Stewart, "Religion, Myths and Beliefs: Their Socio-Political Roles," 589.

45. Ibid.

46. Ibid., 590.

47. Ibid.

very much shaped by the black theology of Marcus Garvey who sought to build a sociopolitical movement to overturn the negative valuations attached to blacks resulting from colonialism. One of its important themes is that of liberation from Babylonian Captivity in the western world and a return to Africa or a greater concentration on Africa along with African culture and practices.[48] As such, the Rastafarians have been most critical of the established church and its theology as they view the church developing an unholy alliance with the state. Wealthy and powerful leaders of the state and society looked to the churches to rationalize their injustices towards the poor blacks. The church in return receives favors from the state leaving the poor poorer and marginalized. Thus, the Christian church is part of Babylon that must also be condemned.[49]

More critically, however, is Rastafarianism's theology of affirmation in which blackness and the black race are badges of honor rather than shame. They have made it their duty to focus deliberately on the rich value of Africa and things African, which, to a large extent, they are way ahead of the Christian church in the Caribbean in relation to some issues such as race. Their radical theology is also a critique of the Caribbean church. Their doctrine of sin, for example, is more in line with the black theology of James Cone and the black theologians, as the Caribbean church has not departed much from that of their European theologians. The Rastafarians do not believe generally in original sin and that humans are born in sin and shaped in iniquity. They claim that the only sin they are aware of in such a scenario is the sin of stealing them away from Africa. The Rastafarian critique of the Caribbean church is an indictment on colonial Christianity as practiced in the Caribbean as they have attempted to contextualize Christianity and to make it more indigenous to Caribbean reality.

CARIBBEAN THEOLOGY

Despite the stranglehold of missionary theology on the Caribbean church some of its leaders who were influenced by liberation theology attempted to indigenize the Caribbean church in the second half of the twentieth century so that it could become more West Indian focused than metropolitan. The focus included social, political, and cultural issues as well as theological and liturgical ones.[50] One of the major initiatives, however, was the development of ecumenism and social action among the traditional churches, namely the Congregationalists, Methodists, Moravians, and Presbyterians. This led to the development of the Christian Action for Development in the Eastern Caribbean

48. Ibid., 561.
49. Ibid., 569.
50. Ibid., 585.

(CADEC) group, and the Caribbean Ecumenical Consultation for Development at Chaguarmass in Trinidad in 1971. By 1973, the regional Caribbean Conference of Churches (CCC) was formed. This was the first such council in the world in which the powerful Catholic Church in the Caribbean was an integral member. The CCC later produced several conferences and academic publications such as essays entitled "Troubling the Waters."[51]

The attempt by the CCC to engage in academic discourse using a multi-disciplinary approach was critical as the church had recognized the need to develop a more authentic Caribbean theology that would be more suited to the Caribbean peoples. More important was the need to remove the theological and institutional legacies of the European and now the North American missionaries and to develop a fully functional indigenous Caribbean church. Despite the necessary and bold attempts by the CCC, their effort remained largely an intellectual enquiry among their churches and among scholars. Their ability to connect to the masses of the Caribbean people was limited, seeing that the Pentecostal and Charismatic churches had much more control of the working-class masses.[52]

PART THREE: NORTH AMERICAN MISSIONARIES AND THE CONTINUED CIVILIZING MISSION

By the middle of the twentieth century, North American missionaries had largely replaced British missionaries, especially in the Protestant churches in the Caribbean. These North American missionaries were also allies of the colonial structure in the Caribbean, since missionaries and colonizers (church and state) largely shared similar ideological values such as the inherent goodness of Western civilization and the need to civilize, Christianize, and humanize the "inferior races and cultures," particularly those from Africa.[53] These missionaries were integral to the philosophy of Manifest Destiny[54] and the belief in the "White Man's Burden" to civilize and Christianize "the heathens" of the "developing" societies in the nineteenth and twentieth centuries. Thus, they conveyed notions of the superiority of Anglo-Saxon culture to the rest of the world. "Referred to as the peaceful conquest of the world, North American

51. Ibid.

52. Ibid., 586.

53. Brian L. Moore and Michelle A. Johnson, *Neither Led nor Driven: Contesting British Cultural Imperialism in Jamaica, 1865–1920* (Kingston: University of West Indies Press, 2004), 167–68.

54. Manifest Destiny is the belief held in the middle to late nineteenth century that it was the destiny of the United States to expand its territory over the entire North America and to expand its political, economic, and social influence.

missionaries dispatched to China, Korea and Africa helped to spur the transfer of American culture and power overseas."[55] Imperialistic expansion was such a feature of North American protestant Christianity in the late nineteenth and twentieth centuries that even university students organized their own foreign missions. Thus, the Student Volunteers for Foreign Missions, which began in the 1880s on college campuses in North America, had placed some six thousand missionaries abroad by 1914.[56]

It is in this context of North American imperialistic expansion that North American protestant missionaries penetrated the Caribbean by the late nineteenth to the early twentieth centuries. One such mission led to the birth of the Church of God in Jamaica by North American missionaries George and Nellie Olson. The couple built the Church of God movement in Jamaica, and their example provides a good paradigm for the ways in which conservative Protestant culture of North America influenced and shaped Christianity in the Caribbean. The Reverend George Olson, his wife Nellie, and their infant son Daniel arrived in Jamaica on July 29, 1907. They landed in Port Antonio, on the eastern part of the island, and the following day they set out for Kingston, the capital of Jamaica. The Olsons arrived in Jamaica at the request of Isaac Delevante, a Jamaican who read *The Gospel Trumpet*, a magazine of the Church of God in North America. Mr. Delevante was impressed with the teaching of the Church of God and wrote to *The Gospel Trumpet* requesting missionaries to come to Jamaica. Interestingly, the Olsons, who worked at *The Gospel Trumpet* in Anderson, Indiana, answered the call to Jamaica.

The Olsons were very successful in establishing churches. By 1932, when the Church of God in Jamaica celebrated its Silver Anniversary, congregations in the Church of God had grown to sixty-six churches with a membership of 1,800 members. By 1942, the congregations increased to eighty while the membership grew to 2,000 persons. The congregations continued to grow through 1955, with the number of churches increasing to eighty-five while the membership increased to 2,800. By 1975, the number of churches continued to increase to around ninety congregations with a membership of around 3,000 persons.[57]

From the outset, Olson intended to build an indigenous church that was self-financing, self-autonomous, and self-propagating. Thus, the strategies employed between Olson and the Missionary Board of the Church of God

55. Norton et al., eds., *A People and A Nation,* 636.

56. Ibid., 636–37.

57. Vilma Bryan, *Revised History of the Church of God in Jamaica* (Kingston: Board of Christian Education, 1989).

in North America, which was financing the mission, was to reduce the salary given to local pastors yearly by fifteen percent. This was to ensure that the local congregations would gradually take responsibility for the pastor's salary. In respect to buildings and other necessary infrastructure, George Olson would still continue to rely on funding from North America.[58]

Under the leadership of Olson, who was the mission secretary of the Church of God Movement in Jamaica, the churches were successful in their self-propagation. However, they had not become self-financing or self-autonomous, although each of the churches had a congregational or democratic form of governance. Despite the geographical growth, much conflict had developed between the Jamaican church and the North American missionaries between the 1950s and the 1960s. A number of the local leaders of the Jamaican church were of the view that the missionaries were no longer needed to provide overall leadership to the church, since they now had the ability to run the church. The local leaders, however, were willing to accept missionary assistance in specialized areas, such as theological training and Christian education.

The Church of God missionaries in Jamaica and in other developing societies where the movement was present seemed to be of a different opinion. They were of the opinion that the younger upstarts or radicals, some of whom were formally educated, were still not in a position to lead the church. Interestingly, many of the older members of the Jamaican church shared the missionaries' view.[59] As such, there were some national church Boards where the missionaries ensured that they themselves occupied all the positions of authority. The missionaries even insisted in the 1950s and 1960s that although they would concede to natives on specific boards and committees of the national church they would not relinquish the positions of mission secretary and national treasurer, since they were the highest leadership positions in the church.[60] Clearly, the missionaries had forgotten that their main objective was to build an indigenous church and not become planted in Caribbean society as the previous plantation owners had done.

The conflict between both groups (Jamaicans and missionaries) was so intense that the leader of the North American Missionary Board had to visit Jamaica all the way from Anderson, Indiana on nine separate occasions from 1955 to 1964 to resolve the thorny transition to what was to become an

---

58. George Olson to Chas. E. Brown, December 14, 1928 and January 3, 1929 (Church of God Papers).

59. Lester A. Crose, Cheryl J. Barton, Donald D. Johnson, eds., *Into All the World: A Century of Church of God Missions* (Anderson, IN: Warner, 2009), 99–100.

60. Ibid., 100.

indigenous church.[61] One particular missionary secretary, Clair Shultz, noticed on his arrival in Jamaica in 1958 that none of the native leaders of the Jamaican church came to meet him at the airport, apart from the Vice President of the Missionary Board in North America, W. W. King, who was in Jamaica to prepare the way for Shultz. Shultz at that time did not view their absence as a serious sign as Jamaica was under a hurricane threat and the local leaders from the church were probably securing their property. However, after a few days on the island, it became quite clear that the Jamaican church was still hostile to both the missionaries and the North American Missionary Board, since they made decisions that were inimical to their interests. Shultz recognized that the distrust of missionaries was so intense that the Jamaican church no longer invited any of them to preach in their churches, visit them, or allowed them to give advice.[62]

One particular issue that insulted some members of the Jamaican church was that the mission secretary had to give a casting vote in board meetings if it was necessary. At this stage of their development, the Jamaican church viewed it as an obvious indictment on their leadership since they were capable of making sensible decisions. They expressed it to Shultz as follows: "This is nonsense. No man no matter his colour or where he is from should have a right like that."[63] Thus, in one of Shultz's first board meetings he was asked specifically his stance on the issue. Shultz skilfully noted that as mission secretary he would not vote on any issue as the Jamaican church was fully capable of making wise choices. If there was a tie on any particular issue, he would ask the Lord's intervention. His response and afterwards his willingness to become more of a facilitator in trusting the Jamaican leaders in decision making helped to some extent in smoothing the tensions between both sides.[64]

Shultz, unlike many of his predecessors, genuinely believed in facilitating an indigenous church as quickly as possible. He gave much latitude to the local leaders to initiate practices in which the North American church would not have allowed. For example, Shultz allowed three women to anoint him and his wife with olive oil all over their heads, neck, arms, fingers, legs and feet, as a symbol of blessing for continued effectiveness in ministry. They placed him and his wife in a room to sit where he had to roll up the leg of his pants. Meanwhile his wife took off her stockings, after which Shultz fully anointed. The gesture could have been interpreted as a sign of "witchcraft and obeah,"[65] which were practices rebuked by fellow missionaries as sinful and codified in

61. Ibid., 107.
62. Clair Shultz, *Wonders in the Deep* (Anderson, IN: Church of God Archives, 1960), 96.
63. Ibid.
64. Ibid.

Jamaican law as evil.[66] Shultz understood the context of the Jamaican church and knew that such activities had become a common feature of the Jamaican and the Caribbean Church of God.

On another occasion, Shultz made it clear to the North American Missionary Board that the Jamaican church already had capable leaders who were qualified to lead the church and equip other leaders. He singled out one individual in particular, Samuel Hines, whom he described as possessing amazing preaching and rhetorical skills. Hines was such an excellent preacher that he could lead an audience spellbound for an hour without anyone falling asleep.[67]

Despite the many positives that Olson brought to the church, one of the major negatives was the Church of God's slowness in fully indigenizing the church. It was not until 1970 that the Jamaican church became fully autonomous and could choose their own Executive Secretary to replace the mission secretary (by that time George Olson had already died). In addition, most of the properties belonging to the Missionary Board were then handed over to the Jamaican church. Ironically, even at that stage, the Jamaican church still could not fund the office of the Executive Chairman and depended on the North American Missionary Board to continue to fund the office but they gradually reduce the salary and benefits by ten percent annually until the Jamaican church could fully fund it.[68]

George Olson's failure to fully indigenize the church is even seen in one of the congregations that he pastored. He served the Higholborn Street church first as pastor and then an associate pastor for over forty years, resigning in 1952. The congregation seemed to have been the one that even initiated his departure, as they chose the exciting local preacher Samuel Hines as pastor. Olson's failure in not speedily indigenizing the church was one of the major factors causing the serious conflict between the Jamaican church and the later missionaries. Olson, as respected as he was by the Jamaican church, sadly expressed his disappointment in the evening of his life that many of the Jamaican leaders and members wanted all the missionaries to now pack their bags and return to the United States.[69]

---

65. Obeah is sometimes spelled Obi, Obea, or Obia. It is a term used to refer to West African folk magic or religion, which was most prevalent in the British West Indies, particularly in Jamaica, during the period of slavery.

66. Shultz, *Wonders in the Deep*, 100.

67. Ibid., 97.

68. General Assembly Booklet of the Church of God in Jamaica, 1970–1971, p. 58.

69. George Olson to Lester Crose, May 28, 1956 (Church of God Papers).

Also, Olson has to be further criticized not only for being slow to indigenize the church, but also for shaping the church with an ultraconservative theology aimed at buttressing colonial Jamaica and not engaging the state and its institutions in their use of power. As such, the missionaries adopted a policy in which critical issues such as race and politics should not be commented on at all. Thus, the church was to be silent on these "controversial issues." Topics such as gambling, however, were commented on to the extent that the General Assembly of the Church of God in 1926 adopted a resolution to the government congratulating the local municipality for voting against a public lottery.[70]

It was quite clear that Olson was not comfortable discussing race, as he always referred to it as "the color question." As a matter of fact, he seemed to have been no different from many whites who believed that persons with fairer skin color, such as mulattoes, were of a better class, were more attractive, and indeed were not black. He spoke glowingly of such individuals and at times lamented that his church did not have more of these persons. Thus, his philosophy was very similar to that of other missionaries in Jamaica who believed that blacks who were usually from the working class should focus on Christianity to improve their morals and to become respectable members of the society.[71] They were to be good and obedient colonial subjects without seeking to engage or challenge the system.

It was not surprising that Olson had a major problem with movements such as the Universal Negro Improvement Association (UNIA) led by Marcus Garvey,[72] who sought to improve the self-image and the socioeconomic and political lives of Afro-Jamaicans. He reiterated in his letters that Garvey was a troublemaker in "constantly stirring up the color question," which was unnecessary. As such, members of his church should have nothing to do with the movement or persons such as Garvey, as he was extremely popular among the poorer class of persons. He dismisses Garvey's movement as anti-Christian, since Garvey fused politics with religion while promoting fun, folly and dancing. Furthermore, he argued that Garvey cursed and swore, and this behavior made him ungodly.[73]

70. George Olson to J. W. Phelps, March 10, 1926 (Church of God Papers).

71. Moore and Johnson, *Neither Led nor Driven*, 167–86.

72. Born in Jamaica, Marcus Garvey was an orator for the Black Nationalism and Pan-Africanism movements, to which end he founded the Universal Negro Improvement Association (UNIA) and African Communities League. Garvey advanced a Pan-African philosophy that inspired a global mass movement known as Garveyism. Garveyism would eventually inspire other movements from the Nation of Islam to Rastafarian. See C. Eric Lincoln and Lawrence H. Mamiya, *The Black Church in the African American Experience* (Durham, NC: Duke University Press, 1990), 125, 166, 177, 209.

73. George Olson to H. M. Riggle, November 5, 1929 (Church of God Papers).

Despite castigating the UNIA as a racist organization whose goal was to create conflict and mayhem, Olson was shocked to know that he as a white missionary was specially invited to speak at the funeral of a UNIA member who had left the Church of God for the UNIA. He was pleasantly surprised to recognize that the UNIA members were respectful and polite, as it was the largest audience to which Olson had ever preached.[74]

Olson was incorrect to argue that the color question that UNIA and even others associated with the Church of God raised was not relevant. Agitation by blacks who were taken advantage of economically, politically, and socially all across the British Caribbean later led to spontaneous labor riots across the entire British Caribbean. These riots led eventually to the British government legitimizing the trade union movement, which later led to political parties becoming legal and eventually to universal adult suffrage and independence by the 1960s.

For Olson to be ministering to a church predominated by working-class blacks who were marginalized by colonial society and to fail to advocate for their interests was poor practice and a bad template for a growing church. No wonder some of his members left the church (E. B. Grant) and, to Olson's surprise, his own members at the Higholborn Street church even questioned his ultraconservative views. They interrogated him on the same color question in 1930 noting that the parent Church of God in the United States has both a black annual convention that is separated from the white church with their own annual convention. Olson admitted that although he tried to answer as best as he could, some of their comments were correct as they were skeptical of Olson's stance on race relations especially since he did not condemn the separation of churches in the United States on race.[75]

CONCLUSION

The Caribbean church has historically been dependent on Europe and North America in that its leadership, its theology, and its polity have been predominantly foreign. Since the Caribbean church had been born out of the context of Spanish colonialism and nurtured by other European nations who ruled the Caribbean, the various missionaries of the Caribbean church were usually more concerned with building a church akin to their cultures than a genuine indigenous Caribbean church. The North American missionaries of the nineteenth and twentieth centuries continued to influence the Caribbean

74. George Olson to H. M. Riggle, June 12, 1930 (Church of God Papers).
75. George Olson to H. M. Riggle, September 9, 1930 (Church of God Papers).

church to their cultural flavor rather than allowing the church to develop its own roots and its real plants. Despite its impact since the 1960s to 1970s, when the Caribbean church could be described as becoming independent of foreign missionaries, the church has had to carry the burden of the colonial and neocolonial values and structures since they have become institutionalized. As such, the critical issues of race, class, and gender discrimination along with the spiritual and social damage done to the psyche of the Caribbean's predominant black and Indian populations are still very much deleterious to the Caribbean church. The Caribbean churches now face the indomitable task of shedding its "potted plants" and strive for greater indigenousness to become a church of the "public square," engaging the sociopolitical and economic structures of the Caribbean. Only then can the Caribbean church become independent of its colonial roots as it practices a theology of affirmation in which the psyche of its predominantly black and Indian populations is repaired and empowered to truly fulfill the mandate and mission of the Lord Jesus Christ.

3

US Colonial Missions to African Slaves: Catechizing Black Souls, Traumatizing the Black *Psychē*

Mitzi J. Smith

INTRODUCTION

The command to teach other nations in Matt. 28:19-20 (24:14; cf. Mark 16:14-18; Luke 24:44-49; John 20:19-23), also known as the Great Commission, eventually became the Magna Carta for missions in the eighteenth century and was canonized in Bible commentaries apparently in the nineteenth century (see my essay in Part 2 of this volume). In his 1792 booklet *An Enquiry into the Obligations of Christians to Use Means for the Conversion of the Heathens,* William Carey, father of modern missions, poses the question whether the Lord's commission given to his disciples is still binding on Christians. Carey identified that commission as "Go and teach all nations" and "go into all the world, and preach the gospel to every creation."[1] He refers to the mission endeavor as "attempts to spread divine knowledge" and argues for the great need for foreign mission (versus domestic missions) where there is no access to knowledge and written resources; missionaries must go where there are no Bibles, written language, ministers, or good civil government, and among people less advantaged.[2] In the nineteenth century, J. Hudson Taylor (1832–1905), the famous missionary to China, asserts in his autobiography that "the Lord Jesus commands, commands me, commands you, into all the world and preach the Gospel to every creature."[3] Taylor may be the first to

---

1. William Carey, *An Enquiry into the Obligations of Christians to Use Means for the Conversion of the Heathens* (London: Leicester, 1792), 6–9, http://www.wmcarey.edu/carey/enquiry/anenquiry.pdf.

2. Ibid., 13.

use the term Great Commission, or at least to popularize it. He found solace in the increase in the number of persons that responded to take the gospel to the wider world and empty themselves to "leave all in obedience to *the great commission*"[4]. While Taylor believed in feeding the hungry, healing the sick, and accommodating indigenous culture, he understood the commission as principally about preaching, teaching, and distributing Bibles, books, and tracts; he did not allow the feeding of hungry children to interrupt Sunday services or preparation therefore.[5]

Nineteenth-century missionaries to the African slaves in the antebellum South, like their predecessors and contemporaries, understood their commission as a call to teach and preach the gospel to *others*. Within the obligatory framework of their commitment to the Matthean Great Commission, missionaries to the African slaves relied on other biblical texts and narratives to convince slave masters of their duty to teach and convert their "poor," "heathen," "brutish," or "savage," Negroes, or African slaves. For example, from the Old Testament the patriarch Abraham provided a model for slave masters: "for I know him, that he will command his children, and his household after him, and they shall keep the way of the Lord . . ." (Gen. 18:19 KJV). Missionaries purposefully deleted the rest of the verse that says "to do justice and righteousness," while emphasizing that Abraham's "household" included his slaves.[6] In fact, the eighteenth-century New England Puritan preacher Cotton Mather (1663–1728) in his essay appended to his catechism asserted the following:

He [Abraham] had some Hundreds of *Servants* belonging to his *Houshold* [sic]: he obtained, that the *Slaves* of his *Houshold* [sic]

---

3. J. Hudson Taylor, *Hudson Taylor: The Autobiography of a Man who Brought the Gospel to China* (Minneapolis: Bethany House, 1987), 118. Originally published under the title *Retrospect*. Taylor founded the China Inland Mission (CIM). The statement "The Great Commission is not an option to be considered; it is a command to obeyed" has been attributed to Hudson Taylor, but no one seems to be able to identify the source.

4. Ibid., 51. Emphasis added.

5. Ibid., 63, 65, 67, 72, 77, 86, 116, 129–30.

6. See Samuel Davies's sermon preached in Hanover on January 8, 1757 entitled "The Duty of Christians to Propagate their Religion among Heathens, Earnestly Recommended to the Masters of Negroe Slaves in Virginia," (London: J. Oliver in Bartholomew-Close, 1757), 10; Cotton Mather, *The Negro Christianized: An Essay to Excite and Assist that Good Work, the Instruction of Negro-Servants in Christianity* (1706), Zea E-Books in American Studies, Book 5, http://digitalcommons.unl.edu/zeaamericanstudies/5, p. 6. See also Tammy K. Byron, "'A Catechism for Their Special Use': Slave Catechisms in the Antebellum South," (unpublished Ph.D. diss., University of Arkansas),109.

should *Know* the *Way of the Lord*; He then *Commanded*, that they should *Keep* that *Way*. Now, *Christianity* is, *The Way of the Lord*. Householder, There are *Servants* pertaining to thy *Houshold* [sic]. It is a mighty Power which thou hast over them; A *Despotick* [sic] *Power* which gives thee numberless Advantages, to call them, and lead them into the *the Way of the Lord*."[7]

Masters could exercise unbridled power over their slaves and compel them to become Christians, at least in name. But slave masters feared that slaves would become unmanageable, desire social equality, and expect or be motivated to seize their freedom. Direct, overt coercion would not yield the desired outcome: content, servile slaves. In the eighteenth century, following the example of the Quakers, the Methodist church, like John Wesley, detested slavery, and they preached both salvation and emancipation until slave masters interrupted and banned their efforts.[8] But in the nineteenth century, Methodist missions to the slaves became "the South's conscientious alternative to antislavery activity—the Methodist Episcopal Church's peculiar work in the peculiar institution" of slavery.[9] In 1844, the Methodist Episcopal Church, which set the example and precedent for missionizing the southern slaves, adopted the *doctrine of noninterference* for church officers. That doctrine said that religious instruction and conversion of slaves could not interfere with civil institutions, particularly the institution of slavery.[10] Between the years 1844 and 1864 the south witnessed a significant increase in slave plantation missions. (Before that period, slave missions were primarily limited to house slaves who attended religious services in and with the master's household.) Over three hundred missionaries were commissioned to the large plantations across the south and more than $1.8 million was given in financial support.[11] These

7. Mather, *The Negro Christianized*, 6, 13. Emphasis in original. In New England in 1700, "negro slaves" accounted for one thousand of the ninety thousand inhabitants. Half of them lived in Massachusetts, being concentrated in Boston, where Puritans traded in slaves and some argued for the conversion of the slaves.

8. Donald G. Mathews, "The Methodist Mission to the Slaves, 1829–1844," *Journal of American History* 51, no. 4 (1965): 615–631 (615).

9. Ibid. See also Albert Raboteau, *Slave Religion: The "Invisible Institution" in the Antebellum South* (New York: Oxford University Press, 1978), 172. The southern Methodist church was the most active among the denominations (Baptist, Presbyterians, and Episcopalians) in plantation missions.

10. W. P. Harrison, ed., *The Gospel among the Slaves* (New York: AMS, 1893), 297. Harrison states that before 1865 "every Methodist preacher, in town or city, became a special missionary to the negroes" (151).

11. Ibid., 297–98, 318–24.

years of missionary increase were motivated by slave revolts,[12] abolitionism, the difficulty and increasing unprofitability of harvesting cotton, encouraging talk of emancipation,[13] and, of course, the Civil War—all threats to the peculiar institution of slavery. Some Christians sincerely desired to "evangelize the poor," but plantation missions were also motivated by a need to create submissive slaves, the aspiration for an exemplary plantation life, and to counter the attacks of abolitionists against the institution of slavery. The Christianizing and catechizing of the slaves functioned both as a salve to relieve the Christian conscience sometimes harassed by the evil nature of slavery and as a justification for slavery.[14]

In this essay, I argue that white missionaries and slave masters, from an overwhelming desire to preserve the institution of slavery, theologically and rhetorically conceptualized and taught the slave to understand himself as a dichotomous being with a soul to be saved and a body to be enslaved, thereby inflicting trauma on his *psyche* "(as defined below). I will examine slave catechisms that were used for the religious instruction of African slaves in the antebellum South. Slave catechisms served as a vehicle for converting slaves to the Christian faith. They were designed for oral instruction since it was forbidden to teach slaves to read, by law or in practice, in most southern states.[15] The instructor or catechist of the slave student (the catechumen) was ideally the slave master or someone sanctioned by him, such as his overseer,[16] his wife or children, a hired white preacher or missionary,[17] and, in rare cases, a black man with an exceptional gift unspoiled by a meticulous sense of and contentment with his place in slave society.[18] Three of the slave catechisms

---

12. A free black man and Methodist, Denmark Vesey attempted a slave revolt in South Carolina in 1822; in 1831, the most infamous and bloody slave revolt was led by Nat Turner in Virginia where sixty whites were killed; in 1839, slave rebels over took the *Amistad*; in 1841, slaves took over the *Creole* ship en route to New Orleans from Virginia and sailed to the Bahamas. See Lerone Bennett, Jr., *Before the Mayflower: A History of Black America* (New York: Penguin, 1982).

13. Harrison, *Gospel among the Slaves*, 120–121.

14. Raboteau, *Slave Religion*, 174.

15. Byron, "A Catechism," 71, 74. Several southern states passed anti-literary laws in the early nineteenth century, including Georgia, North Carolina, and South Carolina. And some states without anti-literary laws sometimes led slaves to believe that they could not legally learn how to read and write.

16. Mather, *The Negro Christianized*, 18. Mather writes, "In a Plantation of many negroes, why should not a Teacher be hired on purpose, to instill into them the principles of the Catechism? Or, if the Overseers are once Catechised themselves, they may soon do the Office of Catechisers unto those that are under them. However, Tis fit for the master also Personally to enquire into the progress which his negroes make in Christianity, and not leave it Entierly [sic] to the management of others."

17. Byron, "A Catechism," 83–85.

that I will analyze were created in that period of increased plantation missions: *A Catechism for Slaves*, an excerpt, (1854); Bishop William Capers's *Catechism for the Use of the Methodist Missions* (1852); *Catechism, to be Taught Orally to those Who Cannot Read; Designed Especially for the Instruction of the Slaves in the Protestant Episcopal Church in the Confederate States* (1862).[19] Prior to creating his own catechisms, Capers probably used an Episcopal Church catechism for instructing children and slaves.[20] A fourth document from an earlier period that I discuss is Puritan minister Cotton Mather's *The Negro Christianized. An Essay to Excite and Assist that Good Word, the Instruction of Negro-Servants in Christianity*, which includes a catechism (1706).[21] This essay also draws upon

18. Harrison, *Gospel among the Slaves*, 139–40. William Capers, the missionary to the black slaves in the south, wrote in 1810 about a black preacher he met in Fayetteville, NC named Henry Evans. Evans is one of those black preachers that was permitted to preach to both white and black audiences. Capers describes him as "most remarkable in a view of his class . . . He was a negro—that is, he was of that race, without any admixture of another." It seems that what was admired most in such negroes was their ability to be content with their social position once converted and to teach other negroes, in word and behavior, so to do. It also appears that Evans was the only capable person allowed to preach to the negroes in his little town. Capers further describes Evans: "I have known not many preachers who appeared more conversant with scripture than Evans, or whose conversation was more instructive as to the things of God. He seemed always deeply impressed with the responsibility of his position, and deeply impressed with the responsibility of his position, and not even our old friend Castile was more remarkable for his humble and deferential deportment toward the whites than Evans. . . . never speaking to a white man but with his hat under his arm, never allowing himself to be seated in their houses, and even confining himself to the kind and manner of dress proper for negroes in general, except his plain black coat for the pulpit." See also Byron, "A Catechism," 96, 101–102. Byron argues that because there were a few instances, one of which she cites, where slave masters set a gifted or competent slave preacher free to preach anywhere he desired, this demonstrated that "some slaveholders were truly interested in slave conversion," (Byron, "A Catechism," 96). But I cannot see how Byron can draw this conclusion given that such a slave could not have preached any message other than one approved by the slave master and that did not oppose slavery (98). So to set the slave free to preach might have been in the interest of maintaining slavery and not due to any unadulterated interest in slave conversions.

19. *A Catechism for Slaves* (1854), "Frederick Douglass's Paper," June 2, 1854, from *The Southern Episcopalian* (Charleston, SC, April, 1854), http://wps.pearsoncustom.com/wps/media/objects/2428/2487068/documents/doc_d066.html; William Capers, *Catechism for the Use of the Methodist Missions* (Richmond: John Early, 1852); *Catechism, to be Taught Orally to Those Who Cannot Read; Designed Especially for the Instruction of the Slaves in the Protestant Episcopal Church in the Confederate States* (Raleigh: Office of "The Church Intelligencer", 1862), http://docsouth.unc.edu/imls/catechisms/catechsl.html.

20. Mathews, "The Methodist Mission," 624. Capers first published *A Catechism for Little Children and for Use on the Missions to the Slaves in South Carolina* in 1833 before creating one dedicated only to slave missions. Capers was a Bishop in the Methodist Episcopal Church and known as "the founder of missions to the slaves." See Harrison, *Gospel among the Slaves*, 279.

21. Mather, *The Negro Christianized.*

Tammy Byron's 2008 unpublished dissertation, "'A Catechism for Their Special Use': Slave Catechisms in the Antebellum South," which is an exhaustive study of eight slave catechisms prepared by the Presbyterian, Episcopalian, Methodist, and Baptist Churches, including Capers's 1852 catechism.[22]

Nineteenth-century catechesis followed the same pattern as in the eighteenth century (except the latter could last for two years) and involved teaching slaves answers to questions spontaneously asked or systematically prepared, as well as the Apostle's Creed, the Lord's Prayer, the Commandments, other prayers and hymns,[23] and sometimes special duties for slaves. Slaves, especially children, were sometimes taught to read in the process of being instructed, but usually solely for the purpose of religious instruction. Slave children were often groomed or taught to read in order to provide other slaves with religious instruction; instead of parents teaching children, children taught their parents. It became a way of converting a "Nation with a Nation."[24]

SAVING BLACK SOULS, TRAUMATIZING BLACK BODIES

Before examining the catechisms, I will briefly discuss the ideology and missionary agenda of converting or saving black *souls*. Slave masters and missionaries used slave catechisms as a means of instructing slaves in the Christian religion in order to save their *souls*. Saving black *souls* became inextricably linked with maintaining slavery and thus the continued traumatization of the black *psyche*. I use the word *psyche* to refer to the total human being, the lives of black folks. White or European missionaries and slave

22. Byron, "A Catechism," 2–3. The slave catechisms Byron analyzes include the Presbyterian catechisms—*A Plain and Easy Catechism, Designed Chiefly for the Benefit of Coloured Persons, to Which are Annexed Suitable Prayers and Hymns* (1828), *Catechism for Colored Persons* (Rev. Charles Colcock Jones, "Apostle to the Blacks," 1834), and *Catechism of Scripture Doctrine and Practice, for Families and Sabbath Schools, Designed also for the Oral Instruction of Colored Persons* (Rev. Charles Colcock Jones, first edition, 1837); Episcopalian catechisms—*Catechism, to be Used in the Religious Instruction of Persons of Colour: To Which are Prefixed, Easy Instructions for Coloured Persons Young or Adult, Who are not yet Baptized* (Christopher E. Gadsden, Paul Trapier, and William Hazzard Barnwell, 1837), *Catechism for the Religious Instruction of Persons of Colour* (1844), and *Manual of Religious Instruction* (John Francis Hoff, 1857); Methodist catechist and minister William Capers's *Catechism for the Use of Methodist Missions* (1852); Baptist Edwin Theodore Winkler's *Notes and Questions for the Oral Instruction of Colored People* (1857). Byron compares the slave catechisms to two catechisms written and used among white Christians: Isaac Watt's *Plain and Easy Catechisms for Children*, first and second editions (1700s) and the Westminster Assembly of Divine's *Westminster Catechism* (1640s).

23. Raboteau, *Slave Religion*, 115.

24. Ibid., 116–17.

masters and colonists grounded their efforts to convert or Christianize black slaves on the ideological metanarrative (controlling mythical story) that black bodies occupy an unalterable, innately inferior social position in relationship to white people; that it was moral to save black souls while oppressing their bodies; that white people and not black people are the intellectual and spiritual custodians of the Christian gospel, and all others are either heathens, pagans, superstitious, religionless, or worshippers of false religions or gods; and that the Christian gospel as conceived by white people, as God's chosen, is pure, objective truth received directly from God. In 1842, Rev. C. C. Jones published a book, *The Religious Instruction of the Negroes in the United States*, in which he advised,

> Having brought distinctly to view this multitude of people introduced amongst us in the inscrutable providence of God, the *original stock* being in a state of absolute *heathenism*, we may inquire into the efforts made for their *religious instruction* . . . Remember that they have immortal souls, and are equally capable of salvation with yourselves; and therefore you have no power to do anything which shall hinder their salvation. Remember that God is their absolute owner. . . . Remember that you are Christ's trustees, or the guardians of their souls . . . Teach them the way to heaven, and do all for their souls which I have before directed you to do for all your other servants. Though you may make some difference in their labor and diet and clothing, yet none as to the furthering of their salvation. . . . make it your chief end in buying and using slaves to win them to Christ and save their souls"[25]

Clearly, enslaving black bodies was not considered antithetical to saving black souls. In diverse ways, missionaries demonstrated their disdain for black bodies seeing them as distinct from their souls. This dichotomous view of black slaves authorized a disregard for the black *psyche* (body and soul) or their full humanity.

Soul rhetoric used in the service of missions, and especially in the context of slave conversions, constitutes a biblical distortion of the Jahwist creation narrative (Gen. 2:4b–2:24). In that narrative, God made the human ('adam) by manually scooping up the dust of the ground and molding it. But the creative act was incomplete until God breathed life, spirit-life, God-life into the dusty

---

25. Harrison, *Gospel among the Slaves*, 38–39. Emphasis in original.

mold, and then the human became a "living soul" (Hebrew: *lənephesh chaiyyah*; Greek: *psychē zōsan*) (Gen. 2:7). It is the body *and* the living breath/spirit from/ of God that constitutes a *psyche*. To fail to acknowledge the *dust* is to fail to acknowledge the common humanity and the God-shaping that is common to all humanity. As Karen Baker-Fletcher asserts, "Dustiness refers to human connectedness with the rest of creation."[26] It is disingenuous hermeneutics, faulty theology, and oppressive pedagogy to propose that one can save one's soul and leave the body in trauma or traumatize the body and leave the soul intact. If salvation is about restoration or redemption of God's original intent for creation, salvation of the soul alone is not salvation, but a tampering with God's creation. Jesus understood this as he traveled throughout the cities and countryside healing folks of their physical ailments and being God with them and when he announced that the spirit of Lord rests on him to "let the oppressed go free" (Luke 4:18 NRSV). But slave ideology framed missional hermeneutics and practice. Davies preached that "a Christian may be happy, even in a State of Slavery. Liberty, the sweetest and most valuable of all Blessings, is not essential for his Happiness: for if he is destitute of civil Liberty, he enjoys a Liberty still more noble and divine: 'he is the Lord's free man.' The . . . invaluable Advantages of being a Christian, which can render the lowest and most laborious Station in Life so insignificant, that a Man need *not care* for it, but continue in it with a generous Indifference."[27] Thus, God would deprive the slave of God's most significant gift to humans: freedom. This mendacious ideology, as some slaves discerned, constituted a blatant and ideologically driven distortion of Scripture and the nature and revelation of God.

Greek ideas about the spirit-body dualism, particularly "spiritualistic dualism" as constructed by Platonic and neo-Platonic thought, gradually impacted Christianity.[28] Arguably, this spiritualistic dualism can be detected in the struggle between the will and the flesh as described by the Apostle Paul in Rom.7:14–25. Kelly Brown Douglas argues that Western Christian tradition of spiritualistic dualism denigrated the body and that disposition also "influenced White cultural dispositions toward Black people. They too would be viewed as the antithesis of 'authentic selfhood' (meaning whiteness). They too would be relegated to the lower half of the dualisms, so that 'spiritualistic dualism' would provide a sacred canopy not only for sexism but also for racism."[29]

26. Karen Baker-Fletcher, *Sisters of Dust, Sisters of Spirit* (Minneapolis: Fortress Press, 1998), 18.

27. Davies, "The Duty of Christians," 20–21. Emphasis in original.

28. Kelly Brown-Douglas, *Sexuality and the Black Church: A Womanist Perspective* (Maryknoll, NY: Orbis Books, 1999), 25.

29. Ibid., 29.

To Christianize a black soul meant to teach him to accept his inferior social position in relation to white people, and to become or act like a happy, content, and grateful slave; to teach her that she was susceptible to the same spiritual condemnation as her white counterparts for committing sins of, for example, sexual immorality, even while she was considered to have a propensity for promiscuity and would be denied the same virtuous status as her white counterparts—her body was used as a breeding playground for perpetuating slavery and was accessible, *ad infinitum*, to her slave master (married or single, Christian and non-Christian). Slaves were taught that their souls could be saved even while their bodies were traumatized. Harrison expresses the sentiment of the Christian missionaries toward the southern black slave in this way: "Poor Ethiopia struggled in the bonds of pagan darkness—*bonds far more terrible than any that bound her bodily*. Her wailing cry fell on the ears of a Christian brotherhood, who heard, pitied, and succored."[30]

Slave owners constructed stereotypes of black male and female sexuality as promiscuous and hyper-sexualized seducers to justify the sexual abuse and control of their bodies.[31] Such stereotypes "reflect the core of the White cultural assault upon Black Bodies and intimacy even as they continued to impact Black lives."[32] Thus, it is no wonder that slave catechisms spent much more time on the so-called sexual vices that slaves were considered most prone to engage in, such as premarital sex, marital infidelity, and polygamy, among others. The gospel was embodied, but in white bodies that epitomized and defined the gospel on their own terms, and in their own image and language. As Willie Jennings argues, a displacement took place: the white European body replaced the Jewish body and the white European body became "the compass marking divine election."[33] The historical missional understanding that white European Christians are divinely elected as the authoritative guardians of the Great Commission and thus the quintessential teachers of other nations and peoples has meant that they alone have decided the content of the teaching and who are best equipped for the task. It is a sacralized pedagogy of oppression.

---

30. Harrison, *Gospel among the Slaves*, 191. Emphasis added.

31. Byron, "A Catechism," 131–35, 146–50.

32. Brown-Douglas, *Sexuality and the Black Church*, 33.

33. Willie James Jennings, *The Christian Imagination: Theology and the Origins of Race* (New Haven, CT: Yale University Press, 2010), 33.

THE LORD'S FREE-MAN AND THE MASTER'S SLAVE

In addition to language and cultural barriers, financial and travel hardships, as well as the shortage of qualified and willing missionaries, the largest hurdle to missionizing the plantation slaves was convincing the slave owners of the efficacy and innocuousness of the enterprise to the slavocracy, especially to their profits. Missionaries had to convince slave owners that saving the souls of their slaves would actually fortify the institution of slavery. Mather's 1706 catechism states the following in that regard:

> Be assured, Syrs [Sirs]; Your *Servants* will be the *Better Servants*, for being made *Christian Servants*. To *Christianize* them aright, will be to *fill them with* all *Goodne[ss]*.... Were your Servants well tinged with the Spirit of *Christianity*, it would render them exceeding *Dutiful* unto their *Masters*, exceeding *Patient* under their *Masters*, exceeding faithful in their Business and afraid of speaking or doing any thing that may justly displease you.[34]

Mathers promised to traumatize the slaves, filling them with fear of doing anything that would upset their masters. In addition to convincing slave owners that Christianity would breed more slaves who would do better and superior work for them than for "inhumane masters," missionaries had to convince them that baptism would not change the slave's social status. In fact, no law could alter their status, since God had made them slaves.[35] Baptism would render slavery sweet and alleviate the exigencies and brutality of slavery, but no law could change the slave's status.

> What *Law* is it, that Sets the *Baptised* [sic] *Slave* at *Liberty?* Not the *Law of Christianity*: that allows of *Slavery*; Only it wonderfully Dulcifies, and Mollifies, and Moderates the Circumstances of it. *Christianity* directs a *Slave*, upon his embracing the *Law of the Redeemer*, to satisfy himself, *That he is the Lords Free-man*, tho' he continues a *Slave*. . . .Will the *Canon-law* do it? No; . . .Will the *Civil Law* do it? No.[36]

In fact, Mather argues that even the English Constitution cannot free the slave because it permits his perpetual enslavement. No, those laws, which were

34. Mather, *The Negro Christianized,* 13. Emphasis in original.

35. Ibid., 3, 13, 14.

36. Ibid., 16–17. Emphasis in original.

enacted between "Lords and Slaves," were done so when both were Christians and are not repealed. Like other chattel and goods, the slave owner has leased the slave for life. Yet, Mather, and others, insist that the slaves are their brothers "on the same level with" them.[37] The matter of perpetuity had to be settled before they could commence with instructing the slaves.

CATECHIZING SOUTHERN SLAVES

Despite attempts to quell their fears, some whites continued to believe that verbal or oral instruction for slaves would increase their desire to learn; they supposed that eventually such instruction would "revolutionize our civil institutions."[38] But feared fits of discontent gave missionaries a renewed zeal and ammunition for convincing slave masters of the necessity of religious instruction for their slaves. In the wake of slave revolts and insurrections, some motivated by religion, more missionaries and ministers solicited slave masters for the Christianization of their slaves.[39]

Again, the overall goal for catechizing and converting slaves was to make them better slaves. Catechists deposited doctrines, dogmas, and creeds into the "souls" of African slaves by rote memorization, the obedience to which constituted evidence of Christian conversion. The doctrines were sometimes supported by scriptures extracted from their historical and literary contexts, proof texts organized around the ideological fears of white slave owners and constructed to reinforce ideas about the sinful nature of slaves, particularly if they engaged in behaviors contrary to expected social norms of white society.[40] Certain pure "truths" contained in the catechisms were intended to maintain and bolster the social hierarchy and its slaveholding system. Based on my analysis, I have divided these truths into the following categories: (1) the Great Creator God speaks out of the Bible; (2) God knows and sees everything; (3) Slaves are sinner children of Adam and Eve; (4) Love your master as your neighbor; (5) Trouble is an act of God (6) Many are the heavenly benefits of baptism; and (7) Let them sing and pray the "truth."

---

37. Ibid., 17.

38. Haven P. Perkins, "Religion for Slaves: Difficulties and Methods," *Church History* 10, no. 3 (1941): 228–45, (240).

39. Byron, "A Catechism," 72.

40. Janet Duitsman Cornelius (*Slave Missions and the Black Church in the Antebellum South* [Columbia: University of South Carolina Press, 1999], 129–30) argues that the slave catechisms overwhelmingly emphasized salvation and not obedience and subordination. But Duitsman would have to disregard, in this assessment, the historical context and the literary context of the catechisms.

THE GREAT CREATOR GOD SPEAKS OUT OF THE BIBLE

In an 1862 Episcopal Church catechism, the catechumen is guided through questions and answers, beginning with teaching the slaves that God made the world and everything in it—a common doctrine that began traditional catechisms. God also sustains and provides for his creation.[41] The slaves were taught that this knowledge about God comes from God who speaks out of the Bible and through the catechist. God has "told" them (the slaves) this information, the catechist claims, even though they cannot read and in some instances cannot touch the Bible itself. Former slave Jenny Proctor testified that they had no way of determining whether "this world am all you ev'r goin' to git' since they had no way of finding out; they 'didn' se no Bibles.'"[42] The slave receives God's word through the catechist and not directly from God (i.e. the Bible). Therefore, the catechist functions like a diviner who transmits knowledge from God through his ability to communicate with God (i.e. the Bible). This God of the book commands the slaves, according to the catechism:

> Q. How do you know this [that God made all things including "you"]?
> A. God has told me so.
> Q. Where has God told you so?
> A. In His own book, called the Bible.[43]

This teaching also challenges and renders false any notion of a God that communicates with the slave outside of the Bible (i.e., nature or revelation) or with a people who cannot read the Bible or do not know the language of their oppressors. Many slaves who were impacted by the eighteenth-century (and early nineteenth-century) Great Awakening and its emphasis on religious experience expressed how God revealed Himself to them through visions, dreams, and the Holy Spirit. As former slave Henry Bibb wrote in his 1849 narrative, "It [his desire for freedom] kindled a fire of liberty within my breast which has never yet been quenched. This seemed to be a part of my nature; it was first revealed to me by the inevitable laws of nature's God."[44] Nineteenth-century black preaching women declared that their callings came from God and

41. Byron, "A Catechism," 91.

42. Ibid., 87.

43. Protestant Episcopal Church, "Catechism."

44. Henry Bibb, "Narrative of the Life and Adventures of Henry Bibb, an American slave, Written by Himself," in *Slaves Narratives*, eds. William L. Andrews and Henry Louis Gates, Jr. (New York: Library of America, 2000), 425–566 (443).

not mortal human beings; that God revealed God's self to them in visions and dreams, like God did with the Apostle Paul.[45] But according to the catechism, God speaks in a written text that the slaves cannot access, and, therefore, they have no direct access to God like the white people do. Allen Callahan in *The Talking Book* relates an incident from the memoir of freed African slave James Albert Ukawsaw Gronniosaw. Gronniosaw hoped "the book" (probably a catechism with prayers) would talk to him in the same way it talked to his master:

> [My master] used to read prayers in public to the ship's crew every Sabbath; and when I first saw him read, I was never so surprised in my life, as when I saw the book [a catechism?] talk to my master, for I thought it did, as I observed him to look upon it, and move his lips. I wished it would do so with me. As soon as my Master was done reading, I followed him to the place where he put the book, being mightily delighted with it, and when nobody saw me, I opened it, and put my ear down close upon it, in great hopes that it would say something to me; but I was very sorry, and greatly disappointed, when I found that it would not speak. This thought immediately presented itself to me, that every body and every thing despised me because I was black.[46]

Slave convert John Jea had a similar experience, but with the Bible: "'I took the book, and held it up to my ears, to try whether the book would talk to me or not, but it proved to be all in vain, for I could not hear it speak one word." It would not talk to him in the same way that it spoke to his master's sons.[47]

When missionaries/catechists claimed that what they taught the slaves could only be verified by reading the Bible, they usurped for themselves sole authority and control over so-called biblical truths that they presented as objective, divine knowledge, knowing as they did that the slaves were denied access or limited in their access to the Bible. They attempted to drive an epistemological and spiritual wedge between God and the slaves. In all of

45. Mitzi J. Smith, "'Unbought and Unbossed': Zilpha Elaw and Old Elizabeth and a Political Discourse of Origins," *Black Theology* 9, no. 3 (2011): 287–311.

46. Allen Dwight Callahan, *The Talking Book: African Americans and the Bible* (New Haven, CT: Yale University Press, 2006), 13.

47. Ibid., 13, 14. Callahan notes that this same talking book metaphor is found in former slave Olaudah Equiano's autobiography *The Interesting Narrative of the Life of Olaudah Equiano, or Gustavus Vassa, the African, Written by Himself* (1789).

the catechisms, this idea of God speaking in/from the Bible and the Bible as the source of the catechetical knowledge is branded into the slave's *psyche* through repetition, memorization, and the insistence that this new knowledge be reflected in the slave's behavior, particularly in relation to their slave owners. Deborah Tannen states in *The Argument Culture* that "culture, in a sense, is an environment of narratives that we hear repeatedly until they seem to make self-evident sense in explaining human behavior."[48] The missionaries sought to enculturate the slaves with white Christian norms within the oppressive social context of slavery.

The catechumen was required to acknowledge that only God, not their parents or anyone else could keep them alive; that God keeps them alive by providing food and drink for them. Immediately after this line of questions and answers, the slave is asked,

> Q. Who do you say made you, and keeps you alive, by giving you what you eat and drink?
> A. God.
> Q. Is God, then a good or bad being?
> A. He is a good Being. . . .
> Q. WHO do you say made all things?
> A. God.
> Q. Did He made them good, or bad?
> A. He made them good.
> Q How do you know this?
> A. He has told me so in the Bible.[49]

Linking together God and the slave's daily sustenance, the catechism effectively and rhetorically constructs an inverted theological triangle/pyramid consisting of God and the slave master parallel to each other—from point A (God) to point B (slave master) at the top of the pyramid and connecting vertically downward to the slave at the bottom point C. The slave master is "the hand" that actually provides food for the slaves. And God (slave master) is good since he provides for the slaves and always commands what is right because "God is too great and good to command what is wrong."[50] So when God commands

48. Deborah Tannen, *The Argument Culture: Moving from Debate to Dialogue* (New York: Random House, 1998), 13. Also quoted in Benjamin Radford, *Media Mythmakers: How Journalists, Activists, and Advertisers Mislead Us* (Amherst, NY: Prometheus Books, 2003), 12. I am indebted to Dr. Sheila F. Winborne for this source.

49. Protestant Episcopal Church, "Catechism," 5.

anything else of the slave in the catechism, it must be good because God never commands anything bad. This includes any practices and ideas that uphold the social hierarchy of the slave system. The 1854 *Catechism for Slaves* plainly states that God ordained slavery and requires that slaves obey their masters:

> Q. Who gave you a master and a mistress?
> A. God gave them to me.
> Q. Who says that you must obey them?
> A. God says that I must.[51]

To do otherwise was to blaspheme "the name and doctrine of God."[52] Capers also includes a section titled "The Duty of Servants" where he cites Scripture (Eph. 6:5-6 and 1 Tim. 6:1-2) as support for the idea that God ordained the maintenance of master–slave relationships.[53] Catechists and preachers also strengthened the master–slave relationship by making an analogy between God as heavenly master and the slave owner as the earthly master. From the earliest possible time, the slave was taught about the heavenly master.[54] Yet, many slaves complained of the unbearable burden of serving both their earthly and heavenly masters.[55]

When direct statements in the catechisms about slaves obeying their masters met with the objections of the slave catechumens, some preachers/ missionaries/catechists would resort to telling the stories of Hagar or Onesimus. When those stories were told to slaves, some slaves stopped listening when it became clear to them that the moral of the story was slave obedience, and then they would either leave or they would stay to confront the preacher/teacher, refuting the existence of such a passage or teaching in the Bible,[56] even when they had not read the Bible themselves.

The God, who according to the catechists commanded slaves to obey their earthly masters, was not only the creator God and ultimate (slave) Master, but also the "Great God." This attribute attached to God is significant. Mather used it often in his catechism.[57] The slave is instructed, for example, as follows:

---

50. Ibid.

51. *A Catechism for Slaves*. See also Byron, "A Catechism," 109.

52. Byron, "A Catechism," 109.

53. Capers, *Catechism*, 22. See also Mathers, *The Negro Christianized*, 30.

54. Matthews, "The Methodist Mission," 625.

55. Raboteau, *Slave Religion*, 181.

56. Perkins, "Religion for Slaves," 236.

57. Mather, *The Negro Christianized*, 24, 27, 31. See also, for example, Davies, "The Duty of Christians," 15.

Q. Do you chuse [sic] the Great GOD for your God?
A. Yes. I chuse God the Father for my Father; I chuse God the Son, for my Saviour; I chuse God the Spirit for my leader. And I Look for the Blessedness, which He has Promised for His people in a better World.[58]

In Mather's "larger catechism, for the negroes of a bigger Capacity" he instructs,

Q. Who is that Great GOD, whom you and all Men are to Serve?
A. The Great GOD, is the Eternal Spirit, who made every thing [sic], and is every where [sic]: And there is no God but He.[59]

I cannot help but to wonder whether this teaching reflects an attempt to subordinate and/or replace the God that some slaves worshiped when brought in chains to America's shores, those who were already Muslims, papists, or practitioners of African Traditional Religions (ATR) or a synthesis of ATR and Christianity.[60] Some slaves maintained tribal or ethnic cultural practices or "Africanisms," and slave owners tried to erase such vestiges from their memory and behavior and replace them with white Christian ideas and norms. This was the case with a Ms. Bodichon who mentioned in her 1858 diary about her "Congos" whom she converted all but one that "clings to his old idolatry."[61] What the *great God* sanctioned and commanded trumped all other gods. And all other gods do not exist, as such; belief in other gods constituted superstition or idolatry. Some slaves' prayers may reflect this line of teaching about the Great creator God and Master. For example, the following prayer by former African slave and pastor London Ferrill, dated 1854, might reflect a successfully catechized slave's prayer:

May the *Great Father of heaven* and earth bless the citizens of Richmond, Virginia, for their kindness toward me in my youthful days, but more particularly, O Lord, be merciful to the citizens of Lexington, Kentucky . . . *make them peaceable, happy and truly religious*; and when they come to lie down on the bed of death, may Thy good Spirit hover around ready to waft *their ransomed souls* to Thy good presence . . . And, O *my Master!*, choose, when I am gone,

58. Mather, *The Negro Christianized*, 31.
59. Ibid., 24.
60. See, for example, Callahan, *The Talking Book*.
61. Byron, "A Catechism," 77.

choose some pastor for them who may be enabled to labor with more zeal than your most humble petitioner has ever done, and grant that it may continue to *prosper and do good among the colored race.* And, Merciful Father bless *the white people who have always treated me as though I was a white man . . .* Amen.[62]

Harrison claims that white people helped raise money to buy Ferrill's freedom so he could preach the gospel to the colored race. [63] However, Ferrill's biography says he was set free after the death of his second master.[64] Black preachers who could be fully trusted to preach the gospel to the black race in the same way they received it from white catechists and/or preachers were rare, but there are instances of white people facilitating the freedom for such preachers to further the cause of birthing more docile, contented slaves for whom religion might indeed become an opiate.

GOD SEES AND KNOWS EVERYTHING: THE PRINCIPLE OF CONSCIENCE

Lesson 2 of the Episcopal catechism discusses how Adam and Eve ate of the tree of the knowledge of good and evil, despite God's *command* to the contrary. God knew that Adam and Eve had disobeyed because God sees everything:

Q. How did God know that Adam and Eve disobeyed him?
A. God sees everywhere, and He saw them do it.
Q. Can God see persons when they are alone in some secret place?
A. Yes; God sees every one of us all the time.
Q. Can He see us in a dark night?
A. Yes; God can see us in the darkest night.[65]

---

62. James Melvin Washington, ed., *Conversations with God: Two Centuries of Prayers by African Americans* (New York: HarperCollins, 1994), 40.

63. Harrison, *Gospel among the Slaves*, 126–28, 139–41, 281, 341–42. Black slave and free preachers who demonstrated oratorical skill and competency in the gospel of the slave master and behaved perfectly according to the norms of white society preached to black and white audiences and were sometimes trustworthy enough to be freed, if they were slaves, to preach to the black race. Harrison mentions the following notable slave preachers: Henry Evans of Fayetteville, NC; Henry Adams of Vicksburg, MS; and Emanuel Mask of Fayette County, TN, whose master gave him a written permit to itinerate around the country preaching to other blacks.

64. London Ferrill, *Biography of London Ferrell, Pastor of the First Baptist Church of Colored Persons, Lexington, KY* (Lexington: A. W. Elder, 1854), 5, http://docsouth.unc.edu/neh/ferrill/ferrill.html#p5. Ferrill's biography states that his master, the Colonel, viewed him as "his faithful servant whom he loved almost as well as one of his own children, and . . . Never did master and servant love each other better than these two."

Slaves gathered clandestinely in the "darkest night" to worship God in their own way and to plan an escape or a revolt. Slave owners wanted to prevent slaves from holding such secret meetings. They also wanted to make the slave think twice before engaging in any subversive behaviors. The catechism continues this idea of God's omniscience and omnipresence in the latter part of Lesson 3:

> A. God knows every thing.
> Q. How does He know every thing?
> A. Because He is always everywhere and sees every thing.
> Q. Does He see actions that are done in the dark and secret places?
> A. Yes; For nothing can hide *us* from God.[66]

God hears all bad words, knows all bad thoughts, and peers into their hearts. If the slave can be convinced of the omniscience and omnipresence of God, the slave masters can curtail and hopefully obliterate all forms of slave resistance. Knowledge of God's omniscience was supposed to deter the slaves from stealing food, resting when they should be toiling in the field, lying to their owners, or any other behaviors that loosened the master's grip on the slave and decreased the value of his human property and thus the master's profit margin. This method of conscientization has a name and a history. In his 1757 sermon to slave masters in Hanover, Virginia, the Rev. Samuel Davies argued that the goal of such catechetical instruction was to make slaves "Christians *indeed*" (Davies's emphasis), which meant "better Servants, than could be accomplished by the Terror of the Lash." He proclaimed the following:

> Then they will be governed by a *Principle of Conscience* towards God: a principle, which will make them as honest and diligent in our Absence, as while under your Eye. Then, according to St. Paul's Injunctions, they will "be obedient to their masters in all *lawful* Things; not with Eye-service, as Men-pleasers, but in Singleness of heart, fearing God.". . . "whatsoever they do, they will do it *heartily*, as to the Lord, and not to Men. . . ."[67]

This *Principle of Conscience* attempted to sear into the slave's *psyche* the fear of God always watching and waiting to pounce should they engage in any

65. Protestant Episcopal Church, "Catechism," 8.
66. Ibid., 12. Emphasis added.
67. Davies, "The Duty of Christians," 28. Emphasis in original.

sinful behaviors, as defined by their masters. This method of catechizing slaves married master-slave ideology with a strategic theology of divine presence designed to soothe the consciences of white folks, missionaries, and slave owners (who were often one and the same), to guarantee the perpetuation of slavery, and to psychologically and spiritually traumatize the slaves into conforming voluntarily and happily to an inferior servile social existence.

SINNER CHILDREN OF ADAM AND EVE

Lessons 2 through 3 of the Episcopal catechism instruct the slaves that God became very angry with Adam and Eve for breaking God's commandment, and as a result God punished them, cursing them and their children because of their sin. The catechism then connects the sin/curse of Adam and Eve with the slave:

> Q. *You said* that God sent evil upon Adam and Eve, and upon their children, for *sinning* against Him; Who are their children?
> A. *We are their children.* . . .
> Q. *Why are we all sinners?*
> A. Because we all break God's commands.[68] (Emphasis mine)

The actual biblical story does not call Adam and Eve's act of disobedience a sin. Any form of slave resistance (i.e., lying, stealing food, running away, stealing away, revolt) constituted disobedience. These forms of slave resistance are addressed, directly or indirectly, in the catechisms as sins.[69] The catechist/slave master taught the slaves that they must live by the ethics of the masters despite their social status as human property and the inhumane treatment generally inflicted upon their bodies and spirits, upon their *psyche*. Slaves ethics, of course, differed from the slave master's ethics that he imposed upon the slave through religious instruction and physical abuse. Cheryl Sanders argues that the slaves developed an alternative or "situation ethics" that justified lying and stealing and other forms of resistance.[70] Sanders writes that

---

68. Ibid., 9. Emphasis added.

69. Capers, *Catechism*, 23–24. Capers includes individual sections entitled "Against Theft and Other Crimes" and "Against Lying," which address lying, killing, and committing adultery through Scripture quotations. For example, he includes "All LIARS shall have their part in the lake that burneth with fire and brimstone, which is the second death. *Revelation* xxi.8." See also Mather, *The Negro Christianized*, 26, 28–29.

70. Cheryl J. Sanders, *Empowerment Ethics for a Liberated People: A Path to African American Social Transformation* (Minneapolis: Fortress Press, 1995), 14–15.

the ethics of stealing from thieves and deceiving the deceivers was empowering to these slaves insofar as they contextualized their thought and behavior with respect to a religious duty to undermine an unjust social order. In fact, the slaves' moral sense led them to define wrong in terms of white moral norms, where white attitudes and conduct were lifted up as counter examples of what was acceptable in the slave community.[71]

Slave resistance stoked fears of abolitionism, as former slave Frederick Douglass wrote in his slave narrative: "If a slave ran away and succeeded in getting clear, or if a slave killed his master, set fire to a barn, or did anything very wrong in the mind of a slaveholder, it was spoken of as the fruit of *abolition*."[72] Missionaries and slaveowners tried to instill a sense of fear and duty to God in the slave's *psyche*. Mathers included in his eighteenth-century catechism the notion that slaves were breaking the tenth commandment if they internalized any kind of impatience and ill content with their enslavement:

Q. What is the Tenth commandment?
A. Thou shall not Covet.
Q. What is the meaning of it?
A. I must be patient and Content with such a Condition as God has ordered for me.[73]

Slaves sometimes resisted their enslavement by a refusal to work or to be worked like an ox. Slave owners generally regarded this type of resistance as proof that Africans were naturally lazy and must be forced to work hard and to value labor. Ohio slave Mrs. Hanna Davidson was so tired one day that she felt "like an inch-worm crawling along a roof. I worked till I thought another lick would kill me." Despite the risk of being whipped, Davidson "crawled in a hole under the house and stayed there till I was rested."[74] An excerpt from the 1854 Episcopalian *Catechism for Slaves* specifically reinforces the ideology that slaves are innately lazy, and that laziness is a sin. It deduces that because Adam and

71. Ibid., 15.

72. Frederick Douglass, *Narrative of the Life of Frederick Douglass. An American Slave. Written by Himself*, in *The Classic Slave Narratives*, ed. Henry Louis Gates, Jr. (New York: Penguin, 1987), 279. Emphasis in original.

73. Mather, *The Negro Christianized*, 29.

74. George P. Rawick, ed., "Ohio Narratives," in *The American Slave, A Composite Autobiography*, vol. 16: *Kansas, Kentucky, Maryland, Ohio, Virginia and Tennessee Narratives* (Westport, CT: Greenwood, 1975), 28.

Eve sinned, cultivating crops became hard work; if the slaves do not do the hard work necessary to grow the crops, they are lazy.

Q. What does God say about your work?
A. He that will not work shall not eat.
Q. Did Adam and Eve have to work?
A. Yes, they had to keep the garden.
Q. Was it hard to keep that garden?
A. No, it was very easy.
Q. *What makes the crops so hard to grow now?*
A. *Sin makes it.*
Q. *What makes you lazy?*
A. *My wicked heart.*
Q. *How do you know your heart is wicked?*
A. *I feel it every day.*[75]

This excerpt taught the slaves to equate feelings of tiredness from their daily labors with wickedness; that to feel tired and not want to work in the field from sun up until sun down was wicked. The catechists attempted to further traumatize the slave's *psyche* by discounting their very real and justifiable bodily pain and attributing that physical pain to a wicked heart or soul.

Another catechism stated that slave disobedience or sin resulted in the murder of others because of the severe punishments and accidents "caused" by violators of the commandment.[76] Any resulting discipline inflicted on the guilty slave, or others, is placed squarely on the slave's *psyche*; it is his fault.

LOVE YOUR MASTER AS YOUR NEIGHBOR.

Love of the slave master as the slave's neighbor is practiced by refraining from acts of resistance to slavery and by unconditional submission. Catechumens were taught that they are obligated to love their slave masters as their neighbors:

Q. How are you to show that you love your neighbor as yourself?
A. I am to show it by always doing my duty to my neighbor, as God has commanded me.
Q. Who is your neighbor?
A. Every body who lives with me, and around me, *and has the control*

---

75. *A Slave Catechism.* Emphasis added.
76. Byron, "A Catechism," 117.

over me.

Q. Can you name some persons?

A. My playfellows, [*my master and mistress*] and my parents. . . .

Q. How are you to show your love to [*your master and mistress*] and your parents?

A. I am never to lie to them, to steal from them, nor speak bad words about them; but always to do as they bid me.[77]

William Capers's 1852 Methodist catechism is more direct, connecting the duty to honor one's parents with the slave's duty to his slave masters as in the New Testament household codes: "*What is the child's duty to his father and mother? To love them, honor them, comfort them, and mind what they say. What is the servant's duty to his master and mistress? To serve them with a good will heartily, and not with eye-service.*" (Emphasis Capers's)[78] Some slave catechisms allotted more space to the fifth commandment about honoring one's parents because it provided an opportunity to focus on slave obedience to their masters (given also that slaves were considered as perpetual children or incorrigibly childlike).[79]

Some slaves rejected the hypocrisy of the missionaries' and slave masters' teachings about neighborly love. For example, Linda Brent, also known as Harriet Jacobs, recognized the double standard of her mistress who taught her about the *golden rule*, but failed to practice it toward Linda; her mistress bequeathed her to the mistress's five-year-old niece instead of manumitting her when the mistress died.[80] Brent wrote the following in her slave narrative: "My mistress had taught me the precepts of God's Word: 'Thou shalt love thy neighbor as thyself.' 'Whatsoever ye would that men should do unto you, do ye even so unto them.' But I was her slave, and I suppose *she did not recognize me as her neighbor*. I would give much to blot out from my memory that *one great wrong*."[81] Byron notes that in Gadsden's catechism the lesson regarding one's duties to one's neighbor started with the explanation "that human beings ought to be good to other human beings, stressing that Christians should love and help

77. Protestant Episcopal Church, "Catechism," 29.

78. Capers, *Catechism for the Use of The Methodist Missions*, 28. Emphasis in original.

79. Byron, "A Catechism," 82, 113

80. For more on Linda Brent's (aka Harriet Jacobs) use of Scripture, see Emerson B. Powery, "'Rise up, ye Women': Harriet Jacobs and the Bible," *Postscripts* 5, no. 2 (2009): 171–84.

81. Linda Brent, "In Incidents in the Life of a Slave Girl," in *The Classic Slave Narratives*, ed. Henry Louis Gates, Jr. (New York: Penguin, 1987), 333–513,(344).

other Christians more so than anyone else."[82] Translation: slaves should do all they can to help their slave masters.

TROUBLE IS AN ACT OF GOD

The Episcopal catechism teaches that slaves are to "submit to God's will" and they do this by "wishing everything to be just as God wishes it to be." Apparently, the slave can know when they have not submitted to God by the afflictions that God sends upon them:

> Q. How are you to submit to God's will as made known in His acts?
> A. *Every thing that happens to us is God's act.*
> Q. Can you tell me one thing, which as God's act, makes known God's will?
> A. When I am *sick*; God makes me so, to do me good. . . .
> Q. How are you to submit to God's will as made known in His acts?
> A. *When God sends trouble, or sickness or death. I am to feel that God does right.*[83]

For a slave, slavery *is* trouble and it becomes a symbol of God's displeasure with him—a ontological symbol embedded in his black flesh and his slavery chains, in his *psyche*. In addition to the trouble of slavery, the catechists sought to traumatize the slave further by convincing him that any sickness with which he might be inflicted (even resulting from hard labor, insufficient food or clothing, and other ills associated with being a slave) was an act of God. If a slave is convinced that *everything* that happens to him is an act of God, then God sides with his oppressors and has little compassion for the slave whose sin perpetually haunts him from sun up to sun down.

Submission to God's will also meant submission to all civil authorities, and all civil authorities deemed that slavery was moral, legal, and in perpetuity. The catechumens were instructed that they should be humble towards all authority figures, particularly toward those considered more wise and religious than themselves. In other words, slaves should be humble towards all white people, including their children, especially those who could read the Bible and communicate with God who ordained all authorities. Gadsen's catechism, like others, stressed the importance of obedience to civil authorities.[84]

---

82. Byron, "A Catechism," 121. Emphasis added.

83. Davies, "The Duty of Christians," 37. Emphasis added.

84. Byron, "A Catechism," 121.

MANY ARE THE HEAVENLY BENEFITS OF BAPTISM

When the slave is baptized, he receives a "Christian name," as well as forgiveness of sins and the Holy Spirit. The Holy Spirit enters the slave's heart and helps him to love and do good, as well as to "hate all that is bad."[85] Therefore, the slave should "always be afraid of disobeying" God who "spieth out" all her ways. At baptism, the slave becomes a child of God, but when he was born he was "the child of the wicked one."[86] This same teaching may be included in the Catechism for white people, but the impact is different for a people who are enslaved and told that there is nothing inherently good about them, who are treated differently simply because of the color of their skin. Their wickedness is an ontological stigma that they can never overcome, and can only be alleviated by conformity in this life. In the catechisms, the white slave masters are repetitively and systematically associated with God and all that is good, but the opposite applies to the slaves. Sheila Winborne argues that "a powerful tool in the continuation of 'Christianizing' nations has been the systematic marketing of created images of the 'Holy Face' of God incarnate as a racially white Jesus of European descent. When used as missionary tools, these images communicate that Jesus' 'whiteness' is necessarily a reflection of his holiness."[87] God is rhetorically cast into the image of the white slave masters in the catechisms.

If the slave does not sin and is compliant, he will receive his reward in the afterlife, the heavenly gift of eternal life. The slave inherits the kingdom of heaven when he is baptized—a kingdom that is only as imminent as the slave's death. And everyday the slave is to strive to get to heaven by being good at all times, even in secret.[88] In order to maintain that hope of an eternal heaven, a reward in the afterlife, the slave must not disobey God and should shun the devil. How does the slave avoid the devil? "By keeping within me no bad thoughts; by speaking no bad words and by doing no bad things."[89] This means that the slave should not hate, wish harm to, or wrong anyone (including attempting to escape to freedom). Charles C. Jones's catechism directly warned his black catechumens that if they were disobedient, they would suffer in this world and the next.[90] All that is taught in the catechism is connected with the getting to heaven:

85. Protestant Episcopal Church, "Catechism," 16–18.

86. Ibid., 19–20.

87. See Sheila F. Winborne's essay, "Images of the White Jesus in Advancing the Great Commission," in this volume.

88. Protestant Episcopal Church, "Catechism," 21.

89. Ibid., 23.

Q. What else must you do to get to heaven?

A. I must believe all that God has told me about the way to get there.[91]

Speaking for the slaves, missionaries argued that they counted it a blessing "to have their attention directed to the higher interests of the soul and the hope of immortality and eternal life."[92] If missionaries and/or slave owners could succeed in convincing slaves of the superior importance of their souls and what happens to them after they die, then they would succeed in creating happy, docile slaves to work for them perpetually in this life—the life of most concern to slave masters, even the Christian slave masters; theirs was no otherworldly gaze, but more of a navel gazing.

LET THEM SING AND PRAY THE "TRUTH"

In addition to the question and answers that slave catechumens had to memorize, the hymns also served to reinforce the master-slave relationship, making better, more productive slaves for Christian masters. Most catechisms contained hymns and prayers. Both were a means to teach slaves the "truth" and norms of white Christianity and to buttress slave ideology.[93] The hymns also functioned to deepen the slave's sense of his own sinfulness. Slaves were required to learn hymns line-by-line and each line was interpreted or explained catechetically "to avoid ridiculous or even natural blunders."[94] Byron found that many creators of catechisms intentionally included hymns in the catechisms because of the African slave's pension for sacred music and the quickness with which they learned songs. For example, in the preface to Winkler's *Notes and Questions*, he asserts that the "most attractive feature" for the catechumen will be the hymns placed after each lesson, and he provides the rationale: "Their [the slaves's] fondness for music is well known. No better vehicle of truth to them can be found, than an appropriate hymn, well suited to a pleasing tune. Their memories stored with sacred songs—and there is nothing they learn so soon—will provide a source of enjoyment and improvement which scarcely anything else can supply."[95] Charles Colcock Jones also expressed how the slave's fondness for music "could 'be turned to good account in their

90. Charles C. Jones, *A Catechism for Colored Persons* (Charleston, SC: Observer Office Press, 1834), 80–81. Cited in Byron, "A Catechism," 141–42.

91. Protestant Episcopal Church, "Catechism," 25.

92. Harrison, *Gospel among the Slaves*, 235–36.

93. Byron, "A Catechism," 171, 185.

94. Perkins, "Religion for Slaves," 235.

instruction'" through hymnody.[96] Hymns functioned to complement, reinforce, or advance the doctrines taught by the questions and answers portion of the catechism; sometimes catechists employed questions and answers to quiz the slave on the content of the hymn.[97] Hymns could consume one-third of the entire catechism, and they could be placed at the beginning as well as at the end of the work.[98]

Although authors of catechisms did not generally write songs especially for slave catechisms but used those already in use by white Christians,[99] the hymns were strategically selected.[100] For example verse 1 of hymn 8 in Capers's catechism reads, "Poor and needy though I be, God, my Maker, cares for me; Gives me clothing, shelter, food; Gives me all I have of good."[101] By connecting the little food, shelter, and clothing that the slave receives with God's benevolence, the master is presented by extension as God's generous earthly agent. Also to connect the slave's poverty with God's generosity implies that there is nothing wrong with the slave's impoverished condition—a condition produced by his enslavement—as in verse 3 of the same hymn: "He who reigns above the sky Once became as poor as I."[102] Hymn 22, verse 2 reinforces the slave's destiny to be a perpetual slave in this life: "To serve the present age, My calling to fulfill; O may it all my powers engage, to do my Master's will."[103] Slavery is a vocation fulfilled in the present age. The use of the word *Master* to refer to God implies that God sanctions slavery; that the institution of slavery originates with God; and that the status of white men as earthly masters reflects God's preferential character. The white masters are God's overseers.

95. E. T. Winkler, *Notes and Questions for the Oral Instruction of Colored People, With Appropriate Texts and Hymns, with an Introduction by James Tupper, Esq.* (Charleston: Southern Baptist Publication Society, 1857), viii as quoted in Byron, "A Catechism," 171.

96. Charles Colcock Jones, *Catechism of Scripture Doctrine*, 5, as quoted in Byron, "A Catechism," 171.

97. Byron, "A Catechism," 175.

98. Ibid., 176.

99. Ibid., 177–80.

100. Contra Byron ("A Catechism," 157) argues that "the hymns in slave catechisms stressed neither obedience nor subordination, nor did they appear to have been chosen simply for their specific appeal to African Americans." She further argues that the major goal of the catechisms and hymns was "teaching salvation to slaves." But even the wording in catechisms like Rev. B. M. Palmer's, "to Which are Annexed Suitable Prayers and Hymns," suggests that the hymns and prayers are strategically attached to the catechism.

101. Capers, *Catechism*, 28.

102. Ibid., 29.

103. Ibid., 38.

The catechisms, through the hymns, promote praise based primarily on what God would do for the slave in the afterlife and what God has done for the slave through his slave master. Such teaching promotes "praise" at the expense of justice and acts of love, and seeks to persuade that hypocritical and empty praise is acceptable to God. Similar to the neglect of justice in the hymns, the slave catechisms encouraged slaves to pray for the "salvation" of their souls and discouraged them "from praying for more immediate desires, such as freedom from slavery and oppression. Believing that such prayers would go unanswered—because . . . God sanctioned slavery."[104] Palmer's catechism encouraged slaves to pray only for "what is agreeable to the will of God,"[105] it having been previously established that slavery was God's will. While the slave is to take her desires to God, those desires must align with God's will as taught to her in the catechism.

The prayers in the catechism also taught slave obedience. Palmer's *Plain and Easy Catechism*, according to Byron, included the following prayer: "Help me to be faithful to my owner's interest . . . may I never disappoint the trust that is placed in me, nor like the unjust steward, waste my master's goods."[106] Missionaries and slave owners draw upon both the deuteropauline household codes and gospel parables in which the master–slave relationship is a metaphor for God and God's interaction with humans. Palmer's catechism included thirteen pages of "Prayers for Servants" providing guidance and models for slaves to follow. It included prayers for their masters, for starting the workday, and for slaves who interacted with non-Christians, among other things. The following excerpt is also from Palmer's catechism:

O enable me to understand the greatness of my privileges, and to feel my obligations, and to improve my opportunities. And while my owners are anxious for the salvation of my soul, may I be deeply concerned for my spiritual welfare, that my condemnation may not be aggravated by abusing my mercies.[107]

104. Byron, "A Catechism," 159.

105. Rev. B. M. Palmer, *A Plain and Easy Catechism, Designed Chiefly for the Benefit of Coloured Persons, to Which are Annexed Suitable Prayers and Hymns* (Charleston, SC: Observer Office Press, 1828), 32. Cited in Byron, "A Catechism," 160.

106. Byron, "A Catechism," 110–11.

107. Byron, "A Catechism," 167.

Conclusion

I have argued that in an effort to create docile and contented slaves who would not resist their enslavement and thus help perpetuate the plantation slave system, slaveholders, for a number of reasons, were convinced to engage in the systematic conversion of the souls of African slaves to Christianize them. This systematic effort relied on specialized slave catechisms used to verbally teach, indoctrinate, and enculturate slaves in white Christian norms within the framework of the social hierarchy of slavery. This focus on the African slave's soul had the effect of traumatizing the black *psyche*, that is the black slave as a full human being before God. As a full human being, the slave, like other human beings, was created by God as a living soul made of flesh and God-spirit/breath. The soul is not something to be separated from the body, and white Christians' attempts to do so had traumatic effects upon their victims. By treating the slave as a soul to be saved while providing a divine rationale for leaving his body in chains, slave masters and missionaries as catechizers and preachers reinforced their understanding of the black race as not fully human. They engaged in doublespeak claiming sometimes that the slaves were equal before God: their souls were equal, but that did not require white folks to treat the slave's body with social parity. They could not see or acknowledge that their own inhumanity toward the African slaves was the greatest hindrance to their salvation rather than something inherent in the African. Missionaries and catechists attempted to convince slaves that Christian masters would be the best slave owners, but the testimonies overwhelmingly tell a different story. For example, former slave Mrs. Joseph Smith testified in 1863 that the most severe slaveholders were Christians. Consequently, Smith said, "I would rather be with a card-player or sportsman, by half, than a Christian."[108] Too many white missionaries and slaveholders were so blinded by and convinced of their own moral and social superiority and their own sense of benevolence and liberality toward the African's soul, that they could abuse the slave's body and not think twice about it. For example, Rev. George Moore, a missionary in the Methodist South Carolina Conference, shared how when traveling back and forth during his mission work he has "ridden horseback, in a gig, and often on a negro's back . . . Often I have had to be pushed some distance through the mud to get to water to baptize the negroes."[109]

Southern conservatives believed that the African slave was morally depraved and forever in need of the instruction of white men and that the

---

108. Raboteau, *Slave Religion*, 166.

109. Harrison, *Gospel among the Slaves*, 208.

emancipated black person was no better or worse than the enslaved blacks. Free blacks were considered idle; however, slavery could keep them from being idle.[110] Harrison writes that "the slave, removed from the influence and example of the whites, was a scene of great depravity."[111] Thus, white people, Christian and non-Christian, saw themselves as the chosen of God sent simultaneously to save the African slave's soul and to perpetuate the idyllic plantation life of the antebellum South.

Slave catechisms (together with hymns and prayers) taught slaves that God, the Great Creator, spoke to them commanding them to accept white Christian norms; that God was their heavenly master whom they should obey; that they have a moral duty to obey their earthly masters too; that God spoke to them in the Bible, even though they were forbidden to or unable to read the Bible; that God sees and hears everything so that attempts to commit any sins (i.e., acts of resistance) would be futile and would result in God's wrath; and that any trouble that afflicts them should be considered an act of God. Never mind that slavery troubled the slave's *psychē*, night and day. While the slave could not expect to be liberated as a result of conversion and baptism, he could expect to go to heaven when he died, if he was good refraining from the wickedness in his heart (e.g. laziness). God would give him the strength to be content with his present predicament. Some slaves were undoubtedly convinced and deceived by the false teachings inflicted upon their humanity. Others rejected Christianity altogether and clung to the religious beliefs and experiences that they brought with them to America's shores, and still others synthesized some aspects of Christianity with their own religious ideas and practices.

110. Ibid., 104–5.
111. Ibid., 101.

PART II

Womanist, Feminist, and Postcolonial Criticisms and the Great Commission

4

The Great Commission: A Postcolonial Dalit Feminist Inquiry

Jayachitra Lalitha

By the eighteenth century, colonial expansion in India had clear links with the paramount missionary agenda of evangelizing the heathen land. William Carey (1761–1834), the father of modern missions, who pioneered Serampore mission[1] from 1800 until his death in 1834 owed his missionary zeal to the Great Commission text, Matt. 28:18-20. Ever since Carey anchored his missionary obligation to the Matthean commissioning of the disciples, this concept had flourished in missionary agencies in colonial India. R. S. Sugirtharajah comments on the impact of Carey's use of Matt. 28:19-20 in a pamphlet published in 1792 (*An Enquiry into the Obligations of Christians to use Means for the Conversion of the Heathen*) asserting that this verse has exercised a considerable influence on the institutionalized missionary efforts of the Christian church in India. Sugirtharajah stated the following:

> What is interesting is that Carey's call to win the souls of the unbelievers in foreign lands and his reactivating of the Matthean command happened at a time of unprecedented territorial conquest by the West. Historians of colonialism have come up with different periodizations of the imperial advance of the West. Carey's call to evangelize distant lands falls within what Marc Ferro categorizes as colonialism of a new type, yoked to the industrial Revolution and to financial capitalism, and marked by expansionist policies. It is highly significant to a postcolonial hermeneutic that Carey's fascination

---

1. Joshua Marshman, Hannah Marshman, William Carey, and William Ward initiated the Serampore Mission in early nineteenth century in Serampore, Hooghly District, West Bengal, India. These four English missionaries were the architects of Serampore Renaissance.

with this dormant verse arose at a time when Europe was engaged in just such a colonialism.[2]

Sugirtharaja's critical approach to colonial India's witness to missionary manipulation of Matt. 28:19-20 reveals the close nexus between colonialism and mission in India since the eighteenth century. The missionary imagination of heathen lands revolves around binary portrayals like the west/the rest, civilized/uncivilized, colonizer/colonized, redeemed/unredeemed, heaven/hell, knowledge/ignorance, privilege/lack, and dominance/subjugation. Gender notions are highly ignored in colonial era as male represented empire and imperialism in perfect collaboration with colonial mission. The Matthean Great Commission pericope (28:16-20) furthers such colonial agenda by limiting the recipients of the Great Commission to eleven disciples, visibly male disciples, thus completely negating the presence of women in this narrative. I would further problematize the vernacular translations during colonial period in India, in which *nations* are translated as *jaathigal* (in *Tamil*), which literally means *caste groups*.[3] Such translations employing an uncritical casteist apparatus in translation has deepened caste divisions in India despite reiterating an already existing female-male binary in the text.

Matthew ends with the resurrected Jesus commissioning the eleven Jewish disciples "to make disciples of all nations" (28:19). What is the implication of this verse for the concept of Jewish particularism in Matthew's Gospel? During Jesus' earthly ministry, he sends twelve disciples on a mission journey with a strict command to "Go nowhere among the Gentiles, and enter no town of the Samaritans, but go rather to the lost sheep of the house of Israel" (10:5-6). Jesus insists on his Jewish mission again at Matt. 15:24, when he replies to the Canaanite woman that he was sent only to the lost sheep of the house of Israel. But does Matt. 28:19 indicate that the Jewish mission has come to an end?

JEWISH PARTICULARISM UNDER POSTCOLONIAL SCRUTINY

Jesus' reinstatement of his mission exclusively toward Jews causes much embarrassment to Matthean interpreters. In Matt. 10:5 and 15:24, Jesus' very own words indicate the Jewish particularism in the sense that they remind readers of God's exclusive covenant with Abraham. This is evident from

---

2. R. S. Sugirtharajah, "A Postcolonial Exploration of Collusion and Construction in Biblical Interpretation," in *The Postcolonial Bible*, ed. R. S. Sugirtharajah (Sheffield: Sheffield Academic Press, 1998), 96–111 (100).

3. *Parisuttha Vedaagamam* (Bangalore: Bible Society of India, 2002), 47.

references to cities of Sodom and Gomorrah (10:15) and children's food (15:26). Sodom and Gomorrah were proverbially wicked cities, destroyed by God for covenantal unfaithfulness (cf. Gen. 13:10; 18:20; 19:24-25; Deut. 29:23; Jer. 49:18). The reference to Jewish towns being treated more harshly if they do not accept the words of the disciples indicates that the disciples' mission has offered greater opportunity for encountering God's saving presence than was given to Sodom and Gomorrah, and the punishment will also be greater on the day of judgment.[4] Similarly, the covenant phrase *children of Israel* is implicit when Jesus says to the Canaanite woman in 15:26 that "It is not fair to take the children's food and throw it to the dogs," which is parallel, but in stark contrast to the implicit term *dog* used for the gentile identity of the Canaanite woman.

Jesus' explicit mission statements with tones of Jewish particularism send dubious signals to interpreters who study the intersectionality of ethnicity, gender, and religion in the New Testament. Do they not indicate unsympathetic bias against gentiles and gentile women in particular? By excluding gentiles from Jesus' missionary agenda, has he not demonstrated explicit nationalist trends? How would one reconcile the favoritism shown toward Jews in clear contrast to the indifference shown to the gentiles? Sugirtharajah thinks the reason for the Matthean unsympathetic approach in general "could be attributed to the persecution the Matthean community faced at the hands of the gentiles during and following the first Jewish war against Rome."[5] He highlights Jesus' discourses on mission in chapter 10 and the apocalypticism in chapters 24 and 25 to support this argument.

Jesus' statements on Jewish particularism continue to intrigue commentators. However, this attitude to Jews changes when Jesus refers to Jewish leaders like Pharisees, Sadducees, chief priests, and scribes. The Jewish leaders' rejection of Jesus indicates collaboration with Roman imperialism. Why do the Jewish leaders oppose Jesus' claims of divine intervention in history? The Jewish leaders function as native elites who collaborate with Roman imperial powers to retain their status quo and to benefit from a hierarchically stratified social set up. Jesus did not clash openly with the Roman authorities, but he directed his anger towards Israel's internal imperialism and the collaborators with the Roman Empire. Samuel Rayan explains it so vividly in an essay written in 1985. He states the following:

---

4. Warren Carter, *Matthew and the Margins: A Sociopolitical and Religious Reading* (Bangalore: Theological Publications in India, 2007), 236.

5. Sugirtharajah, "A Postcolonial Exploration," 100.

Jesus fought imperialism of every sort when he resisted and rejected dominance, and spoke for and worked for autonomy and liberation. He undermined imperialism when he refused to submit or conform to the powers that be, to their prescriptions, their prohibitions and their framework for living; he did it when he encouraged others to refuse too. He was subverting imperialism when he took away people's fear, and challenged them to think and act independently. One remarkable thing about the Gospels is that each of them is the story of a sustained struggle unto death against dominance by religion, tradition, society, State and empire.[6]

Rayan thinks that Jesus' rejection of the Roman Empire was not confrontational, for it might have led to defeat of his earthly mission.[7] Nevertheless, one witnesses how he was confrontational to the Jewish leaders.

The Jewish leaders exhibit a number of corrupt practices: Matthew opens with King Herod plotting to kill the newly born Messiah. In Matt. 2:3, all Jerusalem was terrified with King Herod at the news of the birth of the Messiah. All Jerusalem includes the chief priests and scribes. This response stands in stark contrast to common perception of the joy attached to the birth of the Messiah. The Jewish leaders, according to Matthew, are nothing but hypocrites. Their words and deeds do not match. John the Baptist criticizes the Pharisees and Sadducees as a brood of vipers failing to bear fruit worthy of repentance (3:7-8). Claiming the Abrahamic ancestry without living a life worthy of Abrahamic covenant is doomed to eternal destruction (3:10). When the Pharisees question Jesus' association with tax collectors and sinners, Jesus reiterates higher virtue like mercy rather than sacrifice or, in other words, actions have to supersede mere verbal adherence to law (9:10-13). Matt. 12:7 also refers to Jesus' critique of how these leaders condemn the guiltless with their selfish intentions of using law for their vested interests. The woes proclaimed by Jesus on Chorazin, Bethsaida, and even Capernaum indicate that these cities "perhaps share the elite's misplaced sense of well-being based on ethnicity" (cf. 3:7-10).[8]

Matthew designates a whole chapter (23) for Jesus' severe denouncing of Pharisees and scribes. In 23:1-12, Jesus highlights various illegitimate practices of the Pharisees. They do not practice what they teach. They make their teachings burdensome for others but are least interested to follow the same.

---

6. Samuel Rayan, "Jesus and Imperialism," in *Jesus Today*, ed. S. Kappen (Madras: AICUF, 1985), 98–117 (106).

7. Ibid.

8. Carter, *Matthew and the Margins*, 256.

They do all their deeds to be seen by others. They love to have their place of honor in public occasions such as banquets and synagogue worships. They take pride in being called as rabbis.

In the following verses (23:13-36), Jesus discloses the hypocritical acts of scribes and Pharisees by which they abuse Mosaic law to control common people while they themselves do not practice any of them. The word *hypocrite* appears thirteen times in Matthew. In chapter 23 alone, the term *hypocrite* is used six times exclusively addressing the scribes and Pharisees. Warren Carter recognizes three major aspects: first, this chapter is part of the life-and-death conflict between Jesus and the religious elite; second, Jerusalem's fall is resulted from the rejection of Jesus; and third, this chapter reflects Jesus' taking on religious elites with their own polemical language, which they used to slander other groups.[9]

Jesus uses very strong phrases such as *whitewashed tombs* to refer to the religious elites (23:27). Their outward display of religiosity does not reflect weightier matters of the Law such as justice, mercy, and faith (23:23). Jesus, in fact, raises his criticism in line with his concerns over interpretations of the Law. Thus, Jesus attempts to question the religious authority of the scribes and Pharisees, which in turn had decided their hierarchical social status. It is quite self-revelatory in first-century Palestine that such Jewish religious elitism was heavily safeguarded by their loyalty to imperial structures. This is attested by Carter as follows:

> To fight over interpretations of Torah, for example, is to fight over claims to possess the past and envision present social interaction and structure. To fight with the temple-based Jerusalem leaders is to fight with those who also must negotiate Roman power, allying with it to preserve their own status and power, while selectively representing traditions that are often contestive of imperial power.[10]

Therefore, Jesus' attack on the religious authority of Jewish elites is not just an attack on them alone, but also on the hegemony that continually sanctioned their authority in a hierarchical imperial social set up. By critiquing the Jewish leaders who collaborate with the Roman empire, Jesus challenges Roman imperialism.

9. Ibid., 449–51

10. Warren Carter, "The Gospel of Matthew," in *A Postcolonial Commentary on the New Testament Writings*, ed. Fernando F. Segovia and R. S. Sugirtharajah (London: T&T Clark, 2009), 69–104 (74).

Matthew's reference to synagogues as the dominant place of religious elites exposes the relation between synagogue and Roman government:

> . . . synagogue leaders were defined not by specialized, vocational training and skills (analogous to contemporary clergy) but within a Graeco-Roman euergetistic framework that required significant wealth, power and societal status to effect group benefaction and representation. They are not primarily religious officials with religious duties (in the modern sense), but (sub)community leaders embedded in and representative of a euergetistic and doxic community.[11]

Jesus' severe curses on the Scribes and Pharisees in relation to their evil acts in synagogues, therefore, comes down upon them as rebukes for collaborating with structures of domination. Here, these religious elites play a significant role in determining the fate of social identity of the majority of Jews. Hence, it is a position of power, in fact a position to exercise power over others' social identity and destiny. The interpretations of Torah upheld by these religious authorities promote unjust societal practices that harm the common masses. Therefore, Jesus' fight over issues related to interpretations of Torah is not a simple controversy over doctrinal issues, but rather a deeper struggle to challenge illegitimate and unjust societal frameworks of day-to-day functioning. Hence, it becomes "a struggle with those invested in, allied with, and representative of an unjust societal order that Rome oversees for the elite's benefit and that the Gospel declares to be contrary to God's purposes."[12]

Many scholars argue that the corrupt Jewish leaders who had rejected Jesus had brought God's judgment upon Jewish people in two ways: first, the destruction of the Jerusalem temple, and second, the movement of God's mission to the nations beyond the ethnic boundaries of Israel.[13] Therefore the Great Commission has often been treated as an extension of God's mercy to the world in alleged contempt to the Jewish rejection of Jesus to death on the cross. Such anti-Semitic approach in Western biblical interpretation in the twentieth century has failed to take into consideration Jesus' opposition to Roman imperialism. Jesus' death on the cross is a punishment given to rebels of Roman government. Therefore, it may not be appropriate to attach anti-Semitic sentiments to the Roman execution of Jesus.[14] A majority of

---

11. Ibid.

12. Ibid., 75.

13. Frank Thielman, *Theology of the New Testament* (Grand Rapids: Zondervan, 2005), 100.

the Jewish people in the first century Palestine lived in their own land as aliens and strangers, as socially ostracized people in the hierarchical society of Roman imperial rule. Jesus' movement was a peasant movement to resist the power structures of imperialism and Jewish elitism. Jesus' confrontation of Jewish authorities who collaborate with Roman imperial powers along with his insistence of Jewish priority in God's mission clearly set him against Roman imperial agenda. I argue, therefore, in favor of Jewish particularism in Matthew as a postcolonial act in that it rejects Roman imperialism along with critiquing the Jewish religious elites who collaborate with hegemonic interests of imperial powers. One may argue that the Jewish particularism is focused on narrow ethnic boundaries of the first-century Judaism, however, Jesus' insistence on Jewish exclusivity in Matthew is set against the backdrop of them being colonized by Roman imperial powers. Therefore, by taking side with the salvific privileging of the Jews, Jesus is clearly revealing his stance against the rulers in authority. However, this ethnic particularity of Jews merges with extending mission to nations in Matt. 28:18-20. Therefore, Jewish particularism merging with the Great Commission itself is a postcolonial act of including those who were earlier excluded from the mission due to the colonized political situation. The hegemonic stratification of ancient society based on ethnic identities finds accommodation of all in the universal extension of Jesus' salvific act now through the Great Commission. In other words, this serves as a postcolonial act since the mission moves beyond the narrow ethnic boundaries of Judaism to accommodate others who otherwise would have been *othered* by exclusive claims of access to God through Judaism. However, the criticism still remains that the gender notion is completely missing in both *Jewish particularism* and *universalism* in Matthew. This cannot be brushed aside as narrative amnesia, but it clearly indicates the strategic denial of the agency of women in the patriarchal social structure. When a critical reading of the Matthean Great Commission is thought about from the Indian subcontinent, what immediately comes to mind is the intersection of caste and gender and how that plays a dominant role in determining meaning(s) in a given context.

Brahmanism, Patriarchy, and the Great Commission: A Postcolonial Dalit Feminist Inquiry

Similar to Jewish elitism in collaboration with Roman imperialism, one may find how the caste elites collaborated with the British colonizers since

14. See Neil Elliott, *Liberating Paul: the Justice of God and the Politics of the Apostle* (Minneapolis: Fortress Press, 2006).

eighteenth century in the colonial India. Therefore, any study that deals with the Great Commission in biblical hermeneutics in Indian context ought to address the intersecting dynamics among colonialism, race, caste, and gender during the colonial period when the Bible was translated and propagated through missionary efforts. A postcolonial dalit feminist inquiry serves the purpose of doing justice to this. Before I define dalit feminism, the term *dalit* requires explanation for the readers.

> India's social hierarchy of casteism places people under four major categories (*chaturvarna*) such as Brahmins, Kshatriyas, Vyshias, and Shudras right within the system and one category outside the system, who are called the dalits. About 16 percentage of Indian population are dalits. They are at the brunt of discrimination, due to their outcaste identity, varying from denial of access to nutrition, education, employment and upward social mobility. Their designation to particular menial jobs in India include managing graveyards, disposing of dead animals, and cleaning human excreta apart from being leather workers, street sweepers, cobblers, and landless agricultural workers. Many Dalits are impoverished, uneducated, and illiterate. Dalits form the majority of bonded laborers. Dalits have been socially oppressed, culturally subjugated, and politically marginalized. The purity-pollution binary underlies all the socio-cultural and political discrimination dalits face in India. It is shameful that conversion to Christianity has not guaranteed emancipation from this Hindu religious practice of caste system.[15]

Dalit feminism emerged in India towards the close of twentieth century to tackle primarily the triple oppression of dalit women based on caste, class, and gender. However, now the oppression may be analyzed through multiple identity struggles adding sexuality and age to the above mentioned three factors. Dalit feminism functions as an ideology and literary device in line with its claims of anti-casteism, anti-sexism, and anti-hierarchy. Unlike single issue-based dominant discourses of dalit movement or Indian feminist movement, dalit feminism aims at radically changing society for the benefit of all women and for all religiously subjugated males. In this way, dalit feminist reading tools are efficient in decoding biblical texts for the benefit of the vast majority of oppressed people without excluding any oppressed woman or man.[16]

15. See Manoranjan Mohanty, *Class, Caste, Gender* (New Delhi: Sage, 2004); Manohar Chandra Prasad, *Dalit Christians in Search of Justice* (Bengaluru: Rachana Prakashana, 2011).

To elaborate on postcolonial tools in critical reading of the Bible, Sugirtharajah approves that "the major achievement of postcolonialism is to inaugurate a new era of academic inquiry which brings to the fore the overlapping issues of empire, nation, ethnicity, migration and language. Where it differs from earlier critical theories is that the postcolonial discourse implicates academic learning in colonialism. It challenges the context, contours and normal procedures of biblical scholarship."[17] This comment presumes that the European mode of reading the biblical texts have fallen prey to colonial domination and power and therefore reflect heavy colonial residues. With the arrival of liberation hermeneutics, attempts to take the local context of the interpreter have gained momentum and precedence. This is relevant when the intersection of coloniality, patriarchy, racism, and casteism is taken into account in the Indian biblical reading practices.

Writing from India, a country that has been caste-ridden for ages now, having witnessed the impact of casteism in pre-colonial, colonial, and postcolonial periods of native history, a postcolonial dalit feminist critical lens calls for looking for locations of dominant metanarratives (grand controlling narratives) and ideological systems. Brahmanism, in modern India, represents the caste ideology intersecting with class and gender identities. The underlying power dynamic behind all ideas and identities demands a subversive outlook in exploring colonial nuances in the biblical texts and their interpretations by European academy. Patriarchy, casteism, and classism existed in pre-colonial India, and it was not surprising when the native elites (here the aristocratic Brahmin males) joined hands with the colonial authorities to retain power structures intact. The colonial period witnessed the hegemonic collaboration of casteist Indian elite men and racist imperial foreign rulers (i.e., Portuguese, Dutch, French or British).

---

16. Jayachitra Lalitha, "Deconstructing Christ-Church Power Model: Enhancing the Dignity of Dalit Women in India," *CTC Bulletin*, 20, no. 3 (2004): 14–20; Lalitha, "Jesus and Ambedkar: Exploring Common Loci for Dalit Theology and Dalit Movements," in *Dalit Theology in the Twenty-First Century: Discordant Voices, Discerning Pathways*, ed. Sathianathan Clarke, Deenabandhu Manchala, and Philip Vinod Peacock (New Delhi: Oxford University Press, 2010): 124–47; Lalitha, "Rediscerning Interconnections in Feminist Thinking for a Relevant Social Appraisal of the Bible in a Postcolonial India," in *Christian Theologizing and Social Thinking in India: Discernment Interconnection Transition and New Direction*, ed. Vincent Rajkumar (Bangalore: Christian Institute for the Study of Religion and Society, 2010), 44–68.

17. R. S. Sugirtharajah, "Biblical Studies after the Empire: From a Colonial to a Postcolonial Mode of Interpretation," in *The Postcolonial Bible*, 12–21 (16). See also R. S. Sugirtharajah, *Exploring Postcolonial Biblical Criticism: History, Method, Practice* (Malden, MA: Wiley-Blackwell, 2011).

It was during British colonization of India that the missionary agencies strategically shared imperial values in their missionary agenda. This collaboration occurred mainly to retain their own survival in a British colony as well as for monetary support from well-wishers back in England. In this process, white missionaries from England since the eighteenth century have failed to address the dominant oppressive systems that were already in operation, such as casteism and patriarchy. Therefore, while white missionaries introduced the Bible and interpretative methods, they were categorically foreign and culturally biased against the natives, as well as reiterating the native hierarchies. Such interpretations failed to employ critical lenses to view casteism in the colonial period, thus favoring native cultural and social evil practices.

It is all the more dangerous when one identifies colonial residues in Bible translations embedded with caste nuances. This is evident if we scrutinize vernacular Bibles and their varying translations. The dominant Tamil version of the Bible translates the Greek noun *ethnē* as *jaathigal*, which literally means caste groups. The reference to eleven disciples as the recipients of the Great Commission totally negates the presence of women among Jesus' disciples, as well as their subjectivity in proclaiming the resurrection of Jesus to the world as the first witnesses. The silent play of denying access to women in this grand narrative unearths the text's manipulative power in denying share in the authority of Jesus. Therefore, "Postcolonialism is not simply a physical expulsion of imperial powers. . . . Rather, it is an active confrontation with the dominant system of thought, its lopsidedness and inadequacies, and underlines its unsuitability for us. Hence, it is a process of cultural and discursive emancipation from all dominant structures whether they be political, linguistic or ideological."[18] However, postcolonial biblical scholars have not always employed gender lens while they pointed out the brutal collaboration of colonial mission and biblical hermeneutics. This is definitely a pitfall.

Does the Matthean Great Commission denote the Matthean community's zeal to evangelize the world, which belongs to the terrain outside Jewish identity? Can we link the Jewish identity of the Matthean church to the thrust in the mission statement to the nations? Does it highlight the colonial aspiration of a minority community that struggles for its own identity and security in an empire occupied Palestine? Or is it a move beyond its colonial resonance to strive for an inclusive community under the reign of the resurrected Jesus? Sugirtharajah suggests that against the popular idea of a positive gentile bias in Matthew, there are very unsympathetic statements about gentiles. Such a

---

18. Sugirtharajah, "A Postcolonial Exploration," 93.

negative approach reveals how the Matthean community perceived gentiles as foreigners.[19] On a similar note, Musa Dube's analyses find the Great Commission statement highly imperial. She says, "Ideologically, the mission advocates relations that sanction authoritative traveling teachers and reduces nations to the position of students who must be taught to 'obey' all that Jesus commanded. Since the exportation of the gospel is a nonnegotiable cultural good to its potential consumers, it passes as an imposition."[20] However, Sugirtharajah and Dube do not address how the Matthean Great Commission empowers eleven disciples who hail from colonized Palestine to hold authority to teach all the nations. Including the colonized disciples into the teaching mission is a direct attack on the exclusivist approach of Jewish religious authorities who have collaborated with the Roman empire and denied access to the ordinary mass of religious people. In this particular sense, the Great Commission becomes inclusive of the people who are ignored hitherto in mainline religious authority. However, a critical enquiry pending is this: why has this excluded women disciples of Jesus Christ, particularly the women who have witnessed the resurrected Christ in the immediate literary context? Here a postcolonial dalit feminist lens is helpful to reread this passage from the experiences of dalit women of India.

Any postcolonial literary device that excludes gender as a critical reading subject fails to unmask imperial structures and practices. For instance, dalit reading devices have fallen into a similar trap of not taking dalit women's experiences seriously. A postcolonial reading apparatus that considers dalit women's experiences as subjective needs to explore how the Matthean text has dealt with imperial composition and gender biases. Sugirtharajah comments that "Postcolonial perspectives are interested in unmasking the imperial structures, practices and visions in which Matthew is enmeshed, by which it is shaped, and to which it articulates resistance, as well as in identifying the alternative world and the world of (imperial-imitating) power that the Gospel creates."[21] Does the original Matthean community have such power to impose on the world? If we problematize the use of *authority* in the Matthean Great Commission, then it provides scope for how women are strategically kept away from accessing power.

The conspicuous absence of women in receiving the Great Commission calls our attention back to Matt. 28:10 where Jesus tells Mary Magdalene and the other Mary (cf. 28:1) to inform the brothers to go to Galilee. Here, while the

19. Ibid., 100

20. Musa W. Dube, *Postcolonial Feminist Interpretation of the Bible* (St. Louis: Chalice, 2000), 141.

21. Sugirtharajah, "A Postcolonial Exploration," 75.

eleven disciples are given a special mandate to teach nations, which in Matthew is a clear act of authority, women disciples are excluded from the same mission call. The silence of women in this pericope seems to be a strategic attempt to keep women away from holding control over the nations. Perhaps, it is a call to wait for the establishing of the church as a community of believers. Therefore, the direct commissioning seems to be a matter of male business. As far as the disciples are concerned, this must be an empowering act in itself while they receive the authority to make disciples of all nations, thus making them competent to challenge the structures of power.

The movement of gospel beyond Jewish boundaries is a postcolonial act. However, the early Christian history has unfurled the danger of mission to the nations becoming a colonial agenda. Dube argues that the "great commission presents a Christ figure that has 'absolute and universal authority or dominion' and who commissions his disciples to teach the nations to obey all that he commanded them. This mission discourse does not underline a model of liberating interdependence, but one of subjugation, of conquest, of authoritative teachers, and of travelers."[22] Dube's criticism is relevant when women are deliberately excluded from receiving the command to teach all nations. In the Indian scenario, Dube's criticism also forces us to delve into the nexus between caste and gender. Therefore, a postcolonial dalit feminist lens is relevant to see how multiple hegemonic powers are at work in the Great Commission narrative.

Brahmanism in feminist discourses and patriarchal practices in dalit hermeneutics are common monsters encountered in the rereading of the Bible. Postcolonialism cautions us to be aware of the danger of employing the very structures of hegemony that we try to resist upon ourselves and others. Dalit feminism coupled with postcolonialism ensures reading practices of dalit women against the very systems of casteism/Brahmanism and patriarchy they fight. Brahmanism exposes its ugly manifestation both as a philosophy of life and a social order. B. R. Ambedkar has for a long time identified the philosophy of Brahmanism as predominantly responsible for pushing the dalits and shudras (who fall at the lowest string of four categories of casteism) into a degraded social status devoid of hope and ambitions. For him, Brahmanism is guided by

1) graded inequality between the different classes; 2) complete disarmament of the Shudras and the Untouchables; 3) complete prohibition of the education of the Shudras and the Untouchables; 4) ban on Shudras and the Untouchables occupying places of power

22. Dube, *Postcolonial Feminist Interpretation*, 148.

and authority; 5) ban on the Shudras and the Untouchables acquiring property and 6) complete subjugation and suppression of women.[23]

Brahmanism's hold on education of dalits has been checked to a certain extent through making education accessible through constitutional rights (although the uproar against reservation for dalits in higher education still continues). However, Brahmanism continues to propagate inequality, disarmament, prohibition to power and authority, ban on acquiring property, and complete denial of agency of women. Brahmanism is not just against equality, but it preaches graded inequality, which is evident from grouping people into *chaturvarna* (four categories of casteism) and excluding a group of people (dalits) in the very same unequal stratification on the basis of outcastes. When people are grouped into caste identity by birth, without any room for change or access to power for change, it creates a pathetic yet pathological system of unjust social order. By denying access to knowledge or education, Brahmanism has kept the marginal communities like dalits and women in enforced ignorance for centuries so that they could not recognize their degraded state of existence. This had mutilated their right to rebel against the awful system. Against such a backdrop, one can imagine how the agency of dalit women has been suppressed in questioning Brahmanism for robbing them of their freedom and significance.

Access to power and authority is still denied to dalit women even in an era of dalit identity politics. Dalit politics is an attempt to politicize the existence of dalit communities, identifying themselves as members of a political and ethical community. The unique disabilities of untouchability have demanded specific modes of politicizing the ethical existence of dalits in India. What I problematize in dalit politics in Indian history is the lack of or less importance given to gender questions. When gender is taken as an inevitable factor for critical inquiry, patriarchal practices are unfortunately found in dalit politics as an uncritical internalizing of patriarchy by dalit men. When Brahmanism is viewed through the colonial past of India, one would invariably encounter its contribution toward creating spaces for dalit politics. But this happened through a complex phenomenon of colonial association with Hindu religion and secularization of caste. Colonial powers have renounced their mediating in religious rights and communal standing, thus challenging caste discipline and brahmanic norms. However, brahmanical knowledge played a major role in colonial knowledge production. Colonial intervention in Indian history benefitted dalits in two ways:

---

23. B. R. Ambedkar, "Caste, Class and Democracy," in *The Essential Writings of B. R. Ambedkar,* ed. Valerian Rodrigues (Oxford: Oxford University Press, 2002), 132–48 (146).

It [Colonial modernity] produced new investments in history and caste identity, and it provoked affinity with a new range of modern institutions—schools and colleges, law courts, hospitals—spaces through which social mobility for the downtrodden and exploited might be accomplished. Colonial infrastructure, and its multiple and dispersed effects in the form of a colonial "sensorium," was inextricably linked to new experiences of the self and enabled radical egalitarian ideology to percolate through caste radicals' discourse, from ideas of self-respect and equality among intimates to a critique of the structured political-economic inequities of Brahmanism.[24]

However, the various exclusionary mechanisms embedded in hierarchical social stratification have categorically kept dalit women from accessing power to overcome extreme underprivileged situations, minimal decision making, and inaccessibility to political endeavors of identity formation.

Now analyzing the mission in colonial India, gender has been a neglected category in dominant dalit discourses because of the inherent patriarchal biases. The colonizer and the colonized find common benefits as collaborators with patriarchy. Any nationalistic identity formation is gendered. The institutionalization of gender occurs if nation formation depends on the frustrations and aspirations of men in such a way that "the representation of male *national* power depends on the prior construction of *gender* difference."[25] Dalit women's struggle for making their presence felt in the nationalistic endeavors in colonial period raises some difficult and unpleasant question on dalit identity politics. Dalit men found dalit feminism as divisive of their common dream of emancipation. But dalit feminism was a political response to gender conflict within the dalit communities. The silencing of dalit women's voices existed even during the period of silencing dalit voices in general.

To insist on silence about gender conflict when it already exists is to cover, and thereby ratify, women's disempowerment. Asking women to wait until after the revolution serves merely as a strategic tactic to defer women's demands. Not only does it conceal the fact

24. Anupama Rao, "Caste Radicalism and the Making of a New Political Subject," *The Caste Question: Dalits and the Politics of Modern India* (Berkeley, CA: University of California Press, 2009), 44. http://www.ucpress.edu/content/chapters/11115.ch01.pdf

25. Anne McClintock, "'No Longer in a Future Heaven': Gender, Race, and Nationalism," in *Dangerous Liaisons: Gender, Nation, & Postcolonial Perspectives*, ed. Anne McClintock, Aamir Mufti, and Ella Shohat (Minneapolis: University of Minnesota Press, 1997), 89–112 (89). Emphasis added.

that nationalisms are from the outset constituted in gender power, but, as the lessons of international history portend, women who are not empowered to organize during the struggle will not be empowered to organize after the struggle. If nationalism is not transformed by an analysis of gender power, the nation-state will remain a repository of male hopes, male aspirations, and male privilege.[26]

Dalit women find themselves active in missionary activities along with the white women missionaries, especially to reach out to the caste women and families. White missionaries introduced the Bible as a colonial fetish to Indian dalits to avail literacy as a means of upward social mobility. "Translation of the Bible into several of the Indian languages was the work of missionaries. Their involvement in the systematization and codification of the grammar of Indian languages can also be seen as part of the colonizing activity of the colonizer to take control of the language, the metaphor, and the worldview of the colonized."[27] However, such ministerial opportunities enhanced dalit Bible women's ability to negotiate creative spaces for their own marginalized identities.

WAY FORWARD...

To conclude, can dalit women at least speak or learn—if not teach—as in the case of the Great Commission? Even if India is free from the colonialism in a political sense, the church and theological seminaries owe their existence to the legacy of western missionaries and the continuing theological funding. A major task in today's Indian theological education/formation is that it should empower self-sufficiency of theological institutions in providing theological education in vernacular languages and with indigenous curricula. While several indigenous models of theological formations were introduced in the early 1970s and 80s of the twentieth century in India, western patterns, methodologies, and frameworks are still carried on in many theological sectors.

As far as dalit women are concerned, they feel both in church and society that they are alienated from decision-making and active participation. The Indian church scenario is still entrapped in the caste system, keeping dalit women at the lowest place of anonymity and lack of voice. Here it becomes

26. Ibid., 109.

27. Monica Jyotsna Melanchthon, "Dalits, Bible, and Method," *SBL Forum* , n.p., http://sbl-site.org/Article.aspx?ArticleID=459.

important that dalit women find interconnections between pastoral formation and theological developments in such a way that they enhance their agency in articulating their life experiences theologically. Dalit experience could be gained primarily by developing a critical caste consciousness, which would make sensitive efforts to analyze how dalit women are strategically oppressed within church and society. As far as Indian theological formation is concerned, it caters to analyzing the identity-specific dimensions involved in accommodation of the subaltern groups such as dalits.

It is the need of the hour that the theologically well-empowered women and men participate in the grassroot activities in the church and society. That is where the real Indian church is! About sixty-five to seventy-five percent of Christians in India are dalits. However, our music, liturgies, spiritualities, and practices are still in harmony with western hymns and western methods in scriptural interpretations. New Dalit biblical commentary series[28] have yet to make an impact on the churches. They are more resisted than given opportunity. As far as the future of postcolonial dalit feminist reading practices are concerned, they are closely linked to dalit emancipation in general. Amartya Sen values the freedom of each individual or a community "not merely because it assists achievement, but also because of its own importance, going beyond the value of the state of existence actually achieved."[29] In other words, the loss of opportunity is the loss of freedom, which in turn is the loss of some importance that directly hampers the communities' ability to lay claim on their much desired benefits. Therefore, the concentration should be on alternative social arrangements that critically evaluate a "less just" or "more just" situation than on a transcendental ideal of a fully just society.[30]

28. See T. K. John and James Massey, eds., *Dalit Bible Commentary: New Testament* (New Delhi: Centre for Dalit/Subaltern Studies, 2007).

29. Amartya Sen, *On Ethics and Economics* (New Delhi: Oxford University Press, 1987), 60.

30. Amartya Sen, "What Do We Want From a Theory of Justice?" *Journal of Philosophy* 103, no. 5 (2006): 215–38 (216).

Privilege but No Power: Women in the Gospel of Matthew and Nineteenth-Century African American Women Missionaries through a Postcolonial Lens

Lynne St. Clair Darden

I have prayed to the Lord and asked Him what He would have me to do ever since I became a Christian and I believe He has given me the work of a missionary and He directs my mind and heart to Africa, the land of my forefathers. To those who are living in darkness and sin. To those who are calling to their sons and daughters to come and help them. . . .
—Nancy Jones, African American missionary, 1888[1]

Kindred and friends I bid farewell
To go to yonder's shore.
The love of God is mine to tell
The heathen is my store.
—Eliza Davis, African American Missionary, 1910[2]

---

1. Sylvia M. Jacobs, "African-American Missionaries Confront the African Way of Life," in *Women in Africa and the African Diaspora: A Reader,* ed. Rosalyn Terborg-Penn and Andrea Benton Rushing, 2nd ed. (Washington, DC: Howard University Press, 1996), 89–100 (92).

2. Ibid.

INTRODUCTION

It is the opinion of postcolonial biblical scholars that the Gospel of Matthew, in general, and the Great Commission (28:18-20) in particular, justifies the invasion and colonization of "foreign" or "uncivilized" territories by powerful European Christian nations. This is the likely summation made once the text has been thoroughly foregrounded in the context of imperialism, not only in a modern sense but also in the context of the ancient Roman Empire, the milieu in which the Gospel is written. Highlighting the ancient political situation allows the reader to glean how the Matthean author rhetorically negotiated the community's marginal position in this imperializing background. However, as it is often the case for scholars who approach the texts in this way, the end result can differ depending on the hermeneutical key of the individual, which is in tune to her or his cultural location.

For example, the Botswanian biblical scholar Musa Dube reads Matthew's vision of mission, a vision she sees as grounded in the foundation myth of Israel, as embodying Empire. She says,

> Matthew's model embodies imperialistic values and strategies. It does not seek relationships of liberating interdependence between nations, cultures, and genders. Rather, it upholds the superiority of some races and advocates the subjugation of differences by relegating other races to inferiority. It posits a universally available world, and it advances the right to expand to other foreign nations, to teach them, and to include them without necessarily embracing equality.[3]

While Warren Carter, who is of Euro-American descent, notes,

> Matthew is a complex text not only because it is produced by and productive of worlds of power but also because of the ambiguities and complicities it attests in negotiating its imperial context. It mirrors imperial realities, even while it contests them. It protests imperial power, even while it imitates imperial structures, language and ways of being. It advocates an alternative identity and way of life, even while recognizing a continuing accommodated existence. It envisages the future and violent triumph of God's power and empire over Rome (24:27-31), even while it forms a community that renounces violence (5:43-44) and structures that embody "power over" others (20:25-26).[4]

---

3. Musa W. Dube, *Postcolonial Feminist Interpretation of the Bible* (St. Louis: Chalice, 2000), 155.

Dube and Carter both approach Matthew with a focus on how the text negotiates Roman imperial power. However, Dube's explicit, contextually informed approach to Matthew reads the text as strictly an accommodation to the Roman powers, a "playing up" to Rome, and, in fact, claims that the Gospel actually re-enacts imperializing practices toward those outside of the community. On the other hand, Carter reads Matthew mainly as a counter-narrative in which the Matthean author strives to create an alternative way of life under God's will and not that of the Roman Empire, even though he acknowledges that the Gospel does replicate an imperializing ethos.[5]

This paper adds to the above analyses by reading the missionary vision of Matthew through an African American lens supplemented by postcolonial theory. The aim of the reading is twofold: (1) to illustrate the complex cultural negotiations of African American women missionaries to Africa in the late nineteenth and early twentieth centuries based on a Christian hybrid identity construction, and (2) to use that cultural framework as a springboard to critically examine the role of women in the prologue (1:3-6) and the epilogue (28:1-10) in terms of mission. The purpose of this reading is to reveal the complexity inherent in a hybrid identity construct in that the marginalized often mimic the imperial ideological processes and practices of the dominant society.

AFRICAN AMERICAN *SCRIPTURALIZATION* SUPPLEMENTED BY POSTCOLONIAL THEORY

African American biblical scribes typically employ a particular hermeneutical approach that is,[6] to use a term first made popular by Edward Said, *contrapuntal*[7]

4. Warren Carter, "The Gospel of Matthew," in *A Postcolonial Commentary on the New Testament Writings,* ed. Fernando F. Segovia and R.S. Sugirtharajah (London: T&T Clark, 2009), 69–104 (73). Carter's earlier work, *Matthew and Empire: Initial Explorations* (Harrisburg, PA: Trinity, 2001),which does not employ a postcolonial theoretical analysis, presents the Gospel as strictly a counter-narrative that replaces the *Pax Romana* with the *Pax Christiana* as an alternative reality. However, he evades the conclusion that the *Pax Christiana* mimics the imperial processes of Rome in this earlier work.

5. See Fernando F. Segovia, "Postcolonial Criticism and the Gospel of Matthew," in *Methods for Matthew,* ed. Mark Allan Powell (Cambridge: Cambridge University Press, 2009), 194–237.

6. I use the term African American *scripturalization* to signify the re-cycling of sacred text in which a community's past is remembered and its future prophetically witnessed in the present. Therefore, it is through the process of *scripturalization* that the formation, de-formation, and re-formation of a community is made possible. African American *scripturalization,* therefore, is a shift from the "interpretation" of texts, as the term "African American biblical hermeneutics" or "African American biblical interpretation" denotes, to the more activating sense of "writing" texts, thereby connoting the production of a scribe whose pen is an active agent in the conceptualization and re-conceptualization of a community and its praxis.See Grey Gundaker, "Scriptures Beyond Script: Some African Diasporic

to the Euro-American ideological framework in that it is committed to challenging an ethos that promotes social inequality as the norm. Therefore, African American biblical scribes generally focus on the identification of biblical passages that have special relevance to the community or that have been used to keep the community in a marginal location, and the need for further attention to the history of interpretation within African American religious and cultural traditions.[8] In approaching this task, scribes have mainly adhered to a hermeneutic of liberation, striving to revive a diasporan community that has been burdened by displacement, slavery, disenfranchisement, marginalization, and persistent racism.

Vital contributions to the scholarly guild have been made based on the use of this emancipatory framework. This fact is particularly the case when liberation hermeneutics is fused with complementary theoretical and methodological approaches that effectively reflect new forms of relevant and constructive praxis. Therefore, in addition to the resources of black liberation theology and womanist theology, ideological criticism, narrative criticism, race, gender, and postcolonial theories are just a few of the methodological tools that complement this scribal activity.

Versatility in the use of a variety of methodological tools is extremely necessary in order to better address the complexity of African American identity formation. African American scribes recognize the need for expanding their goals and objectives, and thus their approaches in response to twenty-first century challenges. One of these challenges is the possibility of estrangement within the community, as well as discrimination against outside groups that are deemed to be "inferior" as a result of class division. Of course, this does not mean to advocate for a post-liberation or post-racial sentiment, which asserts that the four great beasts of American society—racism, sexism, classism, and economic deprivation— are no longer threats. What this does mean, however,

Occasions," in *Theorizing Scriptures: New Critical Orientations to a Cultural Phenomenon*, ed. Vincent L. Wimbush (New Brunswick, NJ: Rutgers University Press, 2008), 155–66; Sze-Kar Wan, "Signification as Scripturalization: Communal Memories among the Miao and in Ancient Jewish Allegorization," in *Theorizing Scriptures*, 105–14; Judith H. Newman, *Praying by the Book: The Scripturalization of Prayer in Second Temple Judaism*, SBL Early Judaism and Its Literature (Atlanta: Society of Biblical Literature, 1999). Newman lays out a similar definition of the term *scripturalization* in her introduction although the term is located in a historical critical mode and not a contemporary contextual understanding.

7. See Edward Said, *Culture and Imperialism* (New York: Vintage, 1993), ii. *Contrapuntal* is a phrase that Said used to convey a manner of reading that aims to "give emphasis and voice to what is silent or marginally present or ideologically represented."

8. Randall C. Bailey, ed., introduction to *Yet with a Steady Beat: Contemporary U.S. Afrocentric Biblical Interpretation*, Semeia 42 (Atlanta: Society of Biblical Literature, 2003), 1.

is that African American scribes must expose the more subtle tactics of the beasts by addressing the full complexity of African American identity.

The supplementation of postcolonial theory (specifically the concepts of hybridity, mimicry/mockery, and ambivalence) to the hermeneutical and methodological approaches of African American scribes blends together smoothly and allows a scholar to articulate this broader identity construction in a post-slavery community. The reason why postcolonial theory and African American scripturalization are compatible discourses is because they share common goals and objectives. These common goals and objectives include: revealing the devastating aspects of neocolonialism and the lingering forms of discrimination, inequality, and racism that the system perpetuates; breaking down the barriers of cultural hierarchy and investigating issues of representation, essentialism, and nationalism; focusing on a subversive revision of the dominant historical narrative; giving voice to a text muted by dominant historical referents; providing an opportunity for an imaginative invention of self beyond the limits of historical re-presentations; and, with reference to womanists and postcolonial feminists, critiquing patriarchy as it aligns with the imperial agenda, including white feminist ideology. Thus, both disciplines are compatible and enhance one another. Whereas postcolonial theory contributes to African American scripturalization by resituating it out of its local context and placing it into a global conversation, African American scripturalization is ideally situated to reveal the (neo)imperial practices of the United States.

THE STRANGENESS OF HOME: THE AFRICAN AMERICAN CONTEXT ARTICULATED IN A POSTCOLONIAL HERMENEUTICAL APPROACH

African American scribes share a common cultural context that informs their scripturalizing of the texts, which I term *the strangeness of home*. The term is used to connote the African American communal experience of institutionalized marginalization by a society that produced a biblically informed foundation myth that sanctioned a racist and sexist ideology as its dominant ethos, while it simultaneously conceived itself as a "democratic" nation.[9]

This ambiguous construct of the dominant society influenced the formation of an African American counter-narrative that is also grounded in biblical imagery and that the enslaved and free descendants of Africans first articulated as a means for *talking back* to an oppressive society. The mimicking or copying of the rhetorical tools of their oppressors constituted a way for

---

9. America is founded on biblical narrative and imagery and variously imagined as the New Jerusalem, the promised land, or the "city of on the hill" that is to be a "light to the nations."

Africans to thoroughly mock the Euro-American self-construction. For example, if Euro-Americans identified with the Exodus narrative and defined themselves as the freed Israelites entering the promised land, the enslaved Africans also identified with the Israelites in Exodus, yet when the Israelites were still in bondage in Egypt. By this "almost the same but not quite like" identification, the Africans challenged how the Euro-Americans could justify the enslavement of members of their own community. By learning to speak the alien tongue, therefore, the enslaved Africans were able to claim a level of power within the context of domination. In possessing a shared language and a shared culture, they were able to construct new cultural identities and find a means to create political and communal solidarity.[10]

Through the strategic use of this rhetorical device, the community slowly morphed into ambivalent African Americans, inaugurating a hybrid framework that will be the hallmark of their cultural identity. A cultural identity that simultaneously adopts and adapts, embraces and resists, mimics and mocks, the dominant American ethos.

Therefore, the postcolonial concepts of hybridity, mimicry, and ambivalence can be extremely useful in assisting to elucidate how different segments of the community variously negotiate *the strangeness of home* since these concepts help to dismantle the confining notion of homogeneity and replaces this fixity with a fluid idea of identity construction.

By extension then, it can also be proposed that these concepts assist in understanding the work of African American scribes as an act of critical conscientization.[11] According to Randall Bailey, Tat-Siong Benny Liew, and Fernando Segovia, the editors of *They Were All in One Place?: Toward a Minority Biblical Criticism*,

> . . . conscientization moves in two directions, by no means are mutually exclusive. On the one hand, it may veer toward questions of critical identity: background and motivation. Rather than engage in criticism in unreflective fashion, the critic pauses to ponder who s/he is as a critic, whence and why s/he does what s/he does as a critic. On the other hand, it may favor questions of critical role: procedure and objective. Instead of pursuing criticism on abstract terms, the critic halts to reflect what it is that s/he does, how and to what

10. bell hooks, *Teaching to Transgress: Education as the Practice of Freedom* (New York: Routledge, 1994), 170.

11. Randall C. Bailey, Tat-Siong Benny Liew, and Fernando F. Segovia, eds., *They Were All Together in One Place?: Toward Minority Biblical Criticism* (Atlanta: Society of Biblical Literature, 2009), 31.

end s/he does what s/he does as a critic. Both paths of questioning are closely interwoven: while the first type of intervention lays the ground for a circumscription of critical task, the second builds on the foundations of critical identity.[12]

The fusion of African American scripturalization and postcolonial theory, therefore, presents the opportunity to self-examine the complexity and inherent contradiction of a hybrid identity that is constructed by the double-movement of shifting away from Western constructions of the "other" while simultaneously (and ironically) shifting towards reinscribing the ideological, theological, linguistic, and textual forms of Western power.

THE WORK OF AFRICAN AMERICAN MISSIONARIES EXAMINED THROUGH A POSTCOLONIAL LENS

The strategy of Western colonialism circa the nineteenth century relied on instilling a sense of inherent inferiority in the indigenous communities, which justified the invasion of European nations in various geopolitical territories, particularly on the continents of Africa and Asia. Pre-colonial existence was presented as exotic, uncivilized, and unenlightened by the colonizer. The schema of Western colonialism depended on denigrating the ancestral past in order to convince the colonized to believe that in adopting the colonizer's cultural system, including the religious system, the colonized were protecting themselves against their own selves.[13] Franz Fanon writes in *The Wretched of the Earth*:

> Colonialism is not simply content to impose its rule upon the present and the future of a dominated country. Colonialism is not satisfied merely with holding a people in its grip and emptying the native's brain of all form and content. By a kind of perverted logic, it turns to the past of the oppressed people, and distorts, disfigures and destroys it.[14]

Thus, the strategy of the colonizer was to trespass on and misconstrue the cultural memory of the colonized in order to force the colonized to construct

---

12. Ibid.

13. This may be a reason why white missionary organizations funded African American missionaries to Africa. African American missionaries represented to the "uncivilized" African a "civilized" version of themselves.

14. Frantz Fanon, *The Wretched of the Earth*, trans. Richard Philcox (New York: Grove, 1961), 145.

a self-demonization that legitimated the colonizer's claims of European supremacy, which in turn, justified the rape and pilfering of the "uncivilized nations."

A key purpose for the disabling of the colonized identity is to reproduce the colonized as a mimic of the colonizer. Colonial discourse necessitated that the colonized adopt the cultural habits, assumptions, and values of the colonizer. In *The Souls of Black Folk*, W. E. B. Du Bois's articulation of *double consciousness* presents the "Negro" as the double that is produced by the mimicry of American culture, particularly directed toward the "talented tenth" of African American society. This doubling was said to have been produced in the high educational institutions. In this sense, the production of the double or, in postcolonial lingo, the hybrid, in post-slavery is similar to the postcolonial subject, and Du Bois considers the construction as inevitable, and both desirable and personally disorienting.[15]

It must be noted that Christian mission collaborated in the shaping of an "almost the same but not quite like" identity, which was key to colonial domination. The work of Protestant missionary societies in Africa coincided with European colonialism, beginning in the mid- to late-1700s, with Great Britain leading the way. Other various evangelical Protestant bodies of Europe soon joined the missionary movement. The Second Great Awakening in the nineteenth century led to the formation of a missionary movement in America that evolved almost directly from British mission bodies.[16]

Both European and American missionaries believed that their work was a calling in obedience to the Great Commission in Matt. 28:18-20, as argued by Dave Gosse, Beatrice Okyere-Manu, and Mitzi Smith in their essays in Part 1 of this volume. Missionaries were dedicated to the task of Christianizing the "uncivilized," baptizing, and making disciples of all nations. Not only did the missionaries go out with an amazing degree of confidence in the supremacy of Western Christianity, but they were equally confident, if not over-confident, in the Western social and economic order. This sense of certainty often produced insensitivity to indigenous cultures, and missionaries contended that the African

---

15. One of the reasons for this disorientation, of course, is the peculiar predicament of the legal prohibition of the early Africans to integrate their cultural traditions and religio-political systems in their new home. The prohibition forced enslaved Africans to appropriate Western culture, particularly in terms of religious praxis, which entailed the adoption of the American appropriation of the Scriptures.

16. The Church of Jesus Christ of Latter-day Saints, Church of the United Brethren in Christ, Seventh-day Adventists, Disciples of Christ, and the Lott Carey Baptist Home and Foreign Mission Convention of the United States that entered Africa in 1901 and are just a few of the missionaries that went to Africa.

belief system was not merely the absence of religious truth but was, in fact, evil.[17] The missionary/colonizer's practice of constructing the colonized ancestral concept of the spiritual world and humanity as ignorant and insufficient aided mightily in the self-demonization of the colonized. This destruction of the psyche led to the stifling of the impulse of resistance, a stifling made possible by the belief that the colonized religious system was invalid, and, indeed, impotent. This, in turn, allowed for the formation of a parental relationship between the missionary and the missionized, in which the missionary believed he was called to train the childlike Africans in Western culture.[18]

Out of the eighty African American women missionaries who served in Africa between 1880 and 1920, four general observations can be made. They were all: (1) relatively well-to-do, (2) well educated, (3) from an extremely religious family life, and (4) devoted to the church. This group, therefore, were members of the privileged class of the African American community. They were the "local elites" of a marginalized, disenfranchised community who exercised a limited form of power within their own community. They were part of the "talented tenth," that was to lead the masses into the promised land.

According to Sylvia Jacobs,

> Most middle class blacks (in the late nineteenth and early twentieth centuries) were of the opinion that Africa needed to be "civilized and Christianized" generally concluding that if the interests and welfare of the indigenous African populations were being considered, European activity on the continent would be beneficial. Many African Americans accepted the idea of "manifest destiny" promulgated by whites. They believed they had been brought to America for slavery by "providential design" so that they might be Christianized and "civilized" to return to the "Dark Continent" with the light of "civilization."[19]

It should be noted that Euro-American *and* African American women involved in mission work believed that they occupied an exalted position in Africa.

17. Sylvia M. Jacobs, "The Historical Role of Afro-Americans in American Missionary Efforts in Africa," in *Black Americans and the Missionary Movement in Africa,* ed. Sylvia M. Jacobs (Westport, CT: Greenwood, 1982), 5–29.

18. Ibid.

19. Sylvia M. Jacobs, "Give a Thought to Africa: Black Women Missionaries in Southern Africa," in *Western Women and Imperialism: Complicity and Resistance,* ed. Nupur Chaudhuri and Margaret Strobel (Bloomington: Indiana University Press, 1992), 207–28 (207).

Attributing their privileged location to American Protestant Christianity, they constructed African women as being oppressed by their traditional religions. Women missionaries were motivated by a desire to teach, to a certain degree, a culture promised by both American-style domesticity and Christian identity.[20] Therefore, African American women missionaries trained African women to be subordinate to the men and limited the women's work to the private sphere of domestic life.

Thus, I suggest, that the abstract concept of hybridity becomes succinctly concrete when placed within an African American missionary identity construct. The cultural performance of this community was, indeed, heavily dependent on the appropriation of Western Christianity and ideology. As a result, this particular group's identity construction is extremely contradictory, in that their experience of *the strangeness of home* was a world of half-truths, of embracing and fostering the Western ideology on a marginalized community, yet they, themselves, were considered marginal members of the society that they promoted.

These missionaries believed that it was God's grand plan to use them as a vehicle to convert their fellow brothers and sisters living in the homeland to Christian civilization, to persuade them to accept a culture that denied, deprived, and disenfranchised the African American. How strange, indeed! Alexander Crummwell wrote in favor of Western imperialism saying,

> A grand police force all over the continent, restraining violence, keeping open grand avenues of commerce, affording protection to missionaries and travelers, protecting weak tribes and nations from powerful marauding chiefs . . . I rejoice in this movement. I have the largest expectations of good and benefice from its operations. I have the most thorough conviction of its need, its wisdom, and its practicality.[21]

Lucy Gant Sheppard, the wife of the pioneer missionary William Sheppard, who served with him as a Southern Presbyterian missionary in the Congo from 1894–1910 and who formed the first women's society of the Congo mission in 1903, states, "when I saw the first native woman in her strip of cloth, her hair daubed with paint, her body smeared with grease and her mind filled with

20. Leslie A. Flemming, "A New Humanity: American Missionaries' Ideals for Women in North India, 1870–1930," in *Western Women and Imperialism*, 191–206 (194).

21. Alexander Crummell, *Africa and America: Addresses and Discourses* (Miami: Mnemosyne, 1969), 129–30.

sin and superstition, I could not help but wonder if she could be changed. . . ."[22] The statements of Crummwell and Sheppard reveal the complexity in the cultural negotiation of a particular segment of the African American Christian community. Their statements provide a clear illustration of the curious nature of cultural hybridity in that it can form an extremely conflicted and contradictory cultural identity.

Both the white organizations and the organizations established by the black independent churches required the embrace of Western education and training and thus, Western ideology, as vital for success. African American missionaries faced a basic conflict: the dark, uncivilized, and unruly continent so much in need of saving by the African American missionaries was also the ancestral homeland. The African American missionaries found themselves in a paradox. Their hybrid, fragmented identity was constructed partly by the dominant group's interpretation of the Scriptures and their own acceptance of some of those interpretations that retained at its core the idea of black inferiority.

The independent black churches of the nineteenth century, in their desire to create "full-fledged" institutions, mimicked the missionary processes of the white churches feeling that they had to prove their mark in this area as well in order to be considered as effective as the white churches.[23] Adding to that, the African American missionaries truly believed that they were excellent role models, the ideal "model minority," for the unconverted African. When they returned to their home churches on furlough, they enthusiastically reported on their progress emphasizing the uncivilized condition of the African, in order to gain funding for their work.[24]

Ironically, the racist nature of American society acted as a spur to the missionary societies involved in Africa. For instance, white mission societies believed that African Americans had special abilities to reach the African, that they were better suited to withstand the climatic conditions, and their bodies were immune to certain diseases. And African American missionaries believed

22. In Africa, William clearly enjoyed his privileged status amongst the Africans, a status open only to whites in the United States. He habitually had photographs taken of himself in the "great white hunter" motif: an entirely white suit complete with white helmet, surrounded by Africans in their native garb. See Walter L. Williams, *Black Americans and the Evangelization of Africa, 1877–1900* (Madison: University of Wisconsin Press, 1982), 94.

23. Ibid.

24. According to Sylvia Jacobs, "the missionaries frequently gave a distorted picture of the African because they wanted to exaggerate their own achievements, hoped to capture and hold their audiences, or wanted to illustrate the need for continued missionary activity." See Jacobs, *Black Americans and the Missionary Movement in Africa,* 18.

that by traveling to Africa they could prove their worth and gain more respectability at home by being placed in a superior relationship to the Africans.[25] The rhetorical strategy of the African American missionary was to highlight the inferiority of the African, the same strategy that was used against them in their own country. So while racism propelled the African American missionaries' desire to do missionary work, racism also ultimately undermined its effectiveness. African American women missionaries were split between proving that they were not inferior to whites, yet demonstrating that they were superior to African women. It can be argued, therefore, that their hybridity prevented them from disconnecting from an oppressive, racist ethos that had become part of their identity construction.

To add to this conflicting situation, the African American woman missionary faced inferiority based on race and gender by both Euro-American and African American men, and, yet, in turn practiced race and gender inferiority toward their fellow African brothers and sisters and also toward their less fortunate sisters and brothers at home.

Postcolonial feminists often problematize how the role of "woman" is defined by Euro-American women, arguing that the Euro-American definition connotes a universal, homogenous definition based solely by a specific race and class of women. According to white feminists immersed in Western constructs, the woman is subordinate to the man, and that patriarchy is absolute. Postcolonial feminists accuse Euro-American women of privileging the Western idea over that of other traditions and erasing the fact that gender roles are not universal. In addition, postcolonial feminists argue that Euro-Americans construct women of color as helpless victims, burdened by layers of oppression who must be saved by their Western counterparts.[26] Euro-American women missionaries were accused of being guilty of maintaining an imperial ethos of domination and subordination.

When studying the relationship between African American woman missionaries and African women, however, we are presented with a similar charge usually directed against Euro-American women. The African American woman missionary traveled to Africa determined to convert the African women by privileging the role of a Western understanding of womanhood as domestication. African women were to be taught to remain in the home, learn

---

25. Ibid.

26. Chandra Mohanty, "Under Western Eyes: Feminist Scholarship and Colonial Discourses," in *Colonial Discourse and Post-Colonial Theory: A Reader,* ed. Patrick Williams and Laura Chrisman (New York: Columbia University Press, 1994), 214.

how to sew, rear the children, and cook proper meals—to take on Western feminine ways and therefore submit to gender subordination.

MATTHEW AND MISSION

In approaching the vision of mission in Matthew from a postcolonial perspective, the identity dilemma of African American women missionaries will serve as the point of departure for the following scripturalization that will propose that the women in Matthew faced a similar dilemma due to their hybrid identity construction. This will be accomplished by focusing on the role of women in the prologue and epilogue of Matthew. We will focus on Matt. 1:3-6 and Matt. 28:5-10. Matthew 1:3-6 is the section of the genealogy that lists the names of the four "outside" women who were extremely strong supporters of the Israelite nation and who, each in her own way, denied her own people—Tamar, Rahab, Ruth, and Bathsheba. Matthew 28:5-10 narrates the commission to Mary Magdalene and the other Mary by the angel to go tell the other disciples to go back to their home base in Galilee to spread the word about Jesus. The reading of these two Matthean passages will illustrate that Matthew presents the women as complicit to an ideological vision. The approaches of Musa Dube and Warren Carter, both of whom highlight the imperializing context of Matthew, will be placed in conversation with this scripturalization. The purpose of this African American scripturalization is to provide a critical conscientization for the twenty-first century African American community by providing a reading that reflects the complex challenges inherent in a hybrid or double consciousness identity construction.

MUSA DUBE'S READING OF MATTHEW AND MISSION

Musa Dube's reading of Matthew and mission "regards the presence of imperial power as central to the construction of the narrative."[27] It is not a reading based on historical facts, per se, but a rhetorical reading "engineered within and by a particular historical setting" in order to discern how the narrative reflects the power struggles "that pertain to the Roman imperial occupation."[28]

Dube's close reading of Matthew illustrates that the text actually "plays up" to the Roman Empire while positioning local rival groups against one another. She says, "Matthew is . . . an example of a collaborative postcolonial narrative that arises from among the colonized but deflects the focus from the root cause of oppression, the imperialists, and focuses instead on other victims."[29]

27. Dube, *Postcolonial Feminist Interpretation of the Bible,* 127.
28. Ibid.

In this case, the Pharisees, scribes, and Sadducees, the Jewish religio-political leaders, are portrayed as the sources of oppression "while the Romans (and other Gentiles) are portrayed as benefactors or allies of the Matthean community."[30]

In addition, the Gospel is also immersed in the political history and traditions of Israel. This is made evident in the positioning of Jesus as heir to the Davidic throne in the genealogy, clearly situating Jesus and his mission as a continuation of the sacred narration of the Israelites as God's chosen people who were divinely sanctioned to control the "promised land." Dube understands the historical figures of the past listed in the prologue as setting up a relationship of domination and subordination between the Christian community and all non-Jewish outsiders. This can be discerned by the genealogy's emphasis on Jewish culture and tradition, a tradition that was religio-political. Linking Jesus with David and Abraham from the very start sanctions "the travel to other lands and peoples, ascribes that mandate to Jesus, in who resides all authority."[31] In turn then, the text demands the submission of all peoples and lands, through obedience to the teachings of Jesus. The Gospel's prologue sets the tone for fostering an imperial ideology that runs throughout the text. For example, further on in the text, Dube's comparative analysis of Jesus' attitude toward the centurion (8:5-13) with that of the Canaanite woman (15:21-28) supports her suggestion that the text fosters imperial processes. By emphasizing the commonality in the character's features we can see that both characters are outsiders, both request healing for dependents, and both receive praise for their faith. However, Jesus shows no hesitation regarding the centurion's request (the unit makes a point to compare Jesus and the centurion equally, as yielders of absolute authority), whereas the woman's pleading is not only first ignored; but, much worse, she and her child are denied a holistic life because of racial discrimination, and her appeal is finally granted only when the woman submits to self-humiliation. This comparative analysis allows Dube to argue that Matthew favors Rome to the detriment of non-Christian Jews.[32] By the time Dube gets to the epilogue, she can argue that Matt. 28:18b issues Christian readers "an unrestricted passport to enter all nations in obedience of their Lord without any consultation whatsoever with any of the nations in question."[33]

---

29. Ibid., 135.

30. Ibid.

31. Ibid

32. Segovia, "Postcolonial Criticism," 234.

33. Musa Dube, "'Go Therefore and Make Disciples of All Nations' (Matt. 28:19a): A Postcolonial Perspective on Biblical Criticism and Pedagogy," in *Teaching the Bible: The Discourses and Politics of*

Ironically, Matthew was written among colonized Jews, suffering under the exploitation of the Roman Empire. Logically, therefore, Dube claims that "one would expect it to be a text of resistance, aiming not only to preserve the autonomy of Jewish culture, including the right to worship God according to their own ways in their own land, but also to secure political and economic independence."[34] She goes on to state that just as the Greeks and Romans "promoted their own cultural and religious practices among the subjugated, Matthew also espouses a Jesus, who, in the way of other kings and emperors, sends forth his servants to establish an empire and to teach the subjugated to obey everything he has commanded (Matt: 28:18-20)."[35] Dube reads the epilogue, Matt. 28:18-20, where Jesus, in his absolute authority, commissions the male disciples to go out and make disciples in all the nations as the culmination of the prologue where he is presented as the heir to the Davidic throne and the inaugurator of the new kingdom.

WARREN CARTER'S READING OF MATTHEW AND MISSION

Warren Carter's latest reading of Matthew in the *Postcolonial Commentary* applies postcolonial theoretical concepts to show the conflicted nature of the Gospel as opposition to the Roman Empire and yet complicit with imperial power.[36] Therefore, he exposes the ambivalence that is part of the Matthean author's identity construct as a marginalized Jewish-Christian living in an oppressive system yet striving to inaugurate an alternative imperial power structure. However, Carter wants to focus his reading of Matthew mainly as a counter-narrative. He reads the genealogy as setting up the Matthean Gospel as resistance to Rome, understanding the presentation of Jesus as continuation of God's promise to Abraham to bless all the nations of the earth with life, not just the powerful, wealthy elite and allies of Rome.[37] Jesus' commission to manifest God's saving presence indicates that the present world under Roman control is contrary to God's purposes, despite Rome's claims to be the world's savior.[38] The intertextuality in the first chapter indicates that "God's purposes are not . . . unconcerned with human socio-political circumstances. Rather

---

Biblical Pedagogy, ed. Fernando F. Segovia and Mary Ann Tolbert (Eugene, OR: Wipf & Stock, 2004), 224–46 (230).

34. Ibid.
35. Ibid.
36. Segovia, "Postcolonial Criticism," 227.
37. Carter, "The Gospel of Matthew," 79.
38. Ibid.

God's purposes is manifested in Jesus' confrontation and resistance to false and oppressive societal structures."[39]

However, because Carter, in this particular article, is explicitly working with postcolonial criticism, he also must acknowledge that the intertextuality suggests that "Jesus' commission continues Matthew's imperialist attempt that is initiated with the genealogy, to lay claim to Israel's past in order to sustain his Christological agenda."[40] Therefore, from the very beginning and in a sustained manner, from the prologue to the epilogue, Carter presents Matthew in a binary opposition against Rome, while also exposing the text as "mimicry of imperial power."

Beginning with the genealogy, the text appears to be inclusive, welcoming men and women, the powerful and the powerless. Jesus is portrayed as the liberator of a people that have been oppressed by various political systems in various times of their history. Throughout the narrative, Jesus is portrayed as committed to saving the despised in society, which is counter to a Roman imperial ethos that privileges wealthy, high-status males. In his reading of the centurion in Matt. 8:5-13, the centurion, although an agent of imperial power, subordinates himself to Jesus, acknowledging the limits of his power, setting Jesus' power as far superior and expressing absolute confidence in such power. In addition, by Jesus' praising of the centurion's faith, Jesus places the centurion within the circle of disciples, and portrays him as undertaking a life of "merciful and just actions."[41]

By the time we get to the epilogue, Jesus' mission now encompasses all heaven and earth. His absolute authority has spread from a Jewish environment (that the prologue and the Sermon on the Mount [ch. 5–7] presents) to an engagement in a worldwide mission that parallels and contrasts Rome's worldwide mission and societal order, in his commission to the disciples. Therefore, Carter emphasizes the powerlessness of Rome in the face of the power of Jesus.

However, Carter realizes that no matter how compelling this narrative may be as a reading against Empire, the text cannot be read as simply a counter-narrative when applying a postcolonial lens. Although the Matthean Jesus' alternative community is directed to the unprivileged, his inner circle consists

---

39. Ibid, 80.

40. Ibid. In his previous works on Matthew, such as *Matthew and Empire*, Warren Carter does not dialogue with postcolonial theory. He primarily reads Matthew through the lens of Empire utilizing the historical critical method to present the Gospel as being totally resistant to Rome. He argues that the Gospel presents an alternative system established by God that is counter to Rome.

41. Segovia, "Postcolonial Criticism," 234.

of twelve men, and a woman has to "shame" him in "a verbal contest to gain benefits (15:21-28)."[42] Therefore, Carter says, "the Matthean author adheres to the dominant social stratification in which women have no real power in the public sphere. And, while Jesus may favor the poor and the deprived, only those who are fully committed to submitting to his absolute authority are promised the Kingdom of Heaven."[43] Matthew mimics Rome by employing "typical features of imperial practices that parallel Rome's strategies. These features include defining the other in negative and demonic terms and defining the present or past as inadequate/inferior and in need of saving."[44]

These two readings by Carter and Dube illustrate that the text's negotiation with Roman power depends "on mode and angle of inquiry, as activated by interpreters who are themselves situated and engaged within their own contexts in any number of ways."[45]

MATTHEW, WOMEN, AND MISSION: MATT.1:3-6 AND 28:1-10.

THE WOMEN IN THE MATTHEAN PROLOGUE THROUGH A POSTCOLONIAL LENS (1:3-6)

Matthew's genealogy (1:1-17) situates the whole Gospel within the wide parameters of the foundation myth of Israel. This is evident in the very opening of the text in which Jesus is immediately linked to Jewish royalty as the "son of David, the son of Abraham" (1:1). Thus, the entire narrative must be analyzed in consideration of this imperial "intertextual weave."[46] By analyzing the pericope's intertextuality from a postcolonial perspective, the roles of the four women listed in the ancestry, Tamar, Rahab, Ruth, and Bathsheba, take on an interesting configuration. Each of these women's narratives are to be considered with the broader narration of nation that focuses on the developmental processes of the Israelite political system from tribal formation to unified monarchy and colonizer of surrounding territories. Each of the four women can be considered as "outsiders" or the "other" of the Israelite community who strategically embraced the Israelite political structure.

In analyzing the characterization of Tamar (Gen. 38), we see a woman on the margins of an Israelite tribe, who nevertheless desired to live by the laws, cultural standards, economic standards, and political processes of that group

42. Ibid., 99.
43. Ibid.
44. Ibid.
45. Ibid.
46. Ibid.

rather than return home and abide by the laws and cultural standards of her own people. The marginalized Tamar privileges the culture that diminishes her and does not provide economic stability for her. In order to obtain some power and personal agency, Tamar has to physically occupy a new geographical space and put on a new change of clothes, and in so doing is able to assume a different identity construction (Gen. 38:14). Only by relocating could Tamar strip off the symbols of her marginalization and deprivation and don a new identity that enabled her to have a degree of independence and active agency and the ability to negotiate with power, albeit only in a temporary fashion. Upon Tamar's return to the Israelite tribe, the society in which she desires to call home, she occupies a more central place within the Israelite community.

The character Rahab is literally located in the middle-space of Jericho (Josh. 2). Joshua 2:15b relates, "for her house was on the outer side of the city wall and she resided within the wall itself" (NRSV). From a postcolonial perspective, it can be suggested that Rahab was literally placed in the middle space, residing on the threshold of continuity and discontinuity.

Rahab's request to the spies that infiltrated her land that "you will spare my father and mother, my brothers and sisters, and all who belong to them, and deliver our lives from death"[47] (2:13 NRSV) implies that Rahab was not economically deprived. She schemes like an elitist who is interested in preserving her own family's resources. We would be remiss not to question her actions of betrayal against her own people, in favor of foreigners who were on a mission of conquest and annihilation justified by the claim of being the "the chosen people." Randall Bailey comments that ". . . politically she is a traitor to her people who switched her loyalty from her people and her deity to the Israelite people and their deity."[48] According to the Matthean genealogy, the sell out of her own people apparently paid off for the colonized Rahab as she is listed as a linkage in the royal lineage of Israel.

The Moabite identity of Ruth is of prime importance when examining the women in the Matthean genealogy as supporting imperial ideology. Her identity construction can be understood as that of the "model minority," made particularly compelling because "Ruth is not simply from any foreign nation but from Moab, whose entanglements with Israel have been antagonistic" (Gen. 19:37).[49] Besides being the model convert, Ruth is also an exemplar for the

---

47. NRS version.

48. Randall Bailey, "He Didn't Even Tell Us the Worst of It!" *Union Seminary Quarterly Review* 59 (2005), 15–24, 17.

49. Gail Yee, "'She Stood in Tears Amid the Alien Corn': Ruth, the Perpetual Foreigner and Model Minority," in *They Were All Together in One Place?*, 119–40 (129).

Jewish people.[50] In her hybrid construction, Ruth appears to be more of a Judean than those who are born Judean. The Moabite Ruth seems to totally embrace the culture and political ethos of the dominant society. However, she will never be fully assimilated into that society. She will always be identified by her ethnicity, as Ruth the Moabite. As Gail Yee states, "This displacement implies that . . . the continuation of the patriline toward David's monarchy depend not only on Ruth's exemplary character but also on her marginalization as a foreigner."[51]

Bathsheba, the wife of the outsider Uriah the Hittite, is the daughter of Eliam (2 Sam. 11:3). Second Samuel 23:34 tells us that Eliam was the son of Ahithophel. It would appear that Bathsheba came from a politically influential family since Ahithophel, her grandfather, is noted as one of David's key advisors.[52] Bathsheba, of course, supports the imperial ideology of David's monarchy. She turns away from her husband, the foreigner, and lies with King David, which insinuates that she has returned to her own people.

Most scholars concede that Bathsheba is not a gentile. She is the only woman in the genealogy who was given in marriage to an outsider of the Jewish tradition. Therefore, her situation is opposite of that of the other three women. Through her marriage to Uriah, she was obligated to abide by the laws and traditions of her husband's culture. Being an Israelite, Bathsheba would have identified with the Israelite myth. At this time in the history of her people, Israel's situation had shifted from the marginalized other to the dominator. It is her husband, the foreigner, who submits to the authority of Israel, being a military officer in David's army. Bathsheba, the Israelite, enters her husband's household with a privileged status as a member of the dominant political system, perhaps even possessing a fuller sense of agency outside of her father's household. However, with her marriage to King David, her position in the hierarchical power arrangement shifts. She is now a female subordinate to the King of Israel who is the embodiment of the Israelite political system. Although Bathsheba may have been subordinate to Uriah in terms of sex, she was the representative of the dominant society in Uriah's household. Bathsheba's identity construct is complex and ambivalent in that her social position subtly shifts as she crosses cultural borders.

50. Ibid.

51. Ibid., 131.

52. Randall C. Bailey, *David in Love and War: The Pursuit of Power in 2 Samuel 10–12*, Journal for the Study of the Old Testament Supplement Series 75 (Sheffield: Sheffield Academic Press, 1990), 87.

The Women in the Matthean Epilogue (28:1-10)

Although Mary Magdalene and the other Mary, the two women mentioned in the epilogue (28:1) are not included in the Great Commission (28:18-20) per se, the angel's words to them in 28:7 are, in fact, a commission, as is Jesus' command to them in 28:9-10. They are the first to see the risen Jesus and the first to receive his commandments to go out and tell the male disciples to meet him in Galilee. Although most scholars would argue that their role is more of a supporting role, it is clear that the women do have a function in the missionizing movement. Feminist scholar Elaine M. Wainwright, who focuses on the rhetorical aspect of the text in seeking to understand the way the text functioned for its Matthean readers, looks at the three women at the cross (27:55-56), two of which are Mary Magdalene and (presumably) the "other Mary" mentioned in 28:1, and she sees these women as faithful disciples.[53] She notes a gender reversal in 27:55-56. Wainwright says that "women's mourning was typically characterized by loud wailing and they were often dismissed from the scene prior to death. It was the male family members or disciples of a dying hero who would remain to the end, mourning silently."[54] In Matthew, it is the women who remained at the cross, and the male disciples who disappeared from the scene. According to Amy-Jill Levine, these independent, motivated women are both the first witnesses to the resurrection and the first missionaries of the church.[55]

I would suggest, then, that it would be logical to assume that these women also traveled back to the home base of Galilee, along with the male disciples, as Jesus commanded them to do in 28:7. Similarly, African American women missionaries of the nineteenth century traveled back to the homeland of Africa in response to their commission by the Lord.

The women in the epilogue, as in the prologue, are situated within the framework of the Matthean mission of spreading an imperial ideology. On the one hand, the women Tamar, Rahab, Ruth, and Bathsheba are outsiders who exist on the margins of the Israelite community; nevertheless, they support the formation of the Israelite nation. Rahab, in particular, brings her entire family and all their property into that culture. On the other hand, Mary Magdalene and the "other Mary" are marginalized Jewish subjects of the Roman Empire who adhere to a tradition of the *re-formation* or *re-establishment* of Jewish political

---

53. Elaine M. Wainwright, "Feminist Criticism and the Gospel of Matthew," in *Methods for Matthew*, 83–117 (106).

54. Ibid.

55. Amy-Jill Levine, "Gospel of Matthew," in *Women's Bible Commentary*, rev. and updated, ed. Carol A. Newsom et al. (Louisville: Westminster John Knox, 2012): 465–77 (477).

power through the resurrection of the Davidic kingdom. Therefore, I agree with Musa Dube's assessment that the Matthean Gospel from the beginning to the end supports an imperial ideology. By the time we get to the epilogue, the Matthean author's rhetoric has fully transitioned Jesus from the "King of the Jews," which is intimated in the prologue, to the "King of the nations." It can then be suggested that, although the women in the Matthean community would have been opposed to *Roman subjugation to a Roman imperial ideology*, they would not have been opposed to the total dismantling of an imperial system and replacing that system with an egalitarian form of governance. I agree with Warren Carter that the alternative religio-political system proclaimed in Matthew as a counter to Rome, is, in actuality, a reinscription of imperial domination. The women's response in the epilogue both to the angel and to Jesus makes them complicit in spreading a religio-political system that mimics imperial Rome by employing "typical features of imperial practices that parallel Rome's strategies. These features include . . . defining the present or past as inadequate/inferior and in need of saving."[56] There is simply a displacement of imperial practices and no dismantling of the hierarchical binary formation these practices embody. Therefore, the exploitative sociopolitical tactics of Empire are transferred into the "Christian mission."

The patriarchal structure remained intact, thereby giving these women no real political power. They perhaps had privilege, but no power. The women were used as tools to further a cause in which they would remain subordinate to men. Similar to the African American missionaries's fragmentation, the Matthean women, as characters in the narrative, were split between an urge toward Christian resistance to Empire and the continued—perhaps unconscious—internalization of imperial ideas.

This scripturalization that is aimed as a conscious, critical examination of the subtle internal complexities of a hybrid identity is a shift in the point of departure that defines African American biblical scholarship framed by a hermeneutic of liberation from sociopolitical oppression. This scripturalization was an attempt to reveal the more knotty issues involved in accommodating to a dominant ethos that is established on the exploitation of the "other." African American missionaries of the twenty-first century must critically examine what it means to missionize in the face of neocolonialism by being ever mindful of the past in order not to replicate those actions in the present and future. Awareness of alternate ways of interpreting mission in the Bible is imperative,[57]

56. Ibid.

57. See Mitzi J. Smith's essay, "'Knowing More than is Good for One': A Womanist Interrogation of the Matthean Great Commission," in this volume.

because as Christian workers, their work is justified by Scripture. Therefore, it is the responsibility of the biblical scribe, in the use of various theoretical methods and approaches—with postcolonial theory as one of those approaches—to articulate the intricate nature of African American identity construction. This is not to say that this paper advocates for a post-liberation sentiment, that the two great beasts of American society, racism, and sexism are no longer threats to a holistic and affirming society. What this paper does suggest, however, is that African American scribes must address the community's vulnerability to succumbing to the sway of the third beast of society—classism.

6

'Knowing More than is Good for One': A Womanist Interrogation of the Matthean Great Commission

Mitzi J. Smith

INTRODUCTION

The naming of Matt. 28:18-20 as the Great Commission has had the impact of delimiting and orientating how readers should understand that passage and the entire Gospel of Matthew.[1] This act of labeling has so constrained how we interpret that text that most readers find it difficult, if not impossible, to read it and Matthew through any other hermeneutical framework. Jesus (and God) is perceived chiefly as the one who sends his disciples to teach other nations. And teaching becomes the primary and essential goal of missions.[2]

1. For similar final or summary commissions in other Gospels, see Mark 16:14-18; Luke 24:44-49; John 20:19-23; cf. *Didache* 7:1.

2. For example, see Christopher J. H. Wright, *The Mission of God: Unlocking the Bible's Grand Narrative* (Downer's Grove, IL: IVP Academic, 2006); John Piper, *Let the Nations Be Glad!: The Supremacy of God in Missions* (Grand Rapids: Baker Academic, 2010); Francis M. DuBose, *God Who Sends: A Fresh Quest for Biblical Mission* (Nashville: Broadman, 1983); Ross Hastings, *Missional God, Missional Church: Hope for Re-Evangelizing the West* (Downer's Grove, IL: IVP Academic, 2012); M. David Sills, *Reaching and Teaching: A Call to Great Commission Obedience* (Chicago: Moody, 2010); Adam Greenway and Chuck Lawless, *The Great Commission Resurgence: Fulfilling God's Mandate in Our Time* (Nashville: B&H Publishing Group, 2010); W. Stephen Gunter and Elaine Robinson, eds., *Considering the Great Commission: Evangelism and Mission in the Wesleyan Spirit* (Nashville: Abingdon, 2005); Mike Barnett, ed., *Discovering the Mission of God: Best Missional Practices for the 21st Century* (Downer's Grove, IL: IVP Academic, 2012); Jedidiah Coppenger, *Retreat or Risk: A Call for a Great Commission Resurgence* (Nashville: B&H Publishing Group, 2010). Also, see Rohan Gideon's essay, "Children's Agency and Edinburgh 2010: The Great Commission or a Greater Omission?," in this volume on the Edinburgh 2010 conference and its continued focus on the Great Commission.

Matthew and Matthew's Jesus are interpreted predominantly through the lens of teaching; that is, Matthew's Jesus becomes the quintessential teacher. This results in the exaltation of teaching and the subordinating or rendering invisible any emphasis in Matthew on acts of social justice. And the type of teaching that is exalted as a result of the Great Commission nomenclature is that in which the student (paganized "others") is the passive recipient of knowledge, and is seldom, if ever, treated as a producer or originator of legitimate and authoritative knowledge. The legitimized and authoritative disseminators of such missionizing knowledge have historically and traditionally been European missionaries and other approved agents in partnership with colonialism and neocolonialism.[3]

In Professor Katie Geneva Cannon's article, "Cutting Edge: Christian Imperialism and the Transatlantic Slave Trade," she coins two womanist terms that signify how European missionaries employed the Great Commission together with other theological constructs with deleterious effect upon the Africans to whom the missionaries were sent to Christianize. The two terms are *missiologic of imminent parousia* and *theologic of racialized normativity*.[4] The former phrase refers to the synchronization of the so-called Matthean Great Commission with the belief in the imminent return of Jesus, which served to legitimize the urgent conversion of Africans by any means necessary (including by torture, rape, perpetual slavery, and murder) to transform the "enemies of Christ" into the friends of Christ, the church, and the crown.[5] The latter term, *theologic of racialized normativity*, signifies how European missionaries and imperial colonists claimed that God made black people naturally inferior and innately servile to whites. Thus, some missionaries indoctrinated Africans by imposing upon them the belief that they were obliged to serve Jesus Christ *and* their earthly masters.[6] Many missionaries, in collusion with European colonizers, separated the physical unjust, inhumane treatment and oppression

3. Kwame Nkrumah, the first post-independence president of Ghana coined the term *neocolonialism*. It refers to the practice of using capitalism, globalization, and cultural forces to control a country (usually former European colonies in Africa or Asia) in lieu of direct military or political control. Such control can be economic, cultural, or linguistic; by promoting one's own culture, language, or media in the colony, corporations embedded in that culture can then make greater headway in opening the markets in those countries. Thus, neocolonialism would be the end result of relatively benign business interests leading to deleterious cultural effects.

4. Katie Geneva Cannon, "Cutting Edge: Christian Imperialism and the Transatlantic Slave Trade," *Journal of Feminist Studies of Religion* 24, no. 1 (2008): 127–34 (128).

5. Ibid., 128–30. According to Cannon, this form of missionary activity started in Africa in the fifteenth century.

6. Ibid., 130–32.

of Africans and slaves from the saving of their souls. It was more important for colonized Africans and enslaved blacks to submit to missionary teachings, to learn to recite Scriptures and creeds, and be added to the membership to expand the church's geographical presence as evidence of the successful propagation of the gospel among them and in foreign lands. Teaching and baptizing black souls trumped the liberating of black bodies from the shackles of their white oppressors. While oppressing black bodies, colonizers and missionaries sought to save black souls for the peace of mind of white bodies. Colonizers, missionaries, and slave owners (who were sometimes one in the same) ensured that Africans and enslaved blacks knew only enough to make them good slaves who remained loyal to their oppressors as unto Jesus. By keeping blacks docile and prohibiting them from learning to read and write and by controlling who could preach or teach them and the content of that teaching/knowledge, the slavocracy (the system of slavery) attempted to prevent blacks from constructing knowledge of their own. Nevertheless, some black people rejected colonizer-missionary knowledge and relied on their own ways of knowing.

Apparently in the nineteenth century, the iconization of the missional preeminence of Matt. 28:18-20 as the Great Commission effectively provided the theological rationale and metanarrative for the prioritization of teaching and the subordination of social justice, permitting strict control of sacralized knowledge (secular knowledge christened as sacred truth).[7] While many missionaries and colonizers had generally privileged Matt. 28:18-20 (and 24:14: "this good news of the kingdom will be proclaimed throughout the world, as a testimony to all the nations; and then the end will come," NRSV), scholars and missionaries would eventually extoll it as the Magna Carta of missions and name it the Great Commission. And the nomenclature became putative, iconic, and universal knowledge.

Knowledge plays a significant role in the disempowerment (and empowerment) of oppressed peoples, particularly when it is inscribed in sacred and authoritative texts (i.e., the Bible, commentaries, and human bodies).[8] A critical epistemology assumes that knowledge is "value laden and shaped by historical, political, and social concerns stemming from conditions and positions of power based on race, gender, and socio-economics."[9] When knowledge is

7. For a discussion of the religio-political processes of *sacralization* and *secularization* of biblical narratives see Cain Hope Felder, *Troubling Biblical Waters: Race, Class, and Family* (Maryknoll, NY: Orbis Books, 1989).

8. See Vincent Wimbush, ed., *African Americans and the Bible: Sacred Texts and Social Textures* (New York: Continuum, 2003). Wimbush describes black people's experience as texts to be read, the "reading of the *self* (not the text[s]!)" (29).

oppressive or used to oppress, new knowledge construction is essential for the transformation of individual consciousness and social institutions.[10] Womanists and others must become iconoclasts, breaking up, deconstructing oppressive iconic knowledge, but also constructing, resurrecting, retrieving, and affirming epistemologies that allow black women and other oppressed peoples to survive and thrive.

In this essay, I shall interrogate the so-called Matthean Great Commission (Matt. 28:18-20) and its elevation as an iconic and universally putative, authoritative epistemological framework for understanding and implementing Christians missions. As a womanist iconoclast, I shall examine the Great Commission through a womanist epistemological lens critically engaging it as constructed, oppressive epistemic iconography. This womanist lens privileges and considers legitimate black women's experiences and ways of knowing or epistemologies. A womanist framework honors black women's concern for the survival and health of the entire community. First, I shall describe the womanist lens or framework for interrogating the Great Commission and for critically reading Matthew. Second, I shall discuss the prioritization and exaltation of the Great Commission by biblical commentators as iconic, authoritative, and putative knowledge. And finally I shall suggest other ways to know/read Matthew and Matthew's Jesus that shift from a characterization of Jesus as a paradigmatic teacher of passive recipient-paganized-other-nations to a focus on Jesus as God with us. As God with us, in Jesus social justice and teaching do not strive for mastery over each other. But Jesus' practice of social justice and teaching organically constitute the incarnate, interactive presence of God with us.

THE WOMANIST LENS: KNOWING MORE THAN IS GOOD FOR ONE

In her 1979 short story "Coming Apart," Alice Walker introduces the word *womanist* and describes a *womanist* as a *feminist, only more common.* Walker expands this definition in her 1983 book *In Our Mothers' Gardens: Womanist Prose* as follows:

---

9. JoAnne Banks-Wallace, "Womanist Ways of Knowing: Theoretical Considerations for Research with African American Women (2000)," *The Womanist Reader*, ed. Layli Phillips (New York: Routledge, 2006), 313–26 (317).

10. Patricia Hill Collins, *Black Feminist Thought: Knowledge, Consciousness, and the Politics of Empowerment* (New York: Routledge, 1991), 221.

Womanist is "from *womanish*. (Opp. of 'girlish,' i.e. frivolous, irresponsible, not serious.) A black feminist or feminist of color. From the black folk expression of mothers to female children, 'you acting womanish,' i.e., like a woman. Usually referring to outrageous, audacious, courageous or *willful* behavior. Wanting to know more and in greater depth than is considered 'good' for one. Interested in grown up doings. Acting grown up. Being grown up. Interchangeable with another black folk expression: 'You trying to be grown.' Responsible. In charge. *Serious*."[11]

Walker's definition of a womanist as "wanting to know more and in greater depth than is considered 'good' for one" was and is for black women more than a "*wanting*," but a necessity. It is a subversive, zoetic (life giving' saving and sustaining), and sometimes necessarily belligerent knowing. It is about developing a mature way of knowing, being "grown," before one reaches the age or seasons of maturity, relative to certain experiences. Slavery, racism, sexism, classism, heterosexism, and other isms have necessitated that black women "know more and in greater depth than is consider 'good' for one'" and to teach their children, grandchildren, sisters, brothers, nephews, and nieces to do the same. Black women have had to teach their children to know that white mobs have and will lynch any black male, regardless of age, for looking at a white woman the wrong way or for too long; to know that white men who raped black women were seldom prosecuted and therefore black women had to walk in numbers and their paths were limited; to know that black men falsely accused of raping white women were more likely to be prosecuted and executed;[12] and to know, among other things, that they will be more likely to be imprisoned and given longer sentences than their white counterparts for the same crimes, if their peers serve time at all.[13]

On the one hand, black mothers chide their children for acting womanish. Conversely, black mothers realize that black children living in a racialized, gendered, classicist world must know more than their white counterparts; and that black children must be prepared to live in a world where they will often

11. Alice Walker, *In Search of Our Mothers' Gardens: Womanist Prose* (San Diego: Harcourt Brace Jovanovich, 1983), xi–xiii. Emphasis in original.

12. See Danielle L. McGuire, *At the Dark End of the Street. Black Women, Rape, and Resistance—A New History of the Civil Rights Movement from Rosa Parks to the Rise of Black Power* (New York: Vintage Books, 2010).

13. See Michelle Alexander, *The New Jim Crow: Mass Incarceration in the Age of Color Blindness*, repr. ed. (New York: New Press, 2012).

be treated according to the color of their skin and not the content of their character.[14] Children are impacted early by racial attitudes in home, school, and the media. The subtle racial messages that Dr. Melanie Kellen of University of Maryland calls "implicit bias" are picked up by children very early. In CNN's 2011 study of race and children, Dr. Kellen found that African American parents prepare their children early to know about racial discrimination and a world of diversity.[15]

This need to prepare young black children and adults to know more than their racial counterparts has seen a renaissance among some blacks and has become a new reality for others with the recent not guilty verdict rendered by a nearly all-white female jury in the George Zimmerman (a white Latino) trial. Zimmerman murdered seventeen-year-old Trayvon Martin while he walked toward his father's home with a bag of Skittles, a can of soda, black skin, and a hoodie. Zimmerman was protected under Florida's *Stand Your Ground* law, despite the fact that Trayvon Martin had every reason to be where he was, was unarmed, and posed no imminent threat to Zimmerman who chose to pursue Martin contrary to the police dispatcher's request that he not do so. Similarly, Marissa Alexander, who is serving a twenty-year mandatory sentence in Florida, now knows, and she and other black mothers must teach their children, that they cannot fire a warning shot into the air to keep a physically abusive husband at bay and expect the same protection that Zimmerman received from Florida's *Stand Your Ground* law.[16]

Acting "womanish" at home is not always acceptable, but acting "womanish" away from home is a necessity. This womanish consciousness is akin to that *double consciousness* about which W. E. B. Du Bois wrote.[17] My

14. In his "I Have a Dream" speech, Martin Luther King Jr. remarked that he dreamt of the day when his four children would be judged by their character rather than by their skin color. See David L. Lewis, *King A Biography* (Urbana and Chicago: University of Illinois Press, 1978), 228.

15. See the CNN report "A Look at Race Relations Through a Child's Eyes" at http://www.youtube.com/watch?v=GPVNJgfDwpw&feature=youtube. CNN studied 145 children in six schools in three states, and they found that white children were far more negative in their interpretations of a picture depicting a white and a black child. White children were more likely to think the white and black child in the picture were not friends and that their parents would not approve of such interracial friendships. Young black children were more positive when shown a picture depicting a black and a white child; only thirty-eight percent of black children viewed the picture in a negative light.

16. Because of public outcry and financial donations for legal fees, Marissa Alexander has been given a new trial sometime in 2014. In February 2014 another Florida "stand your ground" case concluded in which a white man named Michael Dunn was convicted of attempted murder for firing into a car full of black teenagers, but Dunn was not convicted of the death of Jordan Davis, whom Dunn killed when he opened fire on the teens.

mother, Flora Smith, schooled my brother Fred about what to do should he encounter the police. She had this talk with Fred twice; the second time was just before he entered the Marine Corps. If the "cops" stopped him, he should not "sass" (talk back), keep his hands out of his pockets, and do whatever the "cops" ask him to do. In the 1955 trial of the white men charged with brutally lynching her fourteen-year-old son, Emmett Till, in Money, Mississippi for allegedly whistling at a white woman, Mrs. Mamie Mobley Bradley testified that "she warned Till 'to be very careful' in Mississippi, cautioning him to 'say *yes sir* and *no, ma'am*' and 'to humble himself to the extent of getting down on his knees' to whites if necessary."[18] Mrs. Bradley had to prove that she had taught her son to "know his place" or to "know his race."[19]

Black women must know more, and in greater depth, in order to teach their children to know more than the status quo allows or makes known. Knowing more than is good for one signifies knowing beyond the boundaries set for one because of one's race, gender, sexual orientation, education, class, or age. It also connotes knowing beyond the intellectual, religious, and political boundaries established by the status quo; to transgress iconic epistemological borders designed to control, restrain, and subordinate. Womanism does not simply espouse knowing more for knowledge sake, but knowing more so that black women can survive and thrive; so that they can be outrageous, audacious, courageous, and willful in the face of oppression; and so that they can grow up, be responsible, and take charge of their lives instead of relinquishing their voices and allowing others, who do not necessarily have black people's best interest in mind, to determine what is "good" for them.

Persons, institutions, traditions, and resources that we consider authoritative and allow to dominate our lives determine our epistemological limits, to a large degree. And those limits are often expressed in terms of authorized vocabulary and nomenclature, acceptable modes of training, and prescribed individuals authorized to disseminate knowledge or to teach us, as

17. W. E. B. Du Bois, *The Souls of Black Folk* (New York: Bantam, 1989), 3. This double consciousness is described by Du Bois as "this sense of always looking at one's self through the eyes of others, of measuring one's shoulder by the tape of a world that looks on in amused contempt and pity. One ever feels his twoness,—an American, a Negro; two souls, two thoughts, two unreconciled strivings; two warring ideals in one dark body, whose dogged strength alone keeps it from being torn asunder."

18. Ruth R. Feldstein, "'I Wanted the Whole World to See': Race, Gender, and Constructions of Motherhood in the Death of Emmett Till," in *Not June Cleaver: Women and Gender in Postwar America, 1945–1960*, ed. Joanne Jay Meyerowitz (Philadelphia: Temple University Press, 1994), 263–303 (280). The justice system let his murderers go free. See also Stephen J. Whitfield, *A Death in the Delta: The Story of Emmett Till* (Baltimore: John Hopkins University Press, 1988.

19. Ibid.

well as what constitutes legitimate hermeneutical frameworks for interpreting authoritative knowledge. Dominant powers in our families, institutions, and communities decide how much we should know, when we should know it, and how we learn what we know. And too often those dominant powers and authorities only act in the interest of the dominant culture. It is up to the marginalized, dominated, or oppressed to critically assess and audaciously reject oppressive, biased epistemologies; to transcend the boundaries of what we have been told "is good for" us to know; and to construct more liberating epistemologies.

A womanist who knows "more than is 'good' for one, and in greater depth" is aware that traditional interpretations of sacred texts and interpretive frameworks constructed by *malestream* biblical scholars[20] and religious specialists, including missionaries, primarily serve the self-interests of men and the white majority. Black women and others have too often been the object of and borne the brunt of oppressive biblical interpretations and theologies that permit, justify, or ignore violence perpetrated against their bodies, and their souls. The naming and iconic elevation of the Matt. 28:18-20 as the Great Commission with its concomitant emphasis on teaching to the exclusion or subordination of social justice action has encouraged, supported, ignored, and sanctioned violence against black women and others. As womanist scholar Linda E. Thomas has argued, Matt. 28:18-20 as the missio Dei has been about, and continues to be so among some Christians, telling "others that we have the keys to the kingdom" and others must get on board so that "we can teach 'them.'"[21] Religious or missional specialists, primarily European white males (and their Victorian wives) consecrated and entrusted with the task of teaching "pagans" have been considered the sole authoritative spiritual and intellectual producers and disseminators of religious truth. The truths or teachings of these missional and religious specialists have primarily consisted of creeds, rituals, and doctrines either detached from social justice concerns and/or indifferent to violence, such as slavery.[22]

---

20. Mary O'Brien (*The Politics of Reproduction* [Boston: Routledge & Kegan Paul, 1985], 5) coined the term *malestream*. It describes the type of sociology that concentrates on men, is mostly carried out by men, and then assumes that the findings can be applied to women as well. It is also a reminder of how completely our cultural discourse is influenced by patriarchal institutions and attitudes.

21. Linda E. Thomas, "Anthropology, Mission and the African Woman: A Womanist Approach," *Black Theology* 5, no. 1 (2007): 11–19 (13). Thomas prefers the Lukan version of the Great Commission and argues that when we engage in the *missio Dei* we can "forget our mission bag with Jesus in it" (18).

22. John Chrysostom (*Homilies on the Gospel of Matthew,* Homily XC, Matt. 27:11–14, *Ante-Nicene Fathers* [Peabody, MA: Hendrickson, 2004], 10:531) sums up Matt. 28:18-19 as concerning doctrines

The naming of one text as the Great Commission implies that other commissioning texts are less significant, not worthy of sustained hermeneutical attention, or are only to be engaged within the hermeneutical framework already created by the approved specialists, primarily malestream. By naming Matt. 28:18-20 as the Great Commission, some interpreters have hijacked some readers' ability to read Matthew in any other way than through that conceptualized iconic epistemological framework. Also, by putatively accepting the Great Commission as the iconic metanarrative (commonly held and controlling grand narrative)[23] for missions and for reading Matthew, some readers are conditioned to read Matthew with the presupposition or expectation of the hyper/über-importance of teaching, specifically teaching doctrines and dogmas, and to understand Jesus as the consummate teacher, with whom they should self-identify in relation to others. Thus, readers are blinded or indifferent to the text's pervasive emphasis on incarnational justice and the integral relationship between incarnational justice and teaching. I disagree with David Bosch's statement that "Matthew's entire gospel can only be read and understood from the perspective of the final pericope [i.e., Matt. 28:18-20]."[24] The conceptualization of Matt. 28:18-20 as the Great Commission has been seared into many Christians' hearts and minds, treated as if written by the very finger of God, accepted by most malestream scholars, in commentary or in practice, as iconic tradition, and exhibited as the objective hermeneutical framework for reading Matthew.

The epistemological challenge for womanists to know more "than is 'good' for" her "and in greater depth," relative to black women's experience, requires that womanists expose, transgress, break down, and counter oppressive epistemologies as the subjective and political constructs that they are. This is not to say that womanist epistemologies are not subjective and political as well; we acknowledge this. But womanists must construct other more liberating

(baptizing) and commandments (teaching). See also the other essays in this same volume written by Dave Gosse, Beatrice Okyere-Manu, and Mitzi J. Smith.

23. Jean-François Lyotard (*The Postmodern Condition: A Report on Knowledge* [Minneapolis: University of Minnesota Press, 1984]) coined the term *metanarrative*. A metanarrative is a grand narrative that constitutes false appeals to universal, rational, and scientific criteria, which are actually very particular.

24. David J. Bosch, *Transforming Mission: Paradigm Shifts in Theology of Mission* (Maryknoll, NY: Orbis Books, 1991), 91. Bosch does articulate this differently earlier in his book, in my opinion, when he says at page 57 that contemporary scholars agree that "Matthew 28:18-20 has to be interpreted *against the background of Matthew's gospel as a whole* and unless we keep this in mind we shall fail to understand it," and he argues that the language in that text is the "most Matthean in the entire gospel" (emphasis in original).

ways of knowing and epistemologies that prioritize the justice needs of black communities and other oppressed groups.

The Hermeneutical Iconization of Matt. 28:18-20 as the Great Commission

It is difficult to know the exact origin of the naming of Matt. 28:18-20 as the Great Commission. According to Robbie Castleman, the term may have been coined in the seventeenth century by the Dutch missionary Justinian von Welz (1621-88), but James Hudson Taylor, the great missionary to China, may have popularized it two hundred years later in the nineteenth century.[25] It appears to be in the nineteenth century that the label surfaces in commentaries. Matthew Henry's eighteenth-century six-volume commentary on the Bible, which first appeared in 1706 but was revised after his death in the early to mid-nineteenth century, does not name Matt. 28:18-20 as the Great Commission.[26] But in the late nineteenth century, John Broadus, in his 1886 commentary on Matthew (a little over twenty years after Lincoln signed the Emancipation Proclamation in 1863 legally freeing the slaves), asserts that in Matt. 28:20a, "teaching them to observe all things whatsoever I have commanded you," we find the "great missionary idea."[27] In his commentary on v.20b, Broadus refers to Matt. 28:18-20 as the Great Commission where he states, "obedience to the Great Commission is based on [Jesus'] universal and complete authority ... And this applies, not merely to the apostles, but to the disciples of every period."[28] Thus, it appears that in the nineteenth century, the Great Commission as an iconic interpretive framework was born; every person subsequently deemed a disciple possessed the authority granted thereby; and no other commission was so highly valued. Some twenty-first century commentators have gone so far as to call Matt. 28:18-20 "Jesus' Great Commission,"[29] thereby sacralizing the hermeneutical nomenclature itself.

This iconic interpretive naming tradition continues in use by many—if not the majority—of scholars and Christians in the twenty and twenty-first

---

25. Robbie F. Castleman, "The Last Word: The Great Commission: Ecclesiology," *Themelios* 32, no. 3 (2007): 68–70 (68).

26. Matthew Henry, "Matthew," *Matthew Henry's Commentary on the Bible*, vol. 5 (Old Tappan, NJ: Fleming H. Revell, 1853).

27. John A. Broadus, *Commentary on the Gospel of Matthew*, ed. Alvah Hovey (Philadelphia: American Baptist Publication Society, 1886), 596.

28. Ibid., 596–97.

29. For example, Tim Stafford, "Go and Plant Churches for All Peoples," *Christianity Today* (September 27, 2007): 68–72 (69).

centuries. Some commentators have identified the Great Commission as the distinguishing feature and the interpretive key for understanding Matthew. For example, Edward Blair (1960) called Matt. 28:18-20 "the key passage of this Gospel."[30] Oscar S. Brooks (1981) argues that since the pericope stresses authority and teaching, themes found throughout the Gospel, it is "basic to the narrative framework of the entire Gospel."[31] Donald A. Hagner (1994) asserts that it has "become the hallmark" of Matthew; that more than any other words, these verses "distill the outlook and various emphases of the Gospel."[32] H. Eugene Boring (1995) gives Matt. 28:16-20 the traditional title *the Great Commission* and asserts that before the resurrection the disciples had not been commissioned to teach; their teaching will consist of "all of Jesus' teaching contained in the Gospel."[33] Interestingly, even the editors of the *Jewish Annotated New Testament* (2011) are putatively, if not hermeneutically, tied to the nomenclature *the Great Commission,* asserting that the label derives from v. 19 where Jesus directs the disciples to go to "all nations."[34] But I contend that while the Greek adjective *pantes* (*all*) is absolute and inclusive, it is not evaluative in the same sense as the Greek word *mega* (*great*) is in Matthew, despite the expansive note it strikes (see discussion below). These and other commentators, including some feminist and liberation scholars, treat the naming of Matt. 28:18-20 as *the Great Commission* as universal, objective, putative, and iconic knowledge.[35] And that knowledge circumscribes how one

30. Edward P. Blair, *Jesus in the Gospel of Matthew* (New York: Abingdon, 1960), 45.

31. Oscar S. Brooks, "Matthew xxviii 16-20 and the Design of the First Gospel," *JSNT* 10 (1981): 2–18.

32. Donald A. Hagner, *Matthew 14–28*, Word Biblical Commentary 33B (Dallas: Word Books, 1995), 881. See also Douglas R. A. Hare, *Matthew*, Interpretation, ed. Paul J. Achtemeier (Louisville: John Knox, 1993), 333.

33. M. Eugene Boring, "The Gospel of Matthew," in *The New Interpreters' Bible*, ed. Leander E. Keck (Nashville: Abingdon, 1995), 8:89–505 (503, 504).

34. Aaron A. Gale, "Notes and Annotations for "The Gospel According to Matthew," *The Jewish Annotated New Testament, New Revised Standard Version*, ed. Amy-Jill Levine and Marc Zvi Brettler (New York: Oxford, 2011), 54, n. 28:16-20.

35. See "Matthew," in *Jamieson, Fausset, & Brown's Commentary on the Whole Bible* (Grand Rapids: Zondervan, 1961); Homer Kent, Jr., "Matthew," in *The Wycliffe Bible Commentary*, ed. Charles F. Pfeiffer and Everett F. Harrison (Chicago: Moody, 1962), 985; Ralph Earle, "Matthew," in *Beacon Bible Commentary* (Kansas City, MO: Beacon Hill, 1964), 254; Ralph Earle, "Matthew," in *The Wesleyan Bible Commentary*, ed. Charles W. Carter (Grand Rapids: Eerdmans, 1979; repr. Peabody, MA: Hendrickson, 1986): 4:122; D. A. Carson, "Matthew," in *The Expositor's Bible Commentary*, ed. Frank E. Gaebelein (Grand Rapids: Zondervan, 1984), 8:594; Hare, *Matthew*, 333; Boring, "The Gospel of Matthew," 503; Donald Senior, *Matthew*, Abingdon New Testament Commentaries, ed. Victor Paul Furnish (Nashville:

ought to read Matthew. As Vincent Wimbush argues, the commentary as a genre, "necessarily forces a certain delimitation"; it forces the interpreter to begin at a place other than "his or her own time . . . or with his or her own world situation."[36]

A few commentators have, to varying degrees, broken with this iconic interpretive tradition. W. F. Albright and C. S. Mann (1971) call Matt. 28:16-20 "Jesus' Final Commission."[37] This interpretive titular break could be because the *Anchor Bible* series claims to not "reflect any particular theological doctrine."[38] Albright and Mann note that of the other three Gospels, only Matthew "has anything that can properly be called an ending."[39] Matthew's "final commission" or ending may in fact be a summary or synopsis of what is made explicit in the text, according to Albright and Mann.[40] Albright and Mann assert that Jesus commanded his disciples to heal and proclaim during his ministry, but now that it is over he commands them to *teach*.[41] While Albright and Mann dropped the iconic label, they continue the interpretive practice of subordinating healing and proclamation to teaching.

Like Albright and Mann, Daniel J. Harrington (1991) sees Matt. 28:16-20 as a summary for Matthew, and he argues that Jesus is "the teacher par excellence," sending his disciples to continue "his teaching mission."[42] Thus Harrington also reiterates and exalts Jesus as the paradigmatic teacher in Matthew, encouraging readers to read the entire Gospel through that lens. I propose that this epistemological and hermeneutical practice obfuscates the holistic and incarnational justice ministry of Jesus to which he called and calls his disciples. In Matthew, teaching is embodied; it is God-with-us teaching.

Abingdon, 1998); Manlio Simonetti, ed., *Ancient Christian Commentary on Scripture*, vol. 1b, *Matthew 14–28* (Downer's Grove: InterVarsity, 2001); Amy-Jill Levine, "Gospel of Matthew," in *Women's Bible Commentary*, ed. Carol A. Newsom, Sharon H. Ringe, and Jacqueline E. Lapsey, 3rd ed. (Louisville: Westminster John Knox, 2012), 465–77 (477).

36. Vincent L. Wimbush, "'We Will Make Our Own Future Text': An Alternate Orientation to Interpretation," in *True to Our Native Land: An African American New Testament Commentary*, ed. Brian K. Blount (Minneapolis: Fortress Press, 2007), 43–53 (44).

37. W. F. Albright and C. S. Mann, *Matthew*, Anchor Bible, ed. William F. Albright and David Noel Freedman (Garden City, NY: Doubleday, 1971), 361.

38. Albright and Mann, *Matthew*, Intro.

39. Ibid., 361. Luke seems to continue in the book of Acts; John (chapter 21) and Mark (chapter 16) have more than one ending.

40. Ibid., 362.

41. Ibid., 363. Emphasis added.

42. Daniel J. Harrington, S. J., *The Gospel of Matthew*, Sacra Pagina, vol. 1, ed. Daniel J. Harrington (Collegeville, MN: Liturgical Press, 1991), 416. See also Senior, *Matthew*, 349.

Similarly, Bosch argues that Jesus' teaching in Matthew combines words and deeds.[43]

Donald Senior (1998) calls Matt. 28:16-20 *the Finale*. Nowhere in Senior's notes does he use the phrase *the Great Commission*. In fact, Senior calls vv. 19-20 a "new commission" that fulfills Jesus' words at 8:11-12 where he states that many will come from the east and west to eat with Abraham, Isaac, and Jacob in the kingdom of heaven.[44] Thus, the dropping of the iconic title allows Senior to read Matthew somewhat differently.

Ulrich Luz (2005) intentionally breaks with the iconic tradition of labeling Matt. 28:16-20 as *the Great Commission*. He provides the interpretative label *the Commission of the Lord of the World for All Nations*.[45] Ulrich gives a brief interpretive history of those versus. He asserts that the famous Baptist missionary William Carey and his 1792 publication *An Enquiry into the Obligations of Christians to Use Means for the Conversions of Heathens* is responsible for making Matt. 28:18 the "Magna Carta of mission."[46] Luz writes the following:

> Through Carey 28:19a became '*the* mission command' that influenced the church and evangelical missionary societies of the nineteenth and twentieth centuries that grew out of the revival movements. I cite as an example the Dutch Calvinist Abraham Kuyper. For him, as for many, 28:19a is an absolute *command*. He understood mission as issuing from God's sovereignty rather than from God's love and correspondingly as "obedience to God's command," "not an invitation, but a charge, an order."[47]

In the latter part of the nineteenth century, according to Luz, Gustav Warneck, the father of modern Protestant mission scholarship, reiterated the idea of Matt. 28:19 as the "charter of missions." Warneck articulated missions as primarily the task of making disciples, "Christianizing" non-Christian nations or of

43. Bosch, *Transforming Mission*, 66–70.

44. Senior, *Matthew*, 347.

45. Ulrich Luz, *Matthew: A Commentary*, Hermeneia, vol 3. *Matthew 21–28* (Minneapolis: Fortress Press, 2005), 614, 618–20. According to Luz, Matt. 28:18b-20 is a "'logion of the Lord' that Matthew composed." He argues that since commissioning narratives have no fixed pattern that would enable Matthew to duplicate it, the form is uniquely Matthean. Verbal agreements with Dan. 7:13–14 lxx demonstrate familiarity with the passage.

46. Ibid., 627

47. Ibid. Emphasis in original.

compelling people to submit to Jesus as their teacher and savior, as Luz puts it. Warneck's perception of mission became foundational for the Catholic understanding of missions with the subordination of papal and episcopal succession to Jesus' mission, as articulated in Matt. 28:19.[48] In fact, Warneck argues that the Reformation raised the consciousness of the church with regard to "mission-preaching," but he criticizes Martin Luther for not taking the Great Commission seriously. Thus, Warneck asserts that "the great reformer's view of the missionary task of the church was essentially defective," having been distorted by his eschatology.[49] Further, Warneck wrote, "With all earnestness he urges the preaching of the gospel, and longs for a free course for it. But nowhere does Luther indicate the heathen as the object of evangelistic work."[50] And so also were John Calvin's missional views defective because he and his co-laborers, according to Warneck, failed to focus on "the mission to the heathen world" as required by the "missionary commission" that states "make all nations my disciples."[51] Warneck wrote that "inside of Christendom [Calvin] missionarized [sic] with demonstration of the Spirit and of power, but the mission to the heathen world had no interest for him or his fellow-labourers."[52]

Luz, by way of Ceslas Spicq, provides the Catholic view of missions that Jesus authorizes his apostles to teach through the power he received from his Father. Further quoting Spicq, Luz writes, "this authority is unlimited. The hierarchy has the right to promulgate the doctrine and the precepts of Christ."[53] This last statement is fundamental for understanding the impact of this "charter of missions." Jesus' authority is filtered through the institutional hierarchy of the church and so-called "secular" or "mundane powers," which control the hermeneutical construction and dissemination of Christian doctrines and precepts. Warneck argues that the missions command is to "make all nations my disciples;" this does not just mean people within all nations, but "the nations in their entirety."[54] He recognizes that it is impossible to Christianize nations without joining forces with "mundane power." While the missionaries are to dedicate themselves to the spiritual component, God will orchestrate the

---

48. Ibid.

49. Gustav Warneck, *Outline of the History of Protestant Missions from the Reformation to the Present Time: A Contribution to Recent Church-History*, trans. Thomas Smith (Edinburgh: Gemmell, 1884), 17. Warneck argues that Luther believed that because the last day was at hand there was no need or hope for converting heathens (19).

50. Ibid., 12.

51. Ibid., 4, 18. Interestingly, Warneck cites initially cites Matt. 24:14 and not Matt. 28:19-20.

52. Ibid., 18.

53. Luz, *Matthew 21–28*, 627.

54. Warneck, *Outline of the History of Protestant*, 4.

cooperation of mundane power, for example, through the conversion of an emperor or local influential chiefs. Warneck claims that both the apostolic and medieval church periods ended with the Christianization of all nations within their territories.[55]

The focus was squarely placed on teaching others or so-called heathen or pagan nations in conjunction with mundane powers; this agenda has basically remained unchanged. However, Luz argues that beyond "evangelical movements" many are more cautious about using Matt. 28:19 as "the missions command" that has served "for a kind of militarization of the practice of missions.'"[56] It has been a matter of building and expanding churches and not of establishing the Kingdom of God in the world.[57]

Nation building and missions were bed-fellows (and this continues to some extent in various ways) and the iconic interpretative tradition of Matt. 28:18-20 as the Great Commission supported and justified this union. In fact, in the book of Matthew itself we find collusion between missions and nation building. As Musa Dube argues, Matthew "is one of those postcolonial texts written by the subjugated that nevertheless certifies imperialism."[58] But we might attribute this collusion we see to a double consciousness often developed (consciously and unconsciously) as a survival mechanism among colonized peoples,[59] as discussed in Lynne St. Clair Darden's essay in this volume.[60] To name it is not to condone it, but to define and critique it.

While acknowledging Matthew's privileging or at least appeasing, at times, the Roman Empire, we can attempt to extrapolate from Matthew a more liberating, social justice oriented reading of Matthew,[61] and particularly of Matt. 28:18-20, and also break with the naming of the text as *the Great Commission*.

---

55. Ibid., 6.

56. Luz, *Matthew 21–28*, 627.

57. Ibid.

58. Musa W. Dube, *Postcolonial Feminist Interpretation of the Bible* (St. Louis: Chalice, 2000), 135.

59. In addition to being oppressed by the Roman Empire, Matthew's community may have been a Jewish minority who experienced rejection and perhaps persecution from Israel's majority.

60. Also interesting is Matthew's use of the master-slave relationship as an analogy (perhaps further evidence for the double consciousness that Lynne St. Clair Darden speaks about in "Privilege but No Power: Women in the Gospel of Matthew and Nineteenth-Century African American Women Missionaries through a Postcolonial Lens" in this volume) for the relationship between the disciple and his teacher. In Matthew, the student does not exceed the teacher, as in John's Gospel (14:12), but it is sufficient "for the disciple to be like the teacher." (10:24-25; cf. 6:24).

61. Warren Carter ("Matthew and the Gentiles: Individual Conversion and/or Systemic Transformation," *Journal for the Study of the New Testament* 26, no. 3 [2004]: 259–82 [216]) argues that Matthew evaluates the Roman Empire and the gentile world as a whole throughout his narrative and

I agree with Luz that contemporary churches and Christians "can no longer read this text uncritically as the Magna Carta of their missionary proclamation" for reasons external to the Scriptures, particularly given "our modern understanding of the relationship between missions, colonialism, and the export of Western civilization and of the more intensive contacts with non-Christian religions."[62] I propose, however, that for reasons *both* internal (Matthew's literary context) *and* external (historical context of missions, colonialism, and neocolonialism) to the Scriptures, womanists, feminists, liberationists, and other justice-minded scholars and readers should no longer apply this nomenclature to or read Matt. 28:18-20 uncritically as the "Magna Carta" of what it means to engage in missional work or as the iconic hermeneutical lens for reading Matthew.

THE WOMANIST AS AN ICONOCLAST: SMASHING THE ICON AND KNOWING MORE

ANOTHER WAY OF KNOWING MATT. 28:18-20

The naming of Matt. 28:18-20 as the Great Commission and the resultant exaltation and myopic focus on "teaching all nations" has supported and provided theological and scriptural justification for subordinating, eclipsing, or obliterating the centrality of social justice acts and incarnation theology in Matthew and for the Matthean Jesus. Matt. 28:18-20 reads as follows:

> And when he came Jesus spoke to them saying. All authority (*exousia*) is given to me in heaven and on earth. Therefore, as you continue to go (*poreuthentes*), make disciples (*mathēteusate*) of all peoples (*ethnē*), baptizing (*baptizontes*) them in the name of the Father and of the Son and of the Holy Spirit, teaching (*diaskontes*) them to keep all that I have commanded you. And know that I am with you (*ego meth' humōn eimi*) all of your days (*pasas tas hēmeras*) until the consummation (*sunteleias*) of the age.[63]

The end of Matthew is not the first time Jesus bequeaths authority to his disciples. It is the substance of the discourse on the mount that evokes the

---

characterizes it as "contrary to God's just purposes" and that God's design as manifested in Jesus "will finally subordinate the Roman-dominated world to God's purposes."

62. Luz, *Matthew 21–28*, 628.

63. Author's translation.

comparison between Jesus' "teaching" and that of the scribes: "for he taught them as one having authority, and not as their scribes" (7:29). Jesus concludes his discourse on the mountain with a triple admonition about the importance of practice or manifesting the Father's will in one's life (7:15-20, 21-23, 24-27). When Jesus declares at Matt. 28:18 that God has given him authority in heaven and in earth, it is an authority granted to Jesus based on a lived life and a dynamic, organic ministry characterized by congruity between his acts of justice and the words he spoke. And so the authority he gives to his disciples to "teach" refers to the continuation of an interplay, an intricate marriage of just practice and words, without which there is no participation in the kin*dom[64] of heaven (7:21). Otherwise, one has a teaching consisting of rhetoric only and detached from just acts.

The second time that Jesus' authority is mentioned is when Jesus demonstrates to his detractors that he has "authority on earth" by causing a paralyzed man to walk, and not merely by the rhetoric that his sins are forgiven. The just act of healing the man serves as confirmation of the authority of Jesus' speech act forgiving the man's sins; otherwise where is the visible proof? And for the crowds, what Jesus has done demonstrates that God has given "such authority to human beings" generally (9:2-8). This final phrase is absent from the other synoptic accounts (Mark 2:1-12; Luke 5:17-26). This is the kind of authority that Jesus bequeathed to his disciples, one that is manifested by just acts and concomitant words. At Matt. 10:1-4 Jesus gave authority to his disciples to do what they witnessed Jesus do (an embodied pedagogy)—cast out unclean spirits and heal diseases and sicknesses or, as Michael Joseph Brown puts it "to meet the needs of the 'crowds,' specifically the poor."[65]

God gave Jesus the authority to commission disciples to continue to replicate what they witnessed Jesus do: "all authority is given to me in heaven and on earth," (28:18).[66] But we cannot understand those words without placing them in the context of Jesus' relationship to authority in Matthew. Unlike Herod, Jesus never used his authority to kill innocent children (2:16). When

---

64. Kin*dom is Ada Maria Isasi-Diaz's replacement for the traditional phrase "kingdom of God" in her article, "Solidarity: Love of Neighbor in the 1980s," in Lift Every Voice: Constructing Christian Theologies from the Underside, ed. Susan Brooks Thistlethwaite and Mary Potter Engel (San Francisco: Harper & Row, 1990): 30–39, 31–40. The term signifies relationship as opposed to kingdom, which connotes hierarchy.

65. Michael Joseph Brown, "The Gospel of Matthew," in True to Our Native Land (Minneapolis: Fortress Press, 2007), 85–120 (99).

66. This phrase is possibly influenced by Dan. 7:14, Exod. 19–20, and 2 Chron. 36:23. See Jane Schaberg, The Father, Son and the Holy Spirit: The Triadic Phrase in Matthew 28:19b (Chico, CA: Scholars, 1982) for a discussion of the connection between Dan. 7:14 and Matt. 28:18-20.

tempted to abuse the power and authority God had given him, Jesus refused to make bread (bread that would not grace the tables of the hungry) for the sake of proving his authority or power. Jesus refused to affirm that the authority and presence of God should be demonstrated by the ostentatious display of that power by the powerful (4:3-10). Jesus does not begin his ministry before he has shown that he will not abuse the power and authority God entrusted to him. Unlike many European missionaries, Jesus did not find it necessary to enter into alliances with mundane, evil and (neo)colonizing powers, in order to own or make disciples of "all the kingdoms of the world and their splendor" or to hasten his mission (4:8-10). Musa Dube argues that when Jesus counsels his disciples to give to Caesar the things that belong to Caesar and to God the things God requires (22:15-25), Matthew has presented the two on par "without suggesting any incompatibility."[67] I would argue differently that Matthew has demonstrated incompatibility by establishing a dichotomy between what belongs to God and what clearly bears the emperor's imprint. The disciples are to imitate Jesus' relationship to authority thereby maintaining continuity with Jesus' example.

Returning to Dube's contention that Matthew promotes an imperialist agenda of entering foreign lands with Jesus' authority and possessing them, Matthew certainly lends itself to such a reading; and missionaries have and continue to read Matt. 28:18-20 accordingly. But it is also possible that the first-century apostles read the text differently, particularly given the reality of the Roman Empire lurking over their shoulders. Most of the apostles, according to the Acts of the Apostles, did not initially travel into foreign lands to preach/teach the gospel but stayed in Judea even after the persecution following Stephen's death (Acts 7:54—8:3) where they formed communities that took care of the least among them (2:44-45; 4:32—5:11).[68] Also, if we read the Greek phrase *panta ta ethnē* as *all peoples*,[69] rather than as *all nations* (28:19), then we might understand Matthew as attempting to transcend nationality, and not to subordinate all nations[70]; issues remain.

67. Dube, *Postcolonial Feminist Interpretation*, 133.

68. Although the programmatic verse 1:8 in Acts sets the stage for geographic expansion of the gospel to the ends of the earth, the author does not tell us exactly how that will happen. And, indeed, it happens in a number of ways.

69. Eduard Schweizer translates the Greek phrase *panta ta ethnē* as *all peoples*: Eduard Schweizer, *The Good News According to Matthew*, trans. David E. Green (Atlanta: John Knox, 1975), 527. Schweizer also does not label the passage as the Great Commission.

70. It is interesting to note that in Acts, Peter's first missional speech takes place among many different nationalities who have entered Jerusalem, and of course, later as a result of some apostles entering into foreign lands (i.e., the Apostle Paul and Thomas). Two stories are placed in relief in Acts: the Ethiopian

Matthew's Jesus may also attempt to present an innocuous view of his disciples in light of the Roman Empire. The tendency of Matthew, as Dube demonstrates, to paint the Roman Empire in a more positive light than the Jewish leadership and Israel's faith[71] may constitute an attempt to placate the Roman Empire. Or as Lynne St. Clair Darden argues in her essay in this volume, it may be, more specifically, a symptom of the double consciousness that colonized peoples have had to construct for themselves—a contextual epistemological consciousness that impacts and governs one's mundane existence and survival.

In Matt. 28:19-20 we also find a semantic and grammatical continuity expressed by the three verbal participles directed at the eleven disciples. The first verbal participle or action directed at the disciples (as objects of the participle) is translated by scholars not as a participle but as an imperative: *Go!* This is a translation of the Greek aorist passive nominative plural participle form of *poreuomai* (*poreuthentes*, going). There is good reason to translate the participle this way. However, it is also possible to translate that Greek participle differently, perhaps as a semantic and grammatical bridge evoking continuity between other commissions in Matthew and the final summary, as a participle that casts a shadow backward and forward. Understood this way, we would translate the participle as *As you continue to go* make disciples. The participle in relation to its immediate context and in relation to the larger context is one of continuity of movement. The disciples have already been commissioned to go; they will continue that commission, and it will become more expansive.

We find a grammatical construction similar to v. 19 at 2:8. At 2:8, Herod instructs the wise men to "Go and search diligently for the child; and when you have found him, bring me word so that I may also go and pay him homage" (NRSV). Here again, we have the aorist passive participle nominative plural of the Greek deponent verb *poreuomai* together with an aorist imperative verb. And again, both verbs are translated as imperatives by most translators. The

---

eunuch traveled to Jerusalem and on his return home the angel of the Lord orchestrates a meeting between the eunuch and Philip (8:26-40); Peter and Cornelius are brought together for Cornelius's conversion and baptism (ch. 10–11). Significantly, for modern missions into Africa, the pattern in Acts is for persons from the African continent to travel and seek as subjects rather to wait passively for missionaries to transgress and possess their lands. However, unfortunately the pattern is for the two Africans (the Ethiopian eunuch and Apollo from North Africa) to be taught (8:26-40; 18:24-28); but they maintain their dignity, agency, and culture. Of course Acts 1:8 set a course for the apostles to travel beyond Judea to Samaria and "toward the ends of the earth," but none of the twelve go the distance, at least not in the canonical Gospels (see for example the apocryphal *Acts of Peter*). The Apostle Paul crosses over into Europe and travels to Rome, as a Roman citizen and to Spain (16:1-15; 28:14; Rom. 15:14, 28).

71. Dube, *Postcolonial Feminist Interpretation*, 140.

participle may again function in Matthew as a referent to past action (i.e., the wise men were already searching for the baby Jesus by following his star, 2:2). The participle also constitutes a grammatical and semantic bridge between the journey (the going) they had already embarked upon and the present command to continue the journey, but with the added task to bring back word to Herod.

Similarly, when Jesus commissions the twelve disciples in chapter 10, we find the same grammatical construction with the present tense participle form of the deponent Greek verb *poreuomai* (going) and the imperative verb *kēroussete* (proclaim) (10:7 NRSV): "*As you go*, proclaim the good news." The words they will proclaim, "the kingdom of the heavens has drawn near," as they are going constitutes good news. But it is good news because it is connected with *going*, and the *going* points back to the commission to heal, resurrect the dead, cleanse from unclean spirits, perform exorcisms, and liberate the people (10:5-8). The news is good because it redresses the people's specific needs. (I will say more about this connection between words and acts below.)

Thus, the use of the aorist or present tense participle of the Greek verb *poreuomai* together with the imperative finite verb is not unusual in Matthew to express continuity and to connect the past, present, and future. And the final or summary commission at 28:18-20 is generally no different grammatically than other commissions in Matthew. On the other hand, when Jesus gives a command that is more narrowly construed and directed at an individual or fewer people, a one-time command, Matthew employs an imperative Greek verb translated *Go*, usually *hupage* (8:4, 13, 32; 9:6; 18:15; 19:21; cf. 8:9), but sometimes the finite present middle imperative *poreuesthe* (go!) (21:2).

The other participles in Matt. 28:18-20 can definitely be understood as subordinate to the aorist active imperative Greek verb *mathēteusate* translated as *make disciples*. Subordinating all participles to the one finite Greek verb in the sentence (*mathēteusate*, make disciples) is not the only legitimate way to read the text. Discipling consists of baptizing and teaching, but not only of baptizing and teaching.[72] Some scholars express surprise that baptism is mentioned here,[73] but Matthew seems to mention baptism no less often than the other Synoptics. Nevertheless, the *teaching* should be understood in a way congruous with the

---

72. Hagner (*Matthew 14–18*, 887) argues that *to make disciples* in Matthew means foremost "to follow after righteousness as articulated" in Jesus' teachings, and I can agree if we understand righteousness as justice. See H. Kvalbein, "Go Therefore and Make Disciples ... The Concept of Discipleship in the New Testament," *Themelios* 13 (1988): 48–53.

73. Luz (*Matthew 21–28*, 631–32) finds it significant that Matthew mentions baptism rather than circumcision since very little is said about baptism in the Gospel, but it is important that they follow Jesus' example and submit to baptism and demonstrate such for others.

manner in which Jesus taught in Matthew. But teaching in Matthew has been diluted to reflect modern understandings of teaching and to support the traditional missionary agenda to teach doctrines. *Teaching* has come to reflect a colonial mindset and the drive to delimit and control the type of knowledge particular converts (i.e., slaves, Indians, Africans, Asians, women and children) received.

When Jesus commissions his disciples, their going is never limited to teaching, per se, but includes healing and other miracles that redress physical and spiritual needs and brokenness; although it seems that healing is not always accompanied by teaching (10:1-4). As Luz argues "the disciples' 'teaching' is also accompanied by their good deeds."[74] Also, "the content of teaching is described as 'keeping the commandments.' Thus at issue is an initiation into praxis."[75] But one cannot initiate into praxis if one does not already practice or embody what one proposes to teach. The evidence of the nearness of God's kin*dom is the powerful acts of justice Jesus performs, and not simply the words Jesus spoke (12:22-32, 13:54-58; Mark 3:22-29, 6:1-6; Luke 11:14-23; also Luke 4:16-30). In fact, Herod thinks that Jesus is John the Baptist resurrected from the dead because of the powerful deeds (*hai dunameis*) he performs (14:1-12; Mark 6:14-29; Luke 9:7-9). John the Baptist was considered to be an Elijah type (17:11-13), known also for his miraculous deeds. And Jesus was like John the Baptist about whom Jesus said there was no greater human being born (11:11).

THE GREAT, GREATER, AND GREATEST IN MATTHEW

While most missionaries, scholars, and Christians have seen fit to continue this iconic tradition of naming Matt. 28:19-20 as *the Great Commission*, the author of Matthew has not called his summary *great*. Matthew is not reluctant to single out individuals, commandments, and activities as *great*, *greater*, or the *greatest*. Jesus' withdrawal to Galilee of the gentiles, after John the Baptist's death, is considered a fulfillment of Isa. 9:2: "a great light has dawned" upon a people who sat in darkness (4:12-16). In the context of Isaiah, the coming King will establish and maintain his kingdom "with justice and with righteousness (9:7)." The phrase *justice and righteousness* constitutes a hendiadys, or two synonymous terms joined with a conjunction.[76] Doing justice is inherent in the royal office.[77]

---

74. Ibid., 634.

75. Ibid., 633.

76. Josè Miranda, *Marx and the Bible: A Critique of the Philosophy of Oppression* (Maryknoll, NY: Orbis Books, 1997), 112.

77. Volkmar Herntrich, "krinō," *TDNT* 3:924.

Matthew, of course, introduces Jesus as coming through the royal lineage of David; he is the anointed, the son of David (1:17-18). As "a great light" we would expect that Jesus would be preoccupied with doing justice.

What is considered great in Matthew is only so in relation to doing justice toward the least. The people who hunger and thirst for justice (*dikaiosunē*) will receive justice (5:6). Those who are bullied and defamed, as were the prophets, will receive a great reward in the heavens (5:12); the kin*dom of the heavens has drawn near in Jesus. The kin*dom does not signify an otherworldly justice; the kin*dom of the heavens is imminent and present in Jesus. Jesus came to fulfill the law and the prophets, which he has summed up as loving God (the *greatest* commandment) and loving neighbor (the second *greatest* commandment) (5:17-20; 22:34-40; cf. 5:44). Anyone who does not love God or neighbor and teaches others to do likewise are least (*elachistos*) in the kin*dom. Notice that *doing* (or not *doing*) is preceded by the *teaching; we are to teach the justice we do; and not teach the justice we fail to practice* (5:19). So if one teaches doctrines, rules, and standards, and yet does not exhibit love, that one or what that one does cannot be considered great. One cannot teach an individual about the *golden rule* without first practicing the golden rule, as former African slave Linda Brent, also known as Harriet Jacobs, recognized.[78] Brent's American slave masters taught a gospel that separated teaching from doing justice, spiritual conversion from physical freedom—at least for the black slaves. Linda Brent, a proto-womanist, knew "more than was 'good for her and in greater depth"; she understood what the status quo would rather she did not know. Brent acted *womanish* when she rejected and wrote about the hypocrisy, the dissonance or disconnect between what her slave mistress taught her and how she treated her. Linda thought that her mother's service as a faithful slave to the mistress would guarantee that her mistress would free Linda in her Will upon the mistress's death. Instead, the mistress bequeathed Linda to the mistress's five-year-old niece. This is Brent's response to the injustice within the atrocity of slavery:

> So vanished our hopes. My mistress had taught me the precepts of God's Word: "Thou shalt love thy neighbor as thyself." "Whatsoever ye would that men should do unto you, do ye even so unto them." But I was her slave, and I suppose *she did not recognize me as her neighbor.* I would give much to blot out from my memory that *one great wrong.* As a child, I loved my mistress; and, looking back on the

---

78. For more on Linda Brent's (aka Harriet Jacobs) use of Scripture, see Emerson B. Powery, "'Rise up, ye Women': Harriet Jacobs & the Bible," *Postscripts* 5, no. 2 (2009): 171–84.

happy days I spent with her, I try to think with less bitterness of *this act of injustice*. While I was with her, she taught me to read and spell; and for this privilege, which so rarely falls to the lot of a slave, I bless her memory.[79]

Linda Brent recognized that even as her mistress taught her to love her neighbor, her mistress did not consider Brent as her neighbor. Knowing the difference between rhetoric and practice, knowing when good doctrinal teaching obfuscated or became a substitute for just practice meant that Linda was not naive about the injustice and hypocrisy of those who held power over her and about the inherent relationship between just action and right teaching. *Just teaching is not just until it is incarnate as just practice.* And Brent's knowing meant that she held her mistress and herself to a greater accountability. Brent's womanish ways of knowing, her womanist epistemology, compelled her to act courageously and audaciously to name her mistress's duplicity and define for herself the relationship between doctrine or teaching and just practice. Linda Brent's mistress propagated the royal law as dogma or doctrine to be taught and not as a mandate for how to live, to be embodied in relation with others.

The least (*elachistos*) who fail to love God and neighbor are not the same as the kin*dom least (*mikroteros*)[80] who are more significant (*meizōn*) than the greatest man, John the Baptist, born to a woman (11:11). Jesus considers himself, as God with us, to be greater than rites, traditions, and laws; mercy and compassion for human beings, which he embodies, is to be valued above sacrifices and ritual (12:1-7; cf. 12:38-42).[81] While sacrifices constitute symbolic rituals, mercy has to do with just and empathetic engagement with people (and creation). Matthew continually demonstrates, with concrete examples, how compassion should trump a strict, inhumane observance of ritual and doctrine, even with regard to cattle (12:9-14; Mark 3:1-6; Luke 6:6-11).

The Canaanite woman would certainly qualify as least among the least, and yet the Matthean Jesus acknowledges and concedes to the Canaanite woman's

---

79. Linda Brent, *Incidents in the Life of a Slave Girl*, in *The Classic Slave Narratives*, ed. Henry Louis Gates Jr. (New York: Penguin, 1987), 333–513 (344). Emphasis added.

80. However, Matthew seems to use interchangeably the two Greek words translated as least—*elachistos* and *mikroteros*.

81. The Matthean Jesus' statement about mercy being preferred above sacrifice, as well as Jesus' explicit and direct indictment of the priests for breaking the Sabbath are absent from both Mark (2:23-27) and Luke (6:1-5). Matthew quotes Hosea 6:6, God requires mercy and not sacrifice, in the context of feeding his hungry disciples (12:1-7) and in the context of the criticism that he eats with "tax collectors and sinners" (9:9-12).

great faith (*megalas pistis*), a complement missing from Mark's version of the story (15:21-28; Mark 7:24-30). Jesus does not require that the Canaanite woman submit to baptism or become Jewish; in fact, she seems to school, or at least convict, Jesus with her persistence and her audacious words, even as she humbles herself for the sake of her child, willing to assume the role of a dog to retrieve the *crumbs* for her sick child. Significantly, the greatest (*meizōn*) in the kin*dom are those who humble themselves like a child (18:1-5). Michael Joseph Brown asserts that to become like a child means to "renounce their privileges" and to "make themselves some of the most vulnerable people in society."[82] The Canaanite woman exceeds the "requirement" for kin*dom membership. And Jesus as God with us is not above being *taught* or challenged by a Canaanite woman. Jesus' practice of responding to questions with questions, and of acknowledging the opposition to and the production of knowledge by people like the Canaanite woman (15:21-28; cf. Mark 7:24-30) demonstrates that Jesus did not practice a pedagogy in which his disciples, the crowds, or those who sought him were passive recipients of rhetoric.

Conversely, the sons of Zebedee presume that they can be made great (*mega*) in the kin*dom by obtaining seats on Jesus' right and left (20:20-28). Not only does Jesus not possess the authority to grant such a request (it is antithetical to what constitutes authority in Matthew), but greatness comes not from position, but from ministry (*diakonos*); greatness is inherently service-oriented (20:20-28), having more to do with just practice than with empty, disembodied rhetoric.

The Matthean Jesus addressed the dissonance between teaching and practice when he saw that certain scribes and Pharisees taught one thing but practiced another (23:1-36; Mark 12:37-39; Luke 11:39-41, 46-51; 20:45-46). And in response to this dissonance, Jesus reiterated what he told the sons of Zebedee that the greatest (*meizōn*) among them will be the one who engages in a ministry (*diakonos*) of justice (*kristis*), mercy, and faith (23:11, 23). The kin*dom of God will consist of people from every nation who practice justice among/for the least (*elachistoi*) (25:31-46), and who do not consider themselves to be just simply because they mention or preach the name of Jesus wherever they go. The least are the hungry, thirsty, strangers, resident aliens, naked, impoverished, sick, and oppressed. And it is in doing justice for the least, that the kin*dom is nearest, takes on flesh, or is embodied. It is as we see Jesus in the bodies of the least and respond with justice that we embody the justice of God's

---

82. Michael Joseph Brown, "The Gospel of Matthew," 108.

kin*dom. By imitating Jesus, we become God-with-us disciples and make God-with-us disciples.

GOD WITH US AS THE JUSTICE OF GOD

Matthew's Jesus is first named *Immanuel*, which is translated *God with us (meth' hēmon ho theos)* (1:23).[83] Matthew concludes with Jesus' promise to be present with *(egō meth' humōn eimi)* his disciples until the end (28:20).[84] Andries van Aarde argues that Jesus, as God with us, is the *viewpoint character* in Matthew, and as the *viewpoint character* he manifests the narrator's *ideological perspective*, which is also the *dominant perspective*.[85] The ideological perspective is integrally connected with the interpersonal (the level at which Jesus interacts with others).[86] Jesus as God with us means that God can be experienced (conceived of, spoken about, imitated, or obeyed) concretely anew because of Jesus' flesh and blood presence.[87] This God-with-us experience evokes womanism's insistence on the interdependence of experience, consciousness, and action. As JoAnn Banks-Wallace asserts, "the interdependence of thought and action allows for the possibility that changes in thinking will be accompanied by changes in actions and that altered experiences may be a catalyst for a changed consciousness."[88]

This designation of Jesus as Immanuel or God with us, derives from First Isaiah (7:14; 8:8, 10) where the prophet's child is born and named as a sign from God for King Ahaz (7:10-12). Matthew quotes the prophet Isaiah more than any other prophet for a total of ten times, and five of those occurrences are distinctive to Matthew.[89] But Matthew also draws from Isaiah an emphasis on teaching that promotes and results in justice (Isa. 1:10-17; 10:1-2), the

83. See Barbara E. Reid, "Which God is With Us?," *Interpretation* 64 (2010): 380–89 for a discussion of the tension between the image of a gracious God who is with us in Jesus and the image of God as a harsh punisher of those who do evil in the parables in Matthew. See also Barbara E. Reid, "Violent Endings in Matthew's Parables and Christian Nonviolence," *Catholic Biblical Quarterly* 66, no. 2 (2004): 237–55.

84. Andries van Aarde (*God-With-Us: The Dominant Perspective in Matthew's Story and Other Essays*, Hervormde Teleogiese Studies Supplement 5 [Pretoria: Hervormde Teologiese Studies, 1994], 34–43 [3]) argues that this motif of presence occurs as well in the middle of Matthew at 18:20 where Jesus asserts that where two or three gather in his name he will be among them.

85. Ibid., 34–35.

86. See Brian K. Blount, *Cultural Interpretation: Reorienting New Testament Criticism* (Minneapolis: Fortress Press, 1995), 11.

87. See JoAnne Marie Terrell, *Power in the Blood?: The Cross in the African American Experience* (Maryknoll, NY; Orbis Books, 1998). Dr. Terrell argues that the crucifix is the greatest reminder of "God's *with-us-ness*" (125).

88. Banks-Wallace, "Womanist Ways of Knowing," 316.

synonymous relationship between justice and righteousness, the embodiment or fulfillment of justice/righteousness, and the emphasis on all nations receiving the teaching of God as justice (2:1-3). In Isaiah, the only way that Judah can be redeemed is by justice and righteousness (1:27). When justice is established, all nations will seek to be taught God's ways so that they might also walk in justice (2:1-3); justice is first established before justice is sought or taught. Justice/righteousness exalts Yahweh, and by justice God demonstrates that he is holy (5:16-17; 9:7). As mentioned above by doing justice, God's people demonstrate greatness. In both Isaiah and Matthew, righteousness and justice are at least organically interconnected (at most synonymous) (Isa. 5:7, 16; 9:7; Matt. 25:31-46). As in First Isaiah, when injustice abounds, the people need to know that *God is with them* and will usher in justice/righteousness.

From the beginning of the birth narratives, justice as a character trait and as an ethical practice is valued or evoked, explicitly and implicitly. Matthew embeds the story of Jesus' birth, as *Immanuel, God with us*, within the historical and political framework of the Roman Empire and its control over Judah through Herod (chapter 2). Prior to the introduction of Herod, Matthew establishes for his readers the character of Joseph as a just (*dikaios*) man who is engaged to the pregnant young girl, Mary; and Joseph is not the father. Implicitly, the justice of God prevails in the wise men's decision not to report back to Herod upon finding the baby Jesus (2:12). Conversely, injustice is committed when Herod orders the murder of all children in and around Bethlehem that are two years old and under (2:16). Acts of justice and injustice are weaved, implicitly and explicitly, throughout the story, the narration of the story, and in the words and practices of Jesus.

The presence of God in Jesus ushers in the justice of God, and the justice of God is evidenced in those who engender justice. When Jesus is tempted by the devil in the wilderness (4:1-11), he chooses not to transgress the boundaries of his humanity (his incarnate God-with-us-ness), while he defies epistemological boundaries by *knowing more and in greater depth* than the devil would like for him to know: "A human being does not live by bread alone but by every word that proceeds from God's mouth" (4:4).[90] Knowing more is a divine trait here, so as not to commit an injustice, be the victim of injustice, or to be complicit with injustice. It is also an act of justice to act (or refuse to act in this case) contrary to the justice one knows. It is a refusal to be duplicitous, to lean clearly toward

---

89. Boring, "The Gospel of Matthew," 151. As with other Gospels, Matthew cites Scripture from the Psalms most frequently.

90. van Aarde (*God-With-Us*, 40) argues that in the temptation scene Jesus acts "from a conscious position of power, being *God-with-us*."

justice rather than injustice. It is also a womanist's necessity. In choosing not to transgress the boundaries of his humanity (trying to be God), Jesus engenders and embodies the justice of God in the wilderness and in his ministry (being like God).[91]

Jesus demonstrated his *God-with-us-ness* in his dealings with the crowds and some Jewish leaders and sects whom he encountered and who pursued him. Richard Beaton argues that 12:15-21 (including the embedded Isa. 42:1-4 quotation) and its immediate context, demonstrate "a developed contradistinction between injustice and justice, namely, the Pharisees' concern for strict halakic observance and their concomitant unjust treatment of the people versus Jesus' own conceptualization of Torah observance and the justice" he engendered among the people.[92] Beaton notes how texts from Deutero-Isaiah's servant songs (Isa. 53:4; 42:1-4), which focus on the justice of God and the unjust treatment of the servant, are quoted after Matthean summaries (8:14-17; 12:15-21).[93] In both 8:14-17 and 12:15-21, a summary of Jesus' healing and exorcism activities is said to fulfill a portion of the Servant Songs (Isa. 53:4; 42:1-4). In fact, Josè Miranda notes that Matt. 8:17 presents an alternative reading of Isa. 53:4 contradicting the "customary interpretation" wherein the Servant takes our pains and sufferings upon himself. But, Miranda notes that in Matthew the Servant takes our pains and sufferings *away*;[94] Jesus fulfills Isa. 53:4 by healing the people of their pains and sufferings, which are acts of justice. Jesus did not require that the crowds listen to his teaching as a prerequisite for receiving healing and wholeness. His acts of justice constitute embodied, incarnational pedagogy. However, teachings and proclamation did at times accompany Jesus' healings and exorcisms (4:23-25).[95]

The Matthean Jesus taught that the poor/impoverished/broken in spirit will not be excluded from the kin*dom of heaven that has been brought near in Jesus (5:3) as *God with us*. The insertion of the words *in spirit* after the word *poor* does not need to be seen as a spiritualizing of poverty. The experience of being trapped in poverty can break one's spirit so that one loses hope of ever

91. Ibid. van Aarde describes Jesus' God-with-us-ness as total obedience to the will of God.

92. Richard Beaton, "Messiah and Justice: A Key to Matthew's Use of Isaiah 42:1-4?" *Journal for the Study of the New Testament* 75 (1999): 5–23 (6).

93. Ibid., 6.

94. Miranda, *Marx and the Bible*, 129.

95. Van Aarde (*God-With-Us*, 36) speaks in terms of Jesus' "concrete proclamation," which is manifest in two inseparable ways: by actions (preaching, teaching, healing) and by attitude (love and compassion). This concretized proclamation is intended to liberate the people from the impact of the Jewish leaders' teaching and thus from Satan's temptations.

changing one's impoverished existence. Conversely, a bankrupt spirit can lead to economic poverty. The fourth beatitude assures that those who hunger and thirst for justice (*dikaiosunē*) will be satisfied (5:6; also 5:10). It is no coincidence that the beatitudes are followed by two significant metaphors admonishing the crowds that they are "the salt of the earth" and the "light of the world" (5:13-14). This connects the promise of justice for the poor in spirit with the global responsibility to impact the world or to engender justice globally. No other Synoptic Gospel makes this connection between justice for the poor in spirit and personal and corporate responsibility to the rest of the world (Mark 4:21; 9:50; Luke 8:16; 11:33; 14:34-35).

Also, in his discourse on the Mount (ch. 5–7), Jesus informed the crowds and his disciples that God cares that they are clothed and have food to eat; that if God clothes and feeds the birds, certainly God cares about human beings and their temporal needs (6:25-34; cf. 7:9-10). In other words, God cares about social justice; God cares that people are fed and clothed, that they do not go hungry or go without proper clothing. Therefore, the disciples can with confidence seek the kin*dom of God first, because justice is an inherent and organic goal of the kin*dom; the mandate does not create a dichotomy between temporal needs and the kin*dom. The gospel is lived and manifested in liberating, just acts (10:40-42; 11:2-6).

As the beloved son, Jesus will bring and proclaim justice (*krisis*) to the nations (12:18-21;[96] Isaiah 42:1-4[97]). It is only in Matthew's version of the commissioning of the twelve that "judgment" or the execution of justice is inserted in the phrase comparing the rejection of the gospel by the cities to which the disciples travel with the fate of Sodom and Gomorrah: "it will be more tolerable for the land of Sodom and Gomorrah on the day of justice (*krisis*) than for that town" (10:15; cf. Luke 10:12). Matthew repeats it again but in the context of the failure of cities to respond to Jesus' powerful deeds (11:20-24). Josè Miranda argues that at 12:20 Matthew has "powerfully" reformulated Isa. 42:4 as: "till he has led *mishpat* [justice] to victory," and proceeds to use *mishpat* three more times to refer to a final judgment.[98] Miranda further argues that this reformulation and repetition obliges "us to think that according to Matthew

---

96. Carter ("Matthew and the Gentiles," 271) translates *krisin* at 12:18, 20 as justice for the nations.

97. Some OT scholars argue that the theme of justice is the key to understanding Isa. 42:1-4, as well as the beginning chapters of Deutero-Isaiah. See M. C. Lind, "Monotheism, Power, and Justice: A Study of Isaiah 40–55," *Catholic Biblical Quarterly* 46 (1984): 432–46; D. Kendall, "The Use of Mishpat in Isaiah 59," *Zeitschrift für die alttestamentliche Wissenschaft* 96 (1984): 391–405; H. Gossai, *Justice, Righteousness and the Social Critique of the Eighth-Century Prophets* (New York: Lang, 1993).

98. Miranda, *Marx and the Bible*, 129.

the triumph of *mishpat* will be the Last Judgment."[99] Matthew sees in "Christ's works of justice [*mishpat*] on behalf of the poor and helpless" the "definitive realization of Judgment."[100]

In chapter 25 of Matthew, in the final judgment (execution of justice), God will distinguish between those who act justly toward the hungry, thirsty, imprisoned, and sick (not exhaustive categories), since Jesus considers such people to be the "least" among us; to treat them justly is the same as acting with justice toward Jesus (25:21-46). But those who consider themselves righteous/just and never engender justice, but merely *teach* about righteousness/justice will not comprise the kin*dom of heaven on earth or in heaven. In Matthew, as Alejandro Duarte has argued, "justice is fulfilled when the law, as interpreted by Jesus is fulfilled"[101] (i.e., in sum, treating others as we would like to be treated, 7:12; cf. 5:17-48). Significantly, Matthew's Jesus prefaces the royal law with the words "in everything"; Luke does not (7:12; Luke 6:31). The royal law of doing to others as one would have them do to us is a summation of God's instruction and commandments in the Torah and in the prophets. As Luz asserts, Matthew's Jesus embodied his message and thus his life was the model for his disciples and for readers, one that inspired and encouraged and who is worthy to be imitated.[102] Through and in Jesus, the presence of God becomes concrete and visible, and as such we are able to see how God would or should function on earth and in human relationships.[103]

CONCLUSION

God is not only or primarily a God who sends, a God of missions.[104] God is a God who is concretely present, intervening in the lives of the oppressed. And Jesus as *God with us* is chiefly concerned with justice. Oppressed peoples have experienced and need to know that God is a God who was present with them before the missionaries arrived and is present with them after the missionaries have left; that God is a God who authors, engenders, and embodies justice. The naming and iconization of Matt. 28:18-20 as the Great Commission subordinates the characterization of Jesus in Matthew as *God with us* and

99. Ibid.

100. Ibid.

101. Alejandro Duarte, "Matthew," in *The Global Bible Commentary*, ed. Daniel Patte (Nashville: Abingdon, 2004), 350–60 (352).

102. Luz, *Matthew 21–28*, 639, 644.

103. Ibid., 644.

104. See Michael Barram, "The Bible, Mission, and Social Location: Toward a Missional Hermeneutic," *Interpretation* 61, no. 1 (2007): 42–58.

continues the missional agenda of elevating the teaching of doctrines and subordinating social justice.

Additionally, this iconic nomenclature has blinded us to more liberating ways to read the Gospel that demonstrate God's care and concern for the oppressed and marginalized. It matters how we read, because how we read impacts how we interact with one another. The execution of an embodied, incarnational pedagogy that privileges justice should flow from the just. The authority of an incarnational, embodied pedagogy rests with the just, those who allow the Spirit of God to transform them into the likeness of Jesus as *God with us.*

If we understand that God has imprinted God's image, the *imago Dei*, on African and African American peoples as well as on any other peoples, then we can acknowledge that even, or especially, black bodies can testify to and embody God's image and be *God with us.* Others can be visited and "missionized" by black women[105] and other peoples of color, by people with no power or authority, and by Haitian women who praise God from beneath the rubble of an earthquake. Thomas argues that a womanist approach to missions calls us to be "missionized"; to be present, with humility, "to listen to the testimony and to witness to the Spirit of God in action, while resisting the desire to proclaim, tell, or contest."[106] We must embody the justice of God so that our actions and words are in sync. We must be open to learning to be just from those who need justice; we must remain open to seeing God's presence in others, because in others God has also imprinted God's image and commissioned them to be *God with us.*

---

105. Thomas, "Anthropology, Mission and the African Woman," 13.
106. Ibid., 14.

PART III

Theology, Art, and the Great Commission

7

Images of Jesus in Advancing the Great Commission

Sheila F. Winborne

Historically, it has not been unusual for any people to represent their deities in their own images. According to Albert C. Moore, throughout history, communities of people have projected their own images onto their God or gods.[1] Although not unusual, it is not necessarily true that every people have done so. As Edward J. Blum and Paul Harvey have argued, to say that racial and ethnic groups necessarily create God or gods in their own images is to accept the myth that the particulars of faith and society such as material, social, and cultural power are meaningless.[2] In other words, in recognizing the influential power of material culture for example, Blum and Harvey highlight the reality that due to western missionary approaches many persons of color around the world embrace images of Jesus as the Christ as racially white, and therefore not in their own racial images. Even when myths such as that of the white Christ are not factually accurate, they are not completely without some truth because they can still communicate much about the beliefs, concerns, and values within a culture. As Karen Armstrong states, it is the effectiveness of myths that makes them true and that gives them the power to influence beliefs, more so than whether they communicate factual information. Myths can transform the ways we believe and behave, in that they function as guides that are ideally meant to inform us about how to live more richly in our given cultures.[3] The visual arts can reflect and impact for better or worse how communities shape beliefs

1. Albert C. Moore, *Iconography of Religions: An Introduction* (Philadelphia: Fortress Press, 1977), 94.

2. Edward J. Blum and Paul Harvey, *The Color of Christ: The Son of God and the Saga of Race in America* (Chapel Hill: University of North Carolina Press, 2012), 19.

3. Karen Armstrong, *A Short History of Myth* (Toronto: Alfred A. Knopf, 2005), 4, 10.

about historical figures such as Jesus. What is the result when a people are forced to accept the Supreme God as represented in the image of their oppressors? The result is a colonial mythical narrative about the white Jesus that continues to be embedded in post- or neocolonial approaches to the so-called Great Commission as Jesus' call to the apostles to "make disciples of all nations" (Matt. 28:19). This narrative has been used to justify Christian conversion by any means necessary, including by economically and politically driven aggression.

History shows that western colonial powers have "Christianized" many around the world by coercive means, including Africans who were taken into chattel slavery during the transatlantic slave trade and forced or coerced into baptism. A powerful tool in the continuation of "Christianizing" nations has been the systematic marketing of created images of God incarnate as a racially white Jesus of European descent. When used as missionary tools, these images communicate that Jesus' "whiteness" is necessarily a reflection of his holiness or that his holiness is manifested in his "whiteness." Christianity understood as a belief system only of "the Word" with Jesus as the "Logos" has contributed to many in the church giving far less conscious and critical thought to how "the Word" has been interpreted visually in support of colonial missionary efforts. Not just oral and written texts, but visual art texts have played major roles in theological approaches to the Great Commission. One of the most powerful ways colonial ideologies about who are defined as *chosen* and *Other* have been communicated is through created images of Jesus rendered as racially white, with these representations marketed as the most "true" or legitimate images of Jesus as the Christ.

The Theological Power of Images

The visual arts have not only played major roles in influencing and reflecting Christian theological beliefs and practices, they have been central to believers' ideas about God's relationship with humanity. To put the role of the white Jesus Christ during the transatlantic slave trade and after into perspective, it is helpful to briefly review how a part of the preceding history reflected the power of images.[4] Like the early theological debates, later arguments about Christian

4. I am not arguing that icons of the Eastern Orthodox Church have been interpreted or have been intended to serve as images of the white Christ as has been the case for many representations in western churches. I recognize that in traditional Eastern Orthodox icons, the less realistically rendered style as well as the darker skin tones of Christ and the saints are meant to be read as symbolic of Christ's and the saints' spiritually or "other-worldliness." Whereas in the western Catholic Church, the artists' choice of the realistic rendering style originally was intended to symbolize the "real presence" of Christ and the saints. But the result in the west has been that the realistic style of church images has resulted in most

colonial art have not just been about how or whether it is possible to visually represent the sacred through art. Closer examination shows that they have been more about power and political control within and outside of the church.

Theologians and other church leaders have argued about images from various perspectives throughout history: from the early iconoclastic controversies in the Eastern Orthodox Church, to the ecumenical council disputes between the Orthodox and Western Catholic divisions of the church, to debates within the sixteenth-century Protestant Reform Movement, to the disagreements that followed between the memberships of various Protestant denominations, to current disagreements within and beyond the church about which type of images can and should serve as "true" or authentic representations of Jesus and other biblical figures. These are issues not only about how stylistic approaches to aesthetic rendering can influence interpretations, but they're about practice, power, and control. The arguments have been as much about institutionalized control as about spiritual faith and practice. In *Icon: Studies in the History of an Idea*, Moshe Barasch states that behind what may have seemed to only have been theological questions were struggles for the establishing of new political and social orders or attempts to stop changes that would have resulted in new classes seeking control.[5] Whether embraced more as icon to be venerated, as art to be admired, or as objects to be completely banded from sight, persons on each side of the arguments have recognized that images have the power to influence human perceptions and therein to influence the shape of religious, political, and other cultural institutions.

Although it may seem logical to conclude that theological approaches that have called for the removal or complete absence of artistic images in the church only support beliefs that art is less significant and less powerful in communicating Christian beliefs than spoken and written words, the historical debates suggest otherwise. The absences of and seeming silences about the visual arts in specific churches carry messages about the theological significance and power of images as strongly as the presence of images in other churches. If they agreed on little else, both the iconoclasts (destroyers of or those who opposed the veneration of images) and the iconophiles (lovers of images) recognized the power of images, even if they disagreed about whether the

viewers reading the art as void of symbolism. See Sheila F. Winborne, "The Theological Significance of Normative Visual Preferences in Visual Art Creation and Interpretation," in *Creating Ourselves: African Americans and Hispanic Americans on Popular Culture and Religious Expression,* ed. Anthony Pinn and Benjamin Valentin (Durham, NC: Duke University Press, 2009), 306–30.

5. Moshe Barasch, *Icon: Studies in the History of an Idea* (New York: New York University Press, 1995), 4.

effects of that power would be more fruitful or harmful for the church. Icons (from the Greek noun *eikōn*, often translated as *image* or *likeness*; see Matt. 22:20; 1 Cor. 11:7) are traditionally defined as religious artistic representations, usually of Jesus, the mother Mary, the saints, or other subjects considered sacred. Such icons are understood as functioning as windows to the meanings of that which is represented.[6]

Early Christian writers developed a variety of theological approaches in arguing for or against images in the church. For example, Quintus Septimius Florens Tertullian, a North African Christian writer of the second and third centuries, argued against created images, based on his belief that they were idolatrous and therefore sinful as "the principle crime of the human race and the highest guilt of the world."[7] The concerns behind his argument were about the impacts that image-worship and image-making would have on believers and on Christianity, in that such activities had been defined in opposition to paganism's association with imagery.[8] Origen, also a North African second to third century Christian writer, argued against created imagery, based on his belief that a human-created image of God could never be a true image equal to the splendor of the original; he declared that spiritual beings cannot be represented through color and shape. His arguments were rooted in concepts about the nature of God in comparison to the nature of humans.[9] In support of images, the seventh-century Syrian monk John of Damascus argued that to venerate an icon was not necessarily the same as worshipping the matter of the icon or interpreting the matter as God. He believed it acceptable to honor matter made by God as Creator, and therein believed an image could be holy. In other words, John of Damascus did not believe that all images were necessarily worshipped. His interpretation of Exod. 20:4 was counter to the belief that to make an icon was necessarily idolatrous or that veneration of an icon was necessarily idol worship. He argued that because the historical Jesus as Christ existed in human form and was seen, representations of Jesus could be created in art. John was concerned with what he considered to be an urgent political matter—the continuation of

---

6. Diane Apostolos-Cappadona, *Dictionary of Christian Art* (New York: Continuum, 1994), 165.

7. Tertullian, *On Idolatry (De idololatria)*, trans. S. Thelwall, Early Christian Writings, http://www.earlychristianwritings.com/text/tertullian02.html.

8. Barasch, *Icon*, 109–23.

9. Origen, *Contra Celsus* II, *De principiis* I, and *Commentary on John*, trans. Roberts-Donaldson, Early Christian Writings, http://www.earlychristianwritings.com/text/origen162.html, http://www.earlychristianwritings.com/text/origen122.html, and http://www.earlychristianwritings.com/text/origen-john1.html; also see Barasch, *Icon*, 127–39.

the church and its theology in the spirit of the founding apostles.[10] An example of a surviving icon of the early church is *Christ Pantocrator* (sixth century).[11]

Later debates in other divisions of the church were at times as similar to as they were different from the early debates. As a part of the sixteenth-century German Protestant Reform Movement, which began as an attempt to reform the Catholic Church and resulted in a new church division, Martin Luther argued for the use of paintings in the church on the grounds that he believed they did no harm and could be used to illustrate the theology of "the Word" to the illiterate. He believed that images could help with "remembrance and better understanding" of "the Word."[12] Toward this end, he collaborated with the artist Lucas Cranach the Elder, and the result was works such as Cranach's *Wittenberg Altarpiece* (1547). This altarpiece consists of a triptych (a work consisting of three painted or carved panels that are hinged together) that shows Luther and other Protestant leaders conducting church sacraments, and in a fourth panel below the triptych Luther is shown presenting the crucified Christ to the membership through preaching.[13]

In more recent years, much of the religious subject art that would have been commissioned by and displayed in churches during earlier periods is displayed in museums and galleries, with debates about the most controversial works often taking place in the public arena through popular news reporting media that include newspapers, television, and the Internet. For example, at the turn of the twenty-first century, a National Catholic Report competition headed by the Catholic nun and art historian Sister Wendy Beckett called for a more inclusive representation of Jesus for the new millennium. Although the winning painting by Jane McKenzie entitled *Jesus of the People* (1999) has been embraced by many, it also has been condemned by those who are unwilling to accept it as an authentic and acceptable representation of Jesus, because it is not the white Jesus they are use to seeing. McKenzie presents Jesus in the image of a black man surrounded by symbols that highlight the multiculturalism of the

10. St. John of Damascus, "Apologia Against Those Who Decry Holy Images," in *On Holy Images,* trans. Mary H. Allies (London: Thomas Baker, 1898), http://www.fordham.edu/halsall/basis/johndamascus-images.asp; also see Barasch, *Icon,* 185–253.

11. *Christ Pantocrator*, 13–14 cent., Byzantine mosaic at Scala Archives, http://www.scalarchives.com/web/index.asp. Also, see Jaroslav Pelikan, *The Illustrated Jesus Through the Centuries* (New Haven, CT: Yale University Press, 1997), 59, 249.

12. Martin Luther, *Church and the Ministry II* in *Luther's Works,* vol. 40, ed. Conrad Bergendoff (Philadelphia: Fortress Press, 1958), 99–100.

13. Lucas Cranach the Elder, *Wittenberg Altarpiece*, 1547, painting, at http://smarthistory.khanacademy.org/cranachs-wittenberg-altarpiece.html.

world.[14] Among the most well-known representations of Jesus as white with European features are in Michelangelo di Lodovico Buonarroti Simoni's Sistine Chapel ceiling (1508-1512),[15] Leonardo da Vinci's *Last Supper* (1495–1498),[16] and Warner Sallman's *Head of Christ* (1941),[17] just to name a few.

Sallman's illustration of Christ with blond hair and European features continues to be the most popular Protestant representation of Jesus worldwide. Not only has this image been widely used for global missionary efforts, it distances Jesus from his Jewish heritage. Sallman had experience as a commercial illustrator, and he approached the creation and distribution of this art piece more as a commercial illustration than as a fine art painting. The widespread popularity of *Head of Christ* has been due to massive marketing efforts. This image was distributed with Bibles, and placed on everything from conversion pamphlets to Sunday school books to church bulletins, billboards, buttons, lamp shades, clocks, posters, cards distributed to US soldiers during World War II, and more. In *Icons of American Protestantism: The Art of Warner Sallman*, David Morgan states that in 1994, Warner Press, as copyright holders of the image, stated in a biography of Sallman that *Head of Christ* has been reproduced five hundred million times.[18] During much of the twentieth century it was not unusual to find this illustration hanging on the walls of some white and black churches as well as in many white and black American households.

In *The Illustrated Jesus Through the Centuries*, Jaroslav Pelikan categorizes Sallman's illustration as a representation of "Christ mysticism" or of Christ as "the bridegroom of the soul." Pelikan defines mysticism in this context as an experience of immediate oneness with Ultimate Reality.[19] Paul Tillich defines Ultimate Reality as that which "underlies every reality, and characterizes the whole appearing world as non–ultimate, preliminary, transitory and finite"; in art, Ultimate Reality expresses the artist's honest search for ultimate meaning in relation to his or her culture.[20] Pelikan associates Christ as bridegroom with the

14. Janet McKenzie, *Jesus of the People*, 1999, painting, at http://www.janetmckenzie.com/joppage1.html.

15. Michelangelo di Lodovico Buonarroti Simoni, The Sistine Chapel ceiling, 1508–1512, frescoes, Vatican, at http://www.vatican.va/various/cappelle/sistina_vr/.

16. Leonardo da Vinci, *Last Supper*, 15th cent., tempera mural, Santa Maria delle Grazie, Milan at Oxford Art Online, http:// www.oxfordartonline.com.

17. Warner Sallman's *Head of Christ*, 1941, illustration, Warner Sallman Collection, at http://www.warnersallman.com/collection/images/head-of-christ/.

18. David Morgan, ed., *Icons of American Protestantism: The Art of Warner Sallman* (New Haven: Yale University Press, 1996), 211.

19. Pelikan, *Illustrated Jesus*, 132.

German hymn "Seelenbraütigam, O du Gottes Lamm!" ("Bridegroom of the soul, thou lamb of God!"), which was written by the founder of the Herrnhut Moravian Church, Count Nikolaus Ludwig von Zinzendorf.[21] People around the world continue to be exposed to Sallman's interpretation of Christ through missionary efforts and Internet exposure, and just as there were debates about it in the twentieth century, the debates about its effectiveness as an authentic sentiment of Christ's image continue.[22] Sallman and others who have participated in the massive distribution of his *Head of Christ* and other Christ illustrations have understood the power of images in influencing perceptions and beliefs in the name of the Great Commission.

Considered the first western Christian theologian to construct a full theology of art, Paul Tillich argued that art can communicate theological and spiritual messages as powerfully and at times more powerfully than words. In his focus on the religious role of fine art painting, he suggested that art can function as a revealer of messages that speak to the spirit, and in doing so can communicate concepts more clearly that words. Tillich declared that language is not just bound to the spoken word but is also present in the silent language of the visual arts. He declared that through their art, artists have the ability to "express the dynamics in the depths of society which come from the past and run toward the future."[23] In that a culture can be understood through its art, what do western representations of the white Jesus as Christ say about western cultures and concepts of *chosen* versus *Other*?

IDEAS OF THE *CHOSEN* VERSUS THE *OTHER* IN THE IMAGE OF GOD

Every artwork functions as an investment by someone to send a message, and many of the more widely successful works are easily comprehended based on simplified and organized systems of representation and rhetoric. Developed for easy interpretations of the world, based upon a simplistic order, colonial systems collapse into stereotypical codes for recognizing the *chosen* versus the *Other* or ideas of *us* versus *them*.[24] In cultures obsessed with sameness versus

20. Paul Tillich, *On Art and Architecture*, eds. John Dillenberger and Jane Dillenberger (New York: Crossroad, 1989), 140, 232.

21. Pelikan, *Illustrated Jesus*, 131–32.

22. For examples of twentieth-century criticisms of Warner Sallman's *Head of Christ*, see Colleen McDannell, *Material Christianity: Religion and Popular Culture in America* (New Haven, CT: Yale University Press, 1995), 189.

23. Tillich, *On Art and Architecture*, xiii, 23, and 29.

24. Maurice Berger, *How Art Becomes History* (New York: Icon Editions, 1992), 79, 109–10.

difference, differences in appearance become important as reflections of the concept of race. Sometimes the artist's intended message and the community's interpretations and uses of the art are in agreement with each other, and sometimes they are not. An artwork may function as an expression of a culture, and therein viewers' reactions to it and uses of it function as measuring sticks of particular beliefs within the culture. Although I recognize that artists can and often do function as critics of mainstream beliefs and perceptions, and some even function as prophetic messengers, I also recognize that they are products and participants in their societies. Through their art, they can reflect and promote messages that can reinforce the more complex and controversial beliefs within their cultures. But for the purposes of this essay, less attention is given to the artist's underlying intent and process than to how communities interpret the art and what they do with it.[25] Martien E. Brinkman recognizes in *Jesus Incognito* that artworks are not just products of individual artists, but also "expressions of a culture in which artists are the antennae" with the capacity through their work to place a spotlight on the major concerns in a culture.[26] Embedded in the continual marketing and popularity of the white Christ are a series of simplistic points of order. For example, continued widespread use of representations for missionary purposes, such as Warner Sallman's *Head of Christ,* can be easily interpreted as supporting the concept of racial hierarchy rooted in western cultures. In the west, and particularly in the United States, where this concept is rooted in the very systems and conventions by which we live, race has been a central issue in the church as well as in the wider political and social cultures. In *Race Matters,* Cornel West defines culture as being "as much a structure as the economy or politics; it is rooted in institutions such as families, schools, churches, synagogues, mosques, and communication industries . . . Similarly, the economy and politics are not only influenced by values but also promote particular cultural ideas of the good life and good society."[27] Deborah Tannen states in *The Argument Culture* that "culture, in a sense, is an environment of narratives that we hear repeatedly until they seem to make self-evident sense in explaining human behavior."[28] The concept of the white Christ is such a narrative. Cultural narratives help to create and

---

25. For examples of discussions on artists' moral and prophetic roles, see M. C. Richads, *Opening Our Moral Eye: Essays, Talks, & Poems Embracing Creativity and Community,* ed. Deborah J. Haynes (Hudson, NY: Lindisfarne Press, 1996), and Deborah J. Haynes, *The Vocation of the Artist* (New York: Cambridge University Press, 1997).

26. Martien E. Brinkman, *Jesus Incognito: The Hidden Christ in Western Art Since 1960* (New York: Rodopi, 2012), 10.

27. Cornel West, *Race Matters* (Boston: Beacon, 1993), 12.

reinforce belief systems, ways of living, and thus communal and individual understandings of what it means to be human. The narrative of white racial superiority is repeatedly communicated in US culture and around the world through missionary efforts and mass media. It is embedded in the very structure of our systems of believing and living. We are influenced by it in ways about which we are consciously aware and in ways that affect us unconsciously.

Marketed use of representations such as Sallman's *Head of Christ* for missionary purposes support the continuation of accepting, without critical analysis, images that aid the continued servitude and lower economic class status of many persons of color. This is done based upon specific interpretations of Scripture in order to support unchanging approaches to class.[29] The arguments presented in the 1706 pamphlet entitled "The Negro Christianized"—widely accepted as written by the New England Puritan minister and slave-owner Cotton Mather—is typical of the types of historical arguments made in support of the Great Commission. Slave owners made up Mather's intended audience of readers. He tells them that it is their duty to "Christianize" their slaves based upon Jesus' commission to the apostles. Although he declares his concern for the souls of the slaves, one does not have to read very closely to realize that Mather's call to his fellow slave owners is more about saving the masters' souls and the continuation of their economic status. Mather justifies the continuation of slave ownership by referring to biblical texts such as Paul's statements in Eph. 6, where Paul instructs slaves to obey their masters as they obey Christ. Mather suggests that it is God's will that the enslaved exist as such. Here he perpetuates the argument that one's class status has nothing to do with human actions and power dynamics, but is a *natural* state based upon a colonial interpretation of what constitutes God's will. Mather argues that it is actually more spiritually and economically profitable to the master to save the "miserable Soul" of the slave from ignorance and sin as an act of charity. He states that the slave owner will receive an "unspeakable Glory" by teaching the slaves the Gospels, bringing them to salvation through Jesus Christ, clothing them, and not overworking them.[30] Mather's arguments reinforce simplistic definitions of what it means to

28. Deborah Tannen, *The Argument Culture: Moving from Debate to Dialogue* (New York: Random House, 1998), 13. Also, quoted in Benjamin Radford, *Media Mythmakers: How Journalists, Activists, and Advertisers Mislead Us* (Amherst, NY: Prometheus Books, 2003), 12.

29. Katie Geneva Cannon, "Cutting Edge: Christian Imperialism and the Transatlantic Slave Trade," *Journal of Feminist Studies in Religion* 24, no. 1 (2008): 127–34.

30. Cotton Mather, *The Negro Christianized: An Essay to Excite and Assist that Good Work, the Instruction of Negro-Servants in Christianity* (1706), Zea E-Books in American Studies, Book 5, http://digitalcommons.unl.edu/zeaamericanstudies/5.

be fully human, through an acceptance of class divides as a normalcy that exists only because of God's will, a will that Mather suggests the "good Christian" should not question.

The continued recycling of stereotypical images of non-western cultures in western art is evidence that our awareness of our common humanity has not developed enough, as Jan Nederveen Pieterse states in *White on Black*.[31] He argues that past fears and antagonisms continue to be encoded in much of the imagery we are exposed to the most, even though some of the past usages are no longer consciously a part of the western mentality. Themes and symbols that have their roots in institutionalized racism of earlier periods, such as the Atlantic slave trade era, continue to be recycled as acceptable imagery. They are recycled in ways that reinforce both old and newly modified stereotypes of non-western cultures and people of color. Pieterse highlights how created images of the white Christ were used in conjunction with images of free blacks to expand definitions of race. He presents C. Jetses's illustration *Freedom as a Gift of Christ* (1913) as an example.[32] In his illustration, Jetses presents a black couple holding their infant up to the white Christ as their Savior and as the giver of the gift of freedom from chattel bondage. This image ignores concepts such as justice and love of others in Jesus' teachings. Instead freedom from enslavement is presented as a gift from the white Christ, with this being the same type of image of Christ that had been previously used to support slavery as a biblical teaching. (cf. Eph. 6:5-9) Jetses's illustration also communicates what had become a normative stereotypical approach to representing and defining persons of African descent in western cultures as "Other" and as lower in the cultural hierarchy, that is to say through the absence of clothing in images with fully clothed persons of European descent. Jetses presents the black female partly clothed, while the black male and the infant are nude; only the white Christ is presented fully clothed.[33] Jetses' illustration embodies what Pieterse describes as the way Europeans understood and represented the African continent and its people, namely as a contradiction of abundance and scarcities:

> The icon of the nineteenth-century savage is determined by absences: the absence, or scarcity of clothing, possessions, attributes of civilization. . . . What Africa did have in abundance, also according to Europeans, was nature. The iconography of Africans as

---

31. Jan Nederveen Pieterse, *White on Black: Images of Africa and Blacks in Western Popular Culture* (New Haven, CT: Yale University Press, 1992), 9, 11.

32. Ibid., 63.

33. Ibid., 35, 63.

savages was determined by the association of nature and flora—often the kind of wild overwhelming landscape which makes human beings appear small. To the image of Africa as wilderness belongs the tropical rain forest with its lush vegetatation, and the jungle which is proverbially "inpenetrable." Explorers with machetes, . . . This explorer imagery suggests the them of *terra nullius*, that is, vacant land, essentially uninhabited or at least uncultivated, and therefore rightfully available to colonization. The assimilation of the African interior to "nature," the denial of African history, the marginalization of African peoples in discourse and imagery—all formed part of a rhetoric that was to culminate in colonialism.[34]

Therefore, images of the white Christ such as Jetses's are as much about what is not represented as they are about what is.

Because it has been distributed and widely embraced as the preferred type of image of Christ, the white Christ communicates and supports the belief that all other representational approaches are not authentic and therein are less important, not only in the church but in the history of art as well. In other words, there is the accepted conclusion that that which has been seen and revered the most is necessarily the most important and justifiably authoritative. Who is entitled to contribute to the canons of faith and history is the issue here.[35] Although changes are beginning to happen in some parts of the church and in the academy, historical representations such as the following were always absent from major historical canons and were considered less authentic and necessarily of secondary importance in comparison to the white Christ: the black Madonna and child statue *Our Lady of the Montserrat* of Spain (artist and date unknown)[36]; Monika Liu Ho-Peh's depiction of an Asian Christ in the painting *The Stilling of the Tempest* (1950s)[37]; Josè Clemente Orozco's painting of the Christ of liberation shown with a raised fist and an axe that he has used to cut down his cross in *The Migration of the Spirit* (1932–34)[38]; William H.

34. Pieterse, *White on Black*, 35.

35. Berger, *How Art Becomes History*, xix–xx.

36. Artworks such as this from early church eras particularly are highly revered in Africa and parts of Europe. Scholars have disagreed about the significance of the dark skin tones in statues and paintings of the black Madonna and Christ child. Some argue that the skin tones suggests that perhaps the historical Mary and Jesus had darker skin tones, while others say the darker skin tones have nothing to do with race and instead are reflective of early pagan influences on Christianity. For more information, see China Galland, *Longing for Darkness: Tara and the Black Madonna* (New York: Viking, 1990).

37. Monika Liu Ho-Peh, *The Stilling of the Tempest*, 1950s. See Arno Lehmann, *Christian Art in Africa and Asia* (Saint Louis: Concordia Publishing House, 1969). Reprinted in Pelikan, *Illustrated Jesus*, 251.

Johnson's painting of a black Christ in *Mount Calvary* (1944)[39]; Prentiss Taylor's litograph *Christ in Alabama* (1932) of a black madonna and child in which the Mother Mary and crucified Christ are shown beside a cotton field[40]; Romare Bearden's abstract painting of Christ in *He is Risen (The Passion of Christ Series)* (1945)[41]; František Drtikol's fine art photograph of a female Christ on the cross in *Female Crucifixion* (1913)[42]; and Renee Cox's fine art photograph in which she poses as a nude black Christ with black apostles, except for Judas who appears to be white, in *Yo Mama's Last Supper* (1996)[43], just to mention a few. The perpetuation of the myth that the realistically rendered white Christ is superior to all other representational approaches supports the perception that the main issue is about appearances as signs of cultural and spiritual value, whereas in reality the main concern is the power to control outcomes in one's own favor. Historical writers such as Cotton Mather who supported slavery along with oppressive approaches to "making disciples of all nations," like leaders throughout church history, understood that "holiness" is power. Therefore, ideas of the white Christ as necessarily the most "holy" of images reinforces the power of this myth's creators and supporters, along with the continued unequal treatment of all others.

Representations of the white Christ that are most effective in their support of traditional western cultural hiearchies are usually rendered in a realistic style. In other words, the style of the art has strong influences in reinforcing general beliefs that as religious subject art, the images are to be interpreted as void of symbolism. If the works that are most successfully mass marketed are those that can be easily comprehended based on simplified and organized systems of representation and rhetoric, and art rendered in a realistic style is perceived by most as easier to interpret, then messages that suggest Christ's "whiteness" and

38. Josè Clemente Orozco, *The Epic of American Civilization: Migration of the Spirit*, 1932–34, fresco mural, Baker Library, Dartmouth College, Hanover, NH, at http://www.bridgemanart.com/asset/33583/Orozco-Jose-Clemente-1883-1949/Modern-Migration-of-the-Spirit-from-The-Epic-of-A?search.

39. William H. Johnson, *Mount Calvary*, 1944, oil on paperboard, Smithsonian Art Museum, Washington, D.C., at http://americanart.si.edu/collections/search/artwork/?id=11894.

40. Prentiss Taylor, *Christ in Alabama*, 1932, lithograph, Library of Congress, Washington, DC, at http://www.loc.gov/pictures/item/92522311/.

41. Romare Bearden, *He is Risen (The Passion of Christ Series)*, 1945, oil on gessoed board, Indianapolis Museum of Art, Indianapolis, Indiana, at http://www.imamuseum.org/collections/artwork/he-risen-passion-christ-series-bearden-romare-howard.

42. František Drtikol, *Female Crucifixion*, 1913, gelatin silver print, The Israel Museum, Jerusalem, at http://www.imj.org.il/imagine/collections/item.asp?itemNum=309058.

43. Renee Cox, *Yo Mama's Last Supper*, 1999, color photography, Renee Cox, at http://www.reneecox.org/.

that are realistically rendered such as Sallman's *Head of Christ* are more likely to be easily interpreted and successfully marketed through missionary efforts. In other words, the average art viewer is less likely to interpret a realistically rendered painting of Christ as embedded with symbolism than he or she would a painting of an abstractly rendered Christ. Therefore, it is to the missionary's advantage to use images of the white Christ such as Sallman's when trying to forward colonial approaches to the Great Commission. This is not to say that from the artist's point of view there is necessarily no intended symbolism in the art.[44]

The white Christ supports a complex and interrelated colonial understanding of "whiteness" as a necessary requirement to be counted among God's "chosen" and among the fully human worthy of power in this world. The American obsession with the concept of race is declared justified through this narrative. The "American Dream" as a capitalistic dream also is rooted in and supports this image. An example of this support can be seen in the placing of Sallman's *Head of Christ* on a US postage stamp in 2010.[45] The capitalism of the "American Dream" is interrelated with and supported by justifications of the white Christ as the most "true" and authentic icon.

In her essay "Representations of Whiteness in the Black Imagination," bell hooks discusses how "whiteness" is seen from the black perspective, and in doing so she gives insights about the concept of the "Other." According to hooks, unfortunately the fantasy of "whiteness" as synonymous with goodness and normalcy detracts attention from the realities of how "whiteness" functions as power and privilege. She discusses how although the legality of racial apartheid is no longer the norm, the habits that support institutionalized white supremacy continue.[46] These habits include the continued marketing of art images of the white Christ as the norm, to the point that these images often are not questioned or deconstructed. According to hooks, the way blacks "see" whiteness is informed and shaped by a psychic state: "Systems of domination, imperialism, colonialism, and racism actively coerce black folks to internalize negative perceptions of blackness, to be self-hating."[47] Yet, within the black

---

44. For more information, see Winborne, "Theological Significance of Normative Visual Preferences."

45. "Warner Sallman's 'Head of Christ' to be Featured on Postage Stamp," The Warner Sallman Collection, 2009, http://www.warnersallman.com/2009/11/30/warner-sallmans-head-of-christ-to-be-featured-on-postage-stamp/.

46. bell hooks, "Representations of Whiteness in the Black Imagination," in *Black on White: Black Writers on What It Means to Be White*, ed. David R. Roediger (New York: Schocken Books, 1998), 41–42.

47. Ibid., 39.

imagination is the ability to also reinterpret images of whiteness with suspicion and in ways that sometimes consciously and sometimes unconsciously allows blacks to put themselves into the pictures of whiteness they see. In other words, there is a complexity in the ways blacks and whites live with the powers of "whiteness," and although originally "Christianized" by forceful means, ultimately as Katie Cannon has said, blacks reimage the faith.[48]

Although much of western visual art has played significant roles in reflecting and advancing the Great Commission in oppressive ways, art also has the capability to instead play major roles in promoting new and more fruitful approaches to the Great Commission. Like John of Damascus, I disagree with interpretations of Exod. 20:4 as stating that icons and visual art are necessarily idolatrous. I agree with Katie Cannon who has defined white supremacy as "the Trojan horse within organized Christianity" and as idolatry.[49] Like Cannon, I believe the real idolatry in the church is through abuses of power in the name of Christianity, such as the myth that God supports white supremacy through uses of the white Christ as a tool that aids forced "Christianizing" in the name of the Great Commission.

The theorist Rudolf Arnheim argues that art has played important roles, not just as illustrations to support oral and written texts, but as original texts in their own rights as well. According to Arnheim, like oral and written forms, visual forms directly influence how we perceive and interpret or "see," and therein how we think and understand the world. He concludes that we understand the things we "see" once we cast them into our particular "manageable models" with our "manageable models" determined by our ways of categorizing the persons and things we "see."[50] Our ways of experiencing the world are influenced by how limited or expanded our ways of categorizing are, and this directly relates to how we act within the world. This includes how we define, interact, and treat others. The white Christ supports limited and simplistic categorizations of God and God's creation. New as well as greater attention to the existing diversity of approaches are needed in order to move past the colonial mythical narrative that supports embracing the Great Commission (Matt. 28:19) in ways that justify economically and politically driven oppressive actions. These new and diverse approaches must include the expansion of our "manageable models" beyond the limited ways most define

48. Cannon, "Christian Imperialism and the Transatlantic Slave Trade," 127–34.

49. Ibid.

50. Rudolf Arnheim, *Visual Thinking* (Berkeley: University of California Press, 1969), and Margaret R. Miles, *Image as Insight: Visual Understanding in Western Christianity and Secular Culture* (Boston: Beacon, 1985), and Winborne, "Theological Significance of Normative Visual Preferences."

persons and the Christian God based upon racial concepts and categorizations. I call for a type of deconstructive analysis of Christian art, in which questions such as the following may be asked: How do the content and form come together in ways to influence interpretation? What biblical and cultural interpretations and beliefs influenced the artist? What were the social, political, and economic conditions of the culture at the time the art piece was created? What was the main concern in the culture of the church at the time? Is there an idea of *chosen* versus *Other* represented? Who benefits the most from the main messages communicated through the representation and why? Finally, I suggest greater focus on how to begin to truly live and embrace Jesus' call to the apostles in ways centered first in his command to love one another as he has loved us (John 13:34-35). Perhaps when all is said and done, the most powerful way to teach others about Christianity is by living it, beginning with a look at our capacity to love in relationship to Jesus' concerns about justice and the poor (cf. Luke 4:16-20, 6:20-21). This may be the most fruitful starting point for countering perceptions of *chosen* versus *Other* as communicated through images of the white Christ. Instead of accepting that a few have the right to define and represent all others, we must be willing to truly see and hear the messages of the interrelatedness of our faith and art histories, if we are to stop making the same mistakes over and over again.

8

———————

The Great Commission in the Face of Suffering as *Minjung*

Michelle Sungshin Lim

"There remains an experience of incomparable value. We have for once learnt to see the great events of world below, from the perspective of the outcast, the suspects, the maltreated, the powerless, the oppressed, the reviled—in short, from the perspective of those who suffer."
– Dietrich Bonhoeffer[1]

"You don't understand what theology is unless you have looked in the face of suffering, unless you have become an atheist in the presence of pain."
– Frederick Herzog[2]

INTRODUCTION

A small group of children ages from eight to ten were running, jumping, and hopping to different cars selling baguettes on the streets of downtown Abidjan.[3] It was around nine o'clock in the morning and it was already hot. As I observed these children through a car window, I was imagining the children in suburbs in America where children of the same age would be going to school, either dropped off by their parents or riding the school bus. As our mission team was

1. Dietrich Bonhoeffer, *Letters and Papers from Prison,* ed. Eberhard Bethge (New York: Touchstone , 1997).

2. Frederick Herzog, "Let Us Still Praise Famous Men," *Theology from the Belly of the Whale: A Frederick Herzog Reader,* ed. Joerg Rieger (Harrisburg, PA: Trinity Press International, 1999): 54–57.

3. Abidjan is the second largest city of *Cote d' Ivoire* on the west coast of Africa.

leaving the city, travelling on the only highway to the northern part of Cote D'Ivoire, I saw many women, young and old, hunching over a small black hill picking up soot from fire grounds. A missionary pastor who has been stationed there for twelve years explained to me that these women make about $1 to $2 a day picking up soot by hand without safety gloves.

On the way to our designated village, I saw many women on the road piggybacking their babies and carrying bundles of wood and other stuff. Many children were topless and barefoot, carrying buckets of water that seemed too heavy for their small bodies to bear.

As a medium-sized jeep carried my body, accustomed to a culture of abundance, of capitalism, and the advanced infrastructures of the Global North, two words echoed in my heart and mind: *dignity* and *justice* for all humanity especially for women and children in the Global South. They are the invisible and voiceless on the map of the world as I write this essay while the media pompously report on the lives of rich and famous in both economic and political spheres. While capitalism and the revolution of digital technologies spread in the name of globalization, the poor in the Global South as well as in the Global North continuously suffer from the lack of basics, such as clean water, food and housing. Currently, "more than half the planet still lives on less than $4 a day, and 2.4 billion people live on less than $2 a day."[4] The reality of the poor is described by Gustavo Gutiérrez:

> [P]overty means death: lack of food and housing, the inability to attend properly to health and education needs, the exploitation of workers, permanent unemployment, the lack of respect for one's human dignity, and unjust limitations placed on personal freedom in the areas of self-expression, politics, and religion. Poverty is a situation that destroys peoples, families, and individuals; Medellín and Puebla called it "institutionalized violence" (to which must be added the equally unacceptable violence of terrorism and repression.)[5]

4. According to Forbes Magazine February 2012, the rank of wealthiest nations is listed below. However, the wealthiest nation does not mean that they would acquire more power to exercise among the nations. Global North and South do not refer geographically but instead are based on the nation-state economy strengths. For instance, newly arising nation-stated such as Brazil and Mexico are located in Global South. 1. Qatar GDP (PPP): $88,222; 2. Luxembourg GDP (PPP): $81,466; 3. Singapore GDP (PPP): $56,994; 4. Norway GDP (PPP): $51, 959; 5. Brunei GDP (PPP): $48,333; 6. United Arab Emirates GDP (PPP): $47,439; 7. United States GDP (PPP): $46, 860; 8. Hong Kong GDP (PPP): $45, 944; 9. Switzerland GDP (PPP): $41,950; 10. Netherlands GDP (PPP); $40,793.

I begin this essay by sketching scenes of the streets and villages of Cote d'Ivoire where, for the last few years, I have been involved in a project called E. T. (Education and Transformation) for children and women in the Global South, especially in the villages of Africa. The devastating and suffering scenes reveal the historical, political, and economic situations that were critically impacted under the rubric of western colonialism: namely, the process of globalization, the spread of capitalism, and the vestiges of patriarchal institutions and environmental degradation.

The poor in the Global South are victims of globalization and the predatory capitalism of transnational corporations that have profiteered from labor exploitation, particularly of women and children in the Global South. Money and political power are inseparably intertwined to favor the "wealthy," especially the superrich of the world, and the system is rigged in favor of "White-Supremacist-Capitalist-Patriarchy"[6] embedded in the Global South since Spanish, Portuguese, French, Dutch, English, and American ships arrived with their modern weapons.

The purpose of this essay is, first of all, an attempt at self-critical analysis through reflection, reevaluation, and inquiry into the purpose and the mission

5. Gustavo Gutiérrez, *A Theology of Liberation: History, Politics, and Salvation*, trans. and ed. Sister Caridad Inda and John Eagleson, rev. ed. (Maryknoll, NY: Orbis Books, 2000), xxi.

6. bell hooks, *Outlaw Culture: Resisting Representations* (Routledge: London, 1994), 197–206. See also Howard Zinn, *A People's History of The United States* (New York: HaperPerennial, 2005), 1–58, 171–210. hooks explains the notion that the domination and colonization of Indians and non-whites by whites starts in grade school in American history class. She recollects her memory in an American class as follows, "We taught that the Indians would have conquered and dominated white explorers if they could have but they were simply not strong or smart enough. Embedded in all these teachings was the assumption that it was the whiteness of these explores in the 'New World' that gave them greater power. The word 'whiteness' was never used. The key word, the one that was synonymous with whiteness, was 'civilization.' Hence, we were made to understand at a young age that whatever cruelties were done to the indigenous peoples of this country, the 'Indians,' was necessary to bring the great gift of civilization. Domination, it became clear in our young minds, was central to the project of civilization. And if civilization was good and necessary despite the costs, then that had to mean domination was equally good" (199). She further explains that the self-righteous acts of the white domination were done as if there was no civilization in other parts of the world other than the "white" race. "The idea that it was natural for people who were different to meet and struggle for power merged with the idea that it was natural for whites to travel around the world civilizing nonwhites. The assumption that domination is not only natural but central to the civilizing process is deeply rooted in our cultural mind-set. As a nation we have made little transformative progress to eradicate sexism and racism precisely because most citizens of the United States believe in their heart of hearts that it is natural for a group or an individual to dominate over others. Most folks do not believe that it is wrong to dominate, oppress, and exploit other people" (199–200).

of the church. It is the pursuit of a community that seeks to do justice and secure equity for all—however idealistic and farfetched that sounds.

Clearly, witnessing poverty stricken Africa in the Global South leads me to reflect deeply on a profound question of what it means to be engaged in a meaningful Christian praxis[7] in this postmodern world. In this essay, I will reexamine "Christ-praxis" by revisiting a leading Minjung biblical theologian's claim that *minjung* is *ochlos*. What kind of "Christ-praxis" should be at the heart of the church's mission in the twenty-first century? What is the task of theological education in preparing future ministers in the face of an oppressive and unjust system of "White-Supremacist-Capitalist-Patriarchy"? Joerg Rieger states,

> The task of theology is not primarily to shore up the field of hermeneutics, which has come under attack in a postmodern world, but to examine the Christian understanding of God's character and the encounter with Christ in light of the encounter with the underside of history, and to join in God's Work.[8]

The Poor as *Minjung, Ochlos*

The "crowds of people" or the multitudes that came to see Jesus Christ during his ministry were the masses at the low end of the social scale. They were the poor, the oppressed, and the sick, often the victims of injustice. They were treated as "non-persons" ostracized from their own by the Pharisees and Sadducees, and the Roman authority. Jesus Christ's main ministry, "Christ-praxis," was focused on feeding, healing, and teaching the crowds—the *ochlos-minjung*—demonstrating what it means to be a Christian disciple and what is the ensuing mission of the church for the future. It was the incarnate God in human form in the person of Jesus Christ who, faithfully and perfectly, revealed God's deepest compassion and mercy in the daily struggle of the poor, the oppressed, and the *ochlos-minjung*.

A Korean epithet, *minjung*[9] has been known by or was at least familiar to both Eastern and Western theological circles since the birth of Minjung

---

7. "Praxis" combines theory and practice or vice versa so that part benefits the other in order to build just and equitable communities within the global villages.

8. Joerg Rieger, *Remember the Poor: The Challenge to Theology in the Twenty-first Century* (Harrisburg, PA: Trinity Press International, 1998), 226.

9. The word *minjung* was and currently is not a popular word for many Korean Christians, including conservative pastors and theologians. It has a "Communist" nuance and the Korean peninsula is technically at war with North Korea, a Communist regime.

theology in the 1970s by a group of Korean theologians and some progressive Christian intellectuals. Minjung theology as a political theology of Korea meant standing and fighting for the liberation of the masses under political oppression and economic exploitation. Followers, urban labor workers, and critical intellectuals were labeled as cultural pariahs during the time of Korea's democratic struggle under severe military dictatorship in 1970s. Minjung theology is "doing theology" and "political theology of Korea" simultaneously. It is fighting against the powerful tyranny of a militaristic government, yearning for democratic government, and fighting for freedom of speech and human rights, especially for young female factory workers whose labor was severely exploited under dire work conditions. It was all swept neatly under the slogan of "Economic Industrialization of Korea in five years."[10]

Historically, the word *minjung* refers to a group of people trapped in the rigid Confucian patriarchal structure and class system of Korean society through the several different kingdoms/fiefdoms that ruled throughout its history. The *minjung* represents eighty percent of the entire population of Korea that belong to the lowest rung in social stratus. Usually, these people consisted of merchants, peasants, slaves, and women that were not of the literati class or members of the royal court. In pre-modern Korean society, one's class identity was passed onto the next generation.[11] The *minjung* were denied even basic education such as reading and writing, as basic and higher education were privileges limited to the ruling elite the aristocrats (literati).

The *minjung* class did not have rights to own land and property, and their purpose for existence was to serve their warlords and aristocrats. The lives of women and children that I have witnessed in Africa and the poor in the Global South replicate the lives of *minjung* of Korea,[12] for, by virtue of their social status, they, too, are economically exploited, politically oppressed, and silenced,

10. Kirsteen Kim, *The Holy Spirit in the World: A Global Conversation* (Maryknoll, NY: Orbis Books, 2007), 117. She describes Minjung theology as "developed on behalf of the *minjung*—that is, the masse, the poor, the oppressed—in the 1970s and '80s by Christian intellectuals, many of whom were arrested and imprisoned as subversives, but whose liberation praxis had worldwide influence through ecumenical channels. Within Korea, Christian activists played a leading role in the movements for democratic reforms in Korean and in ameliorating the workers' conditions."

11. Within five thousand years of Korean history, Korea was ruled by four different kingdoms. The last kingdom was the Joseon Dynasty until it became annexed by Japan in 1910. So the author opines that the pre-modern period of Korea is before 1910. Therefore, the modern period starts from 1910, coinciding with the start of Japanese occupation. After thirty-six years of Japan's colonization, Korea became a modernized state.

12. The usage of the word *minjung* was limited to the particular context of Korea's situation in 1970s in the midst of fighting against a military regime. Nevertheless, I will be extending the use of word *minjung*

and culturally despised. They are classified and opposed by the "Other" through the cultural lens of "white-supremacy-capitalism-patriarchy" of European and North American descent.[13]

The poor are *minjung-ochlos*, according to a leading biblical *minjung* theologian, Ahn Byung Mu, who focused on the social characters of the crowds or multitudes of Jesus Christ.[14] He asserts that *ochlos*, the crowds of Galilee, constituted the poor, sick (both physically and mentally), outcasts, and women that constituted the lowest class in Israeli society. These were the followers of Jesus Christ for whom he had compassion and mercy. Not only did Jesus Christ heal the sick but he also taught and preached on the issues of justice, peace, caring, evil structures, and hope for the "Kingdom of God."

Focusing on the word *ochlos* in the Gospel according to Mark, Ahn differentiates between the uses of the Greek words *laos and ochlos*. Ahn points out that the word *laos*, which refers to "the people of Israel as the people of God," appears approximately two thousand times in Septuagint. On the other hand, the word *laos* is used only twice in the entire Gospel of Mark (14:2), referring to the chief priest and lawyers. According to Ahn, Mark used *ochlos* to indicate the crowds who followed Jesus everywhere and gathered around him (Mark 2:4, 13; 3:9, 20, 32; 4:1; 5:21, 31; 8:1; 10:1). Not only were they called as sinners, but they were also isolated from the center of society (2:13-17).[15] Moreover, Ahn asserts that Mark is the first writer who introduced the word *ochlos* as specifically referring to the crowds of Jesus. It is therefore imperative to pay attention to the social characteristics of *ochlos*. Ahn claims that Mark had attempted to demonstrate Jesus' particular relationship with them (*ochlos*).[16]

> It is certain that in the New Testament, Mark is the first writer to introduce the term *ochlos*. It does not appear in any New Testament

---

and its identity to the people who have been oppressed, alienated, silenced, unheard, and uneducated because they are poor and, therefore, invisible.

13. Edward Said, *Orientalism* (New York: Vintage, 1979).

14. *Minjung* theology is described in the book *Voices from the Margin: Interpreting the Bible in the Third World* as follows, "*Minjung* theology is one of the most provocative and challenging theologies to emerge from Asia. As its starting-point for doing theology and reading the Bible, it takes the *minjung*, the people who are politically oppressed, socially alienated, economically exploited and kept uneducated in cultural and intellectual matters." R. S. Sugirtharajah, ed., *Voices from the Margin: Interpreting the Bible in the Third World* (Maryknoll, NY: Orbis Books, 2006), 87.

15. Byung Mu Ahn, "Jesus and the Minjung in the Gospel of Mark," in *Voices from the Margin: Interpreting the Bible in the Third World*, 85–104 (89–90).

16. Ibid., 87–89.

writing before Mark, but the documents written after Mark, such as the other Gospels and Acts, contain this word many times, proving the influence of Mark. *Ochlos* appears three times in Revelation, which we know to have been written during the persecution of Christians. (7.9; 19.1, 6). It is noteworthy that in the Epistles of Paul, which were written before Mark, this word does not appear even once.[17]

Ahn explains the social character of *ochlos:* they consisted of tax collectors, sinners, and outcasts who located on the periphery of Israeli society. He posits that the *ochlos* "are contrasted with the ruling class of that time and that Jesus was criticized for associating with the *ochlos* . . . it becomes evident that the *ochlos* were the condemned and alienated class."[18] Moltmann identifies the crowds of Jesus Christ, *ochlos,* as follows,

> The "crowd" consists of "sinners", that is, those excluded from, Jewish society. They are the impoverished country people, people off (*ha'aretz*), without property, as John 7 and 12 show, people who are not economically in a position to keep the Law of Israel, and are hence looked upon by the Pharisees as *messa perditioni*, the multitude of lost: "Cursed are the rabble who do not know the Law" (cf. John 7:49).[19]

In addition to emphasizing the social character of *ochlos,* Ahn highlights Jesus Christ's attitude towards the *ochlos* in three points. First, he asserts that Jesus Christ showed a deep compassion towards them and treated them as if they were without a shepherd (Mark 6:34). The shepherd implies a ruler and a caregiver.[20] Second, he emphasizes that Jesus Christ deliberately refers to the *ochlos* as his mother and brother in order to establish "kinship" promoting "a new community (family)."[21] Third, he states that Jesus taught these uneducated *ochlos* by adopting simple metaphoric narratives to ensure and empower them, especially the "Kingdom of God" and God's special love towards to them.[22]

17. Ibid., 88.

18. Ibid., 91.

19. Jürgen Moltmann, *Experiences in Theology: Ways and Forms of Christian Theology* (Minneapolis: Fortress Press, 2000), 253.

20. Byung Mu Ahn, "Jesus and the Minjung in the Gospel of Mark," 90–91.

21. Ibid., 91.

22. Ibid.,

For Ahn, identifying *ochlos* as *minjung* has been critically important for doing the theology of "God-walk," not "God-talk" for the oppressed *minjung* in their effort towards liberation from pervasive oppression. Ahn defines theology as follows:

> Theology was neither for the oppressors nor for the prestigious. It is for sufferers and for the oppressed, to serve. That particular place was the place of incarnation of Jesus, it is the place for his suffering, and place for his second coming, 'Parousia'. That place was Galilee, in the midst of sinners and place of laborers. It was the place of *Ochlos*.[23]

Where are the *ochlos* in the postmodern world? After five hundred years of "White-Supremacist-Capitalist-Patriarchy" and in the process of globalization, the gulf between "rich" and "poor" nations has never been deeper or wider. For instance, the gap between the wealthiest nation in the Global North and the poorest nation in the Global South has become steeper than any time in history. Due to reserves of oil and natural gas, Qatar, the wealthiest nation, has a per capita GDP (purchasing-power parity, hereafter, PPP) of $88,222, compared to the poorest African nations, such as Burundi, Liberia, and the Democratic Republic of Congo, where GDPs (PPP) per capita are $400, $386 and $312 respectively.

In fact, according to the National Bureau of Economic research, the per capita GDP for African nations in sub-Saharan Africa is now less than what it was in 1974 that have been declined over 11 percent. From 1975–2000, the number of poor Africans increased from 140 million to 360 million.

In America, income inequality is steadily increasing. According a Congressional Budget Office (CBO) report, income from 1979 to 2007 for the bottom twenty percent of the population gained less than 20 percent, while income for the top one percent of Americans increased by 275 percent. According to the National Poverty Center and National Women's Law Center, the poverty rate for women climbed to 14.5 percent in 2010 from 13.9 percent in 2009, the highest rate in seventeen years. The extreme poverty rate among women rose to 6.3 percent in 2010 from 5.9 percent in 2009, the highest rate ever recorded. Over seventeen million women lived in poverty in 2010, including more than 7.5 million in extreme poverty, with an income below half the federal poverty line. Moreover, the poverty rate among the black and Hispanic women rose even more than the poverty rate of women in general.

---

23. Byung Mu Ahn, preface to *Jesus of Galilee* (Seoul: Korea Research Institute for Theological Studies, 1990). Preface.

The child poverty rate at 20.7 percent in 2009 jumped to 22 percent in 2010; 16.4 million children lived in poverty.[24]

Additionally, the decision-making power and economic and political strength still reside in the hands of several European nations and the United States. Therefore, policy-making decisions profoundly favor these nations. Not only do they hold and monopolize all the decision-making powers, but they also control the outcome, which by and large benefits them exclusively. Emad Mekay asserts that wealthy nations exercise their political powers at the world organizations. He writes,

> From the World Trade Organization (WTO), the International Monetary Fund (IMF), the World Bank and the United Nations, to Interpol and the World Health Organization (WHO), dozens of international agencies now work to regulate world trade, telecommunications, transportation, labour, business, health and the environment. In almost all of those bodies, poor and powerless nations, like Somalia and Afghanistan, are under-represented while the rich and powerful, like Britain and the United States, operate with almost unchecked authority and overwhelming power.[25]

The political power and money are increasingly held by a small number of individuals and nations as Marx predicted at the birth of industrialization. Thus, the poorer the nations or individuals, the more their presences are marginalized. As they are powerless and invisible to the circle of policymakers, they pay more for the most basic necessities for survival. According to Fiona Harvey in "A Costly Thirst: Proper Pricing of Water Could Ease Shortages," the poorest nations pay more for water than wealthier nations.

> Slum-dwellers in Dares Salaam pay the equivalent of £4 ($8, €5) for 1,000 litres of water, bought over time and by the canister. In the same Tanzanian city, wealthier households connected to the municipal supply receive that amount for just 17p. In the UK, the same volume of tap water costs 81p and in the US it is as low as 34p. Figures from other countries confirm the evidence: it is generally the

24. National Women's Law Center, September 2013.

25. Emad Mekay, "Rich Nations Continue to Wield Power in Global Bodies," *Inter Press Service News Agency*, May 6, 2003, http://www.ipsnews.net/2003/05/politics-rich-nations-continue-to-wield-power-in-global-bodies/.

poorest who pay most for what is one of the most essential of all natural resources.[26]

According to Gutiérrez, the poor are powerless and invisible in the structure of every society, as

> . . . the poor person is "insignificant," a person who is considered a "nonperson," someone whose full rights as a human being are not recognized. We are talking about persons without social or individual weight, who count little in society or in the church. This is how they are seen or, more precisely, not seen, because they are in fact invisible insofar as they are excluded in today's world.[27]

Anup Shah reports that, according to UNICEF, twenty-two thousand children die each day due to poverty. And they "die quietly in some of the poorest villages on earth, far removed from the scrutiny and the conscience of the world. Being meek and weak in life makes these dying multitudes even more invisible in death."[28] Between 27 and 28 percent of all children in developing countries are estimated to be underweight or stunted. The two regions where most of these children live are South Asia and sub-Saharan Africa.

CALL TO MISSION OF THE CHURCH

The *missio Dei,* the mission of God, in the twenty-first century, should be profoundly rooted in the praxis of Jesus Christ, the "Christ-praxis" of "feeding, healing and teaching" the poor and the oppressed in the Global South. They have every right as children of God to receive and enjoy the gift of full life from God: beauty, goodness and truth.

bell hooks claims that we need to interrogate our memory of the past and be ready to be disrupted in the present for the betterment of a future world.

> Fundamentally, we are called to choose between a memory that justifies and privileges domination, oppression, and exploitation and

26. Fiona Harvey, "A Costly Thirst: Proper Pricing of Water Could Ease Shortages," *Financial Times,* April 4, 2008.

27. Gustavo Gutiérrez, "The Situation and Tasks of Liberation Theology Today," in *Opting for the Margins: Postmodernity and Liberation in Christian Theology,* ed. by Joerg Rieger (New York: Oxford University Press, 1993). 89–104.

28. Anup Shah, "Poverty Facts and Stats," in *Global Issues,* http://www.globalissues.org/article/26/poverty-facts-and-stats.

one that exalts and affirms reciprocity, community, and mutuality. Given the crisis the planet is facing—rampant destruction of nature, famine, threats of nuclear attack, ongoing patriarchal wars—and the way these tragedies are made manifest in our daily life and the lives of folks everywhere in the world, it can only be a cause for rejoicing that we can remember and reshape paradigms of human bonding that emphasize the increased capacity of folks to care for the earth and for one another. That memory can restore our faith and renew our hope.[29]

Historically, the mission of the church is based upon an expansion of the Christian kingdom that started in the sixteenth century in Spain and Portugal. Ulrich Luz explains this in his commentary on Matt. 28:18-20, the Great Commission,

> Since the beginning of the *High Middle Ages* "mission" was accomplished primarily through the expansion of Christina territory, for the most part it was also true then that 28:19a was not a basic text of Christian mission. To my knowledge that was also true of the great missionaries of the sixteenth century who on behalf of the church and the Spanish or Portuguese crown went out to incorporate into the Christian world the newly "discovered" peoples, especially America and to a lesser degree also of East Asia.[30]

Luz, however, acknowledges that in the beginning of eighteen century, the Great Commission became the Magna Carta of missions, primarily because of a 1792 document by William Carey of the English Baptists. According to Luz, it is Carey who carried the torch of the mission command that became so popular and became a critical influence of the mission movement that grew into the Protestant church in twentieth century. For example, Luz cited Dutch Calvinist Abraham Kuyper's understanding of Matt. 28:19a as an "absolute command." According to Luz, Kuyper "understood mission as issuing from God's sovereignty rather than from God's love and correspondingly as 'obedience to God's command,' 'not an invitation, but a charge, an order.'"[31]

---

29. hooks, *Outlaw Culture*, 202.

30. Ulrich Luz, *Matthew: A Commentary*, Hermenia, vol 3. *Matthew 21–28* (Minneapolis: Fortress Press, 2005), 626.

31. Ibid., 627. Abraham Kuyper according to Bosch "Structure," 219; cf. idem, *Transforming Mission: Paradigm Shifts in Theology of Mission*, (Maryknoll, NY: Orbis Books, 1991), 341.

By the end of the nineteenth century, Gustav Warneck, father of the modern Protestant mission movement, began a missionary task of converting non-Christians into Christians regarding Christianity as world religion. Luz, furthermore, states that through Warneck, Matt. 28:19a became the basic missionary statement of the Christian Church for the salvation of lost souls in the world as well as a fundamental text for "the Catholic understanding of mission."[32] According to Luz, Warneck's view on the gospel is as follows,

> "all root ideas of the gospel are directed toward a general salvation
> of the world, therefore the gospel story concludes with a missionary
> command, and therefore this mission constitutes a central task of the
> Christian church."[33]

In 1974, at the International Congress on World Evangelization in Lausanne, Switzerland, Matt. 28:19 became the basis of the preamble statement. Luz states that, from this point on, evangelical Christianity has used this particular text as a "mission command" and as a reason for militaristic training of missionaries in an effort of "changing world" into "Christian Kingdom." He also posits that the people outside of evangelical circles, including people of interreligious dialogue emanating from the World Council of Churches, have expressed their concerns with much doubt and are "deeply skeptical" on uncritical interpretation of the text[34] and the mission goal of evangelical circles.

The utmost example for this militaristic training of missionaries and uncritical interpretation of the Magna Carta or the Great Commission are probably the Korean churches in South Korea and North America. The churches in South Korea, including the Korean American Church in North America, send missionaries to the end of earth in order to "make all the nations into disciples, baptizing them in the name of the father, and of the son, and of the Holy Spirit." The number of missionaries is currently about 25,000, many of whom are located in the Global South as well as Muslim communities. The Korean churches have continued to sponsor and send out missionaries with fervent zeal by recruiting young adults on college campuses in South Korea as well as in America. The Korean mission, whether it is short or long term, is basically set out to convert the natives into Christians by providing charitable works such as food, medical aid, and by building identical churches in native villages on the mission fields. I call this short-term missionary

---

32. Luz, *Matthew*, 627.

33. Luz, *Matthew 21–28*, 627. Cf. Warneck, *Missionslehre* 1.94, 100–102.

34. Luz, *Matthew 21–28*, 628.

task "Band-Aid" mission works, using native *minjung* for their own church promotional events. The core of its missionary style is very much that of the American missionary movement of the early twentieth century, which was based on the expansion of Christianity from the evangelical Christian camp. According to Andrew Walls in his book, *The Missionary Movement in Christian History: Studies in the Transmission of Faith*, the spirit and core of Christian mission—and especially the American missionary movement—was based on capitalism and a vigorous expansionism of a white supremacy. He writes, "The linking of entrepreneurial activity, efficient organization, and conspicuous financing, which was characteristic of American business, became characteristic of American Christianity."[35]

Thus, mission based on this kind of "Christian expansionism and imperialism" has been perpetuating a prototype of the structure of "white-supremacy-capitalism-patriarchy" and continues to claim the power of Christianity by "building more churches" without carefully discerning other religious practices in native lands. Usually, the problem is that despite the missionaries' short or long term mission, their mindset and attitude as guests have remained as the "center of power" in objectifying the periphery. Rieger asserts the problem of old practices of the church as follows,

> The church has a long history of serving people at the margins. The modern church in particular, probably more so than at any other time in the history of the church, has been involved in the exercise of charity through special programs and activities. At the same time, however, an older problem has been intensified in modernity. The modern self's blindness to the other as part of the self has led to an increasing perception of charity as a one-way street, something that originates with the charitable self and leads to handouts for those in need. Here the challenge that the other poses to the self is lost. The primary focus of charity in modern time has become, implicitly and explicitly, making the other into the image of the self.[36]

Therefore, as Rieger points out, the critical task is the "de-centering of modern self and creation of a corporate self in the identification with those on the underside."[37]

---

35. Andrew F. Walls, *The Missionary Movement in Christian History: Studies in the Transmission of Faith* (Maryknoll, NY: Orbis Books, 1996), 231.

36. Rieger, *Remember the Poor*, 90. Cf. George E. Tinker, *Missionary Conquest: The Gospel and Native American Cultural Genocide* (Minneapolis: Fortress Press, 1993).

Next, a new kind of mission for the church should be the construction of infrastructures for the poor in the Global South. The church must seek not only to challenge globalization, capitalism, and re-colonization, but it should also seek to empower the poor to, at some point, eradicate the systemic oppressive structure that has caused endless poverty and suffering for the *minjung*. Chandra Talpade Mohnaty accurately states her feminist vision,

> Here is a bare-bones description of my own feminist vision: this is a vision of the world that is pro-sex and woman, a world where women and men are free to live creative lives, in security and with bodily health and integrity, where they are free to choose whom they love, and whom they set up house with, and whether they want to have or not to have children; a world where pleasure rather than just duty and drudgery determine our choices, where free and imaginative exploration of the mind is a fundament right; a vision in which economic stability, ecological sustainability, racial equality, and the redistribution of wealth from the material basis of people's well-being. Finally, my vision is one in which democratic and socialist practices and institutions provide the conditions for public participation and decision making for people regardless of economic and social locations.[38]

The first task of the future mission of the church should focus on resolving the fundamental problems of feeding the *minjung* in the Global South. During Jesus Christ's ministry, he demonstrated many times how important it was for *ochlos-minjung* to eat and drink. Tae Yeon Cho, a New Testament biblical scholar, explains that a fellowship of eating was an absolutely necessary event for Jesus Christ. Jesus assured that the *minjung* were fed while they were around with him (for instance, feeding the five thousand; Matt. 14:13-21, Luke 9:10-17, John 6:1-14). For this, Cho reemphasizes, the Pharisees criticized Jesus Christ and his disciples for their gluttonous drinking habits (Matt. 11:19; Luke 7:34).[39]

Therefore, as I mentioned earlier, if the past mission of the church focused on the expansion of Christianity by providing charitable works through

---

37. Rieger, *Remember the Poor*, 102.

38. Chandra Talpade Mohanty, *Feminism Without Borders: Decolonizing Theology, Practicing Solidarity* (Durham, NC: Duke University Press, 2003), 4.

39. Tae Yeon Cho, "On Eating Table, the Kingdom of God," in *Reading the New Testament From Upside Down*, ed. Tae Yeon Cho, Jung Sik Cha, and Seung Won Yoo (Seoul: Christian Literature Society of Korea, 1999), 47–57.

programs and aid relief, then the future mission of the church should concentrate on developing agricultural systems to produce an adequate food supply and working with various international organizations as well as individual donors. Kofi Annan, a former secretary of United Nations, states that "the poor do not really want a handout. They want to trade and work themselves out of poverty."[40]

For example, I was told by a missionary worker of fifteen years in the Cote d'Ivoire that the rich soil and the perfect weather of Cote d'Ivoire provided excellent conditions for multiple rice harvests annually. (Cote d'Ivoire is, in fact, a leading nation in the production of quality cocoa to European nations.) However, there are two difficulties: the majority of farms are owned by either French or Lebanese farmers who have virtually monopolized cocoa and pineapple production; and the native farmers do not know how to husband rice farming and are in dire need of agricultural expertise.

The second task of mission is the "healing" together of the church with government officials and NGO organizations in order to build infrastructures that provide better medical services for *minjung*. Throughout the four Gospels, Jesus Christ showed his deepest compassion towards the *minjung* and their plight. For example, he healed many at Peter's house (Matt. 8:14-17; Mark 1:29-34; Luke 4:38-41), cast out the demons from the Garasene demoniacs (Matt. 8:28-34; Mark 5:1-20; Luke 8:26-39), healed a paralytic (Mark 2:1-12: Luke 5:17-26), healed two blind men (Matt. 9:27-31), healed a demon-possessed mute man (Matt. 9:32-34), and healed a man with a withered hand (Matt. 12:9-13; Mark 3:1-6; Luke 6:6-11). Mercy and Truth Medical Mission is an excellent example as a leading modern medical mission team, which provides international and local healthcare services especially on the African continent.

The most common reason that *minjung* in Global South suffer sickness and disease is from drinking unclean water, the consequence of an inadequate sewage system. Although there are multifaceted NGO groups and organizations that have extensively drilled water fountains and implemented effective toilet systems, the missionary teams should have done more in terms of installations of these systems in collaboration with private sectors as well.

The third mission task is to provide basic educational system for all, especially women and children in these regions. The *minjung* have no ability to school their children due to lack of money. Many households depend on their children to work for basic survival. Moreover, remote from urban cities, there are no schools in rural villages. Some missionary teams from the Church

---

40. Kofi Anan, *Africa in the 21st Century*, www. 21stcentruychallenges.orgx/faces/kofi-annan-qotes/.

of Korea have built schools and seminaries near and around the mission centers, but there are still large areas that do not have any type of schooling whatsoever.

Amartya Sen emphasizes the need of basic education for all in order to help reduce human insecurity and promote gender equity. Moreover, he asserts that there is a strong connection between education and economic growth, exemplified in Japan, Korea, Hong Kong, China, Taiwan, and Singapore that are members of G20s[41] in last twenty years. He states,

> Not surprisingly, all the cases of speedy use of the opportunities of global commerce for the reduction of poverty have drawn on help from basic education on a wide basis. For example, in Japan, already in the mid-19th century the task was seen with remarkable clarity. The Fundamental Code of Education, issued in 1872 (shortly after the Meiji restoration in 1868), expressed the public commitment to make sure that there must be "no community with an illiterate family, nor a family with an illiterate person". Thus – with the closing of educational gaps – began Japan's remarkable history of rapid economic development. By 1910 Japan was almost fully literate, at least for the young, and by 1913, though still very much poorer than Britain or America, Japan was publishing more books than Britain and more than twice as many as the United States. The concentration on education determined, to a large extent, the nature and speed of Japan's economic and social progress. Later on, particularly in the second half of the 20th century, South Korea, China, Taiwan, Hong Kong, Singapore, and other economies in East Asia followed similar routes and firmly focused on general expansion of education.[42]

Basic education for children is crucial in the formation of identities as people of dignity and self-esteem. It equips them with a set of tools in critical thinking to analyze both politically and historically in order to participate and voice their

41. The members of G20 are finance ministers and central bank governors from nineteen countries plus the European Union. The assembly of the group was proposed at the meeting of the G7 Finance Ministers on September 25, 1999. The purpose of this body is to serve "as a new mechanism for informal dialogue in the framework of the Bretton Woods institutional system, to broaden the dialogue on key economic and financial policy issues among systemically significant economies and to promote cooperation to achieve stable and sustainable world growth that benefits all" (G7 1999, http://www.g20.utoronto.ca/g20whatisit.html.

42. Amartya Sen, "The Importance of Basic Education," *The Guardian*, October 28, 2003, http://www.theguardian.com/education/2003/oct/28/schools.uk4.

own views in fighting injustice, both near and far. Frantz Fanon asserts that the transformation of structure should be changed from bottom up, and that this change be "willed, called for, demanded" by the colonized.[43] Sen posits the importance of providing basic education for the marginalized and the poor.

> Basic education is not just an arrangement for training to develop skills (important as that is), it is also a recognition of the nature of the world, with its diversity and richness, and an appreciation of the importance of freedom and reasoning as well as friendship.[44]

Therefore, a new mission of the church should be directly involved in the building of infrastructures by sharing our resources freely and cooperating with the *minjung* for transformation into an "I-thou" relationship for a "new and better community" for all of us. Frederick Herzog posits the mission of Christian life for the future:

> At the core of this process is a new spirituality, not a new dogma. It is a spirituality that leads Christians closer to each other and to all human kind. The ecumenical movement is one expression of this spirituality, but more important is the perception of Jesus' presence in situations of dire need throughout the world. The base communities in the Third World are one dimension of this encounter. The development and transmission of Christian faith in these situations is no longer a hierarchical matter, moving from the top down, but a corporate one, moving from the bottom up.[45]

I would like to end this section by excerpting a portion of a new mission statement recently published by WCC, which will be presented at the WCC Tenth Assembly meeting in Busan, South Korea on October 30–November 8, 2013.

SPIRIT OF LIBERATION: MISSION FROM THE MARGINS
Why Margins and Marginalization

38. Mission from the margins seeks to counteract injustices in life, church, and mission. It seeks to be an alternative missional movement against the perception that mission can only be done by the powerful to the powerless, by

---

43. Mohanty, *Feminism without Borders,* 7.

44. Ibid.

45. Fredrick Herzog, "A New Spirituality: Shaping Doctrine at the Grass Roots," *Christian Century,* July 30,1986, 680–81.

the rich to the poor, or by the privileged to the marginalized. Such approaches can contribute to oppression and marginalization. Mission from the margins recognizes that being in the center means having access to systems that lead to one's rights, freedom and individuality being affirmed and respected; living in the margins means exclusion from justice and dignity. Living on the margins, however, can provide its own lessons. People on the margins have agency, and can often see what, from the centre, is out of view. People on the margins, living in vulnerable positions, often know what exclusionary forces are threatening their survival and can best discern the urgency of their struggles; people in positions of privilege have much to learn from the daily struggles of people living in marginal conditions.

39. Marginalized people have God-given gifts that are under-utilized because of disempowerment, and denial of access to opportunities and/or justice. Through struggles in and for life, marginalized people are reservoirs of the active hope, collective resistance, and perseverance that are needed to remain faithful to the promised reign of God.

40. Because the context of missional activity influences its scope and character, the social location of all engaged in mission work must be taken into account. Missiological reflections need to recognize the different value orientations that shape missional perspectives. The aim of mission is not simply to move people from the margins to centres of power but to confront those who remain in the centre by keeping people on the margins. Instead, churches are called to *transform* power structures.

41. The dominant expressions of mission, in the past and today, have often been directed *at* people on the margins of societies. These have generally viewed those on the margins as recipients and not active agents of missionary activity. Mission expressed in this way has too often been complicit with oppressive and life-denying systems. It has generally aligned with the privileges of the centre and largely failed to challenge economic, social, cultural and political systems which have marginalized some peoples. Mission from the centre is motivated by an attitude of paternalism and a superiority complex. Historically, this has equated Christianity with Western culture and resulted in adverse consequences, including the denial of the full personhood of the victims of such marginalization."[46]

---

46. I received permission from Dr. Rev. JoonSeop Keum, Director of CMME and editor of IRN at World Council of Churches to excerpt the portion of the new mission statement in this particular essay.

CONCLUSION: TAKE THE CROSS AND FOLLOW ME

"Then Jesus told his disciples, 'If any want to become my followers, let them deny themselves and take up their cross and follow me." (Matt. 16:24 NRSV)

"Christianity without discipleship, is always Christianity without Christ."
– Dietrich Bonhoeffer[47]

The ultimate goal for the Christian requires three serious commitments: first, to follow Jesus with the unconditional prerequisite of denying or emptying oneself; second, to take up one's cross; third, to begin a life journey of following Jesus as long as one has decided to remain as a disciple of Jesus.

What does it mean to become a disciple of Jesus and follow him in this postmodern world? Being a disciple and following Jesus means that one ought to make the Christian commitment and put into practice or imitate his ministry in action and in solidarity with the *poor* based on his teachings.

It is a ministry to the "the crowd," the *ochlos*, the *minjung*, who by virtue of their social location in the society have been politically oppressed, culturally despised or patronized, and most of all, economically exploited for over five hundred years. Chandra Talpade Mohanty describes,

> The twentieth century was also the century of decolonization of the Third world/South, the rise and splintering of the communist Second World, the triumphal rise and recolonization of almost the entire globe by capitalism, and of the consolidation of ethnic, nationalist, and religious fundamentalist movements and nation-states.[48]

Therefore, the theological-ethic should concentrate at the service of the poor, the *ochlos*, the *minjung*, to proclaim and practice the reign of God's love and mercy via Jesus. It is our responsibility and accountability as disciples of Jesus, practicing and mimicking the ministries of Jesus to our neighbors, Others, and most importantly, *minjungs* in our society and the Global South. To "take up one's cross" means to eradicate the poverty from our neighborhoods as disciples of Christ in building up an equitable, just, mutual, and accountable society of caring and sharing. Bonhoeffer succinctly states that "we have literally no time

---

47. Dietrich Bonhoeffer, *The Cost of Discipleship* (New York: Simon & Schuster, 1959), 59.

48. Mohanty, *Feminism without Borders*, 3.

to sit down and ask ourselves whether so-and-so is our neighbor or not. We must get into action and obey—we must behave like a neighbor to him."[49]

"Money, then, appears as this distorting power both against the individual and against the bonds of society, etc., which claim to be entities in themselves. It transforms fidelity into infidelity, love into hate, hate into love, virtue into vice, vice into virtue, servant into master, master into servant, idiocy into intelligence, and intelligence into idiocy." – Karl Marx [50]

49. Bonhoeffer, *Cost of Discipleship*, 78.

50. Karl Marx, "The Power of Money," in *Economic and Philosophic Manuscripts of 1844*, http://www.marxists.org/archive/marx/works/1844/manuscripts/power.htm.

9

Children's Agency and Edinburgh 2010: The Great Commission or a Greater Omission?

Rohan P. Gideon

INTRODUCTION

It would not be inappropriate to start with an obvious negation. Neither in Matt. 28:16-20 nor in its parallel texts (Mark 16:15-18; Luke 24:44-49) did Jesus say that he was giving his followers a *great commission* as it has turned out to be called in the Christian history of missions. Rather, we are certainly aware of passages where Jesus has given a *great commandment* or the *greatest commandment* (Matt. 22:35-40; Mark 12:28-34), through which he summarily captures Mosaic commandments. When uncritical readers read Matt. 28:16-20 with the editorial title *The Great Commission*, they begin their interpretation based on the title without realizing the editorial bias in the title. A significant pitfall of an uncritical and overwhelming acceptance of the phrase *the Great Commission,* in contrast to lesser acceptance of what was emphatically uttered as *the great commandment* or the *greatest commandment,* is the creation of unsolicited binaries. Historically, prioritizing the "great commission" has substantially prioritized a form of mission *to preach and to make disciples* over against a mission *to love God and neighbors.*

Prefixing *great* to the *commission* generates an agency—both in the sense of an organization and as a capacity to act and establish a discourse—that has deeply established in history the binary of "patron-recipient." The implications of such prioritization would mean not just identifying the dynamics that sustain the binary but also to identify common grounds where the binary meets. In short, there has been a history of irreversible colonial missions based on the

Great Commission where Christianity raided, both militarily and culturally, many non-Christian and non-Western "heathens" to convert them into disciples of Jesus Christ. India, my home country, has been deeply impacted by Christian missions, where Christian missionaries from Denmark, Portugal, Britain, and other European countries came to establish themselves as legacies of their empires. They intended to preach, in the words of William Carey, to "Mahometans and pagans."[1] Responsively, Indian theology exhibits both acceptance of and resistance to the above mode of Christian missions. Dana Robert reviews various responses to the Great Commission by different confessional organizations. She mentions that the Lausanne Movement[2] and the A.D. 2000 and Beyond Movement[3] were optimistic that they had reached out with a Christian gospel to 95 percent of the world's population. Robert notices that the twentieth century has witnessed "the great geographic expansion of Christianity since the conversion of Europe." Therefore, those mission organizations that are critical of the expansionist motifs of missions believe that the "Great Commission should no longer be emphasized as the centre of Christian mission because the age of expansion is over."[4] The organizations that abide by the Matthean Great Commission missional strategy give themselves a clear mandate to preach and to convert non-Christians. And thus, the Great Commission missional strategists regard all those they encounter as uncritical hearers of the gospel or as those who do not exercise their critical agency to interact with the gospel. They believe the agency rests with the expansionists. The mission organizations of our times clearly sense a necessity for an alteration to customary grand suppositions about mission dynamics (preacher-hearer binary) and recreate approaches for a "non-imperial" relational basis. The alternative is not about one replacing the other. With an increasing trend to move beyond the conventional notion of the Great Commission, missions

1. William Carey, "An Enquiry into the Obligations of Christians to use Means for the Conversion of the Heathens (1792)," http://www.gutenberg.org/files/11449/11449-h/11449-h.htm.

2. The Lausanne Movement is an evangelical movement fervently involved to "unite all evangelicals in the common task of the total evangelization of the world." Two prominent leaders of the movement have been the famous evangelists Billy Graham and John Stott. The first congress of the movement was held in Lausanne, Switzerland in 1974. For more information, see http://www.lausanne.org/en/about.html.

3. A.D. 2000 and Beyond is a movement of many Christian organizations and denominations equipped with and focused on reaching out to every part of the world with the Christian gospel by the year 2000. For more information, see http://www.ad2000.org/ad2kbroc.htm.

4. Dana L. Robert, "The Great Commission in an Age of Globalization," in *Antioch Agenda: Essays on the Restorative Church in honor of Orlando Costas*, ed. D. Jeyaraj, R. Pazmiño, R. Petersen (New Delhi: Indian Society for the Promotion of Christian Knowledge, 2007), 7–8.

today are called to envision healthier missional debates that convert into mission practices.

In recent decades, there has been a clear shift to evaluate the understanding of agency and the role of the colonizer and the colonized in Christian missions. A recent large-scale review was taken up at the Edinburgh 2010 conference that marked one hundred years of modern missionary movement. Edinburgh 2010 was a conference held to celebrate the Centenary of the World Missionary Conference held in Edinburgh in 1910. The core idea of the Edinburgh 2010 was to review and revise mission strategies in light of rapid sociocultural, geopolitical, and poly-dimensional global change. While the 1910 conference was limited to mainline Protestantism, the 2010 conference claimed participants from a variety of "Christian traditions and confessions including Roman Catholic, Orthodox, Pentecostal, and Independent churches, and show a better gender and age balance."[5]

To understand the role of children in mission, my evaluation in this chapter is based on two important documents that are products of the Edinburgh 2010 conference: *Edinburgh 2010, Volume II, Witnessing to Christ Today*, edited by Daryl Balia and Kirsteen Kim,[6] and *Edinburgh 2010: Mission Today and Tomorrow*, edited by Kirsteen Kim and Andrew Anderson.[7] The documents are anthologies of group reflections based on various themes and of individual presentations and responses. So, I analyze the documents' views and comments with reference to the Great Commission. From this, I first determine what sense of agency is generally perceived. And second, I explore how this sense of agency influences the understanding of the role and participation of children in mission.

Edinburgh 2010 highlights and discusses the preaching motif as an outcome of the Great Commission, albeit as a critical discussion on the place and role of children in Christian mission. Also added to this dynamic is the notion of the "advantage of the adult over children." I want to say how the whole Christian mission motif to preach also translates in adult-children relationships as adults' prerogative to prescribe and control, especially in understanding the place and role of children in mission. This dynamic in adult-children relationships, which is adult-dominant, is not new or just a fall-out

5. "About Edinburg 2010," Centenary of the 1910 World Missionary Conference, http://www.edinburgh2010.org/en/about-edinburgh-2010.html.

6. Daryl Balia and Kirsteen Kim, ed., *Edinburgh 2010: Witnessing Christ Today* (Oxford: Regnum, 2010).

7. Kirsteen Kim and Andrew Anderson, ed., *Edinburgh 2010: Mission Today and Tomorrow* (Oxford: Regnum, 2011).

of the kerygmatic mission. Rather, this age-old dynamic is time and again reiterated with various motifs. In the case of Edinburgh 2010, it is echoed with the preaching motif. Finally, I propose theological directions for children's agency. I draw my idea of agency from a combined reading of Simone Bignall's *Postcolonial Agency* and Rowan Williams's exposition of agential significance of Holy Spirit in Trinity from "Word and Spirit," in his significant work *On Christian Theology*.

PART 1: A THEORETICAL FRAMEWORK FOR AGENCY

For this paper, I draw my framework of agency from Simone Bignall's explanation for a postcolonial agency. Bignall proposes a qualitative postcolonial perspective, expanding upon various forms of "political resistance to Empire." While there is a tendency in postcolonial arguments to create binaries through resistance, Bignall's work seeks to balance the binary tendency by retrieving the agency of the colonized as well as recognizing the "responsibility and transforming capacity of formerly colonizing subjects."[8] In Bignall's words,

> the process of postcolonialization therefore requires not only an appropriate philosophy of transformation encompassing a general theory of historical discontinuity . . . but also a particular concept of transformative agency that enables one consciously to enact a postcolonial ethic of relation to others, and to engage a collaborative politics of material transformation in order to construct postcolonial institutions and communities of practice with others.[9]

A starting point for my working definition of agency is to explain agency as the "human capacity to act"[10] or for people to react in their contexts.[11] In a context where violence is embedded in social structures, human agency is due

---

8. Simone Bignall, *Postcolonial Agency: Critique and Constructivism* (Edinburgh: Edinburgh University Press, 2010), 4; also see Musa Dube, "Towards a Post-colonial Feminist Interpretation of the Bible," *Semeia* 78 (1997): 11–26, for a postcolonial reading of the Great Commission. Dube sees an analogy of the first-century mission–Roman Empire collaboration in the nineteenth-century mission–Western Mission collaboration. What I argue for is agency in mission in what is a postcolonial mission time.

9. Bignall, *Postcolonial Agency*, 3–4.

10. Laura M. Ahearn, "Agency," *Journal of Linguistic Anthropology* 9, no. 1 (2001): 12–15 (12).

11. Donald Davidson, "Agency," *Essays on Actions and Events* (Oxford: Oxford University Press, 1980), 3–19, 46; Raymond Caldwell, "Agency and Change: Re-evaluating Foucault's Legacy," *Organization* 14, no. 6 (2007): 6–7.

to two factors: (1) to a social structure where human agency is a consequence of structural constraints or cultural stresses, and (2) to human agency or action as a product of self-will. The self-willed agency could challenge a structure inadvertently. The explanation of agency is classically connected to social structures, and how agency and social structure reciprocate in constituting or reconstituting each other. Discussions on agency gained prominence with a critical assessment of structuralism that either negated or diminished the role and actions of individuals as significant in shaping a discourse. To explain it further: Foucault, for instance, does not completely rule out the connection of the agency of subalterns to their subjectivity, albeit agency appears and disappears in subjectivity without clarity to the notion of agency. Subjectivity and agency exhibit a state of flux. Foucault questions agency as a unitary rational entity of Enlightenment. Yet it allows for space to discuss differences, and therefore allows a notion of agency that is not necessarily a rational, autonomous agency, but an agency that projects itself as an effect of subjectivity.[12] Therefore, subjectivity becomes a key formative factor of agency, an agency not as a completely separate entity, but as a response that emerges out of such questioning of autonomy or privileging of one form of agency over the other.

The ambiguous relationship between subjectivity and agency has been revisited among postcolonial thinkers. Edward Said sees in Foucault a disapproval of structures, which is not enough to separate self-willed agency from subjectivity for a considerable moment.[13] In Said's thoughts, critics of structures, such as Foucault, hesitate to allow the significant success of counter discursive attempts: they could first be the way counter powers have been misrepresented, especially concerning the way physical and political repression takes place to safeguard a dominant culture; and second, they do not emphasize the ensuing discourse of liberation.[14] Said's thoughts open up to what Bignall calls "causal and purposeful" agency. For Bignall, "'agency' primarily refers to action that is both causal and purposefully directed, although never free from constraints."[15] She attempts to separate "agency" from "action."[16] For this paper, my explanation for the agency-action binary relation that Bignall creates is that agency is a cumulative notion of perceptions, actions, voices, and aspirations

12. Caldwell, "Agency and Change," 6–7.

13. Edward W. Said, *Reflections on Exile and Other Literary and Cultural Essays* (New Delhi: Penguin, 2001), 242.

14. Ibid., 243–44.

15. Bignall, *Postcolonial Agency*, 12.

16. Ibid.

that interrogate a structure at various levels. It envisions a new display of relationships that identify, esteem, and assert the agency of the least.

The above discussions have set a few parameters for further discussions about agency and children in Edinburgh 2010 discussions. New subjectivities such as the missionally colonized peoples, including children, have the ability to provide agential significance. The abilities of missionally colonized adults and children to provide agency exists alongside the capacity of dominant mission agents to adapt to the growing needs of the contexts. One of the dominant mission agents in the context of this discussion is adults. Specifically, the agencies of the new subjectivities have inherent powers that could be further explored to constantly enhance the possibility of newer or unrecognized trajectories of agency. In the case of emphasizing children's agency, some questions would be: How long should children strive to establish themselves as equally significant without being completely submissive to adults? What is the level of openness adults should exhibit for children given the historical danger that they subsume and overpower children? These questions to some extent could ward off the danger of the new agency creating a new hierarchy and new power equations. They also create spaces for various "assemblages of 'the multitude.'"[17]

The conference has raised a crucial question, keeping in mind new forms that power takes contextually and draws us to act in the face of the power: "The question of agency is pertinent. Christians may find themselves in positions of power or being given powerful positions, but how are they utilizing that power and to whose advantage?"[18] That question offers a sense of desire among mission-organizations for an alternative where changes in organizations would effect transformation. For Bignall, given various kinds of responses to power, a "postcolonial" condition describes a holistic change that has happened "in practices defining social construction, self-concept and attitudes of being, relating and belonging."[19]

PART 2: THE GREAT COMMISSION AND AGENCY IN EDINBURGH 2010

[I]t is frequently acknowledged that the interconnections between the modern missionary movement and colonialism damaged the Christian endeavor by presenting a powerful Christendom model of the religion from a Western world view.[20]

17. Ibid., 2.

18. Balia and Kim, *Witnessing Christ Today*, 179.

19. Bignall, *Postcolonial Agency*, 2.

In this section I discuss how proclamation (kerygma) of the Christian gospel by preaching and making disciples in the name of the Triune God continues to be a critical point of reference in Edinburgh 2010. With this, it becomes clear that the mission motif to preach lingers on as a predominant strategy while themes such as reconciliation, love, dialogue, and inclusive community work around the main theme. This is not to negate equally significant attempts to radically reverse the colonial method of preaching by exhibiting "attentiveness to the experiences of those affected by this agenda of colonial expansionism." It is to challenge power dynamics within mission history by now promoting the "agency of indigenous people in contextualizing Christianity from their earliest engagement with it."[21] It can, however, be noticed that expansionist motif in mission continues to be a pressure-exerting strategy by many missional agencies, but by wisely accommodating and negotiating with the agency of the colonized. This strategy retains the powerful notion of the dominant that one's knowledge is better than the other's as a missional tool, especially in its interaction in multi-faith and multicultural contexts. It creates constructs like preacher-recipient. Exposition of such binaries will help to further explain that preaching does not remain only as a geopolitical expansionist activity, but also as a dynamic of knowledge-transfer intergenerationally (between adults and children).

The conference sets the tone for future missions in *Theme One* on biblical bases for mission. One of the biblical bases of mission is being "sent forth" based on a Trinitarian formula where God sends his Son and the Son in turn sends the Spirit. The conviction of being "sent" demands of Christian mission a rigorous conviction to continue a Trinitarian affair. However, with the recent contextual challenges, the "procession" model assumes a dialogical tone towards "being with others in loving communion." "Mission among other faiths," which is the emphasis of *Theme Two*, traces continuity and discontinuity in theological themes such a dialogue, conversion, and pluralistic theology. *Theme One* of parallel sessions highlights a survey conducted among churches and mission agencies on their theological understanding of missional practices. An important element pertinent to our discussion is a discussion on *missio Dei* that seems to vie for attention alongside the overarching theme of the Great Commission:

> From the three models of mission adopted on the survey—proclamation, liberation and justice and *missio Dei*, it was

---

20. Balia and Kim, *Witnessing Christ Today*, 13.
21. Ibid.

found that proclamation was the most commonly described as the driver for mission in the local survey. The national survey was more concerned with integrating all three models. *Missio Dei* was found to be a weak driver for mission. Despite the prevalence of the language of *missio Dei* it was not found to be a prominent driver of mission in the interview stage. Matthew 28:18-20, the "Great Commission", appeared to be the primary biblical driver for the local survey and interviews and this verse was also used in website texts.[22]

Edinburgh 2010 shows a great awareness of "oppressive misinterpretations" of the conventional idea of the Great Commission, and yet it sustains the postresurrection instruction of Jesus by rereading the "mandates given by the resurrected to his disciples." Dialogue is envisioned in multi-faith setups, however, not without an apprehension about compromising one's own convictions in dialogue.[23] The conventional commission has nonetheless been "proved" a stimulus for missions. Edinburgh 2010 has tried to see new challenges for mission in light of the conventional *commission* framework. It sees that Matthean priorities for mission are concerned with forgiveness, love, and the "formation of communities across ethnic boundaries." Furthermore, reading the Markan indicator for the *commission*, the conference explains how the disciples of Jesus are lead to "a specific commission" (16:15-20). It is the only version of the Great Commission passage indicating the act of "preaching the gospel" beyond geographic and cosmic boundaries: to "all creation." Preaching leads to spiritual healing ministry and miracles ("signs").[24]

There is strong reason to see further why the conventional idea of the Great Commission still holds sway amidst growing awareness of the need to move away from it. For example, in *Theme Seven,* under the subsection *Mission, Migration, Diaspora and Ethnicity*, the East African presentation described Christian mission as purpose-driven and God-centered in order to address some of the immediate issues that bother the region socio-politically. In Eastern Africa, which faces uninterrupted encounters with poverty, disease, and ignorance amidst enormous resources, the mission of the church is trying to confront these anomalies as its priority. For this focus, the church is invested with the agency to empower and not disempower, bring peace, healing, and reconciliation, and not to cause conflict, injury, and segregation.[25]

22. Kim and Anderson, *Mission Today and Tomorrow*, 125.

23. Ibid., 131.

24. Balia and Kim, *Witnessing Christ Today*, 20.

25. Ibid., 189.

It is also interesting to note that the East African perspective of mission is strongly driven by the conventional imperative of mission beyond home geography. The region's internal challenges significantly contest the conventional notion of mission as beyond one's own geographic boundaries. Even as the church's empowering agency is called to focus on internal troubles, it is strongly believed that "beyond mission at home, the church in Eastern Africa has to go out to all corners of the earth to make disciples as per the great commission. In this the church has to identify the various mission fields in order to discern the engagement, proclamation and presence required of it."[26]

The conventional Great Commission now sees the swapping of actors, but the message and the method remain largely intact. It would not be appropriate at the moment to assert that the world outside Eastern Africa, be it other parts of Africa or outside the African continent, which could be the former colonizers like Europe or Asian countries, should receive the gospel. The focus of concern is that the mode—preaching and teaching —seems to be mission-essential.

In *Theme Eight* under *Biblical and Theological Foundations of Mission in Unity*, mission is constructed on unity manifested in the Triune God. Just as the Father in the Trinity sent his Son to be fully human, the Word becomes incarnate. The intention of the Son's sending "starts with the *kerygma* of *metanoia* [repentance]." Here the theological foundation of mission begins with *kerygma* [proclamation] and ends by "calling" the nations to be baptized in the name of the Triune God. It is to "spread" and "bring" the "good news to the ends of the earth." What has to be noticed here is that a reference to Triune God is a readily implied connection to kerygma. While there have been hints on how the Triune God's model is a sign of unity and reconciliation, the emphasis is laid only on Jesus' salvific work in the world rather than as a wider intention of the Trinity to strive dialogically for a harmony. In its explanation of the mission of the Triune God, the mission of Jesus to proclaim, to call all nations to baptism, and to preach, takes priority—but with a twist. The language of "solidarity with the suffering people" finds its place alongside preaching and baptizing the nations.[27] It becomes noticeably evident that the liberationist language of "solidarity" is employed to ease the gravity of the conventional *commission* and accommodate a solidarity stance as a new trajectory for the Great Commission. Even as the *theme* continues to dwell on *mission in kenotic love,* it is presented that sharing, as in Christ's self-emptying and sharing, is to share the gift of love that Christ freely gave. Therefore "opening up of the

26. Ibid.
27. Ibid., 209.

church" is a "fundamental condition" of the church.[28] As Cathy Ross concludes in her essay on Great Commission Christians, "Christianity is now a faith of many centres, and mission is multi-directional—from anywhere to anywhere. Christians in various parts of the world engage in mission differently and in new ways. We are experiencing Christianity as a kind of multi-coloured and multi-layered quilt with many shapes, sizes, fabrics and textures."[29]

A few observations can be made here on the method and content of the preaching motif. Preaching as a method in the conventional understanding of the Great Commission in Edinburgh 2010 still insists on moving beyond one's own geographic boundary. In the baggage of such a notion are dialogue, reconciliation, and solidarity. One can also notice a sense of self-evaluation by home mission agencies. This back and forth movement of contents within an old method of preaching tends to retain and establish strongly some older contents as baptizing the non-Christian communities and rigorously spreading the gospel of Jesus as relevant methods. What too often goes unnoticed is negotiation of power equations: With whom should power lie more: With the preacher or the hearer? Or, in the context of conflict and the need for reconciliation, the question about power is: With whom does power lie more? With the perpetrator or the victim? On whose terms should reconciliation occur? How much power could be shared in working out a reconciliatory position? What I try to argue and present here ahead of understanding children's agency in an adult-dominant theological landscape is that the overarching emphasis of the Great Commission situates its power equation still in a dominant mode. There have been committed efforts, however, to pan the power across among the different participating groups in missions. This seems to be the case in understanding the agency of children in missions in Edinburgh 2010.

PART 3: CHILDREN AND CHILDREN'S AGENCY IN EDINBURGH 2010

After having established that the preaching motif of the Great Commission continues to be a dominant thought in Edinburgh 2010, I will critically present how children and children's agency have been presented in the Edinburgh 2010 conference. In the run up to the conference, the significance of children and their agential significance in missions were some of the crucial issues that preparatory study groups of Edinburgh 2010 invested more time in than in the

---

28. Ibid., 208–209.

29. Kim and Anderson, *Mission Today and Tomorrow*, 196.

previous missions conferences. A quick critical gist of how children's issues were dealt with in some of the preparatory groups at the conference is appropriate.

Wendy Strachan explained a significant vision for children's active presence in her presentation *Welcoming Children: Reinstating Children in our Theological Reflections on Mission*. Strachan calls the insignificant attention to children in Christian mission "a scandal." She refers to "a few fleeting references to children" and calls the conference to "inspire the church beyond its existing paradigms so that children become an integral part of the life and mission of the church."[30] The paradigm shift would happen through theological reflections and research. Strachan also refers to the centrality of children proposed through the Child Theology movement[31] and other theological movements as suggestions to take this issue further. The persuasive argument of Strachan is to know from the conference whether children's issues would feature prominently on the agenda of subsequent mission conferences and whether children would be active and equal participants at the conference.[32]

Mission and Power, which was the focus of *Theme Four*, has picked up on a noteworthy gap in missions by dealing with educational motives of dominant models among younger generations of many indigenous communities. The group report mentions that *missions* has always been associated with *power* much against Pentecost's objective that the power of the Spirit would empower the powerless (Acts 2:17-18). A case study of Canadian Residential School style education during the colonial period captures the typical perpetuation of a grand scheme of imperialism. Education as a colonial tool is a point of discussion. "From the earliest days, Christians were interested in providing a European-style education to indigenous children."[33] While generally it is presumed that the colonialists were completely successful in imparting their cultural legacy through educating the younger generation, in reality, this may not be the case. In the discussion, there is a clear rejection of the suggestion

---

30. Balia and Kim, *Witnessing Christ Today*, 283–84.

31. Child Theology is an emerging movement retrieving the notion of centrality of children in Christian theologies. It "reexamines not only conceptions of children and obligations to them but also fundamental doctrines and practices of the church. Drawing on analogies to feminist, black and liberation theologies, child theologies have as their task not only to strengthen the commitment to and understanding of a group that has often been voiceless, marginalized and oppressed—children—but also to reinterpret Christian theology and practice as a whole" through the lens of children. Marcia J. Bunge, "Theologies of Childhood and Child Theologies: International Initiatives to Deepen Reflection on Children and Childhood in the Academy and Religious Communities," *Dharma Deepika* (2008), 33–53 (35).

32. Balia and Kim, *Witnessing Christ Today*, 289.

33. Ibid., 88.

that "indigenous peoples were without agency, ignorant and devoid of the capacity to engage and decide for themselves."[34] They weighed new teachings in the light of their own experiences and made "crucial decisions whether to accept the new faith." However, the missionary impact was deemed maximum by implementing colonial ideas in residential schools. The "aboriginal children were to be 'caught' young to be saved from what is on the whole the degenerating influence of the home environment."[35] It is here highlighted that children's vulnerability and their unquestioned innocence to accept a thought uncritically is taken advantage of. In a survey conducted later on to analyze the impact of the colonialists' objective, it was found that the children taken into residential schools "were ashamed of their ancestry" and aboriginal culture, and wanted to disconnect themselves from their original cultural teachings. Those who tried to run away from the system were punished. Punishments were also sexual in nature.[36]

Vulnerable groups participating in mission, like aboriginal children, do have their positive dynamics, according to the *Theme Four* group. They mention that those who are vulnerable have little to lose and are therefore prone to take more risks and be more open to others and other conditions. By keeping windows of vulnerability open, we might experience new things, and gain new insights for our lives and our understanding of God, the world, and humanity. Then "there is an element of mystery when the dynamism of mission does not come from the people in positions of power or privilege . . . but from below, from the little ones, those who have few material financial or technical resources."[37] Otherwise, children are bundled up in a conventional "women, children and the marginalized" way! Or, whenever scarcely children are mentioned, children are the most vulnerable and need empowerment. And the question was how Christian education could empower them for missions. The agency of each marginalized group in this bundle is ignored or not fully considered as a relevant theological category.

Theme Seven deals with the topic *Christian Communities in Contemporary Context*. Taking the African context seriously, the group highlights the limitations of Edinburgh 2010 with regard to the number of people who can be physically present in the conference. What is emphatic is the group's call for an "equitable representation of people from the global South (Africans included), women, children, youth, disabled, African independent Pentecostal

34. Ibid., 90.

35. Ibid.

36. Ibid.

37. Balia and Kim, *Witnessing Christ Today*, 124.

and indigenous churches, people living with HIV/AIDS (PLWHA), indigenous peoples, and so on."[38] This emphasizes the missional need to listen to the voices of the marginal groups directly and not through their representatives external to themselves. The representation could diminish the agency of the marginalized groups.

Mission and Unity, Ecclesiology and Mission, the focus of *Theme Eight*, deals with the signpost of ecumenicity in and around Edinburgh 1910 and broader conceptual issues, as this group finds "unity" to be the pressing need of the time. The first-century Pentecostal unity was engendered by the Holy Spirit that was sent by Jesus. This unity should not be overwhelmed by the traditional missionary zeal of expanding and dominating. *Theme Nine* with its focus on *Missions Spirituality and Authentic Discipleship* powerfully suggests the importance of depending on the work of the Holy Spirit and the reading of the Scripture, which would enlighten us to engage ourselves directly towards "caring for the orphans and children." It calls us to cultivate discipleship in youth and children.[39]

However, of utmost interest for our discussion, I feel, is the document of the *Theme Five* group that discussed *Forms of Missionary Engagement*. That theme states that "these forms of missionary engagement include mission with the vulnerable, partnership, mission with children, 'receiving' mission, and the mission of the media. These specific themes are emphasized since they bear significant consequences for missionary engagement in our time."[40] The context for this discussion is clearly set. It happens in varying and overlapping contexts as globalization, neo-liberalism, multiculturalism, unprecedented urbanization, religious fundamentalism, situations of growing economic injustice, multi-faith and beyond faiths situations, and the "'shift of the centre of gravity' of Christianity from global North to global South."[41]

The "Listening Group" of the Conference in its report raises optimistic thoughts about the role of children as "a new energy for twenty-first century mission." It notes with concern from the past many instances of misuse of power in the treatment of children. The group deems it important to adapt an accommodative language devoid of power notions, which respects children with dignity. It also highlights how in many Christian communities children are perceived as passive recipients of adult-centric thoughts and inactive participants in fellowships for adults.[42] A critical revision of such theological

38. Ibid., 181.
39. Ibid., 225.
40. Ibid., 116.
41. Ibid., 117.

positions ensures children's "full participation as members of the Body of Christ [and] makes us realize anew that God has used children as his willing instruments throughout Christian history."[43] In Strachan's thought, children's agency could be recovered by introducing child-centered theological thinking that cuts across disciplines, thus creating a "synergy between theory and practice" that responds to children's aggrieved situations.[44]

It is heartening to see how *Theme Five* attributes to the Holy Spirit the power to transform the structured and institutionalized churches that through their power structures are shown to co-opt or pass over some members of the community. These power structures are highly influenced by market forces that have not spared children in their contexts. In fact, neo-liberalization has put children at greater risk than ever. In this context, the group has this to say about the working of the Spirit: "Renewal of the local church begins when the Holy Spirit calls a congregation or group back to their true identity and source (Luke 15:17). This identity is found in God, God's coming kingdom, in the Word made flesh, the Bible and the Tradition of the Church universal. Local church renewal occurs when the Holy Spirit transforms the people and the community into the likeness of Christ through repentance (*metanoia*) and openness of hearts to God."[45]

The conference publication has also dedicated a considerable section to understanding the ability of children to participate in mission, which could open up to new avenues within missions. The publication considered how in the biblical sense children are "welcomed and deployed for service," how children could be "agents of transformation," and how children could be "the untapped force for mission." It is, therefore, inspiring to know that much later than never, the issues of children and their agential significance has made way into the thought process of missional projects.

PART 4: A NEED FOR CHILDREN'S AGENCY IN MISSION: EDINBURGH 2010 AND BEYOND

How can children be active participants in missions where their views and perceptions could be considered as significant? What are some theological directives for children's active agency in missions? Strachan's analysis highlights, as a starting point, some liberating alternatives for children's agency in mission.

42. Kim and Anderson, *Mission Today and Tomorrow*, 315.

43. Ibid.

44. Ibid., 286.

45. Balia and Kim, *Witnessing Christ Today*, 119.

It is now clear from the earlier sections that children's agency has to be projected in a context where preaching as the dominant motif of the Great Commission weighs heavily as a priority in many mission organizations and institutions.

However, many organizations wisely accommodate and negotiate with voices that vary from the conventional Great Commission. Despite this, the accommodative strategy tends to retain the powerful notion of the dominant. In situations as this, we see that new subjectivities such as children have always the potential to provide transforming views and perceptions alongside the agential capacity of adults as the dominant mission agents. Children's agencies open up innovative or unrecognized courses of action for their agency. In Cathy Ross's thoughts, Christianity has been adapting itself to the many-centeredness and multi-directionality of faith and mission activities. This adaptation has the potential to challenge any one continent or empire-centric agency and, therefore, to invest agency in every community and beyond. Such exposures build into mission the ability to identify and project the agency of the sidelined.

Even a significant mission paradigm as *missio Dei* (as discussed in Part 2) that could engage the Great Commission has been, as Jayakiran Sebastian suggests, a dominant paradigm. Sebastian proposes what could make *missio Dei* an engaging paradigm. He argues for "Mission to God" as a novel and critical missiological position. A bold mission *to God* fearlessly perceives means to interrogate normative ideas of mission and "yet create a notion of mission that is simply not built on any form of nativism." [46]

A theological paradigm that begins to challenge the Great Commission's conventional notion of being "sent" and therefore licensed to "preach" is Rowan Williams's theological provocative on the Trinity. The conventional Trinitarian "procession" formula continues to be a theological challenge too in perpetuating the expansionist mode of the Great Commission. However, the Trinity also encompasses in it a potential to create an agency for the Holy Spirit, which in Williams's thought is not just "a supplement" to the Father and the Son. Williams provides insights on the Spirit's agential distinction in the body of Trinity, where the assemblage of the Father, the Son, and the Holy Spirit is understandably dominated by the Father. The commission of the Son is significantly considered too. But what about the transforming power of the

---

46. J. Jayakiran Sebastian, "Interrogating *Missio Dei*: From the Mission of God toward Appreciating our Mission to God in India Today," in *New of Boundless Riches: Interrogating, Comparing, and Restructuring Mission in a Global Era,* ed. Max L. Stackhouse and Lalsangkima Pachuau (Delhi: ISPCK) 1:42–44. He has shared this thought in the Edinburgh 2010 preparatory meeting. See Balia and Kim, *Witnessing Christ Today,* 69–70.

Holy Spirit? How significant is it in relation to the Father and the Son? For Williams,

> The Spirit's 'completion' of Christ's work is no longer to be seen epistemologically, as a supplement or extension to the teaching of Christ, or even as that which makes it possible to hear and receive the Word. It is rather a completion in terms of liberation and transformation: it is *gift*, renewal and life. It is not possible to speak of Spirit in abstraction from the Christian form of life as a whole: Spirit is 'specified' not with reference to any kind of episodic experience but in relation to the human identity of the Christian.[47]

Williams redefines the concept of transformative agency of the Spirit not as an add-on of the Father and the Christ of the Trinity, but as the one who consciously enacts an ethic of relation with and to the Father and the Son. This is breaking grounds in Trinitarian discourse that conventionally treats the latter as a procession from the former: the Son proceeds from the Father, and the Spirit from the Son. Moreover, the Spirit is not just via media for the Word to take roots in its hearers and practitioners. It also has a precise role to play. This makes the agency of the Spirit stand out at various moments in the working of the Trinity. The Spirit complements and enhances the scope of the Trinity in its liberative pursuit. Therefore, the working of the Spirit is concrete just as is its presence. So also is its agency. It continues to interact with the Father and the Son; it shapes their vision and work, and is shaped in the process. The work of the Spirit, if you like, is not of a "flash–in–the–pan" mode. Williams then goes on to emphatically present the agential significance of the Spirit:

> If what we are speaking of [i.e, Holy Spirit] is the agency which draws us closer to the Father by constituting us children, we are evidently speaking of any agency not simply identical with "Father" or "Son", or with the sum or amalgam of the two. That perhaps is obvious, or even trivial, but it may be that no more can be said of the Spirit's distinctiveness.[48]

The unique voice of the Spirit is given the privileged notion of the agency that is traditionally attributed to the Son, the Word. What more? The Spirit is not

---

47. Rowan Williams, "Word and Spirit," in *On Christian Theology* (Oxford: Blackwell, 2000), 123. Emphasis in original.

48. Ibid., 123–24.

just "bridge" builder, but one who "spans" the divine and the human. In that sense, the Spirit as an agency, in Williams's understanding, is an agency that brings a sense of hope. In Williams's words,

> If there can be any sense in which "Spirit" is a bridge-concept, its work is not to bridge the gap between God and the world or even between the Word and the human soul, but to span the unimaginably greater gulf between suffering and hope, and to do so by creating that form without illusion but also without despair.[49]

The Spirit as spanning the work and presence of the Triune God could be brought in here as an analogy for children to help understand children's presence and their agency significantly. While children physically proceed from adults, understanding childhood as a stage in itself recognizes children's unique place and contribution. Children nevertheless are present in adults through adults' own childhood and through their own selves, therefore in a sense carrying with them. This bridges the gap that the adult-child binary creates. Such a presence creates for mission a strategic participation of children and childhood memories. This participation is of hermeneutical significance. Children's experiences, memories, and creativity provide agential space that interacts with other mission dynamics to enrich the idea of mission. As Bignall explained, a body (human as well as institutional) is at one and the same time individual and multiple. However, for Bignall, not all bodies are agents. Her sense of agency emerges from a view that a body exhibits constant need for relationships and uses various conditions to create agency.[50]

By deconstructing a processional understanding of the Trinity as Williams did, we see that the theological agency of the neglected is very much at its core. The deconstructive activity is not just to flag up the marginalization process. It is also about committedly claiming to be enriched by the agency of the marginalized. A renewed understanding of the Trinity also opens up more towards children's issues than just about the generic disclosure of agency. A theological insight and hope is that Christ of the Trinity—Jesus, the Word—was a child himself who exhibited prodigious agency amidst his vulnerable context. This brings our understanding of the Trinity closer to children's reality than just a propositional discourse.[51]

49. Ibid., 124.

50. Bignall, *Postcolonial Agency,* 12.

51. Thanks to Dr. Mitzi J. Smith for her insight on this issue, and to Smith and her co-editor Dr. Jayachitra Lalitha for their comments.

To re-view children as active agents in mission, we need to reconsider the roles of "children in our midst." As a theme and a theological method, "Child in the Midst" is suggested by the Child Theology movement (referred to by Wendy Strachan), which tries to bring children's agency to the center of theological discussions and missions practices. The method challenges a power-centered model for mission that derives its theological language from military campaigns.[52] Christian mission should move from being an aggressive colonizer to a humble interactor. Humility in mission translates into a god-like approach of accepting everyone, including children. Abstract notion of childhood or children would deter salvation. A contextual exposition of children's stories and their tapestries help develop a relevant mission.[53] Therefore, violation of their dignity and rights is a clear stumbling block for children to develop their own agency.[54]

Missions are discursive spaces, spaces that open up for active and critical participation and interactions. Such interactions are in the best interest of the fullness of life for all participants and as such welcomes the hitherto unheard voices. The fullness of life could be termed either *liberation* or *shalom* (wholeness). Moreover, these discursive spaces are not necessarily geographical spaces, and they detest the traditional understanding of missions as conquest-oriented and expansionist. It is the missions that recognizes the agential significance of the marginalized and listens to their critical views of the traditional notions of mission. Their views are not necessarily a method of critique of the structured missions based on a driving force such as the Great Commission or any one normative propeller. The agency, here of children, could be novel, and therefore, both a radical moving away from the normative as well as a critique of the structure. The span-ability of the agency of the so-understood insignificant children can be well placed alongside the analysis of their vulnerability. It provides us with two vantage points for missions with and for children: (a) it opens up to a world of mysterious interpretations on

52. Sunny Tan, *Child Theology for the Churches in Asia: An Invitation* (London: Child Theology Movement, 2007).

53. Jan Grobbelaar, *Child Theology and the African Context* (London: Child Theology Movement, 2012).

54. See Rohan Gideon, *Child Labour in India: Challenges for Theological Thinking and Christian Ministry in India* (Delhi: ISPCK/NCCI, 2011). While children are very much part of our families, churches, society and God's kingdom, many of us continue to believe that childhood is an insignificant stage. As a result, today's theologies do not give serious attention to the issue of children's rights as it deserves. I challenge these notions in the light of the Scriptures and the recent developments in the field of Child Theology.

the significance and role of children in redefining missions as they seamlessly span the activities of the adult world in their own wisdom; and (b) it invigorates children's unsung abilities amidst their vulnerabilities. As Bignall concedes, it is not an easy task. The difficult task is to practically address the adult–child dichotomy and the sharing of power.

The missions that listen and theologies that are open-ended to receive new agencies are inherently interdisciplinary. These listening and open-ended postures emerge at the intersection of generations. Missions in the recent past are highly verbiage and unilateral in their approach based on the Great Commission's extreme emphasis on authoritative preaching/telling. A listening mission that recognizes the presence of the so-understood insignificant has been of secondary interest. In the case of children, a positivistic and essentialist worldview makes children objects, appropriate only for controlled analysis and social operation, perhaps, but removed from the indispensable correlation with the wider adult community. The idea of "participation" as a model for missions means taking seriously children's own insights, coming from a stage in itself but also, at the same time, spans generations.

The Great Commission and Christian Education: Rethinking Our Pedagogy

10

Interrogating the Matthean Great Commission for US Christian Education: Reclaiming Jesus' Kingdom of God Message for the Church

Karen D. Crozier

You must lay your lives on the altar of social change so that wherever you are there the Kingdom of God is at hand![1]

The task of those who work for the Kingdom of God is to Work for the Kingdom of God. The result beyond this demand is not in their hands. He who keeps his eyes on results cannot give himself wholeheartedly to his task, however simple or complex that task may be.[2]

INTRODUCTION

In 1931, W. E. B. Du Bois (1868–1963), a preeminent scholar of sociology and sociology of religion, activist, and *race man*,[3] published an article entitled "Will the Church Remove the Color Line?".[4] Du Bois raised a critical question for the

---

1. Howard Thurman, "Religion in a Time of Crisis," in *A Strange Freedom: The Best of Howard Thurman on Religious Experience and Public Life*, ed. Walter Earl Fluker and Catherine Tumber (Boston: Beacon, 1998), 130.

2. Howard Thurman, *The Inward Journey* (Richmond, IN: Friends United Press, 1961), 65.

3. A "race man" was a male who was committed to addressing the problem of white supremacy, racism, and segregation through critiquing and resisting the prevailing social, public, and ideological discourse on race. Du Bois's second wife, Shirley Graham, was called a "race woman."

4. W. E. B. Du Bois, "Will the Church Remove the Color Line?" in *Du Bois on Religion*, ed. Phil Zuckerman (Walnut Creek, CA: AltaMira, 2000), 173–79 (173).

church in the United States nearly thirty years after his publications of *The Souls of Black Folk* (1903) and *The Negro Church* (1903) in which he described, in the former text, the problem of the color line and a vision to remove the vicious and debilitating socially constructed marker of demarcation. In the latter text, Du Bois described the role of the Negro church in responding to and being victimized by the color line. Unfortunately, for Du Bois and the millions of emancipated Africans on United States soil, the color line was becoming an integral part of the nation's identity and practice that was in many ways created, endorsed, and perpetuated by the Christian church in the United States.

In 1949, pastor, preacher, prophet, theologian, mystic, and educator Howard Thurman (1899–1981) tells of an encounter with a Hindu gentleman in India while he (Thurman) was on a Christian delegation in 1935. According to Thurman, the Hindi gentleman politely but sternly asserted his opinion that he believed Thurman to be "a traitor to all the darker peoples of the earth,"[5] and he challenged Thurman to defend his Christian position. Thurman's response led to the publication of *Jesus and the Disinherited* (1949) in which he articulated the radical, redemptive religion of Jesus that gave him, a dark-hued colored man in the United States, the ability to live with creativity and dignity. Thurman identified with a poor and oppressed Jesus who found a way to navigate the Roman Empire of the first century and externalize a vision for oppressed peoples in any epoch.

Thurman's reinterpretation of Jesus and, hence, Christianity in the United States for those who were the victims of European colonization, conquest, and enslavement is antithetical to the European notion of the Matthean Great Commission. Thurman's two quotes open this chapter because they point to the significance of Jesus' message for enslaved Africans and their descendants on United States soil. For Thurman, and for many others like him, Jesus' proclamation of the kingdom of God enabled him to acknowledge yet transcend a hostile, oppressive, unjust, and immoral nation that is supposedly founded on Christian principles. As an African American born in Daytona Beach, Florida, he is remembered for being both timeless and timely in the ways he plumbed the depths of his interior and subjective structures in order to externalize a different vision for humanity grasped by various sociopolitical and religious tensions and strife.[6] Living in, through, and beyond the Jim Crow South, two world wars, the Vietnam War, and the Civil Rights Movement of

---

5. Howard Thurman, *Jesus and the Disinherited* (1939; repr., Richmond, IN: Friends United Press, 1981), 15.

6. Kim Lawton, "The Legacy of Howard Thurman: Mystic and Theologian," *Religion & Ethics Newsweekly*, January 18, 2002, www.pbs.org/wnet/religionandethics/week520/feature.html.

the 1950s and 60s, he challenged European triumphalist, abusive practices and ideologies of Christianity and the church that were—and still are—perpetrated on the indigenous peoples in Africa, Asia, and the Americas. Both Thurman and Du Bois decried the Christian church's direct involvement with and biblical endorsement of "African holocaust, enslavement and colonization; the 'failure' of reconstruction, the ritual of lynching and the rise of Jim Crow segregation in the United States; and, white colonial and racial rule throughout Africa, and especially apartheid in South Africa."[7]

In light of the historical and contemporary effects of the pathology of white supremacy in the Christian church in the United States, this essay focuses on envisioning a new day of Christian education through Howard Thurman's critical interpretation of Jesus. I presuppose that what is commonly coined and understood as the Matthean Great Commission (hereinafter referred to as the Great Commission) is a distortion and misappropriation by the European colonizers and missionaries of Jesus' final message to the disciples in Matt. 28:16-20. Jesus instructed his disciples to model and disseminate his message of liberation, life, and love to Jews, Samaritans, and Gentiles. Regardless of national origin, all were to have access and participation in the new faith community that was inclusive of cultural, gender, age, and class difference. Deviating from Jesus' instructions, the European colonizers and missionaries brought and modeled violence, enslavement, death, and hatred. Apparently, in their minds, fulfilling the Great Commission was synonymous with European enculturation, expansion, and the subjugation of humans who were of a much darker hue. With this distorted ideology, the Euro-American Protestant colonizers and missionaries taught and modeled Christianity to enslaved Africans in the United States that, on one hand, promoted the eternal subservience of black souls. However, on the other hand, they taught a Christianity that separated the material world from the spiritual one by asserting that in the other-world, heaven, the enslaved Africans would experience freedom from slavery. Christian education was, and for many people still is, a tool to maintain white domination over non-white people in the United States and beyond.

My interrogation of the Great Commission explores reclaiming Jesus' kingdom of God message that invited people, especially poor, oppressed, and enslaved people, to a radical, new way of being human. This radical, new way of being required being in right relationship with self, others, the divine, and all of creation. First, I provide a brief overview of Christian education and black souls during the antebellum era in the United States. Next, I elucidate

7. Reiland Rabaka, "The Souls of White Folk: W. E. B. Du Bois's Critique of White Supremacy and Contributions to Critical White Studies," *Journal of African American Studies* 11, no. 1 (2007), 1–15 (2).

Thurman's understanding of Jesus' proclamation that "the kingdom of God is within you" (Luke 17:21). Third, I briefly discuss contemporary womanist theological scholarship that interrogates the Matthean Great Commission. The womanist critique is shorter in length than the two preceding sections although it is nevertheless substantive. Womanist scholarship is much younger than scholarship on Christian education, African Americans, and the kingdom of God. Nevertheless, the contributions in this volume of Mitzi J. Smith and Lynne St. Clair Darden help to broaden the womanist and feminist perspectives on interrogating the Matthean Great Commission. Finally, I conclude with poetic prose to provoke the imagination of my colleagues in the academy and church as we find new ways of educating in the Christian faith that take seriously Jesus' kingdom of God message and its potency to redeem humanity from the various racial and social evils and injustices. The primary goal of this essay is to provide Christian education content for humanization and liberation in light of the uncritical acceptance of the Great Commission.

CHRISTIAN EDUCATION AND BLACK SOULS

Thurman launched an explicit critique on the Christian church because of the extent to which too many Christians viewed the disinherited[8] as "objects of missionary endeavor and enterprise, without being at all willing to treat them either as brothers or as human beings."[9] The "Christian" objectification of black souls on United States soil by Euro-American colonizers and missionaries was a process of dismissing the well-developed religious worldview of enslaved Africans that they possessed prior to their arrival in the United States and that was retained even during the Middle Passage.[10] This religious worldview of

8. In light of the overuse of terms such as "disinherited," "oppressed," and "poor," I will offer a brief explanation of Thurman's understanding of the "disinherited." Thurman understood the disinherited in both specific and non-ontological ways. A person or group is disinherited if they lack social, political, and economic status and resources to act on their environment with creativity and dignity due to the oppression and suppression by another person or group. Hence, as an African American in the twentieth century, due to race and racism, Thurman considered himself to be a member of a disinherited group. Moreover, he considered Jesus of Nazareth and the Jews to be disinherited, too, in light of Roman social, political, and economic control and suppression. However, for Thurman, the socially, politically, and economically disinherited can look to religious and spiritual resources in order to act on their environment in ways that engage and transcend the disinherited, oppressive material status. In his reinterpretation of Jesus and Christianity, Thurman discovered how to move within and beyond "the problem of the color line" as a human with creativity and dignity.

9. Thurman, *Jesus and the Disinherited*, 13.

10. E. Franklin Frazier, *The Negro Church in America* [published with] C. Eric Lincoln, *The Black Church Since Frazier* (New York: Schocken Books, 1974), 17; Peter J. Paris, *The Spirituality of African*

the enslaved African encountered a religious worldview in the Euro-American that deemed them as infidels who were not worthy to ascend to the superior Christian religion of Europeans and Euro-Americans.[11] Along with this perception of enslaved Africans as infidels, the Europeans had an unwritten law that Christianity and slavery could not be concomitant.[12] Hence, if an enslaved African became a Christian, she or he would no longer be a slave. Consequently, proselytizing the enslaved African or Negro was not a top priority for obvious reasons. Another component within the religious worldview of the Euro-American was the fear of insurrection by the enslaved Africans if they received religious instruction.[13] For many Europeans in the United States, Christianity was a religion that was designed for the superior white race and could potentially obliterate the slave and master, black and white oppressive relationship. In the antebellum period, Euro-American Christianity was practical in its thought and practice concerning the Negro.

Despite this pervasive religious ideology, there were some denominations or religious groups that were dissenters. For example, the Quakers sought not only to convert the enslaved Africans, but also to abolish slavery. Though not abolitionists, the Puritans did consider it appropriate to proselytize the enslaved Africans.[14] The Methodists also took interest in providing religious instruction to the Negroes, once a royal decree indicated that conversion to Christianity would not constitute manumission.[15] In this vein, the tension or dilemma of propagating the gospel as Christian service and social and economic profit was resolved as freedom of the soul from damnation could occur even though one's physical body was still in bondage.[16] The enslaved Africans or Negroes were considered by these denominations or religious groups to be worthy of Christianity without their religious conversion resulting in social freedom. Unlike the other Euro-American Christians, the Puritans and Methodists bifurcated or polarized the body and soul as if two distinct and parallel worlds existed where the spiritual one functioned without any relevance

Peoples: The Search for a Common Moral Discourse (Minneapolis: Fortress Press, 1995), 22–26; Henry H. Mitchell, *Black Church Beginnings: The Long-Hidden Realities of the First Years* (Grand Rapids: Eerdmans, 2004), 16–18.

11. Carter G. Woodson, *The History of the Negro Church*, third ed. (Washington, DC: Associated Publishers, 1972), 1–2.

12. Ibid., 2.

13. Anne H. Pinn and Anthony B. Pinn, *Fortress Introduction to Black Church History* (Minneapolis: Fortress Press, 2002), 2; Woodson, *History of the Negro Church*, 3.

14. Pinn and Pinn, *Fortress Introduction*, 3.

15. Woodson, *History of the Negro Church*, 5.

16. Pinn and Pinn, *Fortress Introduction*, 4–5.

in the social, material world. Moreover, this kind of Christianity seems to be truly otherworldly because the enslaved Africans' freedom was something to be experienced in another lifetime, in a different world. Or, the Puritans and Methodists' guilt were assuaged as they promulgated the gospel to those they considered to be redeemable heathens yet chattel property.

The political and economic influence on Christianity during the antebellum period highlights the integration that existed between church and state. The majority of the Euro-American Christians refused to share the gospel with their (human) chattel property because the enslaved Africans could view themselves as equal to their masters and consequently disrupt the economic system of slavery that exploited and raped both slave and master of their humanity. The status quo of separation, oppression, and racial and social caste had to be maintained because, if not, Christianity would enfranchise the enslaved African with the right to vote and to be free.[17] Then, the modicum of Euro-American Christians such as the Puritans and Methodists became more aggressive in proselytizing the Negro only when the church endorsed the notion that baptism or initiation into Christianity did not threaten the economic and social status of either party. In both of these Christian camps, the desire to maintain power over a people in society, politics, and religion shaped their religious ideology and practice. Noted historian of black culture and life Carter G. Woodson asserts that "while struggling for liberty themselves, even for religious freedom, these Americans [many of British descent] were not willing to grant others what they themselves desired."[18]

Prior to the Revolutionary War, a religious revival emerged in colonial America that transformed the theology of certain denominations—mainly the Methodists and Baptists— concerning the Negro and Christianity. The period of the first Great Awakening (1730s–1740s) was marked by a sense of religious fervor that called into question human sin and God's judgment on such immoral acts.[19] The will of God had to be adhered to or else sinners would endure suffering and pain or eternal damnation as the result of disobedience.[20] Furthermore, many of the revivalist preachers who proclaimed such a message considered themselves to be part of an extraordinary work of God where they were discovering rather than designing the move of God.[21] Basically, "when

17. Mitchell, *Black Church Beginnings*, 27.

18. Woodson, *History of the Negro Church*, 35.

19. Pinn and Pinn, *Fortress Introduction*, 6–7.

20. Ibid., 6.

21. Frank Lambert, *Inventing the "Great Awakening"* (Princeton, NJ: Princeton University Press, 1999), 4.

scores of men and women came under 'conviction' for their sins and seemed to undergo 'conversion,' the revivalists declared the existence of revival."[22] For the first time in colonial America, both the free and the bond were given equal access to become a part of Christianity.[23] However, the greatest influx of enslaved Africans into Christianity did not occur until after the first Great Awakening in 1760s and 1770s.[24] During this period of revivals, which were different from the 1730s and 1740s, the Presbyterians, Methodists, and Baptists offered the Virginian colony a different perspective of Christianity than the Anglicanism that had formerly dominated the region.[25] With this different way of preaching and teaching Christianity that was filled with emotional and overt expression, "the Holy Spirit, broke out of the mold of the literate, formal, structured Anglican liturgy and 'got loose' in the radically new 'dispensation.'"[26]

During the period of the Great Awakenings, many enslaved Africans began to move beyond rigid, doctrinal borders and orders. It is noted that "Slaves filtered the revivalists' message through their experience in bondage."[27] Furthermore, some white historians even contend that African Americans saw baptism and freedom as being synonymous, and consequently, many African Americans became emboldened and empowered to resist the unjust institution of slavery.[28] Gayraud Wilmore, church historian, affirms this experience of the enslaved Africans in the following statement: "But blacks have used Christianity not so much as it was delivered to them by racist white churches, but as its truth was authenticated to them in the experience of suffering and struggle, to reinforce an enculturated religious orientation and to produce an indigenous faith that emphasized dignity, freedom, and human welfare."[29] Hence, during and following the Great Awakening, the enslaved Africans appropriated a Christian theology and manner of worship that differed from their slave masters. What they observed and heard from their slave masters was deemed as hypocritical and, in many instances, disparaged.[30]

The Christianity the enslaved Africans learned or caught as embodying freedom came from a source other than their slave masters and missionaries. Or,

22. Ibid., 6.

23. Pinn and Pinn, *Fortress Introduction*, 7.

24. Lambert, *Inventing the "Great Awakening,"* 16.

25. Ibid.

26. Mitchell, *Black Church Beginnings*, 37.

27. Lambert, *Inventing the "Great Awakening,"* 142.

28. Ibid.

29. Gayraud S. Wilmore, *Black Religion and Black Radicalism: An Interpretation of the Religious History of Afro-American People*, second ed. (Maryknoll, NY: Orbis Books, 1983), 4.

30. Ibid., 10.

it can be argued that while the enslaved Africans were denied access to, and had not gained reading, writing, and speaking fluency in the English language, their African linguistic system, cognitive capacity, and worldview were keen in helping them to perceive falsities. For example, Frederick Douglass, an abolitionist and former slave, adamantly asserts,

> What I have said respecting and against religion, I mean strictly to apply to the slaveholding religion of this land, and with no possible reference to Christianity proper; for, between the Christianity of this land, and the Christianity of Christ, I recognize the widest possible difference—so wide, that to receive the one as good, pure, and holy, is of necessity to reject the other as bad, corrupt, and wicked. . . . Indeed, I can see no reason, but the most deceitful one, for calling the religion of this land Christianity. I look upon it as the climax of all misnomers, the boldest of all frauds, and the grossest of all libels. Never was there a clearer case of "stealing the livery of the court of heaven to serve the devil in." I am filled with unutterable loathing when I contemplate the religious pomp and show, together with the horrible inconsistencies, which everywhere surround me. We have men-stealers for ministers, women-whippers for missionaries, and cradle-plunderers for church members. The man who wields the blood-clotted cowskin during the week fills the pulpit on Sunday, and claims to be a minister of the meek and lowly Jesus.[31]

Refusing to associate Christianity with what was being manifested in colonial America, Douglass reveals the free and bonded African's ability to discern authentic Christianity from the superficial posturing of their slave masters. It must have been extremely difficult for the enslaved African to imagine or conceive of a religion that promised freedom of the soul without the body. According to social ethicist Peter J. Paris, the African and African American cosmology saw no bifurcation between the spiritual and material worlds; all of life was sacred.[32] This holistic perspective of the cosmos is contrary to the Western, Christian slaveholding logic that espoused a clear line between the sacred and the profane, the spiritual and material, the body and soul. For the African in the United States, an all-powerful God who gave them eternal salvation could not be so removed from and unconcerned about their

---

31. Qtd. in Pinn and Pinn, *Fortress Introduction*, 12.

32. Peter J. Paris, *The Spirituality of African Peoples: The Search for a Common Moral Discourse* (Minneapolis: Fortress Press, 1995), 33–34.

present dehumanization and oppression.[33] However, according to religious historian Albert J. Raboteau, a fifteenth-century Portuguese chronicler, "for though their bodies were now brought into some subjection, that was a small matter in comparison of their souls, which would now possess true freedom for evermore."[34] Beyond the intentions of the revivalists, the enslaved Africans seemed to have known intuitively what Catholic theologian M. Shawn Copeland records of Gregory of Nyssa: "God would not reduce the human race to slavery, since [God], when we had been enslaved to sin, spontaneously recalled us to freedom. But if God does not enslave what is free, who is he that sets his own power above God's?[35] Consequently, the enslaved Africans exercised power when they developed the invisible institution, a place and space, as a means to worship independently of their slave masters so that freedom of both body and soul could become a reality.

In the invisible institution, conversion was not based on "English language skill and successful rote memorization of such Christian standards as the Lord's Prayer and Psalm 23."[36] This Anglican way of conversion was supplanted with one that was commensurate with the revivalist fervor in the need to show remorse for one's sin and to turn away from such worldly activities as drinking, dancing, and certain styles of music.[37] Furthermore, as the enslaved Africans would steal away to have worship on their own terms, they met in secret places called hushed harbors where they preached sermons, sang songs, danced, and released deep intimate emotions without words, but with a shout or deep moans and groans, all which addressed their yearning for freedom as well as religious development.[38] This invisible, yet empowering religious institution was nascent of those more visible, concrete assemblies of dark bodies and souls that were yet to come as constant reminders of the unjust legacy, ideology, and practice of the Great Commission.

THE KINGDOM OF GOD IS WITHIN YOU

According to Thurman, the centrality of Jesus' message that the kingdom of God is within you is more than a private, personal experience. He found

---

33. Wilmore, *Black Religion and Black Radicalism*, 11.

34. Albert J. Raboteau, *Slave Religion: The "Invisible Institution" in the Antebellum South* (Oxford: Oxford University Press, 1978), 96.

35. Cited in M. Shawn Copeland, *Enfleshing Freedom: Body, Race, and Being* (Minneapolis: Fortress Press, 2010), 23. Parentheses in original.

36. Mitchell, *Black Church Beginnings*, 28.

37. Pinn and Pinn, *Fortress Introduction*, 14.

38. Ibid., 13–14.

Jesus' message in Luke 17:20-21 (NIV) to be empowering, inclusive, public, universally accessible, relational, and most importantly, disruptive of social and political systems and structures that fail to be life affirming and humanizing. More specifically, Thurman claimed,

> His [Jesus'] words were directed to the House of Israel, a minority within the Greco-Roman world, smarting under the loss of status, freedom, and autonomy, haunted by the dream of the restoration of a lost glory and a former greatness. His message focused on the urgency of a radical change in the inner attitude of the people. He recognized fully that out of the heart are the issues of life and that no external force, however great and overwhelming, can at long last destroy a people if it does not first win the victory of the spirit against them.[39]

As an African on United States soil, Thurman was able to draw parallels between the disinherited status and position of his people and that of Jesus and the Jews in Palestine under the Roman Empire. Furthermore, he understood Jesus' message to be descriptive and prescriptive, timely and timeless for the socially, politically, and economically oppressed of any age.

Thurman's perception of Jesus' message and ministry explicitly focuses on the House of Israel, those first-century Jews who were "sick and tired of being sick and tired."[40] Not every Jew accepted Jesus' message. Yet, for those Jews who could accept Jesus' message, his life and teachings invited them to recognize, receive, and enter into the kingdom of God.[41] In recognizing, receiving, and entering into the kingdom of God, the House of Israel—or the oppressed of any era—were acknowledging and adhering to a divine power other than Caesar's or the respective "emperor." Noncooperation with or maladjustment to the Roman oppressor enabled the House of Israel to recover their dignity and sense of self. They had another way of responding to the enemy because God's liberating power and reign was, according to Horsley, finally being manifested and modeled in and through the person of Jesus, Jesus' disciples, Jesus' predecessor John the Baptist, and other marginalized Jewish

39. Thurman, *Jesus and the Disinherited*, 21.

40. Fannie Lou Hamer (1917–1977), a civil rights leader, political activist, and community organizer of Mississippi, declared that she was "sick and tired of being sick and tired," which catapulted her into a public presence and force in the midst of the Jim Crow South.

41. Richard A. Horsley, "The Kingdom of God and the Renewal of Israel," in *The Bible and Liberation: Political and Social Hermeneutics*, ed. Norman K. Gottwald and Richard A. Horsley, rev. ed., (Maryknoll, NY: Orbis Books, 1993), 408–13.

groups such as the poor, children, and the persecuted who were recognizing, receiving, and entering into the kingdom.[42] God had not forgotten the socially, economically, and politically disenfranchised House of Israel. In short, their oppression was not final, and Jesus' message was a profound, powerful reminder that God was not only with the House of Israel, but also present to engender social and political renewal.[43]

Thurman was not a biblical scholar; nevertheless, his emphasis on Jesus' kingdom of God message for any oppressed group predates Richard A. Horsley's biblical scholarship on Jesus' intense politically oppressed context, and a corresponding radical resistance ethic of proclaiming and demonstrating the kingdom of God.[44] Moreover, Horsley unequivocally asserts that "the modern Christian mission enterprise is not historically unprecedented"[45] because many of the ancient Near Eastern empires imposed their culture and "gods" on the subjugated, dominated people groups.[46] Hence, the European Christian colonizers and missionaries have behaved in a fashion more akin to the infidel than to their professed founder and savior Jesus. The indigenous, colonized peoples in Africa, Asia, and the Americas, whom the European colonizers and missionaries considered to be uncivilized savages, were subjected to something similar to what Jesus and Jews experienced under the Roman imperial rule.[47]

Thurman's understanding of the kingdom of God as proclaimed by Jesus clearly challenges the church in the United States to rethink its historical and contemporary legitimatization of various forms of violence and evil that is contrary to God's intention for humanity and all of creation. First and foremost, the kingdom of God is an internal, interior reality. In Luke 17:20-21 (NIV), Jesus responds to the Pharisees' inquiry regarding the future establishment of God's kingdom by stating *how* it will not come and *where* it resides. Jesus explicitly asserts that the kingdom of God will not come with things that can be observed, but, in fact, it is something that is within you. Far too many of the Europeans who practiced the Great Commission focused on the expansion of an external kingdom through conquering, trafficking, killing, lynching, stealing, raping, and enslaving those whom they considered not human. Seemingly void of an interiority regarding the breadth, height, and depth of the kingdom of God, the

42. Ibid., 409.

43. Ibid., 410.

44. Richard A. Horsley, *Jesus and the Spiral of Violence: Popular Jewish Resistance in Roman Palestine* (San Francisco: Harper & Row, 1987).

45. Ibid., 8.

46. Ibid.

47. Ibid., 11.

Europeans became conquerors, colonizers, traffickers, and slave-masters who were economically and politically oppressive instead of liberating. In short, the overwhelming majority of the European colonizers and missionaries were unlike Jesus who trusted God for provision and embraced the humanity of his neighbor.

Thurman's interpretation of the significance of Jesus' message transforms Christian education from a mere inculcation of doctrine, creeds, and Scriptural passages into a process of knowing and being that manifests and models how to recognize, receive, and enter into the kingdom of God. In this model of Christian education, the church and Christianity are not the center, but the kingdom of God is central. This emphasis on the kingdom of God pushes the church beyond itself as the local and denominational bodies assume a different posture than merely passing on tradition based on theological presuppositions that usually lack power to speak to the exigencies of the day. Furthermore, teaching people of any or no faith tradition to recognize, receive, and enter into the kingdom of God somewhat constitutes a fellowship of shared humanity because, as human beings, we all need to grow in our awareness of self and beyond our particularities. With the kingdom of God as the center, we are educating and modeling how to encounter a neighbor, embrace difference, and nurture human flourishing regardless of one's religious particularity. If taken seriously, the church in the United States and Christian education can experience the boundless, open, and celebratory nature of the kingdom of God and thereby be on its way to addressing the problem of race and various other "isms" that divide.

Thurman named his broader understanding of Christian education while in India when a gentleman approach him who was alarmed that the Buddhist students who attended Christian schools ended up not only abandoning their faith, but also showed no interest in accepting Christianity.[48] This was problematic to Thurman's inquirer because, in his mind, there was little difference between Christianity and Buddhism. Thurman's response was as follows:

> It seems to me that Christian education has succeeded if it makes a man an authentic Christian, or it may make him a better and more completely devout Buddhist. For I believe that Jesus reveals to a man the meaning of what he is in root and essence already. When the prodigal son came to himself, he came to his father.[49]

48. Howard Thurman, *With Head and Heart: The Autobiography of Howard Thurman* (San Diego: Harcourt Brace, 1979), 114–15.

Thurman admits that in the moment the question came, he was able to articulate and announce what had before been an elusive thought.[50] Although he does not elaborate on the nature and scope of his understanding of Christian education, nevertheless, he seems to be saying that Jesus' revelatory power as a religious subject informs one and all on how to be and become fully human regardless of one's religious or national identity. For Thurman, Jesus, and consequently, Christian education at its best, illuminates who we, as humans, really are beyond the non-ontological particulars such as religion, race, color, creed, gender, class, sexuality, denominations, and national origin that alienate us from self, others, the world, and the divine. Moreover, Thurman knew a Jesus ". . . who was so conditioned and organized within himself that he became a perfect instrument for the embodiment of a set of ideals—ideals of such dramatic potency that they were capable of changing the calendar, rechanneling the thought of the world . . ."[51] This Jesus and his teachings, offered Thurman, a second generation, emancipated slave, yet still disenfranchised involuntary immigrant,[52] "a promising way to work through the conflicts of a disordered world."[53]

No doubt, Christian education, for Thurman, was grounded in Jesus and his message of the kingdom of God being within us as humans, and not in the transiency of social and political issues or movements. This insight and persuasion informed his leadership first as a co-founder of the Church for the Fellowship of All Peoples in San Francisco in 1943, and then as the first black dean of chapel of any predominantly white educational institution at Boston University. As co-pastor working alongside Alfred Fisk, a White colleague, Thurman eventually became the solo pastor of the first interracial and intercultural church in the United States.[54] This church began as an experiment to answer critical questions for Christianity and democracy.[55] Towards this Christian democratic end, the church attempted to embody in thought and

49. Ibid., 115.

50. Ibid.

51. Thurman, *Jesus and the Disinherited*, 16.

52. John Ogbu, a Nigerian born yet US trained sociologist educated at the University of California at Berkeley coined the term *involuntary immigrant* when referring to black people in the United States who were brought to the country against their will in comparison to black people from the continent of Africa and other Asian and Latin American ethnic groups who come to the United States more so out of their own volition as voluntary immigrants.

53. Thurman, *With Head and Heart*, 114.

54. Fluker and Tumber, eds., *A Strange Freedom*, 220.

55. Howard Thurman, "The Fellowship Church of All Peoples," in *A Strange Freedom*, 222.

practice the lofty ideals of democracy within the framework of Protestant Christianity.[56]

How Thurman taught, preached, and practiced inclusivity, social and political engagement, humanization and redemption as pastor of a new faith community was driven by the following key questions:

> First, is it possible to establish islands of community or fellowship in a sea of religious and social strife, with any hope of their resolving the strife? Second, is it possible for an authentic interracial and intercultural church to develop—a church that will not be largely dominated by one particular group with some other group on the fringes? Third, is it possible for a Negro and white minister to share the leadership of such a church on the basis of their respective gifts rather than on the basis of their group affiliations? In other words, in any given venture of this sort will the Negroes tend to gravitate toward the Negro pastor for leadership and counsel, and white people gravitate toward the white pastor for these same services? Fourth, how fundamental, and of what kind, will be the opposition to the development of the idea in practice, both from ecclesiastical interests and other interests of the community? What steps will be taken to neutralize its effect and to defeat its purpose?[57]

In response to these questions, Thurman developed curriculum that taught both children and adults from diverse backgrounds concerning other nationalities and races.[58] Furthermore, within the curriculum and church, women were included as a cultural group in which their lived experiences were affirmed and celebrated.[59] Hence, Thurman's questions became a compass for religious instruction and Christian education as he and the church endeavored to make Christianity relevant for contributing to a democratic society through its appropriation of the centrality of Jesus' message. He noted in his autobiography that "increasing numbers of people who were engaged in the common life of the city of San Francisco found in the church restoration, inspiration, and courage for their work on behalf of social change in the community."[60]

---

56. Ibid., 220.
57. Ibid., 222.
58. Ibid., 222–24.
59. Ibid., 223.
60. Thurman, *With Head and Heart*, 144.

Thurman is instructive for the church in the United States (institutional Protestant and Roman Catholic congregations and denominations including the Black Church and black churches) that has yet to address "the problem of the color line" and various other lines around gender, class, ability, and sexuality. He provides another way of being, thinking, and relating in the world that is not grounded in the false science of race or other nonessential categories, but rather as a human nurtured in dignity and creativity. He envisioned a world in which the politically and economically oppressed of any age would be able to experience life and God on earth while resisting social or political violence and injustice. In the process, oppressive systems and relationships are disrupted and new relations and structures emerge that foster Jesus' message of and commitment to the kingdom of God that is within.

We in our black religious institutions must find new creative ways of responding to the old and new forms of violence and injustice through Christian education that puts the kingdom of God at the center. In the age of faith-based organizations receiving federal funding, far too many of our black religious institutions continue to educate in the faith in ways that perpetuate—instead of disrupt—the status quo. More African American religious leaders and institutions should be mindful of and align with the Samuel Dewitt Proctor Conference, Inc. (SPCD). As an organization of progressive African American pastors and congregations, the SPCD educates and empowers its constituents towards human and social justice.[61] They are combating chronic, unjust unemployment, inadequate homes and neighborhoods, miseducation in public schools, and mass incarceration in the twenty-first century. They are on the front lines of a new abolition movement in response to what legal scholar Michelle Alexander calls "the New Jim Crow"—the legal system of discrimination against poor, African American males (and their communities) who have been convicted as felons for petty drug crimes and thereby lose access to vote, jury duty, financial aid, federally subsidized housing, gainful employment, and mainstream society.[62] SPCD moves beyond mere social action and cultic practice in their faith commitments, and speaks truth to power. African American religious institutions in particular, and the church in the United States in general, must refuse to be consoled or appeased by the government. As during Jesus' day:

---

61. "About Us," Samuel DeWitt Proctor Conference, Inc., sdpconference.info/about-us/.

62. Michelle Alexander, *The New Jim Crow: Mass Incarceration in the Age of Colorblindness* (New York: New Press, 2010), 4.

The Romans allowed the exercise of Jewish religion so long as it took no form other than mere cultic celebration, personal belief, and the reinforcement of local social order. The minute it became more collective in its expression and had political implications, the Romans intervened with renewed physical repression.[63]

May we, the church, educate in ways that are collective and political in scope as we carry our cross in bearing witness to God's redemption in recognizing, receiving, and entering the kingdom.

CONTEMPORARY WOMANIST CRITIQUES

For many womanist theologians, ethicists, and biblical scholars, the phrase *kingdom of God* has been appropriated in a similar way that Jesus' words to the disciples have become interpreted as *the Great Commission*. Today, for these particular scholars, both phrases connote an oppressive, patriarchal ideology that dehumanizes women and non-white people groups, and further subjugates them in the name of Jesus.[64] In short, the European male elite (economically and politically) used Christianity to perpetuate violence and injustice on people groups who welcomed them as the stranger or the traveler. Womanist ethicist Katie Cannon unequivocally argues that Prince Henry of Portugal (1394–1460) was motivated by Christianity to implement the aggressive assaults on Africans in the transatlantic slave trade.[65] In the midst of the religious crusades between European Christians and Moorish Muslims, the papacy granted authority to the European regimes to spread Christianity through the use of clerics for evangelization and thereby propagate European interests.[66] Here, Cannon unveils that the first missionaries were priests from the religious orders that existed during the time of Prince Henry, and who were supported by his economic, political, and military might. Moreover, the earliest European,

63. Horsley, *Jesus and the Spiral of Violence*, 45.

64. Thurman predates womanist and feminist scholarship. My extensive focus on reclaiming Jesus' kingdom of God message through Thurman allows me to challenge those who have distorted it and those who have been severely wounded by the distortion to see and experience it differently, if possible. My introduction of womanist scholarship engages those who cannot—or choose not to—return to Christianity due to the irrevocable damage that has been done by the misappropriation and distortion of the kingdom of God and the Matthean Great Commission. The womanist scholars, in my mind, are in continuity with Thurman as they raise another important marginalized group, black women, which was not explicit in Thurman.

65. Katie G. Cannon, "Cutting Edge: Christian Imperialism and the Transatlantic Slave Trade," *Journal of Feminist Studies in Religion* 24, no. 1 (2008): 127–34 (127).

66. Ibid.

Western forms of sharing or spreading Christianity were informed by "an unholy alliance of contorted logic"[67] of what Cannon calls the *missiologic of the imminent parousia*[68] and the *theologic of racialized normativity.*[69] European expansionists and imperialists came to believe they were the ones to help usher in Christ's return and the establishment of a new world order, God's kingdom on earth, that reflected the "Christianizing" of the nations by the supposedly pure, white race.[70]

Linda E. Thomas, a womanist theologian and anthropologist, rightfully notes that the phrase *Great Commission* does not exist in the Matthean narrative and, like Cannon, interrogates the European imperialist notion of the mission of God.[71] Moving away from the Matthean narrative, Thomas employs the Lukan narratives at 9:1-9 and 10:1-10 to explicate the mission of God which focuses more on how Jesus sends the twelve out ". . . not to call people to receive Christ but, quite contrarily, to stand at the door of the stranger, both hungry and tired, with the hope of that the good people of the house or street will receive them, feed them, and save the disciples from the elements."[72] In this vein, the disciples had to depend on hospitality as a way of entering into the villages or being welcomed by the people. They had to trust Jesus, the one who sent them, and simultaneously rely on the people Jesus was sending them to as they went forth proclaiming and manifesting the kingdom of God. In the process, the people were being called to recognize the kingdom of God, the peace of God in their midst.

Both Cannon and Thomas, along with Thurman, are critical of the triumphalist notion of European imperialism through Christianity. They provide us, the church in the United States, with new lenses and models for Christian education that take seriously Christianity's painful, atrocious past of aiding and abetting imperialism and colonialism and the legacy of the Matthean Great Commission on the present. In summary, they help us to reclaim the significance of Jesus' message for those who were and still are in deep need of social, political, economic, and religious relief. Moreover, they open up new ways of being and becoming human that challenge political and

---

67. Ibid., 128.

68. Ibid.

69. Ibid.

70. Ibid., 130.

71. Linda E. Thomas, "Anthropology, Mission, and The African Woman: A Womanist Approach," *Black Theology* 5, no. 1 (2007), 11–19 (12).

72. Ibid.

economic systems that promote death and oppression instead of life and human progression.

Conclusion

"Will the church remove the color line?" is a question, unfortunately, that is yet to be answered. However, following Du Bois, the church in the United States must raise this question in the twenty-first century and reclaim Jesus' kingdom of God message as a central component to their Christian education vision and practice. Slaveholding Christian education and its legacy must be combatted because it existed to maintain the master–slave relationship that was void of the life-giving message of the kingdom of God that Jesus proclaimed. Further, in loyalty to and as an extension of the Matthean Great Commission, slaveholding Christianity dismissed the humanity of enslaved Africans in the United States, created dichotomies foreign to the African worldview, and promoted a false message of social bondage as God's design. Thurman's Jesus encourages us to teach the faith that engenders perpetual healing and justice in light of the trauma inflicted by those who enacted the Matthean Great Commission. What he launched at the Church for the Fellowship of All People in 1944 is exemplary and relevant today as we respond to cultural diversity, and religious difference within and beyond Christianity. Moreover, he, along with Cannon and Thomas, invite Christian educators in the academy and the church to consider new lenses, practices, and sources for doing Christian education. Thurman funds us Christian educators with an ability to reclaim an old concept that has potency to address the pressing issues of the day. Then, Cannon and Thomas, as womanist scholars, supply us with new concepts, theoretical frameworks, and practices that allow for fresh insights and critiques of the Matthean Great Commission.

The contributions of Thurman, Cannon, and Thomas can inform some logical next steps in Christian education. First, Thurman's concept of the kingdom of God and pastoral leadership can be used to develop contemporary Christian education models that critique institutional and social structures while exposing the most vulnerable populations today. As individuals and faith communities grow in critical consciousness, they would be discerning how to live as witnesses to God's redemptive activity on earth and reimagining a more authentic way of carrying out Jesus' instructions and commissions in the Matthean Gospel. Second, Cannon's theoretical concepts and language challenge Christian educators to explore the historical and contemporary impact of the terrorist, traumatic experience that occurred in the European expansion. Employing the terms *missiologic of the imminent parousia* and the *theologic of racialized normativity* constitute a major departure from the traditional uncritical acceptance of Christian missions and education. Cannon's language affords us the opportunity to talk about global encounters and Christian education in a way that examines the intersection of race, gender, religion, capitalism, and anthropology. New ways of educating in the faith at the local and global levels could emerge from such a serious, disciplined conceptual analysis. Third, Thomas points us to specific practices of hospitality and trust in God and others that are integral to Christianity. We can create lessons or role-play activities that invite students in the academy and church to value and practice hospitality, the welcoming of friend and stranger, and to document their experiences. These experiences and narratives could help to illuminate the vulnerability of practicing radical hospitality as either recipient or giver to a friend or stranger. Students could even reenact the initial encounters between Europeans and the people in Africa, Asia, and Americas to get yet another perspective concerning hospitality, or the lack thereof. Finally, I conclude with poetic prose as another way of doing Christian education towards humanization and liberation in my interrogation of the Matthean Great Commission.

The European Matthean Great Commission perpetrated evil and sin on indigenous people and their respective occupied lands of dwelling

Africa, Asia, and the Americas they ENCOUNTERED, and not discovered

The commodification of people and land was the primary end

Creating unbalanced, disharmonious, master-slave relations

Dismissing their humanity viewing them as savages, and thereby created a fallacy of White control and superiority

Inflicting bondage, violence, and injustice, the Europeans were somehow convinced that Jesus endorsed such inhumane acts

The pathology of such an ideology and theology, unfortunately, is still among us

We, in the Church, have yet to recover from the death-dealing blows of such spiritual, religious, and mental dysfunction

We seem to be tainted forever unless we re-member the time before European invasion

Our indigenous sisters and brothers welcomed the European stranger, traveler, and modeled for the world a radical hospitality

A hospitality that embraces instead of excludes, and lives in freedom

A hospitality that did not fear or mistrust the apparent differences between them

A hospitality that shared resources for human sustainability

A hospitality that contributed to and affirmed one's creativity and dignity

A hospitality that understood the way of the migrant or immigrant among them

A hospitality that included a spiritual, cosmological awareness that was possibly more akin to Jesus as the God with us

A hospitality that was abused and misused, and transformed the welcoming neighbor into an enemy

Genocide, economic exploitation, rape, stealing, lying, blood lusting and continuous warmongering were the evil fruit of the European explorers

Colonizing and settling on already inhabited land while simultaneously dismissing the indigenous people's vision and practice of civilization, or righteous relationship between people and land

"Separate, hostile, and unequal" "Separate, hostile, and unequal" "Separate, hostile, and unequal"[73] are adjectives that reflect a twisted, deranged practice known as "the Matthean 'Great Commission.'"

Now, there are visas and passports for anyone to travel,

Governments dictating and controlling our natural, human movement

The redefining of boundaries and settling on land reconstituted the nature of our creative, human encounters

Upon closer analysis, our biblical forefathers and mothers, too, interrogate the Matthean Great Commission

Yahweh told Abram to get up and leave his land of Ur the Chaldeans

Traveling to an unknown land he had to trust God and the hospitality of the stranger whom he was yet to encounter

Jesus' mother and stepfather were told to flee to Egypt due to Herod's fear of replacement

Movement was a necessity to avoid the decree of death that claimed far too many of the Jewish male babies

---

73. This phrase is drawn from Andrew Hacker, *Two Nations: Black and White, Separate, Hostile, Unequal* (New York: Ballantine, 1995).

The disputed conquest narratives found in the first testament may seem to be a direct connection[74]

Look, Yahweh promised the emancipated Hebrews the land of Canaan

Violence, rape, conquest, and warfare dominate the biblical narratives

Yet it is believed they lived in an era where it was kill or be killed, an ancient form of savagery

This kill or be killed mentality was not the case for the European explorer

We know how they were welcomed by the African, Asian, and American indigenous sisters and brothers

Welcomed and embraced the European stranger was not "othered"

Yet, today, over 500 years of African, Asian, and Indigenous American displacement can be traced directly to the European's Matthean 'Great Commission'

Who were the uncivilized, savage ones? Critical questions must be raised in order to reclaim Jesus' message of healing and hope

Here is some of the fruit of such insanity as W. E. B. Du Bois declared: "the church today is the strongest seat of racial and color prejudice."[75]

The Rev. Dr. Martin Luther King, Jr. challenged the Church and the United States of America to change unjust laws and deep-seated immorality

King's nonviolent direct action helped to expose the depth of such violence and hate that resided among those who claimed Jesus as their "Lord and Savior."

He endured the accusations of criminalization as a disrupter of law and order just like the historical Jesus if our Euro-American sisters and brothers care to remember

This similarity I draw between King and Jesus is not new

Here is Du Bois' comparative analysis between Jesus and the African on US soil:

---

74. Norman K. Gottwald, *The Hebrew Bible in its Social World and Ours* (Atlanta: Scholars, 1993).
75. Du Bois, "The Church and The Negro," in *Du Bois on Religion*, 99.

Yet Jesus Christ was a laborer and black men are laborers; He was poor and we are poor; He was despised of his fellow men and we are despised; He was persecuted and crucified, and we are mobbed and lynched. If Jesus Christ came to America He would associate with Negroes and Italians and working people; He would eat and pray with them, and He would seldom see the interior of the Cathedral of Saint John the Divine.[76]

The enslaved black woman, man, and child on US soil were perceived to be soulless and thoughtless, and who were taught the Bible so they could remain subservient

Infidels, emotionless, soulless beasts were the pejorative stigmas applied

No longer shall we continue as Christian educators in the church, academy, and community in such a deficient manner of what constitutes the core of our shared humanity

I hope and pray we vow to reclaim, to recover Jesus' kingdom of God message so that wherever we are there the kingdom of God will be in response to contemporary empires and kingdoms, both local and global, towards an increasing faithfulness regardless of the corrupt, violent circumstances

I hope and pray we vow to reclaim, to recover Jesus' kingdom of God message so that our lives can become a living sacrifice unto the only true leader and divine emperor of all creation and people groups

I hope and pray we vow to reclaim, to recover Jesus' kingdom of God message that denounces results and success as defined by systems of oppression where we become consumed by mindless production that cuts at the core of our high, holy calling

I hope and pray we vow to reclaim, to recover Jesus' kingdom of God message as a new political and educational vision that informs the US church's identity and mission

76. Ibid., 99–100.

11

Beginning Again: Rethinking Christian Education in Light of the Great Commission

Anthony G. Reddie

TEACHING AND LEARNING THE CHRISTIAN FAITH

The impulse to propagate the Christian faith is often attributed to the words found at the very end of Matthew's Gospel, in the nomenclature often identified as the Great Commission. For the purposes of this essay, the relevant words of the Great Commission are to be found in Matt. 28:20, which states "and teach them to do everything I have told you." The teaching ministry of the church has arisen from the mandate to "make new disciples" of Jesus Christ. The establishment of new churches in the Mediterranean during the second half of the first century of the Common Era was often predicated on the replication of Christian ideas, combined with human socialization in the power of the Holy Spirit, in which, new recruits were placed in proximity with more established believers within a powerful framework of an emerging Christian narrative.[1]

The teaching ministry of the church that has often been utilized to make new disciples has been that of Christian education. The term Christian education can be defined and understood in a variety of ways. Jeff Astley and Colin Crowder provide a helpful starting point for a definition and a rationale for Christian education. The authors describe Christian education as

---

1. See Stanley Hauerwas, "The Gesture of a Truthful Story," in *Theological Perspectives on Christian Formation: A Reader on Theology and Christian Education,* eds. Jeff Astley, Leslie J. Francis, and Colin Crowder (Grand Rapids: Eerdmans, 1996), 97–105. See also Craig Dykstra, "No Longer Strangers: The Church and its Educational Ministry," in *Theological Perspectives on Christian Formation,* 106–18.

> The phrase...often used quite generally to refer to those processes by which people learn to become Christian and to be more Christian, through learning Christian beliefs, attitudes, values, emotions and dispositions to engage in Christian actions and to be open to Christian experiences.[2]

In the context of this essay, we are looking at the practice of Christian education as a facet of the *missio Dei*. In using the term *mission* I am referring to the overarching activity of God in the world in which the church seeks to participate in the saving work of Christ as it relates to all dimensions of the God–human encounter in various cultures and contexts across the world.[3]

Central to the notion of Christian education as an expression of mission, in light of the Great Commission, is the importance of identity and self-esteem. Namely, what does it mean to be a human being created in the image and likeness of God and what is the nature of our existence and worth in the world? Christian education is concerned not only with the narrow propagation of the Christian faith, but also with wider questions of human growth and development.

Mission attends to the holistic nature of God's saving activity in the world and what makes for human flourishing. Christian education is the discipline that enables people to reflect upon and actualize their experiences that contribute to the life of faith. The role of the Christian educator is not solely confined to enabling people to *know more* about the Christian faith (namely, a strictly cognitive exercise), but it is also linked to assisting people to *be more*, which is an affective or emotional perspective.

THE PSYCHOLOGICAL DAMAGE ARISING FROM WESTERN CHRISTIAN MISSION

The Great Commission, allied with Eurocentric notions of superiority complicit with European imperialism, gave rise to a form of mercantilist expansion. This, as a corollary, resulted in the exploitation of non-white bodies. Womanist theologian Linda Thomas critiques the Matthean tradition of mission, arguing that the locus of power lies with those who are sent as opposed to those who are the recipients of such missionary activities.[4] The missionary

2. Jeff Astley, Leslie J. Francis, and Colin Crowder, eds., *Theological Perspectives on Christian Formation*, x.

3. Arguably, one of the most important and influential texts in our understanding of Christian mission is David J. Bosch, *Transforming Mission: Paradigm Shifts in Theology of Mission* (Maryknoll, NY: Orbis Books, 1991).

impulse of the Great Commission was interpreted as a means of imposing Eurocentric values on the cultures of non-European peoples across the world.

Western Christian mission formed a collusive relationship with white European hegemony that assisted in providing the theological underscoring for the transatlantic slave trade. When Europeans, particularly in the Elizabethan age, began to engage with Africans on a prolonged basis, mainly through trade, it did not take much imagination to deduce that the preexisting, underlying notions of "otherness" made black Africans ripe for exploitation.[5] The tensions between religion, faith, ethnicity, and nationality were exploited by means of "specious" forms of biblical interpretation. One of the main prooftexts that resolved the issue for justifying the enslavement of Africans within a Christian framework arose from Gen. 9:18–25, "The Curse of Ham." Noah punishes his son Ham by cursing his own grandson Canaan (the son of Ham), condemning him and all his descendants to slavery.[6]

African American scholars, such as Asante, estimate that upwards of fifty million African people were transported between Africa and the Americas over a four hundred year period.[7] Inherent within that black, transatlantic movement of forced migration and labour, was a form of biased, racialized teaching that asserted the inferiority and subhuman nature of the black self.[8] The continued struggles of black people that arise from the era of slavery can be seen in the overarching material poverty and marginalization of black people across the world.[9]

Anthony Pinn perhaps, more so than any other contemporary scholar, has charted the contested relationship that exists between the existential, material realities of black bodies and the overarching construction of Christianity into which so many of the former were both herded and socialized of their own volition.[10] In *Terror and Triumph*, Pinn outlines the long hinterland of demonization and virulent denigration that provided the essential backdrop to

4. See Linda E. Thomas, "Anthropology, Mission and the African Woman: A Womanist Approach," *Black Theology* 5, no. 1 (2007): 11–19.

5. See Ron Ramdin, *Reimaging Britain: Five Hundred Years of Black and Asian History* (London: Pluto, 1999), 5–10.

6. See Stephen R. Haynes, *Noah's Curse: The Biblical Justification of American Slavery* (Oxford: Oxford University Press, 2002). See also Sylvester A. Johnson, *The Myth of Ham in Nineteenth-Century American Christianity* (New York: Palgrave Macmillan, 2004).

7. See Molefi Kete Asante, "Afrocentricity and Culture," in *African Culture: The Rhythms of Unity*, ed. Molefi Kete Asante and Kariamu Welsh Asante (Trenton, NJ: First Africa World Press, 1990), 3–12.

8. See Eric Williams, *Capitalism and Slavery* (London: Andre Deutsch, 1983).

9. See Dwight N. Hopkins, *Heart and Head: Black Theology, Past, Present and Future* (New York: Palgrave Macmillan, 2002), 127–54.

transatlantic chattel slavery.[11] Outlining the apparent ease and the complicity with which Christianity colluded with epistemological frameworks that underpinned the machinery of slavery, Pinn writes,

> In short, Scripture required that English Christians begin their thinking on Africans with an understanding that Africans had the same creator. Yet they were at least physically and culturally different, and this difference had to be accounted for. As we shall see, a sense of shared creation did not prohibit a ranking within the created order, one in which Africans were much lower than Europeans.[12]

The sense of a deep prevailing anti-black sentiment replete with notions of Greek antiquity[13] and practiced within English, imperial, mission Christianity was given added piquancy in the deliberate attempt to use the developments of early Christian theology as a means of reinforcing the essentially depraved and base status of the black body.[14] Kelly Brown Douglas demonstrates how a particular outworking of Pauline, Platonic influenced theology (one that downplays the concrete materiality of the body in favour of the abstract and the spirit) was used as a means of demonizing black bodies.[15] Kelly Brown Douglas writes,

> Accordingly, it is platonized Christianity that gives rise to Christian participation in contemptible acts and attacks against human bodies, like those against Black bodies. Not only does platonized Christianity provide a foundation for easily disregarding certain

---

10. See Anthony B. Pinn, *Terror and Triumph: The Nature of Black Religion* (Minneapolis: Fortress Press, 2003). See also Anthony B. Pinn and Dwight N. Hopkins, eds., *Loving the Body: Black Religious Studies and the Erotic* (New York: Palgrave Macmillan, 2004) and Anthony B. Pinn, ed., *Black Religion and Aesthetics: Religious Thought and Life in Africa and the African Diaspora* (New York: Palgrave Macmillan, 2009).

11. Pinn, *Terror and Triumph*, 1–80.

12. Ibid., 6.

13. This phenomenon and theme has been explored by Robert E. Hood, *Begrimed and Black: Christian Traditions on Blacks and Blackness* (Minneapolis: Fortress Press, 1994).

14. This idea is taken from Kelly Brown Douglas's excellent study on black bodies and how they have been policed and controlled within the religious framework of Christianity. See Kelly Brown Douglas, *What's Faith Got to Do With It?: Black Bodies/Christian Souls* (Maryknoll, NY: Orbis Books, 2005).

15. Ibid., 3–38.

bodies, but it also allows for the demonization of those persons who have been sexualized.[16]

One can amplify the prevailing sense of an incipient anti-black strain within the corporate edifice of western mission Christianity when one considers the ways in which black Christianity itself has imbibed the strictures against the black body in their own corporate operations of religiosity. Anthony Pinn, drawing on a similar analysis of Platonized, Pauline theology, argues that black Christianity has imbibed the prevalent suspicion surrounding the black body and has taught many black Christians to remain at best indifferent to the material needs of the black body or to seek to transcend the despised nature of the black body as depicted in all its demonized and based images of European demagoguery.[17]

This sense of dislocation is manifested in both psychological and physical terms. The forebears of these children were plucked from the ancestral cradle of Africa and transplanted to the Caribbean and the Americas. In the light of the rupture and breach in African Diasporan history, the past five centuries have been a perpetual and substantive struggle for self-definition—a search for a sense of identity that has not been dictated and imposed by white power.[18] For many Diasporan Africans, the search for identity and a sense of positive self-esteem has been found from within the frameworks of the Christian faith. Faith in Christ has provided the conduit by which issues of identity and self-esteem have been explored.

CHRISTIAN EDUCATION FOR THE PURPOSES OF IDENTITY AND SELF-ESTEEM

The development of Christian education in the twentieth century has utilized the emergence of development psychology and the impact this discipline has made on our understanding of the human self. Particularly liberal Protestant models of Christian education have drawn upon the seminal work Erik H. Erikson. In his pivotal work on "identity crisis" amongst youth, Erickson takes pains to detail the assumptions that arise from what is often a pejorative term.[19]

16. Ibid., 37.

17. Pinn and Hopkins, *Loving the Body*, 1–8.

18. See the work of the great African American historian Carter G. Woodson for work that reflects on the notion of identity struggle of black people that often arises from various forms of miseducation organized and perpetrated by white power. See Carter G. Woodson, *The Mis-Education of the Negro* (1933; Trenton, NJ: Africa World Press, 1990).

19. Erik H. Erikson, *Identity: Youth and Crisis* (New York: Norton, 1984), 16.

Erikson contends that our understanding of what one might term an identity crisis should be seen as something that is normative and part of a general development of the intellectual processes of cognition.[20]

Erikson is most notable for the detailed work he has undertaken in the field of identity, with specific reference to the identity formations and crises of adolescents. In his writings, Erikson chronicles the various stages of the individual's development, and the increasing importance of the *Ego identity*, a term borrowed from Freud. *Ego identity* relates to the conscious knowing self of the individual. It is that part of our make-up of which we are aware. *Ego identity* is the awareness of the fact that there is a self-sameness and continuity to the ego's attempts to construct meaning for the individual. By this I mean that the conscious part of our mind is attempting to make sense of the world and to find a coherent pattern to the external world that confronts the individual. Coupled with this is the style of one's individuality, which is linked crucially to the style that coincides with the sameness and continuity of meaning for significant others who are in the wider community.[21] To put this in more basic terms, one's identity is not only constructed by the individual, but it is influenced also by one's relationship with others. Namely, that the "group" as well as the "self" influence the construction of the identity of an individual.

A good deal of Erikson's work rests upon the pioneering research and practice of Sigmund Freud. Freud, speaking of his own sense of identity as a Jew in post-World War I Austria, described himself as slowly becoming aware of the attractions of his Jewish identity and of being a Jew. This awareness for Freud was a consciousness of his inner identity and the perception that he owed the basis of his character to his "Jewish nature."[22]

The question of identity, so fundamental to human beings and their mental construction, can be understood and expressed in a variety of ways. William James, in the course of writing to his wife, describes his identity in the following terms:

> A man's character is discernible in the mental or moral attitude in which, when it came upon him, he felt himself most deeply and intensely active and alive. At such moments there is the voice inside which speaks and says "This is the real me."[23]

20. Ibid., 17.

21. Ibid., 208–12.

22. Sigmund Freud, *Address to the Society of B'Nai of B'rith,* 1926 ed. (London: Hogarth, 1959), 20:273.

23. Henry James, *The Letters of Henry James* (Boston: Atlantic Monthly, 1920), 1:199.

The importance of Christian education, as a corrective to the ongoing psychological negation of the black self, cannot be overstated. Christian education directed towards people of African descent must assert the importance of self-esteem. The need for this is to counter the disinformation that has been unleashed on black people via the imperial version of Christian faith arising from the Great Commission that has led to a demonization of the African self. The teaching and learning process must be concerned with enabling black people to have a profound appreciation and love of self. This self-love can be fostered by reminding black youth that God, in whose image they are created, loves them and desires all that is good for their continued existence. Jawanza Kunjufu reminds us that

> . . . self-esteem is greatly enhanced by putting God first. "If God be for us, who can be against us," and "greater is He in me than he who is in the world." [P]lacing God first in your life should provide greater strength for struggle against oppression. The problem with many religious people is reading only half the sentence, "Love thy neighbour" – the remaining part is "as thyself." Many Black Christians love their neighbours better than they love themselves . . .[24]

Romney Moseley argues that by identifying and surrendering self to God, a person can begin to transcend the finite limitations of the self, in order to appreciate that God, through Jesus Christ, has transformed the world.[25] Craig Ellison, like Moseley seeks to fuse the discipline of developmental psychology with an interpretative approach (or hermeneutic) that is a common feature of theological inquiry. He argues that positive self-esteem does not come through self-denial of the human realities and one's existential needs. Rather, it is located in the recognition of God's unconditional love for us and in the relationship that the individual builds with God.[26]

The teaching and learning of the Christian faith for the purposes of promoting positive identity and self-esteem is of vital importance as it seeks to repair the damage unleashed on black people by the legacy of the Great

24. Jawanza Kunjufu, *Developing Positive Self-Images and Discipline in Black Children* (Chicago: African American Images, 1984), 27–28.

25. Romney Moseley, *Becoming a Self before God: Critical Transformations* (Nashville: Abingdon, 1991), 102–104.

26. Craig Ellison, ed., *Your Better Self: Christianity, Psychology, and Self-Esteem* (San Francisco: Harper & Row, 1983), 11.

Commission. In utilizing the insights of developmental psychology, progressive models of Christian education have sought to provide a rich array of conceptual tools to enable Christian learners to interpret their experiences for greater meaning.

RETHINKING CHRISTIAN EDUCATION IN LIGHT OF BLACK THEOLOGY AND TRANSFORMATIVE LEARNING

Black theology can be broadly understood as the self-conscious attempt to undertake rational and disciplined conversation about God and God's relationship to black people in the world, looking at the past, the present, and imagining the future.[27] The God that is at the centre of black theology is one who is largely, although not exclusively, understood in terms of God's revelation in Jesus Christ in light of the historical and contemporary reality of being black. The understanding of blackness or indeed, of being black is one that is often seen in terms of suffering, struggle, marginalization and the oppression of black people. The importance of black theology needs to be tempered, however, with the necessary caveat proffered by womanist theology. Womanist theology arises from the definitional intent of the African American novelist and social critic, Alice Walker. The term *womanist* was coined by Walker as a way of defining the subjectivity of black women in the United States.[28] Womanist theology is the theological articulation of God as understood through the lens of the experiences of black (predominantly African American) women.[29] It seeks to address the tripartite jeopardy of being black, female, and poor in the wealthiest nation in the world. Womanist theology emerged as a necessary corrective to the patriarchal, androcentric myopia of much that was

27. An important aspect of black theology is the extent to which it attends to existential realities of lived experience of black people within history, both in the past and present epochs. This emphasis upon the lived realities of black people is one that seeks to displace notions of theology being "distant" and unresponsive to the needs of ordinary people in this world and is less concerned with metaphysical speculations about salvation in the next. For a helpful discussion on this issue, see Dwight N. Hopkins, *Introducing Black Theology of Liberation* (Maryknoll, NY: Orbis Books, 1999), 1–14.

28. See Alice Walker, *The Color Purple* (London: Women's Press, 1983) and Walker, *In Search of Our Mothers' Gardens: Womanist Prose* (London: Women's Press, 1984).

29. Some of the early *classics* in the womanist theology canon include: Jacquelyn Grant, *White Women's Christ and Black Women's Jesus: Feminist Christology and Womanist Response* (Atlanta: Scholars, 1989); Delores Williams, *Sisters in the Wilderness: The Challenge of Womanist God-Talk* (Maryknoll, NY: Orbis Books, 1993). See also Kelly Brown Douglas, *The Black Christ* (Maryknoll, NY: Orbis, 1994); Emile Townes, *Womanist Justice, Womanist Hope* (Atlanta: Scholars, 1993); Renita J. Weems, *Just a Sister Away: A Womanist Vision of Women's Relationships in the Bible* (Philadelphia: Innisfree, 1988); Katie G. Cannon, *Black Womanist Ethics* (Atlanta: Scholars, 1988).

black theology that emerged in the late 1960s, through to the 80s, as well as a critique of the same phenomena in the black community and the black church.[30]

In the context of rethinking the educational mission of the church, particularly, as it applies to black people, I am exploring the relationship between black theology and transformative models of Christian education. I believe that the adoption of transformative models of Christian education, coupled with black theology, is the means by which black people can be located within a formational process that is geared towards the sole purpose of liberation and a life of existential freedom. Creating a new model of Christian education, one that is informed by its engagement with black theology, is necessary in order to provide a new framework for Christian formation; this is a model that seeks to overturn the prevailing negativity arising from the Eurocentric captivity of the Great Commission.

My own engagement with transformative learning has its roots in my engagement with Paulo Freire, Ira Shor, and James A. Banks. The latter describes transformative knowledge (which is the precursor to learning) as that which challenges the dominant theories and paradigms that constitute normative frames of epistemology.[31] Transformative models of education focus on critical forms of epistemology.[32] Central to the epistemological framing of transformative knowledge is the challenging of the alleged objectivity of western scholasticism. Banks asserts that "the assumption within the Western empirical paradigm is that knowledge produced within it is neutral and objective and that its principles are universal."[33]

This model of transformative education is one that seeks to incorporate black theology within the educative process in order to create a new form of knowledge that challenges the hierarchical claims for white superiority and supremacy.[34] In rethinking the educative task of the church in light of the Great Commission, it is my belief that using transformative models of education is

30. See Jacquelyn Grant, "Black Theology and the Black Woman," in *Black Theology: A Documentary History*, ed. James Cone and Gayraud Wilmore (Maryknoll, NY: Orbis Books, 1979), 1:418–43. See also Kelly Brown Douglas, "Womanist Theology: What is Its Relationship to Black Theology?" in *Black Theology: A Documentary History*, 2:290–299; Douglas, *The Black Christ*, 92–93.

31. James A. Banks, ed., *Multicultural Education, Transformative Knowledge, and Action: Historical and Contemporary Perspectives* (New York: Teachers College Press, 1996), 9.

32. See Jürgen Habermas, *Knowledge and Human Interests* (Boston: Beacon, 1971).

33. James A. Banks, *Race, Culture, and Education: The Selected Works of James A. Banks* (London: Routledge, 2006), 148.

34. See Emmanuel C. Eze, ed., *Race and the Enlightenment: A Reader* (Oxford: Blackwell, 1997).

necessary in order to critically assess the veracity of particular truth claims and the processes that produce hegemonic, interlocking systems and structures that constrict and inhibit the God-given selfhood of black peoples.

I believe that linking black theology to transformative models of education is necessary as a means of illustrating the illusory dimensions of the white, Euro-American western world order. This new approach to Christian education provides a means by which the negative impact of the Great Commission's legacy of Christian mission on black people can be dissipated. This model of Christian education is one that seeks to enable ordinary people to apprehend the emancipatory appeal of God's kingdom that is envisioned in Isaiah 11. In that chapter, Yahweh will create a new reality when Yahweh's spirit rests, giving rise to a re-emerging Davidic kingdom: Yahweh will execute justice for the poor, and Yahweh will recover the remnant of his people from Egypt and Ethiopia as well as from other nations (11:1, 4, 11).

The changing perceptions of reality and what constitutes the "real" is what lies at the heart of this renewed approach to education in light of one's rethinking of the efficacy of the Great Commission. This model of education presses for a symbiotic relationship between black theology and the transformative frameworks of knowledge production and learning that enables ordinary people to become critical agents in a dialectical process of apprehending the visionary reality that is God's kingdom rule or reign. It is my belief that the process of cognitive and affective change, which has sometimes been likened to the notion of conversion, is one that begins in the imagination of the self before it can be enacted as a form of concretized praxis.

The re-envisioning of reality that is central to this work is one that calls for ordinary black people to be empowered to envision a new reality that is beyond the warped intimations of life that has been bequeathed to us by the white supremacist tentacles of the Western imperial mission paradigm. This approach to Christian education, informed by black theology, forms a theological break from what often defined the church's mission in light of the Great Commission. The learning that I have in mind that is central to this work is one that emerges from the experiences of the marginalized and the oppressed: that to envision a new reality requires one to be able to apprehend such from within the deepest contours of the new black self.

This work is one that seeks to affirm those whose voices have rarely been heard outside of a few select situations, where such individuals experience a sense of being valued and feel "safe."[35] This approach to black theological

---

35. I have termed this phenomenon "cultural dissonance." See Reddie, *Nobodies to Somebodies: A Practical Theology for Education and Liberation* (Peterborough: Epworth, 2003), 97–99, 105–106.

reflection is one that enables poor, marginalized, and oppressed peoples to reflect upon their experiences within the context of the church, which remains at its best, an intergenerational, redemptive community.

In attempting to use this method for theological reflection in an intergenerational context, I wanted to tap into some of my previous research, and link the experiences of older people with those who are young.[36] In using the form of black theology–inspired model of Christian education, I want to enable black people who are poor and oppressed to find the necessary resources for more holistic and fruitful living. The import of this work also rests in the necessity of developing a means for enabling different generations to speak to one another.[37] Given the concerns expressed at the vulnerability of black youth in the present epoch, this approach to the teaching and learning process seeks to pull together the fragments[38] of the experiences of the poor and the oppressed in the postcolonial world that continues to live in the shadow of the Great Commission.

My scholarly work, approaching twenty years now,[39] has been an attempt to harness the emotive power of the Christian faith in order that those who have traditionally been without a voice might be enabled to gain one for the purposes of their ongoing liberation. My approach to this form of scholarship is one that combines theological reflection with forms of social analysis that attempts to bring theory and practice into a dialectical conversation. Black religious

36. See Anthony G. Reddie, *Faith, Stories and the Experiences of Black Elders: Singing the Lord's Song in a Strange Land* (London: Jessica Kingsley Publishers, 2001).

37. Ibid., 54–61.

38. The theme of fragments comes from David Tracy. See David Tracy, "African American Thought: The Discovery of Fragments," in *Black Faith and Public Talk: Critical Essays on James Cone's Black Theology and Black Power,* ed. Dwight N. Hopkins (Maryknoll, NY: Orbis Books, 1999), 29–40.

39. See, for example, Anthony G. Reddie, "Being the Enemy Within: Re-asserting Black 'Otherness' as a Riposte to the Homogeneous Construct of Whiteness," *Modern Believing* 53, no. 4 (2012): 408–18; Reddie, "Teaching for Social Justice: A Participative Approach," *Teaching Theology and Religion* 13, no. 2 (2010): 95–109; Reddie, "Re-thinking Biblical and Theological Perspectives: Christian Nurture of Children," *International Journal of Practical Theology* 14, no. 2 (2010): 171–88; Reddie, "A Dialectical Spirituality of Improvisation: The Ambiguity of Black Engagements with Sacred Texts," in *Black Religion and Aesthetics,* 153–71; Reddie, "Not Just Seeing but Really Seeing: A Practical Black Liberationist Spirituality for Re-interpreting Reality," *Black Theology* 7, no. 3 (2009): 339–65; Reddie, "Black Theology in Britain," *Expository Times* 120, no. 1 (2008): 16–23; Reddie, "People Matter Too! The Politics and Method of Doing Black Liberation Theology," *Practical Theology* 1, no. 1 (2008): 43–64; Reddie, "African-centered Approaches to Education as a Resource for Christian Education," *British Journal of Religious Education* 25, no. 1 (2002): 6–17; Reddie, "Developing a Black Christian Education of Liberation for the British Context," *Religious Education* 98, no. 2 (2003): 221–38.

scholars, such as Robert Beckford[40] and Emmanuel Lartey,[41] have directed their research and writing energies to enable poor and oppressed peoples to become fuller human subjects. My work differs from the aforementioned, chiefly in terms of method. As an educator in addition to being a theologian, I have been intent upon creating schemes of teaching and learning that reflect, inform, and affirm the existence and experience of black people on the margins.

This approach to black theological reflection is one that makes recourse to the ways of knowing, or the epistemological foundations of black people of diasporan African descent on the margins in the shadow of the Great Commission. These are bound up in their on-going experiences of struggle. This approach to the teaching and learning process seeks to enable subjugated black subjects to actualize many of the central themes of black liberation theology, in order to remake their present consciousness, which in turn leads to renewed forms of Christian praxis for an imagined and hoped for future.[42]

Working alongside marginalized people using this form of educational methodology is nothing less than a process of critical advocacy. It is a way of assisting marginalized people to learn more about themselves and the world through the framework of religion. It is a process of being nurtured and educated into such a worldview and being enabled to understand more about the kind of faith that can sustain and empower. This, I believe, can be achieved by means of an interactive and participatory model for undertaking black theological reflection in which marginalized and oppressed black people are central agents in the learning process.[43]

Finally, this approach seeks to affirm the oral traditions of non-European cultures and contexts that are concomitant with the lived realities of these peoples. We know that the mission imperative of the Great Commission of the European powers was one that denigrated the historic cultures and traditions of peoples who had long experienced a reality of the divine before the Europeans ever set foot in their contexts.

40. See Robert Beckford, *Jesus is Dread: Black Theology and Black Culture in Britain* (London: Darton, Longman & Todd, 1998). See also by Robert Beckford, *Dread and Pentecostal: A Political Theology for the Black Church in Britain* (London: SPCK, 2000); Beckford, *God of the Rahtid: Redeeming Rage* (London: Darton, Longman & Todd, 2001); and Beckford, *God and the Gangs* (London: Darton, Longman & Todd, 2004).

41. Emmanuel Y. Lartey, *In Living Colour: An Intercultural Approach to Pastoral Care and Counselling* (London: Cassell, 1997).

42. See Paulo Freire, *Education for Critical Consciousness* (New York: Continuum, [1973] 1990).

43. This work has been explored in the following texts: Anthony G. Reddie, *Acting in Solidarity* (London: Darton, Longman & Todd, 2004); Reddie, *Dramatizing Theologies* (London: Equinox, 2006); and Reddie, *Working against the Grain* (London: Equinox, 2008).

Ella P. Mitchell describes the oral tradition of black people as being the summation of the cultural vehicles through which the essential nature of black existence and experience has been channelled. These cultural vehicles assist African people in their knowledge of self, both individually and corporately. These cultural vehicles are manifested in many forms, ranging from storytelling, festivals, celebrations, parties, role-play and acting, through to religious worship. The origins for these communicative modes of cultural transmission are to be found in Africa.[44]

It is not my contention that African people are alone in possessing an oral tradition. Clearly, there are many ethnic, cultural, and religious groups who possess oral traditions that are the repository of experience and that provide the narrative thread of biography and existence. I would argue that this facility has played a particularly important role in the ongoing life experiences of African people.

I make this contention aware of the central importance of black theology, and the aim of that discipline to affirm and legitimate the black experience as a valid source for talking about God's interaction with God's people. James Cone says that "there is no truth for and about Black people that does not emerge out of the context of their experience. Truth in this sense is Black truth, a truth disclosed in the history and the culture of Black people. Black theology is a theology of and for Black people, an examination of their stories, tales and sayings."[45] Cone continues by suggesting that these experiences and expressions often crystallized in stories, folk sayings, the spirituals, the blues, and sermons, cannot be subdivided into secular and religious. Rather, they sit alongside each other in a unitary whole of human experience.[46]

While this approach to undertaking theological reflection has been undertaken with predominantly black individuals (as a black contextual theologian, my point of departure are the realities of the black experience), I believe there is an integrity and utility to this method that renders it applicable for other communities and cultures. As Lartey reminds us, whilst there are very real differences between people, we are, in many other ways, very much alike.[47] The great potential of this approach to undertaking theological reflection is the opportunity it provides for marginalized lay people to name their own subjectivity and be active in that process of naming. Rethinking Christian

---

44. Ella P. Mitchell, "Oral Tradition: Legacy of Faith for the Black Church," *Religious Education* 81, no. 1 (1986): 93–112 (94–95).

45. James Cone, *God of the Oppressed* (San Francisco: Harper San Francisco, 1975), 17–18.

46. Ibid., 23.

47. Lartey, *In Living Colour*, 9–14.

education in light of the Great Commission, as it applies to black people, is focused on the need to repair past damages to their identity and self-esteem. This form of pedagogy is one that utilizes aspects of developmental psychology, black theology, and transformative learning. The aim of this approach to Christian education is to critique the negative legacy of the western, imperialistic appropriation of the Great Commission. It reminds black learners that there is another dimension and interpretation of Christianity and that this faith can be the conduit for black liberation and a more expansive, holistic form of living.

12

Christian Moral Education and the Great Commission in an African Context

Lord Elorm-Donkor

INTRODUCTION

It is forecasted that in the near future the form and face of Christianity will be shaped from Africa and that religion and culture may become areas of Africa's greatest contribution to the "global village".[1] Apparently, the Great Commission has succeeded tremendously in making many Africans believe in Jesus Christ. The exponential growth in Christian membership in Africa in the last fifty years and the general contribution of this to the future of the global faith is widely celebrated.[2] However, ironically, as missiologists and other observers laud the growth in Christian membership in Africa, economists and social scientists also lament the socioeconomic and political woes of Africans.[3]

---

1. Kwabena Asamoah-Gyadu, "Pentecostalism in Africa and the Changing Face of Christian Mission: Pentecostal/Charismatic Renewal Movements in Ghana," *Mission Studies* 19 (2002): 2–38 (33). See also Philip Jenkins, *The Next Christendom: The Coming of Global Christianity* (New York: Oxford University Press, 2002).

2. See Gerrie ter Haar, *How God Became African: African Spirituality and Western Secular Thought* (Philadelphia: University of Pennsylvania Press, 2009); Jenkins, *The Next Christendom*; Lamin Sanneh and Joel Carpenter, *The Changing Face of Christianity: Africa, the West and the World* (Oxford: Oxford University Press, 2005); David Barrett, "Annual Statistical Table on Global Mission," *International Bulletin of Missionary Research* 27, no. 1 (2003), 24–25.

3. See Ewusi Kwadwo, *The Political Economy of Ghana in the Post Independent period: Description and Analysis of the Decadence of the Political Economy of Ghana and Survival Techniques of the Citizens* (Legon: University of Ghana, 1984) and Kwadwo Konadu-Agyemang, *IMF and World Bank Sponsored Structural Adjustment Program in Africa: Ghana's Experience 1983–1999* (Aldershot: Ashgate, 2001).

Political instabilities, poor governance, widespread corruption, and poverty are characteristic of most African societies, including Ghana.[4]

That a successful Christian evangelization takes place alongside general sociopolitical and economic degeneration is absurd and begs the question whether the Great Commission is really successful in making disciples of Jesus Christ in Africa as it should. In their general assessments of the evangelization of Africa, scholars agree that the earliest messengers of the gospel to Ghana misunderstood or disregarded the African culture by projecting and teaching the Western cultural perspectives as the norm by which Africans should live.[5] In the process of the evangelization, African minds were considered as empty slates (*tabula rasa*) upon which Europeans were to engrave their religious, political, economic, and educational doctrines.[6] It is claimed that as a result of the method of evangelization used, there has been a loss of cultural identity that Africa needs to restore into its Christian practice and to follow a thorough contextualization of the gospel in Africa.[7] Although scholars have written on African Christianity broadly, the damage that the Great Commission has done to the moral compass of the African is not yet under focused discussion. The damage to the moral conceptual scheme of Africa is responsible for the political, social, and economic woes of Africa today.

Two things seem to have happened. First, because the African Traditional Religion (ATR) was rejected, the moral conceptual scheme that it sanctioned was also destroyed. The destruction of the moral system is a major problem, the consequences of which are felt in the political, social, economic, and psychological spheres today. Second, by focusing on teaching as the primary

---

4. George Ayittey, *Africa in Chaos: A Comparative History* (New York: St. Martin, 1999).

5. S. G. Williamson, *Akan Religion and the Christian Faith: A Comparative Study of the Impact of Two Religions* (Accra: Ghana Universities Press, 1965); Harris Mobley, *The Ghanaian's Image of the Missionary: An Analysis of Published Critiques of Christian Missionaries by Ghanaians* (Leiden: Brill, 1970); Kwame Bediako, *Theology and Identity* (Oxford: Regnum Books, 1992); Bediako, *Jesus in Africa: The Christian Gospel in African History and Experience* (Akropong: Regnum Books, 2004); John Pobee, *Christ would be an African Too* (Geneva: World Council of Churches, 1996).

6. Raphael Njoroge, *Education for Renaissance in Africa* (Bloomington, IN: Trafford, 2004), 190. Cornel West and Eddie S. Glaude Jr., *African American Religious Thought: An Anthology* (Louisville: Westminster John Knox, 2003), 618. *Tabula rasa* was a philosophical view that the mind of the baby is like a clean slate on which new things were to be written as the baby grows. It later became a widely intellectual view in Europe that the African mind was a clean slate on which the Christian missionary was to write or inculcate Christian faith and morals. See Kwame Bediako, "Africa and Christianity on the Threshold of the Third Millennium: The Religious Dimension," *African Affairs* 99 (2000), 303–23.

7. Bediako, *Theology and Identity*; John Pobee, *Toward an African Theology* (Nashville: Abingdon, 1979).

means for carrying out the Great Commission, the Christian messengers to Africa promoted individuality that dented the strong sense of community of the Africans.

In this essay, I use the evangelization of the Akan people in Ghana as case history, and I argue that the method of the Great Commission in Ghana has been problematical. I will show that the missional approach of the earliest Christian messengers, which was in some ways imitated by their successors, was greatly influenced by an understanding of the Great Commission as consisting mainly of teaching a new worldview. This destroyed the solid African traditional conceptual framework upon which a sustainable Christian moral education could have been realized. So, although the membership numbers in churches show that evangelization of Africa has been successful, the church has failed to make sufficient disciples of Christ who understand the Great Commission as the practice of love of God and neighbor in concrete ways. I will also show that because the method involved the extension of the Western Enlightenment worldview and imperialism, it was impossible for Ghanaian converts to develop and maintain a Christian moral thought that extends and integrates their traditional moral scheme with the Western Christian worldview. I will then suggest the virtue framework as a heuristic tool for integrating the two rival traditions.

THE GREAT COMMISSION RECONSIDERED

It is important to consider the so-called Great Commission in its Matthean context to understand how it ought to be done before assessing how it has actually been done among the Akan people in Ghana (28:19-20). Unlike other commission texts in the Gospels and the book of Acts, which focus on proclamation, the mandate of the Great Commission is to make disciples of all nations, baptizing and teaching them to do all that Jesus commanded.[8] This suggests that disciple-making is central to Matthew's view of the church's mission to the nations.

Moreover, the three appearances of the Greek verb translated *to make disciples* (mathēteuō) are all in Matthew and nowhere else in the other Gospels do we find this verb in a commission text (13:52; 27:57; 28:19).[9] From the Matthean account, disciple-making is central to the mission of the church to the nations around the world.[10] Also, in Matthew, Jesus did not leave the apostles to

8. References to other commission texts are Matt. 10:24-25; Luke 10:1-20, 24:44-53; Acts 1:4-8.

9. David Bosch, *Transforming Mission: Paradigm Shifts in Theology of Mission* (Maryknoll, NY: Orbis Books), 73.

figure out how to make disciples. Here, it is stated clearly that the apostles were to baptize and teach the nations to obey everything Jesus had commanded them (28:20).

In his discussion of the Great Commission, David Bosch considered this passage and stated that "everything Jesus commanded his disciples" is summed up in the great commandment, "love your neighbor as yourself" (19:19, 22:39). This commandment is greatest in importance, second only to the first, which is to love God. Thus, essentially, making disciples is about teaching the nations to know the will of God, which is to love one's neighbor. This love command must be the central theme, the guiding principle and content of disciple-making. With this view, the Great Commission should be understood as the teaching of the great commandment to the whole person and the whole society in the whole world. As Bosch puts it, the Great Commission ". . . is the church sent into the world, to love, to serve, to preach, to teach, to heal [and] to liberate."[11] In other words, making disciples is about teaching the nations to love God and to love their neighbor as themselves in every aspect of their daily interactions in society. But how exactly is this to be done?

The eminent Evangelical theologian John Stott made a clearer point on this when he said,

> The Great Commission neither explains, nor exhausts, nor supersedes the Great Commandment. What it does is to add to the requirement of neighbour-love and neighbour-service a new and urgent Christian dimension. Our neighbour is neither a bodyless soul where we could love our neighbour's soul, nor a soulless body that we care for its welfare alone, nor even a body-soul isolated from society. Therefore, if we love our neighbour, as God made him, we must inevitably be concerned for his total welfare, the good of his soul, his body and his community.[12]

Three important points may be drawn from this quotation. First, the Great Commission is a command to teach the great commandment. Second, the great commandment is the driving principle of the gospel, the good news. Third, the great commandment is the essence of discipleship and must be taught in ways that concretizes love in all human relationships and in all communities

10. In Acts 1:8, the apostles will receive power from the Holy Spirit to become witnesses of the Jesus' death and resurrection. In John, they will receive the Holy Spirit and bring forgiveness to all people.

11. Bosch, *Transforming Mission*, 412.

12. John Stott, *Christian Mission in the Modern World* (Leicester: InterVarsity Press, 1975), 30.

throughout the world. Stott thought that if we said that we love our neighbors, then we could not avoid sharing the good news of salvation with them. By this, he was exposing the full scope of the Great Commission. He meant that our love for neighbor should not be restricted only to our neighbor's spiritual and physical welfare, but inescapably, love must be related to all social interactions and institutions in the community in which our neighbor lives. The implication here is that the total concern for our neighbor includes the "quest for better social structures in which peace, dignity, freedom and justice" is available for all.[13] But is that what we see in the nations that are described as Christian?

Jacques Matthey also considered the Matthean Great Commission and concludes that, mainly, the love commandment implies the prophetical reproof of repression and a charge to work for change, to struggle for justice, or to support such struggles.[14] For example, this means that Jesus sent us to teach people to refuse submission to any ruler who exploits the poor and allows for the maintenance of systems that work to the disadvantage of the needy.[15] But the question is how could this be done practically, especially as messengers move from their own cultural contexts to other contexts that are very different from their own? How should Christian messengers consider the cultures in which they teach love, and how should they show this love?

Again, Stott is instructive.

Jesus did not touch down like a visitor from outer space, or arrive like an alien bringing his own alien culture with him. He took to himself our humanity, our flesh and blood, our culture. He actually became one of us and experienced our frailty, and our suffering and temptations. He even bore our sin and died our death. And now he sends us "into the world", to identify with others as he identified with us (though without losing our Christian identity) to become vulnerable as he did.[16]

Here, Scott used Jesus as the model for how we are to make disciples and teach the nations. It is important to stress that Jesus did not arrive in Judea with a full blown worldview and cultural perspective on life in Palestine that was totally foreign to what the Jews were familiar with. In fact, Matthew reports Jesus'

13. Ibid.

14. Jacques Matthey, "The Great Commission According to Matthew," *International Review of Mission*, vol. 69, no. 274 (1980): 161–73.

15. Ibid., 172.

16. Stott, *Christian Mission*, 25.

affirmation of the Law and Prophets and his declaration that he had come not to abolish them but to fulfill them, that is, to fully demonstrate what they mean practically (5:17).

Considering this brief discussion of the Great Commission, it should be noted that the whole enterprise of the gospel is about making disciples and teaching the restoration of God's original intention for relationships through practical demonstration of love as Jesus did with his life. Basically, "teaching them to observe all things I have taught you" should rather focus our efforts on restoring and developing the right relationship that is expected from humanity towards God, which consequentially translates into the right and good relationships among humans. The Christian life envisaged in the Sermon on the Mount (Matt. 5–7) is about good human–divine and interpersonal relationships in the present and the future kingdom of God. Thus, essentially, the Great Commission could be considered as moral education based on God's terms through love and obedience.

CHRISTIAN MORAL EDUCATION

Moral education involves teaching how we actually live out our beliefs about what is right and good; where such conduct as oppression, stealing, cheating, and lying are regarded as bad and wrong.[17] It includes instruction on behavior patterns, responses, or attitudes that are in conformity with the accepted moral beliefs, social rules, and norms of people in a society.[18] Morality is the actual practice of ethics, which is the study of the principles and rules or laws that govern behavior. Whereas ethics "investigates the foundational concepts and principles underlying our judgments of good and evil, right and wrong, obligation and optional," morality focuses on the actual living out of what is considered good and acceptable behavior for the community. It guides and regulates the people's conduct in every relationship.[19] It is important to note that each community must determine what their acceptable norm is, not another community deciding for the other. This means that the determination of what are good and acceptable norms of a community is based on the philosophical and religious conceptions of a people in that community.

17. Stanley J. Grenz, *The Moral Quest: Foundations of Christian Ethics* (Leicester: Apollos, 1997), 23.

18. Kwame Gyekye, *An Essay on African Philosophical Thought: The Akan Conceptual Scheme* (Cambridge: Cambridge University Press, 1987), 130.

19. Kwasi Wiredu, *Philosophy and an African Culture* (Cambridge: Cambridge University Press, 1980), 171.

In light of this understanding of moral education, the practice of the Great Commission among the Akan people in Ghana could only be seen as problematical. This is because instead of building on Akan traditional religious and moral conceptions (a similarity to what in Jesus' culture was the Law and Prophets) to redefine and transform them, the missionaries worked hard to abolish these beliefs in the Ghanaian communities. The outcome is separation of morality from spirituality, where people could be serious Christians without necessarily being morally competent. To discuss this further, first let us catch a glimpse of how morality and religion in the Akan community looked like before the advent of the messengers of the Great Commission.

AKAN RELIGION AND MORAL EDUCATION

Before the missionaries arrived in the Gold Coast, now Ghana, the Africans had their religion, customs, and culture. They had social and political institutions by which their communities were organized. This African religion is the outcome of humans pondering their loneliness and vulnerability in the midst of the unpredictable situations in the world.[20] Such an attitude toward religion is utilitarian, in that it is motivated by the quest for the well-being of the community, a well-being that is sustained by mutual moral responsibility.[21] The African traditional religion (ATR) is a "nature religion" based on a numinous awareness of the natural environment. Its practices are directed towards the continuance of the vitality in the life and community of humans.[22] ATR does not have prophets appointed by God, nor does it have revelations or sacred scriptures like the Bible or Koran. There are no creeds to be recited because the creeds are believed to be already written in the hearts of individuals, and they are transmitted through oral traditions, rituals, and religious personages.[23] It is held in ATR that the material world and natural phenomena are not all that there is to reality. Another important factor in ATR for moral education is that humans are believed to be sharing the universe with other realms of deities and hosts of spirit beings. This belief in other realms of existence is the main force of ATR because it is the reference point of both natural and supernatural phenomena and for moral behavior. The traditional belief in a Supreme Being, deities, ancestors, and other personalized spiritual powers shows and promotes

---

20. Segun Gbadegesin, "Origins of African Ethics," in *Blackwell Companion to Religious Ethics*, ed. William Schweiker (Oxford: Blackwell, 2005), 413–14.

21. Ibid., 414; also, see Gyekye, *Essay on African Philosophical Thought*, 143–45.

22. Williamson, *Akan Religion and the Christian Faith*, 139.

23. John Mbiti, *African Religions and Philosophy* (London: Heinemann, 1969), 3.

the interdependence of the created order, human and non-human, animate and inanimate.

Centrally, it is believed that when left on their own to provide for the spiritual, physical, and psycho-social resources that they need for mastering their environment, individuals are found to be limited and inadequate.[24] Therefore, mutual interdependence and hospitality are used as crucial means for maintaining community and ensuring that every individual is properly catered for and lives well. To achieve this goal a sense of kinship is created. These relationships require the individual to act in consonance with certain social values and norms such as mutual help, hospitality, honesty, and loyalty without fail. The failure to conduct one's self in this manner affects the health of the relationships in the cosmic, natural, and social realms. Also, the relationship of humans to each other and to other beings in this universe, especially to the deities, in a way, determines how human life in its totality progresses or regresses. In fact, this sense of human finitude (the need for the other) is the rationale behind the communitarian life promoted by African religions.

In this African scheme, the well-being of the community is achieved by the development of effective moral relations that promote both communal existence and individual interests.[25] The congenial coexistence of humans is the most important factor for ensuring the well-being of an African community. It means that the survival of the Akan community was achieved through mutual moral responsibility. Here, morality is vital for controlling and enhancing the institutions in a community for the well-being and flourishing of its individual members.[26] However, because of the inherent weakness of humans to remain moral in all their interactions, religion is employed to regulate behavior and conduct. The most obvious role of religion is found in its sanctioning of morality. [27] In other words, religion becomes an important means for preventing immorality because of the inherent moral weaknesses of humanity.

This function of religion should not mean that people endeavor to be moral for fear of retribution that comes through religion. It is rather that with this African traditional scheme, good moral conduct predisposes humans favorably towards other humans and the supernatural realm so that one may receive the benevolence of the divinities in the form of health, wealth, and peace

---

24. Gyekye, *Essay on African Philosophical Thought*, 154–58.

25. Ibid., 80–83.

26. Gbadegesin, "Origins of African Ethics", 415.

27. Kwasi Wiredu, "Moral Foundations of an African Culture," *Person and Community: Ghanaian Philosophical Studies I*, eds. Kwasi Wiredu and Kwame Gyekye (Washington, DC: Council for Research of Values and Philosophy, 1992), 194.

and the constant support of other people. Kwasi Wiredu affirms that although the fear of punishment from the deities may focus people's mind on the path of virtue "it is not this that creates the sense of moral obligation."[28] Rather, it is because one's own flourishing and well-being is believed to depend on moral competence. Ronald Green was right when he observed that Africans live in a morally saturated religious universe in which all-important interpersonal relationships, including essential relationships between humans and spiritual beings, have moral content and are governed by moral considerations.[29]

The Akan people regard individuals to be autonomous in the sense that they could choose to act in conformity, or otherwise, to what their society prescribes as good conduct. Yet this autonomy comes with a responsibility that stretches far beyond the individual in terms of the relationships to the family (clan), tribe, the natural order, and the spirit realm. Accordingly, morality is realized basically by means of a relational network that is "equally anthropocentric, cosmic and theocentric."[30] For instance, a greedy act of a "head of family," such as denying a member of the extended family the appropriate share of the clan's inheritance, say, a piece of land for farming, becomes a breach of the moral requirements of his position as *Abusuapanin* (Family Head), as well as a breach against the ancestors.

The harmonious coexistence of people and well-being of the community depended on how humans maintained a balance through their conduct in their relationships with all the realms. From the foregoing discussion, African oriented spirituality is by necessity holistic. Every deed or act has both spiritual and social implications. A separation between morality and spirituality cannot be entertained because these are inseparable. This brief description of the use of religion and morality among the Akan to maintain community and ensure the wellbeing of individuals in it will help us see clearly how the Matthean Great Commission becomes problematic in this context.

THE GREAT COMMISSION AMONG THE AKAN

To begin with, it is apt to note that the messengers that were sent to disciple Ghanaians for Christ were mainly ill-prepared for the arduous task. The caliber of missionaries sent to Africa in the nineteenth and early twentieth centuries

---

28. Ibid.

29. Ronald M. Green, "Religion and Morality in the African Traditional Setting," *Journal of Religion in Africa* 14, no. 1 (1983): 5.

30. Bénézet Bujo, *Foundations of an African Ethic: Beyond the Universal Claims of Western Morality* (New York: Crossroad, 2001), 2.

may have contributed to the general outcome of the Great Commission in this context because of the foundation they laid for moral education. This is evidenced by a commissioned report of Edinburgh 1910, which revealed that the missionaries sent to Africa lacked the necessary skills for gaining and articulating a deeper appreciation of the ATR. Discussing the preparation of missionaries at the conference in Edinburgh in 1910, Rev. Dr. Alexander P. Camphor affirmed the general view that standards for the preparation of messengers for Africa were not high. Dr. Camphor stated that "Africa has in the past greatly suffered from poorly prepared missionaries. They generally lacked either the physical or intellectual quality since comparatively low students will do for Africa."[31]

Apart from this, it is also fair to note that they were influenced by the imperial powers and their own culture. Bosch has shown that whether deliberate or not, evangelical missionaries also became promoters of Western imperial interest in the colonized nations around the world.[32] Also, he noted that Victorian Britain, where most of the missionaries to Ghana came from, had two faces: a public face that spoke of high morals, and a private face that manifested all sorts of moral decadence.[33] With this background, the messengers of modern Christian mission to Ghana disregarded the religion and culture of the communities they were sent to disciple, and in the process, perhaps inadvertently, destroyed the moral potentiality of their converts. This is because, as stated above, although ATR sanctioned morality, which informed and regulated behavior in society, the earliest missionaries to Ghana failed to recognize the religion as such. That ATR was not even treated as a religion at the first International Missionary Conference in Edinburgh in 1910 is indicative of how it was regarded. It was mentioned only scantly in the study of Animism.[34] Dr. T. Jays of the Church Mission Society (CMS) was seriously concerned about this and said, "I cannot help the feeling that there is not enough from those who have been working in West Africa.[35] I think a great many very different answers would have been given, and would have modified

31. "Report of Commission V: The Training of Teachers. With Supplement: Presentation and Discussion of the Report in the Conference on 22nd June 1910," *World Missionary Conference*, p. 311.

32. Bosch, *Transforming Missions*, 282.

33. Ibid.

34. World Missionary Conference. Report of Commission IV, *The Missionary Message in Relation to Non-Christian Religions; With Supplement; Presentation and Discussion of the Report in the Conference* (June 18, 1910), 6.

35. The Church Missionary Society was established in London in 1799 by evangelicals associated with the Church of England and other Protestants. It was initially known as Society for Mission to Africa and the East.

some general statements that have been made."[36] Some of the statements that were made to justify disregard for ATR was that the animists had no moral sense and could hardly differentiate the good from the bad. This gave the European messengers the right to teach the African about the gospel that was seriously tainted by the Western culture. Mitzi Smith is right when she states in this volume that "the type of teaching that is exalted as a result of the Great Commission nomenclature is that in which the student (paganized "others") is the passive recipient of knowledge, and is seldom, if ever, treated as a producer of legitimate and authoritative knowledge."[37]

In the process of the missionaries teaching the nations, Africans were told that belief in witches was psychological delusion and belief in the spiritual realm (ancestors, deities, and spirits) is superstition.[38] So, the missionaries considered the "destruction of traditional superstition and the implantation of the Christian faith" as their primary task.[39] This was despite the fact that Ghanaians still believed in the reality of the spirit realm and witchcraft. In this missionizing process, they also dismissed a very important African belief, which is that retribution follows moral failures in this life. After dispelling the fear of retribution in this life, the missionaries did not make any provision for addressing the apprehension Ghanaians have about crises in life. What J. E. Ayandele said about the effect of the Great Commission on the moral life of Nigerians is also true of Ghana. In both contexts the messengers were indicted for destroying the high moral principles and orderliness of African indigenous societies.[40]

John Pobee, an Anglican minister and a Ghanaian theologian, was once asked to explain why it is that when Ghanaians swear by *Tigare* or *Antoa Nyamaa* (traditional shrines that claim to be powerful and quick to punish immorality), they honor their word, but when they swear on the Bible, they break their word.[41] This type of question is common and has become one of the strongest indictments against the method used for the Great Commission in Ghana. Such questions are unavoidable because ATR is seen as more reliable in sanctioning morality in African societies than the Christian faith.

36. Ibid., 298.

37. See Mitzi J. Smith's essay, "'Knowing More than is Good for One': A Womanist Interrogation of the Matthean Great Commission," in this volume.

38. Williamson, *Akan Religion and the Christian Faith*.

39. Ibid., 54, 139.

40. J. E. Ayandele, *Missionary Impact on Modern Nigeria 1842–1914: A Political and Social Analysis* (London: Longman, 1966), 329.

41. Pobee, *Christ would be an African Too*, 25.

Similarly, Segun Gbadegesin affirms that in many African religions such as that of the Yoruba of Nigeria, the divinities punish moral infringements. "Whoever swears on the altar of *sango* the god of thunder and justice and breaks the oath is punished with death."[42] He contrasts this with Christianity and notes that although Christians may swear on the Bible and many times contradict their oath, there is no belief that any empirical punishment will follow their action. So, Christianity is regarded as having weakened people's moral integrity, while the traditional cults are said to hold people to their word.[43]

This is not a disparagement on the important work the missionaries did in providing education, health, commerce, and political institutions, many times at the peril of their own lives.[44] However, despite these achievements, perhaps sometimes inadvertently, the missionaries missed the integration that was needed between the gospel and the traditional religion and culture. Western modernity and its technology could not offer the socio-psychological and spiritual answers that were needed in the Ghanaian context.

Outcomes of the Focus on Teaching

Unsurprisingly, this approach to the Great Commission produced what Mathias Forson has described as split-level Christianity.[45] This is where converts held to the Christian faith but still believed and interpreted their daily life events through the prism of the African traditional conceptual scheme. Split-level Christianity has had a crippling effect on African Christian spirituality and moral competency because it creates uncertainty about social values and religious beliefs and forces a general confusion on moral reasoning.

A statement presented to the International Missionary Council at Willingen in Germany in 1952 reveals that many Ghanaian Christians live on two conflicting levels because of the way the gospel was presented to them.[46] They subscribed to the proclamation of the Christian gospel and maintained

---

42. Gbadegesin, "Origins of African Ethics," 417.

43. Ibid.

44. Mobley has argued that Christianity was the "guardian angel" of African nationalism because it was the educated Africans who led the way to independence. Harris Mobley, *The Ghanaian's Image of the Missionary: An Analysis of the Published Critiques of Christian Missionaries by Ghanaians 1897–1965* (Leiden: Brill, 1970), 132.

45. Mathias Kwesi Forson, *Split-Level Christianity in Africa: A Study of the Persistence of Traditional Religious Beliefs and Practices among the Akan Methodist of Ghana* (Ann Arbor, MI: UMI, 1997), 4. "The co-existence within the same person of both traditional and Christian beliefs often leading to a conflict either consciously or unconsciously within the individual."

membership in a church. However, beneath their conscious Christian belief, they also believe in profoundly embedded African traditions and customs, which entail interpretation of the universe and the world of spirit that is quite different from what Christian interpretations would offer. For instance, during crises in life, many Christians are more likely to use African traditional interpretations of reality than the Western/Christian views to deal with their situation.[47] What is even more distressing is that the statement reveals that even in younger people who had never really known clearly what their forefathers believed (the African traditional scheme), there were some ATR inheritance in their minds, some fear of vague unknown forces of evil "which made them easy converts to some fetish shrines."[48] Asamoah observed that the unsuccessful attempt to replace the ATR with the Western Christian worldview has rendered African Christians sociologically (and psychologically) wretched with a divided personality that was neither here nor there. He believed that there was a section of the African mind, "a sphere of the African soul world," that missionary Christianity had not succeeded in penetrating.[49]

Also, Kofi Busia, an eminent scholar and a former Prime Minister of Ghana made a poignant observation of the process of the Great Commission in Ghana during the second part of the twentieth century. After conducting sociological studies of the church in certain Akan communities, Busia detected that the lack of engagement between the Western Christian worldview and the African traditional scheme had made Ghanaian Christianity both superficial and alien. He said,

> Those who have been responsible for the propagation of the Christian gospel in other lands and cultures have not shown sufficient awareness for the need for an encounter between the Christian religion and the cosmology of the people alongside European culture and traditions. It is this which has made Christianity either alien or superficial or both.[50]

---

46. E. A. Asamoah, "The Christian Church and African Heritage," *International Review of Mission* 44 (1955): 289–301.

47. African traditional interpretations allow people to ascribe the causation of events and crises in life to the activities of the spiritual realm.

48. Asamoah, "The Christian Church," 293.

49. Ibid., 299–300.

50. Kofi Busia, "Has the Christian Faith Been Adequately Presented?," *International Review of Mission* 50 (1961): 86–89 (87).

Moreover, Forson's study of the Methodist church in Ghana just twenty years ago reveals that in the churches we find evidence of continuous belief in ATR.[51] This implies the use of two worldviews, the Western and the African traditional. Since worldviews serve as our lenses by which we view reality, the process of knowing the truth and what is good is largely influenced by it. Therefore, whenever we use two different lenses to observe the same reality, our perceptions are significantly hampered, if not confused, unless we synchronize the lenses.

Thus, focus on "teaching the nations" without due regard for the religious and moral conceptions that made them people is problematic because it creates conflicts between indigenous values and Western ones. It also causes displacement of the authority of traditional rulers and leaders, as the understanding of the gospel that the new converts receive makes them flout the authority of the unconverted chiefs. [52] These converts treat their unconverted parents and extended family members with contempt, and such behavior is immoral in an African society.[53] Therefore, this method of pursuing the Great Commission did not only remove the old religious sanctions, but it also tore down those social structures that, however simple or complicated, held "the members of society to some measure of mutual understanding, of trustworthiness, and often of deep and loyal affection."[54] Ephraim Amu a Ghanaian church leader lamented this situation and stated the following:

> The fear of the evil consequences of immoral behaviour which existed with superstition and the fear of evil spirits have been dispelled by Christianity. As things are now, we are like a seedling taken out of its bed, its root cut off and then planted in another bed; it stood all right in the cool weather of the morning but withered with the hot sun. We have no root to support us, how can we stand how can we grow?[55]

---

51. Forson, *Split-Level Christianity*, 182–83.

52. J. Kofi Agbeti, *West African Church History: Christian Missions and Church Foundations: 1482–1919* (Leiden: Brill, 1986), 162.

53. Ibid.

54. "Report of Commission V," 9.

55. Ephraim Amu, "The Position of Christianity in Modern Africa," *International Review of Mission* 29 (1940): 477–85 (479).

The New Redeemers

Today, Pentecostal Christianity, which takes the African traditional cosmological views seriously, has blossomed in Ghana and has affected the traditional missionary churches to the extent that it could be used as a descriptive category for Ghanaian Christianity.[56] Kingsley Larbi has stated that the failure of the traditional mission churches to meet the deep yearning of their members for spiritual power for healing helped the Pentecostal churches to reap where the historical churches had sown.[57] But these newer expressions of the Great Commission have also missed the important point of making true disciples because of their inappropriate appropriation of the African traditional religion.[58]

By using the gospel to respond practically to the existential needs of their members, it is often assumed that the African initiated churches bridged the gap between Christianity and the African worldview.[59] While this view cannot be totally dismissed, a deeper evaluation of Pentecostal contextualization in Ghana reveals that on the most crucial points the efforts of these churches to contextualize the gospel result in just a superficial appropriation of some aspects of the traditional religiosity. [60] In fact, most often their contextualization relate to prognosis of hardships, especially sicknesses and poverty, and subsequent prescription of rituals to overcome these without adequate consideration of the causes of such situations from the perspective of the traditional moral scheme.

In terms of making true disciples, the indigenous churches are not better than their forerunners. Whereas the missionaries regarded traditional beliefs as superstitious and did not dwell on them, the indigenous churches generally make the cosmic battle between Jesus and the powers of darkness their main concern. In creating a battle between traditional religion and Jesus Christ, the Ghanaian Pentecostal churches believe they show the concrete effectiveness of

56. Cephas Omenyo, *Pentecost Outside Pentecostalism: A Study of the Developments of Charismatic Renewal in the Mainline Churches in Ghana* (Zoetermeer: Uitgevcerij Boekcentrum, 2002); Omenyo, "From the Fringes to the Centre: Pentecostalization of the Mainline Churches in Ghana," *Exchange* 34, no. 1 (2005): 39–60; Omenyo, "The Charismatic Renewal Movements in Ghana," *Pneuma* 16, no. 2 (1994): 169–185.

57. Emmanuel Kingsley Larbi, *Pentecostalism: The Eddies of Ghanaian Christianity* (Accra: CPCS, 2001), 182.

58. See Elorm-Donkor, "Christian Morality in Ghanaian Pentecostalism: A Theological Analysis of Virtue Theory as a Framework for Integrating Christian and Akan Moral Schemes," (unpublished PhD diss., University of Manchester, 2011), chapter two.

59. Elom Dovlo, "African Culture and Emergent Church Forms in Ghana," *Exchange* 33, no. 1 (2004): 28–53 (33).

60. See Elorm-Donkor, "Christian Morality," 48–71.

the power of Jesus over the spiritual realm in ATR, which they refer to as the powers of darkness. This power war has its usual climax in the confrontation that is believed to happen between the cosmic powers and the power of the Holy Spirit during the healing and deliverance services where people are believed to be set free from any form of bondage that they suffer.

But even on this, Ghanaian indigenous churches are not getting it right because their prognosis neither fits the Christian nor the traditional religious view of causation. For example, whereas in the traditional religious scheme people always have to take moral responsibility for their actions and what happens to them or their community, the indigenous churches seem to place the blame for every misfortune on evil spirits. Ogbu Kalu has noted that some of them even consider despotic and dictatorial political leaders as subalterns of the devil and thus resort to prayer rather than sociopolitical activism for the resolution of the suffering brought about by the moral failures of the politicians.[61] This prognosis of unjust political suffering is contrary to the view of the ATR. In the Akan traditional scheme, even if sufferings are not immediately understandable, they are regarded as morally deserved.[62] For example, the cause of chronic sicknesses could be attributed to factors that can be natural or spiritual. Kofi Appiah-Kubi has shown from his research on health and healing among the Akans that the causes of suffering and misfortune "may be one's own doing brought on by an offence against another person or the community, or by failure to perform a religious duty."[63] In addition, some sufferings may be caused by individuals who fail through moral incompetence to comply with moral requirements.

Kalu believed that the idea of spiritual causation that some African Christians appropriated from the ATR is responsible for their attitude towards social injustice. But, actually, as I have shown thus far, it is not the traditional conceptions per se that are the problem. The problem is that because of the way the Great Commission was carried out, whenever Africans accept the Christian message, they sign up to holding another worldview without abandoning their African traditional worldview. To a very large extent, commitment to the Christian faith is also an acceptance of, and adherence to, a Western worldview, philosophy, and ethics, which differs conceptually and metaphysically from the African traditional worldview. The main issue is thus the confusion that the

61. Ogbu Kalu, *African Pentecostalism: An Introduction* (Oxford: Oxford University Press, 2008), 180.

62. Green, "Religion and Morality," 13, 14.

63. Kofi Appiah-Kubi, *Man Cures, God Heals: Religion and Medical Practice among the Akans in Ghana* (New York: Friendship Press, 1981), 12.

holding of the two worldviews causes. This is a major problem for Christian moral education in Africa.

Even with the indigenous churches, although the courtyards and prayer camps of Christian prophets have replaced that of African traditional priests and diviners, there are dissimilarities in the way they reveal causality of events and provide solutions to them. For example, African traditional diviners may reveal that the sickness of a supplicant is caused by the person's abuse of another person or a moral infringement the person or a related forebear has caused in the community. But the new Christian prophets always seem to find the causes outside of the person in the demonic forces that many times operate as witchcraft in a close relative.

Another major difference between the two worldviews makes using them simultaneously problematic: In Western Christian thought, the Enlightenment worldview has separated the experiential world that is "governed by reason and subject to scientific enquiry" from the unseen world. This resulted in a two-tiered universe that separates the world of science from the world of religion.[64] But for most Africans, the two worlds are one reality. The African traditional worldview considers the unseen world as real and impacting on the physical world. ATR sees the world as holistic and makes no bifurcation between secular and religious or sacred and profane.

So far, the point has been made that by focusing on teaching the nations, the Great Commission among the Akan people has only succeeded in appending another conceptual scheme (Western Christian worldview) to the African traditional scheme instead of integrating the two. The confusion that this has brought about hampers moral education, which is the actual demonstration of the great commandment. Therefore, a framework is needed to bring the two traditions together and I suggest the use of the virtue framework for this task.

Virtue Ethics in African Christianity

The influence that traditional beliefs have on behaviour and policy in contemporary African societies compels an in-depth study of its prominence and resilience.[65] So an explicit response to the challenges of African traditional beliefs, such as belief in the reality of evil spirits, pose to theological moral reflection is now central and not peripheral to the church's theological task in

---

64. Timothy C. Tennent, *Theology in the Context of World Christianity: How the Global Church is Influencing the Way We Think About and Discuss Theology* (Grand Rapids: Zondervan, 2007), 178.

65. Kalu, *African Pentecostalism*, 170.

Africa.[66] Some scholars who have taken up the challenge to reflect on Christian moral education and ethics in African Christianity argue that Western modern universalist ethics is unsuitable for the integration of the Christian and African moral traditions.

Neville Richardson, Bènèzet Bujo, and Brian Jennings have all published works on the integration of the Christian and African ethics and shown that the virtue tradition is more suitable for the African traditional culture and its moral systems than other Western models.[67] A review of those studies shows that although they offer significant contributions to Christian moral education in an African context, a framework that can integrate the African traditional and Western Christian moral schemes is still needed.

Bujo's work focuses mainly on the Catholic Magisterial and its relation to African morality. Bujo asserts that although the main goal of African morality is the promotion and preservation of the vital life force of the community, the spiritual dimension is one of its most essential components. He states that in Africa, communal life is very essential just as community is central for moral formation in the virtue tradition. The African community depends on individuals for ethical conduct, which is realized through a relational network that is "equally anthropocentric, cosmic and theocentric."[68] By this, Bujo affirms the importance of the African traditional belief in spirit beings for moral education and behavior. He also makes a very important observation that African thought cannot be simply subsumed under other modes such as Western thought, but demands to be taken seriously as a dialogue partner. Bujo's positive regard for African traditions and culture is commendable and his view of moral contextualization is a bold attempt.

---

66. Tennent, *Theology in the Context of World Christianity*, 267.

67. Peter J. Paris, *The Spirituality of African Peoples: The Search for a Common Moral Discourse* (Minneapolis: Fortress Press, 1985); Bujo, *African Christian Morality at the Age of Inculturation* (Nairobi: St. Paul Publications, 1990); Bujo, *Foundations*; Brian Jennings, *Leading Virtue: A Model for the Contextualisation of Christian Ethics* (Frankfurt am Main: Lang, 2009); Jennings, "Christian Virtue in a West African Context: A Study of the Interaction and Synthesis of Methodist and Fanti Moral Traditions as a Model for the Contextualization of Christian ethics," (PhD. diss., University of Birmingham, 2007); Neville Richardson, "On Keeping Theological Ethics Theological in Africa: The Quest for a (Southern) African Theological Ethics," *Annual of the Society of Christian Ethics* 21 (2001): 361–78; Richardson, "Can Christian Ethics Find its Way, and Itself, in Africa?" *Journal of Theology in Southern Africa* 95 (1996): 37–54; Richardson, "Ethics of Character and Community," in *Doing Ethics in Context: South African Perspectives*, ed. Charles Villa-Vicencio and John W. De Gruchy (Maryknoll, NY: Orbis Books), 89–101; Richardson, "Community in Christian Ethics and African Culture," *Scriptura* 62 (1997): 373–85.

68. Bujo, *Foundations*, 2.

Richardson has published articles and a book chapter on ethics in African Christianity.[69] Richardson maintains that Western Enlightenment thinking, which is individualistic with its view that there is a universalizing ethic that is shared by all people despite their cultures, has generally dominated Christian ethics in Africa.[70] He argues that the Enlightenment framework is not practical for theological reflection on African ethics because African morality stands contrary to the Enlightenment view in many essential ways.[71] Richardson asserts that Western Enlightenment-based ethics make contextualization of Christian ethics in an African Christian context difficult because it presents Western moral concepts as universal, "one-size-fits-all," and expect all other cultures to adopt it. But whereas the Enlightenment-based ethics hampers the integration of Christian ethics in African Christianity, the virtue tradition provides a theoretical framework for achieving this goal.[72] Richardson affirms strongly that it is only through virtue theory that "Christian ethics can find its way in Africa."[73] He argues that the virtue framework has both similarities with some of the essential features of African moral tradition such as community, tradition, and practices, and it has a prospect of being especially beneficial in Africa.[74] Richardson also considers virtue ethics as a solution to the general sense of loss of community and the individualism that characterize Western societies and which is becoming a norm in contemporary Africa.[75]

Although, Richardson himself does not demonstrate sufficient evidence of his understanding of the African traditional system, especially with regard to belief in spirit beings, his recognition of the need for integration of the two traditions is commendable. However, it could be deduced from Richardson's discussions that he does not see the possibility of expressing Christian moral thought in a way that responds to the African spirit world. He comes across as implying wrongly that the gospel has a culture of its own that must be maintained at all cost.

However, since, as I stated above, Jesus is the model for discipleship, the gospel is rather supposed to find embodiment wherever it travels and should not have a culture of its own.[76] Consequently, the question about contextualization

69. Richardson, "Can Christian Ethics Find its Way?" 37–54.

70. Ibid., 41.

71. Ibid., 47.

72. Richardson, "Community in Christian Ethics," 378.

73. Richardson, "Can Christian Ethics Find its Way?" 53.

74. Ibid., 37–54.

75. Richardson, "Ethics of Character," 97.

76. Kathryn Tanner, *Theories of Culture: A New Agenda for Theology* (Minneapolis: Fortress Press, 1997), 93–120; Adrian Hastings, *Church and Mission in Modern Africa* (London: Burns & Oates, 1967), 60.

should be concerned with how Africans integrate the Christian narrative within their traditional narrative without the former losing its essence. In other words, the Christian narrative should be rooted (incarnate) in the African conceptual milieu rather than replacing it.

In his doctoral thesis at the University of Birmingham, Jennings used Alasdair MacIntyre's concept of *practices, tradition, virtues,* and *narratives* to show the interaction that exists between the Christian moral scheme and the Akan (Fanti) moral scheme in Ghana.[77] He focused on six practices of the Akan people in Ghana to explore the nature of the interaction of the moral teaching of the Methodists with the Akan practices to show it is possible to contextualize the Christian moral conception in Africa Christianity.[78] Jennings makes a very significant contribution that by applying the virtue framework to the studying of particular Akan practices one is able to observe the contextualization that has already taken place.

Although these scholars identify virtue ethics as a more suitable model for the contextualization of Christian ethics in Africa, the need still exists to show how this integration may be achieved. It has been shown that there is continuity of the belief in ATR in Christian practices of Ghanaians and that the two traditions are held simultaneously. The holding of the two rival worldviews simultaneously causes confusion in moral reasoning. Therefore, a dialectic synthesis is being proposed as a heuristic tool for integrating the two traditions.

DIALECTIC SYNTHESIS OF TRADITIONS

Alasdair MacIntyre argues that instead of regarding rival traditions as being mutually exclusive and incompatible ways of perceiving the world, we should regard them as providing perspectives that are very different but complementary for understanding reality.[79] He considers the dialectical process through which Thomas Aquinas synthesized Aristotelian virtue ethics with Augustinian theology as the most viable solution to the problem of rival traditions.[80] ATR and the Western Christian traditions are considered here as rival traditions that need to be harmonized to ensure successful moral education in African Christianity.

---

77. Jennings, "Christian Virtue."

78. Ibid., 64–86.

79. Alasdair MacIntyre, *Whose Justice? Whose Rationality?* (Notre Dame, IN: University of Notre Dame, 1998, repr. 2003), 352.

80. Ibid., 363.

MacIntyre notes that Aquinas wrote out of at least two traditions, extending each as part of his task of integrating them into a systematic mode of thought.[81] First, Aquinas revealed that the Augustinian view of sin claimed that humans have a perverted will, ". . . a rooted tendency to disobedience in the will and a diversion of their passion . . ." that obscures reason and sometimes causes systematic cultural deformation. Second, in relating the Aristotelian virtue ethics to this Augustinian view, Aquinas detected that it upsets the Aristotelian moral framework.[82] Aristotle's view was that when fully trained, the human intellect is capable of obtaining both theoretical and practical truth, which then orders a person's acts towards a good moral life. Aristotle did not have a notion of the will and had no explanation for the inherent defect of human capacity for knowing and doing good. MacIntyre thinks that this was an error in the Aristotelian scheme for which it needed another scheme.[83]

On the other hand, Aquinas understood the Augustinian view to mean that no amount of training or exercising of the virtues can help people to advance towards the ultimate good, due to the perversion of their will by sin. He saw in this willful evil the possibility of humans achieving their moral goal. For Aquinas, the revelation of God in Augustinian theology complemented the Aristotelian view to provide a more adequate description of practical reason, and for providing a means to achieve this ultimate goal.[84] He thought that the revelation of God introduces free grace from which faith, hope, and love ensue. MacIntyre believes that the approach of Aquinas did not derail the Augustinian view of perverted *will*. It rather complemented it by making the Augustinian view of the human condition a bit more encouraging. In the same way, it also strengthened Aristotle's framework, because although it upheld that humanity has capacity for knowing and doing good, it also accepted the limitation of humanity to singlehandedly know and be able to do what is good. It is in this regard that Aquinas is regarded as the father of the method of correlation, which has been alluded to and used widely in practical theological reflections.[85]

From the foregoing, it is clear that acknowledging the differences between the Akan and Christian moral traditions does not mean that their

---

81. Ibid., 164; Thomas Aquinas, *Summa Theologica*, vol. 1, section 2.

82. Alasdair MacIntyre, *Three Rival Versions of Moral Enquiry: Encyclopaedia, Genealogy and Tradition* (Notre Dame, IN: University of Notre Dame Press, 1990), 140.

83. Ibid., 111.

84. Luke Bretherton, *Hospitality and Holiness: A Christian Witness Amid Moral Diversity* (Aldershot: Ashgate, 2004), 22.

85. Elaine Graham, Heather Walton, and Frances Ward, *Theological Reflections: Sources* (London: SCM, 2007), 269–75.

incompatibility cannot be rationally resolved. A proper characterization of rival viewpoints yields an understanding that makes it possible for the rival traditions to work together and to benefit from each other's strengths. But how does this integrated approach to the human moral condition transform previously promising but now inadequate conceptions? How does an integration of the rival traditions resolve the moral dilemma and still maintain some continuity with some central conceptions of the traditional scheme? To answer these questions, a contemporary moral issue is used as a practical example of how the integration would work to benefit the Ghanaian society.

The Issue of Nepotism as Social Injustice

It must be recognized that although African kinship attachments work well in mono-cultural rural settings, in urbanized and globalized societies, they can promote affections and passions that would potentially inhibit good moral acts towards people who are considered as not belonging to one's tribe or clan (ethnic group). Moral issues such as economic corruption, nepotism, dictatorship, and various forms of injustices in Ghana may be seen simply as a continuation of previously accepted social obligations that did not change when global changes hit African societies. In the traditional system, social obligations were primarily understood to be toward people from one's family, clan, and tribe. But in the modern nation state, fulfilling social obligations in this way may be seen as an immoral practice and an injustice, especially if one was a government or public functionary charged with the distribution of goods and services. So, the practice of mutual responsibility entailed in the traditional kinship ties can be construed as injustice in the modern system.

Communal relationships worked well in the traditional communalistic rural society because they exemplified a sense of mutual moral responsibility that has the well-being of the community as its goal. On the other hand, because of the individualism brought about by the Western Enlightenment and promoted through the Great Commission in Africa, people's focus in life changed from the community to the autonomous self (individual).[86] Due to this self-centered tendency, one's achievements in life these days often depend on the power of the people one is connected with rather than on skills, talents, and hard work.[87] Although one may not have the requisite skills, talents, and experience in comparison to other competitors in a job search, yet he or she

---

86. Alasdair MacIntyre, *After Virtue: A Study in Moral Theory*, 3rd ed. (London: Duckworth, 2007), 6–12.

87. This is known in Ghana as *Connections*.

could be given a job by virtue of knowing and being connected to a person of power (a big man). These injustices are general to humanity. However, in Ghana, the confusion that holding two rival worldviews (traditional and modern) prevents people from realizing and standing up against these social injustices. When the Christian messengers dismissed the ATR belief that the spirit realm punishes immoral behaviour, self-centered people became less inclined to act in ways that the traditional system regards as moral.

A major weakness of the traditional scheme is that ATR only sanctions morality and does not provide any effective means by which a person's innate moral weakness is transformed for moral character formation. People do not expect any supernatural help from the deities and spirit beings in their pursuit of morality. This weakness can be resolved when the traditional scheme is integrated with Christian worldview. With the Christian view, although humanity is created in the image of God (Gen. 1:26-28), it is limited in at least two ways. First, humanity is limited by sin, which includes personal disobedience or turning away from God, and corporate injustice caused by corrupted social structures, institutions, and other social relationships.[88] In turning away from God, humanity is locked up in self-centeredness and obsessed with personal security and existential needs.[89] The second limitation is that humanity is not totally free in its decisions and actions because in our freedom, we often tend to contradict God's desire for "mutuality in intimate affairs, brotherhood and sisterhood in public affairs and fellowship with the divine."[90]

However, unlike the anthropology of the Akans discussed above, in the Christian view, humanity has the capacity to transcend its finitude imaginatively and to relate reflexively to itself and also to God.[91] The possibility that humans can transcend their natural innate limitations and be able to relate directly to God in order to have the power to live moral lives is affirmed in the Christian scheme. Thus, the believer is expected to depend on the grace of God and the power of the Holy Spirit to help him or her live according to God's will. So, by integrating the two traditions, an improved understanding of the human moral condition that is hopeful is obtained. The grace of God and

---

88. Joseph Kotva Jr., *The Christian Case for Virtue Ethics* (Washington, DC: Georgetown University Press, 1996), 90.

89. John Wesley, "On Perfection," in *The Works of John* Wesley, ed. Albert Outler (Nashville: Abingdon, 1985), 2:170–85.

90. Don Browning, *A Fundamental Practical Theology: Descriptive and Strategic Proposals* (Minneapolis: Fortress Press, 1991), 146.

91. Ibid., 144.

the power of the Holy Spirit that the Akan system lacks for dealing with the question of human moral weakness are provided in the Christian scheme. On the other hand, the individualistic tendency that the Western Enlightenment promotes would be corrected by the relational community that the African religious tradition stresses and that forms the basis of all relationships. In that way, social injustice that is promoted by self-centeredness would be reduced as people try to live by the grace of God in the framework of kinship relationships that are no more limited to one's race or ethnicity but open to the whole human family. Ghanaian society would benefit from a moral system in which the traditional complements the modern to provide consistency in moral reasoning and conduct.

CONCLUSION

It has been shown that the universalizing method used for teaching the Great Commission among the Akan people in Ghana resulted in a split-level Christianity whereby converts still hold both the African traditional beliefs together with Christian belief and that this situation makes Christian moral education problematic. Although the Akan community depended on the mutual moral responsibility of its members for its well-being and used religion to sanction moral behavior, because the missionaries dismissed the traditional beliefs as delusion and superstition, a great damage was done to the foundations upon which Christian moral education could succeed. It is also shown that the indigenous Ghanaian churches are not better in this regard because although they take the traditional conceptions seriously, their prognosis of suffering blames everything on spirits and absolves humans of their moral responsibility. Therefore, it has been proposed that a framework for a dialectic synthesis (integration) of the two rival traditions be pursued. The suggestion in this essay is that the virtue tradition offers a congenial framework that could serve as a heuristic tool because of its stress on community and sensitivity to rival conceptual viewpoints. By characterizing the moral concepts of the two traditions, it is possible to bring their strengths together for the benefit of the Ghanaian society.

PART V

Interrogating the
Commission from Beyond
the Academy

13

A United States Inner–City Oriented Great Commission

MarShondra Scott Lawrence

Our love is bigger than the strongest of arguments / we are the ones we've been waiting for / we won't believe what we're told to believfe in / we are the ones we've been waiting for . . . love is what we are.[1]

If you have come here to help me, you are wasting our time. But if you have come because your liberation is bound up with mine, then let us work together.[2]

INTRODUCTION

A shocking thing happened on Saginaw High School's prom night in 2013—a deadly shooting occurred at a pre-prom event. Students had come together at a local conference facility to take pictures and begin their prom night celebration, as onlookers from the community gathered outside. Shots were heard from the parking lot, students scattered seeking safety, and in the end this shooting injured and hospitalized three women ages 18 through 39, and left one young seventeen-year-old woman dead . . . on prom night.[3] My young cousin was attending the prom on that fateful night, and the victim was her friend. Anxiety was especially heightened for the city, as the other public city high school in

---

1. Sky Nelson, "We Are the Ones (We've Been Waiting For)," *Other Singles*, http://www.skynelson.com/track/303745/we-are-the-ones-we-ve-been-waiting-for?feature_id=39921.

2. Aboriginal activists group, Queensland, 1970s.

3. Jessica Shepherd, "17-year-old Female Killed during Saginaw High Pre-prom Shooting; 3 Other Females Injured," *MLive*, May 23, 2013, http://www.mlive.com/news/saginaw/index.ssf/2013/05/17-year-old_female_killed_duri.html.

Saginaw, Michigan—the one I graduated from—was scheduled to have its prom the next night. For many days that followed, I read the news stories about the victims and the search for their attackers. I watched the pain of the students inscribed on Facebook, and I hurt along with them. How horrible was the senseless and tragic loss of a young life, the terror made of such a special night.

Shootings are no stranger to cities like Saginaw. Saginaw is a city plagued with inner-city challenges—gun violence, today, being just one of those issues. Many neighborhoods in Saginaw have all of the marks of a typical inner city. David Wilson, for example, defined the black inner city, or "ghetto," as a space "with more than 95 percent of residents African American and with 35 percent or more of households living below the poverty level" that is "within the city's political boundaries."[4] According to recent statistics, 56.6 percent of Saginaw city residents live in poverty.[5] And, as 46.1 percent of the entire city population is African American, there are no doubt a number of neighborhoods within the city with over 95 percent African American residency.[6] In recent years, the city of Saginaw has been hit hard by the economic downturn and the fledgling manufacturing industry. Like Detroit to the south, the metropolis where I now live, Saginaw has had to contend with decreasing population, increasing segregation, and the chilling effects of globalization.

Saginaw sits just thirty miles north of Flint and less than one hundred miles north of Detroit. Both cities have recently been named as numbers one and two, respectively, of the United States' most dangerous cities.[7] Saginaw, Flint, and Detroit are all Michigan cities situated within the Rust Belt, along with cities like Indianapolis, St. Louis, Chicago, and New York—a region that some demographers seemingly derogatively call the "Ghetto Belt."[8] What has been happening in Saginaw around gun violence is reminiscent of the news we hear out of Chicago these days—murder by the numbers has become a daily occurrence,[9] creating entirely too much pain.

4. David Wilson, *Cities and Race: America's New Black Ghetto* (New York: Routledge, 2007), 13.

5. "Saginaw, Michigan (MI) Poverty Rate Data – Information About Poor and Low Income Residents," City-Data.com, http://www.city-data.com/poverty/poverty-Saginaw-Michigan.html#ixzz2biAYc3BB.

6. United States Census Bureau, "State and County QuickFacts," U.S. Department of Commerce, January 7, 2014, http://quickfacts.census.gov/qfd/states/26/2670520.html

7. 24/7 Wall Street, "Most Dangerous Cities in America," Huffington Post, June 21, 2013, http://www.huffingtonpost.com/2013/06/21/most-dangerous-cities-in-america_n_3478091.html.

8. Douglas Stanglin, "Two Views of Census Bureau Data and Integration," USA Today, December 14, 2010, http://content.usatoday.com/communities/ondeadline/post/2010/12/nations-neighborhoods-more-integrated-than-for-at-least-a-century/1#.UggZdNKTj6U.

I have to admit that even though I live near and work in the inner city and am familiar with many of its challenges, the prom night shooting stunned me. This happened in my hometown, and I truly cared. I was affected, though not so directly, by this violence. And as I ruminated on it, as I prayed for the pain of the students and parents and families that were impacted in Saginaw, as I considered the suffering in inner-city communities all over America, I again began to wonder: Do we, as Christians and the church, think about the reality of the black inner city—the ghetto? Do we understand that we are called there, too?

I can drive through just about any inner-city neighborhood and see churches dotted throughout. There are numerous, sometimes stunningly beautiful, churches in the suburbs and the downtown centers that are near and around our inner cities. Yet, even with so many dedicated, church-going Christians, there is still so much yet to do. In this essay, we will first examine closely the history and reality of urban American life. Then, we will discuss the Matthean Great Commission for what it tells us about our Christian responsibility to our inner cities. Finally, we will discuss how and what we can do to engage or to effectively *go* to and with the ghetto.

A Long Way From Beloved

It is 2013 and the state of the United States urban community seems a far cry from the loving, inclusive, and just beloved community that Martin Luther King, Jr. envisioned in 1956.[10] Of course, Martin Luther King did not have today's inner city on his mind—he never saw quite these communities, fraught with their current issues. What is now the inner city is a community phenomenon that has evolved over many years and with a number of national and international economic changes. A closer look at the inner city community reveals virtually nothing loving, inclusive, or just about the practices, policy changes, and realities that have made it what it is.

As a middle-class African American woman, born after the civil rights movement, it would have been too easy, I suspect, to live my life and never know much of what was going on in the ghetto or how it came to be. As I began to work in the city, however, my mentors—both African American and Anglo—thankfully encouraged me to learn its history. The very first black

9. Rebel Pundit, "Chicago Murders Soar: 67 Shot, 11 Killed Over July 4 Weekend—So Far," Breitbart, July 7, 2013, http://www.breitbart.com/Big-Government/2013/07/07/Chicago-Murders-Soar-67-Shot-11-Killed-over-July-4-Weekend-So-Far.

10. Charles Marsh, *The Beloved Community* (New York: Basic Books, 2005), 1.

communities in the Unites States beginning with Virginia in 1619 were, of course, slave communities on plantations. After slavery, the black community—still, then, living primarily in the South—was bound by Jim Crow laws and heavily depended on slave-like agrarian and extractive employment.[11] The Great Migration of American blacks into the cities and to the north, which brought my grandparents to Michigan from Mississippi, created another big change in the structure of the United States African American community. Many blacks now lived in the city, especially in the north where they found job opportunities in the industrial plants. The more affluent black people lived next door to less economically prosperous blacks. Certain housing practices, such as redlining, kept us all together then. And though our mixed-income communities were created unjustly, they benefitted from the strength of financial and occupational diversity. And so it was, until the civil rights movement resulted in federal policy changes that had surprising effects.

In the pre-civil rights movement era, life was hard if one was black. The forced residential communities in the north became more and more overcrowded, and in this way also less and less stable.[12] In the south, especially, blacks still had very limited to no rights to the economic stabilizers provided by even the 1935 Social Security Act—still no access to pensions, disability, or unemployment compensation and very little job stability.[13] The civil rights movement and the push for more equal rights came largely from the South, but a hundred years after the abolition of slavery, policy changes toward social and economic equality were still needed all over the country. Then in 1964 and 1965, the government's attention turned toward the black and poor peoples, and important pieces of legislation were passed, including the Civil Rights Act in 1964 and the Voting Rights Act in 1965. These policy changes created education, employment, and housing opportunities for a number of blacks—again my family was a part of this history. Both of my parents became the first generation in their families to go to college; both landed good and stable jobs in education. Eventually, they also moved away from the black neighborhood. Herein, was the problem for the black community. The civil rights legislation helped some, but not enough. It made it possible for blacks to begin to live away from each other, weakening the black city neighborhoods by taking the most educated, most professional, and most economically contributing residents out. Also, it created a noticeable and growing class rift in the black community that has continued to grow to this day.[14]

11. Wilson, *Cities and Race*, 12.

12. Helene Slessarev, *The Betrayal of the Urban Poor* (Philadelphia: Temple University Press, 1997), 8.

13. Ibid.

Helene Slessarev-Jamir, in her book *Betrayal of the Urban Poor,* makes an interesting case about the limited effectiveness of the civil rights legislation of the 1960s. She charges that the forming of this legislation was an act built on only a "partial commitment to equality."[15] In fact, while blacks had little to no voting power (Southern blacks did not achieve full rights to vote until 1965), powerful groups lobbied the government to limit the scope of the legislation and protect their own interests.[16] These lobbying efforts resulted in legislation that could only help a relative few, and it included little in the way of job development. Perhaps the biggest problem here is just that—limited jobs equaled limited equality. William Julius Wilson described changes in the inner-city communities after so many were left with no job training and little in the way of sustainable job opportunities. Wilson argued that the rates of such social dislocations as out-of-wedlock births, female-headed families, and violent crime have continually risen over the years.[17] Where 25 percent of black births were outside of marriage in 1965, by 1980, the number rose to 57 percent; whereas in 1965 almost 25 percent of black families were headed by females, 43 percent of black families were by 1980; and the rates of violent crime have "increased sharply in recent years."[18] While these social problems do "disproportionately plague the ghetto underclass" and the greater public's awareness of such reinforces racial and class stereotypes, the real truth is that "these growing social problems have accompanied increasing black rates of joblessness."[19]

What is even worse, and even scarier, concerning the inner city is that life in the inner city today is yet growing more and more difficult due to the impact of globalization. David Wilson termed this new iteration of the ghetto the *glocal ghetto,* a space carved out by the global "political economic force" since 1990 that he calls *the global trope.*[20] The problem of the *global trope* is more about rhetoric than anything else; it is rhetoric that drives fear and urgency of what must be done to be a vibrant city in this new world of globalization.[21] The inner city, with the ugliness of its blight and the seeming immorality in

---

14. William Julius Wilson, *The Truly Disadvantaged,* 2nd ed. (Chicago: University of Chicago Press, 2012), 110.

15. Slessarev, *Betrayal,* 1–24.

16. Ibid., 41–45.

17. Wilson, *Truly Disadvantaged,* 20.

18. Ibid., 21.

19. Ibid.

20. Wilson, *Cities and Race,* ii.

21. Ibid., x.

its social problems, becomes a literal threat to our survival. City finances are directed at areas that are being remodeled and upscaled, as resources are cut off to the areas left for the poor. This new inner city, the *glocal ghetto*, experiences marginalization—social and public policy marginalization—to an extent that we have not seen applied to spaces in this country before. This is the 2013 ghetto.

I see this process in full swing in Detroit today. The church that my family pastors sits in an east side Detroit neighborhood that has been slated for increasingly limited support services as the city makes itself brand new in the city center. As the city is yet more violent outside the center, those with some financial means are still being forced out of the city altogether, while many people who used to live in the suburbs have moved into Detroit's downtown and university areas, like the Wayne State corridor. This process of city revival and gentrification has happened similarly around the country, and especially in Rust Belt cities like Cleveland and Chicago. Good people who have been living in the inner city for years are being upended or have to live in a space supported by few of the city services for which their tax dollars pay.

It has been commonly said that when white America gets a cold, black America gets pneumonia. Or, it seems that, as the United States fights its way through economic and policy changes, the black and Latino inner cities take the brunt of the hit. The inner city, and those of us who live in it, are invisible in this society. Black feminist Michele Wallace writes the following about the experience of invisibility for black women:

> What most people see of the black woman is a void, a black hole that appears empty, not full. The outsider sees black feminist creativity as a dark hole from which nothing worthwhile can emerge and in which everything is forced to assume the zero volume of nothingness, the invisibility, that results from the intense pressure of race, class, and sex.[22]

Alexander's words appropriately describe what it is like for both women and men of the inner city, for the homeless, for those that have been forever marked as criminal, and all too often for the mentally ill of the city. It is as though most of the rest of the world cannot see the frustrations, the pain, or the humanity in inner-city life. Too many do not ever think of this space or these people. And, when we do, too many of us do not expect any more than nothingness—in fact we fear that the existence of these places and *those people* is a threat to us somehow. Invisibility and marginalization make for a lonely place, but it need

---

22. Stephanie Y. Mitchem, *Introducing Womanist Theology* (Maryknoll, NY: Orbis Books, 2002), 19.

not be, not with so many of us out here who are a people called to love, called to care, and called to go.

JESUS SAID *WHAT?*

Civil rights activist, community developer, and founder of the Christian Community Development Association (CCDA), John Perkins taught us in his 2011 CCDA Immersion class that the purpose of the church is to love and to teach how to love. Perkins taught us this as he was preparing us to work with people in the inner city toward better community and better living standards. Though we know that love is a necessity in a disciple, and we know that learning to both receive and give love is a requirement for our optimal personal and spiritual development, this may seem a strange place to begin thinking about what Jesus told us to do.[23] I realize and admit that it is this description of purpose that provides a framework for my understanding of the so-called Great Commission and its relevance toward the work that we are called to in the city. I recognize that there is no more perfect bringing together of the spirit of what Jesus commanded with the tone of mission and evangelism that is necessary to effectively join our inner city neighbors. We are to love and to teach how to love.

Historically, the application of Matt. 28:18-20 as the Great Commission, especially as it pertained to disciple-making the oppressed, was not centered on love. Mitzi J. Smith, in her essay in this volume titled "'Knowing More than is Good for One': A Womanist Interrogation of the Matthean Great Commission," discusses how too often missionaries made disciples with a "by any means necessary" vitriol that validated "torture, rape, perpetual slavery, and murder" and focused on baptizing and teaching, ignoring any scriptural references and inferences toward justice.[24] Such an understanding of the Great Commission was disastrous when it was applied during the transatlantic slave trade. It continues to be suppressive for the poor and the marginalized in our society as a gospel impetus void of social justice, and further strips those in the inner city of their human rights and dignity as many of us continue to apply it in such a way in our work today.

Instead, as I consider my Christian motivation to work with the inner city, and as I think about how Jesus would have me do this ministry, I am struck by the relational tone of what Jesus commanded. I understand that Jesus told his

---

23. Timothy P. Jackson, ed., *The Best Love of the Child* (Grand Rapids, MI: Eerdmans, 2011), 28–34.

24. See Mitzi J. Smith's essay, "'Knowing More than is Good for One': A Womanist Interrogation of the Matthean Great Commission," in this volume.

disciples to make disciples (and we believe by extension that it applies to us). He said to make disciples in all the nations, within all people, in all places of the earth, as we are going. In fact, I argue that if we are to *go to all people*, this going *must* include the people of the inner city—this place so close to so many of us. I know that Jesus said our disciple making is to include baptizing and teaching. I, then, think about the fullness of this instruction.

Disciple building is not easy work. Dave Buehring says that "disciple-making involves a hands-on approach: people teaching and investing, modeling and demonstrating."[25] Disciple making is the work of connection. Done Jesus' way, disciple making is built on love. Jesus expanded on this for us. He said to baptize and to teach. Baptism is a special occurrence—a time when an individual, a community, and God join together. This is sacred joining bonded by and through God's love and with each other. This is joining based not on our personal commonalities, but on our love in and for God. Teaching, as Jesus taught, builds on our community standing. This teaching is about so much more than telling someone what to do or how to be. This teaching of all that Jesus taught involves a relationship so intricately engaged that both the teacher and the student feed into each other's growing. Black feminist bell hooks shared the words of Vietnamese Buddhist monk Thich Nhat Hahn who says that "in a true dialogue, both sides are willing to change. We have to appreciate that truth can be received from outside of—not only within—our own group. We have to believe that by engaging in dialogue with another person, we have the possibility of making a change within ourselves, that we can become deeper."[26] Paulo Freire, who greatly influenced bell hooks and her theory of engaged pedagogy, said it this way:

> To exist, humanly, is to name the world, to change it . . . Dialogue is the encounter between men, mediated by the world, in order to name the world. Hence, dialogue cannot occur between those who want to name the world and those who do not wish this naming—between those who deny others the right to speak their word and those whose right to speak has been denied them . . . Dialogue cannot exist, however, in the absence of a profound love for the world and for people. The naming of the world, which is an action of creation and re-creation, is not possible if it is not infused with love.[27]

25. Dave Buehring, *The Jesus Blueprint: Rediscovering His Original Plan for Changing the World* (Oviedo, FL: HigherLife Development Services, 2012), 21.

26. bell hooks, *Teaching Community: A Pedagogy of Hope* (New York, NY: Routledge, 2003), xv–xvi.

This is the dialogue and exchange necessary for teaching disciples. And, this is where exciting things may begin to happen while we lovingly disciple between races, classes, and cultures.

The possibilities grow yet greater when I think of all that Jesus taught. It was Jesus who read, "The Spirit of the Lord is upon me, because he has anointed me to bring good news to the poor. He has sent me to proclaim release to the captives and recovery of sight to the blind, to let the oppressed go free, to proclaim the year of the Lord's favor" (Luke 4:18-19 NRSV). It was Jesus who in his Sermon on the Mount said, "Blessed are the poor in spirit, for theirs is the kingdom of heaven" (Matt. 5:3 NRSV). And, it was he who once spoke about our right response to the hungry, thirsty, stranger, sick, and the imprisoned, saying, "Truly I tell you, just as you did it to one of the least of these who are members of my family, you did it to me" (Matt. 25:40 NRSV). Toward the end of his teaching, it was Jesus that told his disciples, "I give you a new commandment that you love one another. . . . By this everyone will know that you are my disciples, if you have love for one another" (John 13:34-35 NRSV).

It is important that we remember all of this as we set out to disciple. As we aim to be both true to Jesus' gospel and relevant to the new disciples around us, the faith that we live and share must include both personal salvation and present and collective social justice. For many of us, it seems that this could be especially tricky. Jim Wallis reminds us that "the kind of Jesus we believe in will determine the kind of Christianity we practice."[28] When I think of all that Jesus said, I know that we cannot turn our backs on the living conditions and realities of our *glocal ghettos* or partake in the ugly comfort of upholding the system of inner-city invisibility. If I am to teach all that Jesus taught, then I must live out love and justice. So then, that is my position toward the inner city as I am there to disciple: to join with the people and to do justice.

Doing As We Have Been Told

Robert Franklin, in *Crisis in the Village*, identified five phases of public ministry that he sees churches engaged in. I contend that individual Christians also often participated in certain of those phases. The five phases include:

- Charity, a "focus on direct, immediate relief of pain and suffering;"

27. Paulo Freire, *Pedagogy of the Oppressed* (New York: Bloomsbury Academic, 2000), 88–89. See also Namulundah Florence, *bell hooks' Engaged Pedagogy: A Transgressive Education for Critical Consciousness* (Westport, CT: Praeger, 1998).

28. Jim Wallis, *On God's Side: What Religion Forgets and Politics Hasn't Learned about Serving the Common Good* (Grand Rapids: Brazos, 2013), 13.

- Support, "longer term . . . counseling and assistance that facilitates the journey from dependence to self-sufficiency and self-determination;"
- Service, the provision of "regular social services to a community;"
- Justice, "representing the needs of people to the public systems and structures of power;" and,
- Transformation, "the ministry of comprehensive community transformation and development" around "a vision of the beloved community."[29]

It is interesting how each of Franklin's phases, taken in order, describe almost exactly the path that my engagement with the inner city has taken. Many years ago, I started volunteering in Detroit with a group that did regular charity work; we worked in food pantries, cleaned the facilities and helped organize non-profits working to provide food and housing, and for the poor, helped facilitate clothing drives and passed out donated Christmas gifts. After a few years, I graduated, if you will, from lightly engaged volunteer work to employment at a non-profit that provided counseling as part of transitional support aimed at helping families to become financially stable. Around the same time, I began to work with residential programs—including one for homeless women and their children and another that houses women in drug recovery—that offer an interesting blend of transitional support and necessary social services. It was in these years that I started to develop the practice of *joining with*. Now, I got to know many of the people I worked with more personally. We could talk about our lives and families, and I would listen to their challenges, seeking to support them in finding solutions. We heard each other, and I better understood their experiences and choices.

An interesting thing happened as I worked my way through these phases of public ministry: The people I met inspired me with their courage, challenged me by the differences between our resources and experiences, which they were often happy to lovingly point out, and they motivated me through their determination. It was my association and love toward the people in the inner city that launched me into pursuing ministries of justice and transformation.

It saddens me, somewhat, that most of the work I have been able to do had to be done outside of the church. I worked with non-profits that were self-motivated: one that was founded as part of a church ministry, but no longer is, and a couple that claim to be religious-based, but have varying levels of ties to the church. Though I do not know that the church has always done better,

29. Robert M. Franklin, *Crisis in the Village: Restoring Hope in African American Communities* (Minneapolis: Fortress Press, 2007), 162–63.

I saw in many of the places that I worked what often looked like a greater commitment to being a helping agency than to actually doing what was most helpful. I also observed disillusionment on the part of both the employees and the citizens they served. Perhaps the real issue was that "programs based solely on the principle of equality of individual opportunity are inadequate to address the complex problems of group inequality in America."[30]

As I continued to work and began to study, I became aware of another problem inherent to the early phases of public ministry. To work in a public ministry in an African-American inner-city ghetto is to work with some of the poorest of Americans. American poverty is not only an issue of the scarcity of material necessities; it can be shameful and belittling. Many programs of charity are designed to simply give to those in need. But Robert D. Lupton says, "perhaps the deepest poverty of all is to have nothing of value to offer in exchange. Charity that fosters such poverty must be challenged."[31] Such a ministry is easier and is prevalent. "One of the biggest problems in many poverty-alleviation efforts is that their design and implementation exacerbates the poverty of being of the economically rich—their god-complexes—and the poverty of being of the economically poor—their feeling of inferiority and shame."[32] What is required is a ministry involving more time, effort, thought, and creativity—and aimed at honoring the gifts of the recipient.

Moving into the world of seeking social justice and working toward community transformation has taken me into ministry that yet more easily fits my inner-city applicable understanding of the Great Commission. Now I find that relationships with those I work with are longer term and allows for more true and mutual disciple making. Doing this work requires me to ask more and deeper questions, to listen more closely and to care about what the community cares about. This is the work of *joining with* the inner city community's issues, and working together with the community for good. It is here that my public ministry path veered a bit from Franklin's proposed order. In fact, it was through my work in community development, a transformation ministry, that I got my first real experience in community organizing, a justice ministry.

Community organizing is just one form of justice work, but one that is available to us all. Though a number of churches are involved in church-

30. Wilson, *Truly Disadvantaged*, 113.

31. Robert D. Lupton, *Compassion, Justice and the Christian Life: Rethinking Ministry to the Poor* (Ventura, CA: Regal Books, 2007), 26.

32. Steve Corbett and Brian Fikkert, *When Helping Hurts: How to Alleviate Poverty Without Hurting the Poor . . . and Yourself* (Chicago: Moody Publishers, 2009), 65.

based congregational community organizing with their neighborhoods, Helene Slessarev-Jamir says that there are also many who set out to do this work more independently, based on their own convictions and not motivated by their churches.[33] Community organizing as *prophetic activism*, as Slessarev-Jamir calls it, is concerned with the well-being of the poor and their access to basic legal and substantive rights.[34] This is an urban answer to the racial and economic discrimination experienced in the inner city. *Prophetic activism* is amazing in that it has the power to bring different classes together, bonded by ethical foundations.[35] The four largest, mostly congregational, organizing networks—the Industrial Areas Foundation (IAF) based out of Chicago, the People Improving Communities through Organizing (PICO) National Network, the Gamaliel Foundation, and the Direct Action and Research Training Center (DART)—have affiliates all over the country, and in some cases abroad. The Regional Congregations and Neighborhood Organizations Training Center (RCNO) "brings together small African American congregations in California, Pennsylvania, Illinois, Alabama and Georgia."[36] Congregation-based community organizing has been one way to fight against the fast moving gentrification that cities like Detroit have experienced, or are now facing.

Community development is also an amazing way to *join with* a neighborhood for its good. I have seen such groups transform homes and streets into safe and beautiful living spaces. Mature community development corporations are able to bring business, jobs, and job training to the inner city. Some have even opened groceries stores to combat the injustice of food deserts in the city. Christian community development can be especially beautiful as one of the principles of the CCDA is leadership development, which, practiced as CCDA style, is discipleship at its finest.[37]

There are so many ways to join with and support the poor in our cities and live out the city Christian's Great Commission responsibility that every church and every Christian can participate in and begin to work. Jesus sent us out to disciple, to connect, and to love. Let us love our whole communities together.

---

33. Helene Slessarev-Jamir, *Prophetic Activism: Progressive Religious Justice Movements in Contemporary America* (New York: New York University Press, 2011), 6.

34. Ibid., 8.

35. Ibid., 7.

36. Ibid., 82.

37. Barry Burch, Jr., "Chicago Priest Mentors Gang Members, Murders Decrease Drastically," Black Blue Dog, August 5, 2013, http://www.blackbluedog.com/2013/08/news/chicago-priest-mentors-gang-members-murders-decrease-drastically/.

Conclusion

It can be so scary to go into any place where we do not belong, where we likely will not be trusted, and where we may not be wanted. And working in the inner city, whether it involves traveling a distance to get there or simply stepping outside the doors of our homes or churches, is more frightening still when we only focus on the inner-city stories of violence. If we can get past the fear, trusting God to cast out fear, there is still the fact that ministry this way—being commissioned for this work—is such hard work. It requires our presence, our time, our patience, and our commitment. No doubt, this might be a deterrent for many. But if we can accept this too, I can still think of one more thing that might give us pause. I am guessing many of us are wondering, what is the point? For too long the inner city has suffered the way it has, and who are we to change it? Or, maybe it is the people—that they seem, at first glance, too far gone.

Inner city work, for me, is about the possibilities. If Jesus sent me and promised he would always be with me, I will always expect miraculous things when I commit myself. The inner-city work is also about our love, the special piece that puts everything in motion. Finally, it is about the people and what is right. There are so many issues in the public forum today that affect the stability of inner city life—including the fight for living wages, for fair immigration policy, for effective gun policy, for reform of mass incarceration laws. People's lives and well-being are being stolen. And if Jesus cares (and Jesus does care), then so should I.

I recently read about Father Michael Pfleger, a Chicago priest who entered one of the city's most dangerous neighborhoods and started a weekly basketball league. Violent crime decreased. According to Pfleger, "there has not been a single shooting amongst his players."[38] Four area gangs have actually partnered with Pfleger to send young guys to him. "Pfleger also helps the players obtain a GED, job training, and also job placement at one of the 100 companies that have made a decision to partner with the league."[39] Pfleger does the hard work to connect with his guys, and the program works because they know that any shooting equals no job. Oh, the possibilities, when we accept our commission—when God, courage, love, creativity, and presence come together and get to work.

38. Ibid.
39. Ibid.

14

The Great Commission's Impact on a Short-term Missionary and Lay Leader in the Church of God in Christ

June C. Rivers

"Religion that is pure and undefiled before God, the Father, is this: to care for orphans and widows in their distress, and to keep oneself unstained by the world."
(James 1:27 NRSV)

My perspective of the Great Commission's impact on me and my service as a short-term missionary emerged from the legacy of my grandmother, my father, and the founder of my denomination (the Church of God in Christ), who because of their humility never denied that they descended from an enslaved people. As a child, I learned that all are called to serve others and to preach and teach the gospel of Jesus Christ; that there are many ways that one can serve others, as the Scriptures have commanded. We are admonished to serve at home and abroad or as Luke puts it in "Jerusalem, Judea, Samaria, and to the ends of the earth" (Acts 1:8 NRSV). My paternal grandmother, Alberta Vinson Green, took her calling seriously. With nine children and a husband who worked menial jobs, she served in her "Jerusalem" and "the ends of the earth." Grandmother Alberta, born in 1899, had only a sixth-grade education. She accepted Jesus as her personal savior as an adult through the outreach of a Holiness Pentecostal church. She carried out her calling to serve at home and abroad. Mrs. Green incorporated the Charitable Workers Institute and charged a small fee of twenty-five cents a week for securing jobs for people who needed employment. She heard about the plight of people in Haiti and Liberia, West Africa from missionaries Elizabeth White and Francina Wiggins and committed herself to supporting the work in these two countries. Elizabeth White planted the first Church of God in Christ mission in Wissikeh, Liberia in 1929 or 1930 and, in 1949, Francina Wiggins was appointed to assist Mother White.[1] My grandmother acquired brand new, unsold clothing from several major department stores, one known today as Macy's. Alberta also collected books from a middle-class school district near Detroit, Michigan. She sold miniature sweet potato pies for ten cents and used these funds for shipping trunks full of the things that she had gathered. To involve her denomination, she instituted "Pennies for Missions" during the yearly convocation of our denomination in Michigan to acquire additional financial support for international missionaries. Even then my grandmother was revolutionary in her thinking about helping others. Her vision of the Great Commission was the embodiment of love and social justice. My father, Rev. Havious Green, embraced his mother's mission legacy. As a child, I heard of his desire to go to Africa after a colleague of his went to teach in Ghana. Like his mother, he served others at home and abroad. He left his lucrative job as a tool and die maker for one of the three automobile industries to become a special education teacher of *socially and emotionally maladjusted boys* (categorized today as *emotionally impaired*). Sometimes in the summers, he had to return to the factory in order to provide for his family of eight children, but he remained committed to the art and science of teaching his "boys." My dad mastered the skill of teaching children to read and so I grew up feeling that he could teach anyone to read. His focus was on social justice as much as it was on preaching and teaching the gospel. Rev. Green served his community by providing tutoring for children in reading and also by paying a professional musician to teach youths to play musical instruments. In 1972, he started a daycare center, which expanded to include all grades through eight; the school has always been known for its high academic achievement.

Rev. Green's work abroad started in Haiti and later extended to countries in Africa, South America, and the Caribbean. As a public school educator, he was always most concerned about the education, housing, and healthcare of children around the world. He financed the building of schools and orphanages. He even funded the building of a clinic in Liberia. He purchased land for farming so that the school children could be properly fed. He provided funds to build churches in several countries as well as at home. To date, with the support of his local church, Rev. Green has given approximately one million

---

1. Glenda Williams Goodson, *Royalty Unveiled: Women Trailblazers in Church of God In Christ International Mission 1920–1970* (Lancaster, TX: HCM, 2011), 85, 123, 240–41.

dollars to help the widows, orphans, and the poor around the world. Not normally one to become emotional, his tears flowed when my dad recounted an experience in the Democratic Republic of Congo. For several years, he travelled to this country with lifetime missionaries, Mother Mary Beth Kennedy and her husband, the late Rev. Charles Kennedy. In the villages, Mother Kennedy would give the children a vitamin to prevent blindness, along with a peanut, and a jellybean. The children's delight over such a small treat gained tremendous significance when my dad recounted the incident in the context of the abundance in the United States, causing him to be overcome with emotion.

The founder of my denomination, Bishop Charles Harrison Mason, the son of enslaved Africans, fought to maintain the worship influences of the enslaved Africans in the Church of God in Christ. He left Arkansas Baptist College because he yearned for an experience with God that was demonstrated in the lives of the old enslaved Africans. "Mason decided that the college would be of no help in preventing the loss of slave religion's vitality because of its assimilation into the culture at large."[2] White colonizers and missionaries, and even some African Americans, condemn the culture of the enslaved African people as heathen and primitive. So in many denominations, African Americans were forced to assimilate to the worship practices of whites. The National Baptist Convention expelled Mason and his colleague C. P. Jones because they promoted Wesleyan perfectionism and slave worship practices.[3] "Rising middle-class educated blacks seeking assimilation in the majority white culture preferred European worldviews shaped by the enlightenment."[4] Mason and Jones confessing holiness or sanctification were an enigma to the holiness movement because of their ethnic values and black cultural identity. Public displays of emotions such as shouting and dancing were frowned upon by various denominations. C. H. Mason wrote a tract entitled "Should the Saints Dance?" in defense of the holy dance. Baptist and Methodist pastors preached against the use of instruments such as drums, guitars, and other instruments that are now commonplace in the worship experience of many denominations. Playing drums as a part of worship was not allowed in white churches and some African American churches as well. Mason and the saints refused to adopt this assimilationist ideology; "They did not believe acceptance by mainstream American society required the rejection of slave religious culture. They believed the ancestral culture to be rich, vital, and worthy of preservation as blacks

2. Ithiel C. Clemmons, *Bishop C. H. Mason and the Roots of the Church of God in Christ* (Bakersfield, CA: Pneuma Life Publishing, 1996), 6.

3. Ibid., 21.

4. Ibid., 21–22.

moved upward in wealth."[5] Pedrito U. Maynard-Reid cites an ordinance passed in Kingston, Jamaica to prohibit the practice of African religious traditions.[6] It was the holiness, Pentecostal, and later the Charismatic movements that allowed people to express themselves in culturally relevant ways during worship. A criticism of European missionaries has been their disregard for the culture of the people to whom they were carrying the Great Commission. Not only was there a disregard for the social justice of converts but some missionaries attempted to denigrate the culture of the converts because they considered it inferior and pagan. And thus their converts were forced to adopt the western culture.

The Church of God in Christ was an interracial denomination like the Azusa Street Revival where Bishop Mason received the baptism of the Holy Spirit.[7] This 1906 revival was a series of religious services lasting three and a half years where the outpouring of the Holy Spirit was manifested by speaking in tongues and other gifts of the Holy Spirit such as miracles of healings, interpretation of tongues, and prophecy. The impetus for this spiritual phenomenon was the preaching about the baptism of the Holy Spirit with the evidence of speaking in tongues by William Seymour, pastor of a holiness church. The services were moved to an old abandoned and dilapidated building at 312 Azusa Street in Los Angeles, California when it outgrew its facilities due to the national and later international attention. At its inception, Azusa was interracial, ecumenical, and interreligious.[8] Charles Fox Parham, who taught William Seymour about the "glossolalia" or speaking in tongues, vehemently objected to the races worshipping together in a way that he perceived as animistic. Parham, known for his racist views, sought to persuade whites away from Azusa Street. So Seymour's dream of integrated Pentecostalism was not sustained.

Mason was determined to maintain the slave religious worship, and so he would not allow whites to modify or transform it. The Assemblies of God organized as an Anglo denomination and seceded from the Church of God in Christ in 1914.[9] Despite the fact that the members of the Church of God in

5. Ibid., 34.

6. Pedrito U. Maynard-Reid, *Diverse Worship: African-American, Caribbean & Hispanic Perspectives* (Downers Grove, IL: InterVarsity, 2000), 116–17.

7. C. Eric Lincoln and Lawrence H. Mamiya, *The Black Church in the African American Experience* (Durham, NC: Duke University Press, 1990), 81.

8. Walter J. Hollenweger, *Pentecostalism: Origins and Developments Worldwide* (Peabody, MA: Hendrickson, 1997), 19–20.

9. Vinson Synan, *The Holiness-Pentecostal Tradition: Charismatic Movements in the Twentieth Century* (Grand Rapids: Eerdmans, 1997), 126.

Christ initially came from the lowest economic strata of people in the United States, it is considered to be the largest holiness Pentecostal denomination in the world today. So as a youth growing up, I did not fit in because I belonged to a "sanctified" church. As an undergraduate, I can recall using sociological factors to determine my social class, and then I proceeded to write a paper about it as a course assignment. Even though my parents were educated, our ethnic background and the fact that I was not an Episcopalian or Presbyterian greatly reduced my socioeconomic position. The social status of sanctified or holiness denominations were ranked at the bottom of the social ladder. "Holiness, spiritual encounter/empowerment, and prophetic social consciousness, rooted in Slave Religion and preserved in black holiness-Pentecostalism"[10] was the worldview bequeathed to me by William Seymour and Bishop Charles Harrison Mason.

It was this worldview lived out by my grandmother, my father, and Bishop Mason that propelled me into my experiences as a short-term missionary coordinator for Youth on a Mission (YOAM), an auxiliary of the International Department of Missions, for the Church of God in Christ (COGIC). Bishop Carlis L. Moody, the president of missions, founded YOAM to provide an opportunity primarily for youths to learn about the role of a missionary and to fill the void left by the decline of long-term missionaries. Therefore, each summer for two weeks, teams composed of youths and adults travel abroad. We have travelled to countries in Africa, South America, Caribbean islands, and Asia. YOAM carries out five ministries. During our stay, team members along with the nationals[11] provide what is called Vacation Bible School. Training for the adults or leaders on requested topics is led by the adults on the team. Team members assist skilled laborers by getting water for cement, carrying bricks, and painting for construction projects. The hospitality ministry distributes the supplies and clothing that we take. Evangelism may be going door to door, or an indoor or an outdoor service. We also have a medical ministry that provides minimal care, workshops about health, and prayer for each person that comes for medical attention.

Six hours of training is required prior to YOAM participation. One of the required texts is *Ministering Cross-Culturally: An Incarnational Model for Personal Relationships*.[12] The authors, Sherwood G. Lingenfelter and Marvin K.

---

10. Clemmons, *Bishop C. H. Mason*, 57.

11. I use the term *nationals* to refer to the indigenous citizens of a country; it provides a more positive connotation.

12. Sherwood G. Lingenfelter and Marvin K. Mayers, *Ministering Cross-Culturally: An Incarnational Model for Personal Relationships*, 2nd ed. (Grand Rapids: Baker Academic, 2003).

Mayers, emphasize the importance of analyzing one's value differences or biases resulting from one's cultural background and then the need to modify one's behavior in order to effectively develop cross-cultural relationships in ministry. Responses are given to various statements to determine one's orientation toward time and event, dichotomistic and holistic thinking, crisis and non-crisis, task and person, status and achievement focus, and concealment of vulnerability and willingness to expose vulnerability. I am more oriented to time rather than event and task more than person, so over the years I have modified my orientations in order to be more effective on my job as an educator and in my role on the mission field. Jesus is our perfect example and the book provides many examples about how Jesus was able to minister effectively in every situation.

Dr. Lingenfelter lived on Yap, a small island in the western Caroline Islands of Micronesia, for two years to collect research for his doctoral dissertation. He preferred to live on an isolated section of the beach with an exquisite view, as would most middle-class Americans, but a national urged him to live among the people if he wanted to learn their language and their culture. Therefore wherever possible we live within the community we are serving. Sometimes we live in the homes of people who are not Christians. Establishing relationships with the nationals is critical to spreading the gospel. Following two trips to Cuba, Cuban nationals of our denomination were complimented by their government officials because we stayed in the town of Caimito rather than in Havana, the capital, like the other missionary groups. We experienced what it is like to have the water turned off while showering each morning. The town barber accepted Jesus as his Savior after the men on the team went to him for haircuts and befriended him by discussing topics of interest to him.

One of the criticisms of some Euro-Western missionaries is that they are afraid to venture outside of capital cities where they feel safe. Instead these missionaries require the nationals to come to a warehouse in the city where supplies are stored for distribution. In most underdeveloped countries, the nationals do not have transportation and so getting to the city is an arduous task. Our most recent mission trip required that we sleep in the "bush" for two nights on a dirt floor in a home that had no running water or electricity and the toilet was an outhouse. Mission trips should not afford us the opportunity to stay in a five-star hotel. Some people have asked me if such trips are dangerous, and I reply that I live in an urban city (Detroit) with a notorious reputation. I took a team to Liberia during civil unrest, and we were detained at the Ivory Coast and Liberian border by the military who were murderers, rapists, and thugs. Hours later they released us as we took pictures together with the guards.

We are no longer blind to poverty and social injustices around the world. While working with the street children in Jinja, Uganda, we noticed their dirt-encrusted feet and so we washed their feet, massaged their feet with lotion, and then gave them new flip-flops to wear. We saw children's hearts, hardened by the circumstances of life, soften when the love of Jesus Christ was exemplified through us. Some of the children had been maimed by shopkeepers for stealing. During the second week in the village of Mpigi, Uganda, team members shampooed and treated the scalp of children at an orphanage and school due to the proliferation of ringworm. We were shocked when we discovered that children who were the size of five year olds were really twelve years old but malnutrition had resulted in their delayed physical development. Our mission was more than preaching and teaching, but attending to the healthcare and other physical needs of the children. Our medical team served at the community clinic for several days training the staff to use equipment and the birthing kits that we provided. In this village and others, a few miles from the capital of Kampala, there is no running water or electricity. Part of our team was working in Buyala, a neighboring village, to assist with building a facility for a church and school. One day I went to check on the progress of that team and my daughter Carla insisted that I see the community well. As I carefully struggled down a rocky hill, I was thinking of the first-class well built by the American Red Cross that was near the mission station where we stayed several years ago in Manolu (Monolu), Liberia. I was shocked to discover nothing more than a "mud hole" that the entire community used to get water for cooking, bathing, and even for building the church. For several days that team ate the most delicious meals cooked by the pastor's wife with water she carried from that hole. On the last day as we left the orphanage, school, and church complex, we were moved to tears as the children dropped their heads and cried due to the bond of love that had been formed between us in one week. The children of Uganda were no longer invisible or nonexistent to us, but they had become our children.

Our love for the people allows us to hug them even though they may be infectious. Carla has been traveling with us on mission trips since she was eleven months old. Despite warnings from my pastor and the bishop not to take her, she has made twenty-two trips with my husband, the team, and me and she has experienced diarrhea only once. After a layover in South Africa on the way to Malawi several years ago, we attended church services where my daughter held babies and hugged the children. From across the church I smiled as I observed her. Several weeks later after arriving home, she commented on the fact that everyone at Pastor Vincent Matthews's church had malaria, tuberculosis, or was HIV positive. Pastor Matthews and his family went to Johannesburg, South Africa as resident missionaries and he was later assigned as pastor when the founding pastor died. Later, Carla developed a cough and mentioned that maybe she had TB. Tests at the hospital proved negative but that experience has never deterred her from "loving on" the children and the adults that we encounter regardless of their appearance or state of health.

In other countries, the injustices against poor children are sometimes more blatant than in our native land. For example, one summer immediately after we left Sao Paulo, Brazil, street children were shot to death by off-duty police officers on the steps of a cathedral, a supposed place of safety and refuge. This was the merchants' method of "pest control" because the children beg their clientele for money. Another summer while in the Dominican Republic, I observed a pre-adolescent girl dressed in an eye-catching red lace dress, matching socks, and an "Easter" hat strolling dejectedly along the beach across from the motel where we were staying in a poor section of the country, and the beach was filthy with debris. The young girl seemed so out of place that I mentioned it to my husband. How naive of me not to recognize a child that was a part of the sex trade! In most of these inhuman actions against children there is a response from secular organizations but rarely an outcry from the religious community.

These and numerous other experiences have given those who go on short-term missionary trips—and me—a broader perspective of the work that God has called us to do. The elevation of the Great Commission above the issue of social justice and love was never an issue for me because of the caution of hanging ones' faith on a single scripture. We are warned about taking Scripture out of context rather than looking at the Word of God as a whole. Throughout the Old Testament, especially in the prophetical books, God punished both the Israelites and foreign nations for their failure to care for the poor, widows, orphans, and the stranger. A recent study of Amos 2:1-16 reinvigorated me about my responsibility to the less fortunate. God, according to the prophet, allowed his chosen people to be taken into exile because of their injustices to the poor. God sentenced the Israelites for selling the just and poor for the cost of a pair of sandals (2:6). Their treatment of the poor was equivalent to horrendous physical abuse (2:7). The wealthy Israelites charged exorbitant taxes on the food purchased by the poor to finance their lavish lifestyles (6:4-6). Micah also records such injustices of leaders against the poor by using the imagery of cannibalism (3:9-11a). First Isaiah in his message to Judah directs them to defend the fatherless and to plead for the widows (1:17). The Old Testament is clear about God's hatred of the social abuse of the poor, widows, and the orphans.

Even in the New Testament, the expectations are the same for us to care for the disenfranchised and the downtrodden. In Matt. 25:31-46, individuals of all nations are told to depart from Jesus into eternal damnation because they did not feed the hungry; they did not give drink to the thirsty; they did not welcome the stranger; they did not give clothing to the naked; they did not visit the sick and those in prison. When we fail to take care of the least of humanity, we fail those with whom Jesus identifies. This passage of scripture, referred to as the works of love, is in the same book as the scripture called the Great Commission, yet somehow greater emphasis is given to the Great Commission than to taking care of the less fortunate. The role of the church is not just to preach and teach the gospel but to embody the love of Jesus Christ by exemplifying acts of charity known as *diakonia*.[13] Love is the foundation for all scripture, for Jesus responded to the lawyer that the greatest commandment was to love the Lord God with all your heart, soul, and mind and to love your neighborhood as yourself (Matt. 22:35-40).

I have three recommendations for all Christians, but especially to African American Christians, because we must accept our responsibility for carrying out the mandate of Matt. 25:32-40 rather than perpetuate the negative impact of the Great Commission. First, we must refocus the message of the church. To refocus the message of the church would be to study and to deliver a series of messages about the position of God and his son Jesus as it relates to social justice for the poor and needy. Messages from the Major and Minor Prophets provide volumes to preach about on this issue. The church will preach about the miracles of Elijah and Elisha, but rarely is the social justice message of the other prophets preached. The message of the church must be that God holds us accountable to significantly impact and alleviate poverty, as we preach the gospel.

Second, we can involve people in projects locally and internationally that will provide immediate help to people. There are numerous ways in which the church can support projects, initiatives, and institutions to improve the plight of the marginalized and disenfranchised people in their communities and beyond. The first step is to analyze the gifts of the church membership and then identify how the gifts match the needs of those in their community. Years ago, as a public school principal, I challenged pastors to adopt the local school and support it. At one school, the pastor and congregation of the church (across the street from the school) served the school in numerous ways based on the talents of its members. Some members served as tutors for students that were

---

13. Ulrich Luz, *Matthew: A Commentary*, Hermenia, vol 3. *Matthew 21–28* (Minneapolis: Fortress Press, 2005), 268.

having academic difficulties. This church gave holiday baskets to needy families of our students and funds to subsidized school projects to increase student achievement.

Churches can provide financial support for schools, orphanages, pastors, and villages in remote parts of the world. One resident missionary to Haiti for eighteen years, and who is now retired from the field, returns to Haiti several times a year. Her latest project is to ask churches to sew dresses from pillowcases for orphans. She prayed for one thousand dresses and in a few months she has been given over 1,500 beautifully decorated garments. Public education is not free in some countries and though the fee may seem minimal to us, many parents in underdeveloped countries cannot afford even a few dollars a month to educate their children. One teen, after participating as a YOAM team member, has joined with several non-profit organizations to assist projects in Africa. One project is the African Library Project that has a book drive for an elementary library in Swaziland. The other project called Building Hope Project is supporting forty-six students by paying for their tuition, uniforms, and meals. These students attend Kirra Primary School in Jinja, Uganda where we provided health workshops for the entire student body when we served there. A friend, who has served as a short-term missionary to several countries, recently sent me pictures of a boys and girls lavatory built out of cement from funds raised from several churches. The "before" picture was of tattered cloths draped for privacy. Another YOAM team member after our trip to Malawi has formed a non-profit and returned to Malawi to establish a birthing center after observing women delivering babies on the floor. She continues to return to this country to provide assistance to various projects based on the needs that she sees. In addition to medical care, she finances the purchase of bicycles for pastors who travel great distances preaching the gospel and caring for their congregations. Also, her non-profit funds the building of boreholes (less sophisticated wells) in remote villages. A past YOAM team member travels to Malawi to monitor whether such projects are completely properly. Adopt-a-child and feeding programs are critical to the survival of children in non-western countries. I visited a school with seventy-eight students in a remote village where the forty orphans receive only two meals a week.

Short-term missionary trips are incredible for exposing youths and adults to the service aspect of the Great Commission rather than the exploitation that has been practiced by many missionaries. A description of the components for short-term missionary trips was given in the earlier part of this essay. I went on several trips and was trained before I was given the responsibility of taking a group. Several people from past teams now serve as our church representatives in various countries. Two others serve fulltime as resident missionaries, one in Brazil and the other a family in Johannesburg, South Africa. One young man in his twenties, a year after our trip to Trinidad, went to serve several months in Cape Town, South Africa *under the supervision of an indigenous pastor.* This young man is preparing to return to South Africa and serve as a resident missionary for one year.

My third recommendation is that we must engage in politics that will change the laws and hold institutions responsible that contribute to poverty and social injustice throughout the world. More strategic steps must be taken to remedy the poverty at home and around the world. Thomas W. Pogge cites statistics from the Human Development reports produced by the United Nations Development Programme about the severity of global poverty: "Out of a total of 6.2 billion human beings (2002), some 799 million are malnourished; more than 880 million lack accesses to basic health services, 1 billion are without adequate shelter, 1.1 billion without access to safe drinking water, 2 billion without electricity, and 2.4 billion without access to basic sanitation."[14] Many churches and organizations have provided financial support to build schools and orphanages in underdeveloped countries but the instability of the governments negates the help that is given. According to Dr. Melba Maggay, "Besides relief and development, we need to engage in politics, recompose power elites, restructure social arrangements, and engage in advocacy on behalf of those who cannot speak for themselves [those who are silenced] (Proverbs 31:8-9)."[15]

Our denomination had established a viable work in Liberia that was significantly reduced by the end of Charles Taylor's presidency when many of our members barely escaped death by fleeing to surrounding countries. Western powers have exploited many countries and the leaders of the countries have colluded with various world powers to keep their own people marginalized. For example, in 1984, I visited a rubber plantation established in 1926 by Firestone Tire and Rubber Company that became the largest rubber plantation in the world. On this site hundreds of employees live in what some people would consider substandard housing. In 1992, President Charles Taylor protected Firestone for $2 million a year. Few Liberians have benefited from the rubber industry while American citizens have become millionaires from the production of rubber and other industries that resulted from the production

14. Thomas W. Pogge, "Human Rights and Human Responsibilities," in *Global Responsibilities: Who Must Deliver on Human Rights?*, ed. Andrew Kuper (New York: Routledge, 2005), 3–36 (3–4).

15. Melba Maggey, "To Respond to Human Need by Loving Service," in *Mission in the 21st Century: Exploring the Five Marks of Global Mission,* ed. Andrew Walls and Cathy Ross (Maryknoll, NY: Orbis Books, 2008), 46–52 (50).

of rubber. In the documentary, *Iron Ladies of Liberia*, current president Ellen Johnson Sirleaf disclosed the struggles in trying to establish her country with financial support from China and only promises from the United States.[16] However, United States politics prevailed by dispatching the United States Marines who arrived August 2003 in Monrovia on the day that Mr. Taylor had planned to massacre thousands of Liberians as he exited the capital. In 2012, Charles Taylor was tried and convicted of heinous and brutal war crimes against people of Sierra Leone and was sentenced to fifty years.

Christians must become activists and more vocal about the injustice of poverty in our own communities than about same-sex marriage and abortion. Is there an outrage that the United States has the largest prison system in the world?[17] Is there an outrage that there is a direct correlation between education and incarceration and that the growth in spending on corrections was 2.5 times greater than on education?[18] At the age of eight or nine, minority children—especially our males—are relegated to a life in prison because many educational institutions do not prepare teachers to teach them to read.[19] Public education is being dismantled across our nation, and the education is turned over to those who wish to make a profit at the expense of poor and minority children. There are schools funded by tax dollars that only teach our children reading and mathematics even though careers of the future require science, technology, and engineering.[20] Due to the grim statistics about the ranking of the US education in these subjects, President Barack Obama has set STEM (science, technology, engineering, and science) as a priority for teacher recruitment and training and student learning.[21] In my state of Michigan, some lawmakers are attempting to pass legislation to overturn the world language

16. *Iron Ladies of Liberia,* directed by Daniel Junge and Siatta Scott Johnson, produced by Henry Ansbacher and Jonathan Stack (New York: Just Media and Gabriel Films, 2007). This program was produced by Just Media and Gabriel Films, which are solely responsible for its content.It was aired on PBS by Independent Lens.

17. Adam Liptak, "U.S. Prison Population Dwarfs that of Other Nations," *The New York Times,* April 23, 2008, http://www.nytimes.com/2008/04/23/world/americas/23iht-23prison.12253738.html.

18. Bruce Western, Vincent Schiraldi, and Jason Ziedenberg, *Education and Incarceration* (Washington, DC: Justice Policy Institute, 2003), 4, http://www.prisonpolicy.org/scans/jpi/EducationandIncarceration1.pdf.

19. Louisa C. Moats, "Teaching Reading is Rocket Science: What Expert Teachers of Reading Should Know and Be Able To Do," *American Federation of Teachers,* (Washington, DC: AFT Teachers, 1999), 7, 28, http://www.aft.org/pdfs/teachers/rocketscience0304.pdf.

20. The information is based on a telephone conversation I had with a management company of charter schools and a conversation on a flight from Baltimore with a teacher teaching ninth grade biology in a charter school in Baltimore, Maryland.

requirement because Americans do not need to learn another language. Yet most telephone operators for customer service are not native English speakers because in almost any other country children quickly learn to speak more than one language. States had representatives to serve on a committee to develop common core standards so that academic expectations and student learning would be consistent across the country in order to raise academic achievement in English language arts and mathematics for our nation that is failing miserably in comparison to top performing nations. However, some lawmakers are also attempting to pass legislation to prevent the implementation of the Common Core Standards.[22] The lack of quality education and the incarceration of the poor are social justice issues that Christians must address politically. Members of our churches should be engaged in effectively turning the tide on such travesties at home and comparable issues in other countries.

According to Peter Singer, the question is not whether we are responsible for those in poverty, but the question is how can we best serve them? Singer dialogues with Andrew Kuper about the responsibility of morally ethical people. Singer feels that Americans should give part of their income to help the poor.[23] Kuper's position is to work through organizations to reduce poverty.[24] The church needs to be actively involved in this discussion. In the book of Acts, members of the early church sold their possessions and shared with those in the community who had need (Acts 2:44-45). How many of us as Christians are willing to forsake some of our luxurious living and share with others? To have a napkin to wipe ones face or hands at a meal is a luxury in all poor countries. Safe water, electricity, three meals a day, adequate clothing, an indoor toilet,

21. ". . . Leadership tomorrow depends on how we educate our students today—especially in science, technology, engineering and math."— President Barack Obama, September 16, 2010. The US ranks twenty-fifth in mathematics andseventeenth in science among industrialized nations. "Science, Technology, Engineering and Math: Education for Global Leadership," http://www.ed.gov/sites/default/files/stem-overview.pdf.

22. "The Common Core State Standards provide a consistent, clear understanding of what students are expected to learn, so teachers and parents know what they need to do to help them. The standards are designed to be robust and relevant to the real world, reflecting the knowledge and skills that our young people need for success in college and careers. With American students fully prepared for the future, our communities will be best positioned to compete successfully in the global economy." "Common Core State Standards," National Governors Association Center for Best Practices, Council of Chief State School Officers (Washington, DC, 2010).

23. Peter Singer, "Poverty, Facts, and Political Philosophies: A Debate with Andrew Kuper," in *Global Responsibilities: Who Must Deliver on Human Rights?*, 173–84 (179).

24. Andrew Kuper, "Global Poverty Relief: More Than Charity," in *Global Responsibilities: Who Must Deliver on Human Rights?*, 155–72 (161).

and toilet paper are luxuries in undeveloped countries (as in places in North America), yet they are so common place in the United States that we take them for granted. Unbelievers cannot see Christ in us if we are not willing to love them by assisting them and being advocates for them. I have to repent when I sometimes fret about how much my husband and I have sacrificed financially in our calling as missionaries. However, God has made us stewards over what he has given us and our needs have always been met as we helped others. One of my grandmother's favorite scriptures was Proverbs 19:17, "whoever is kind to the poor lends to the Lord, and will be repaid in full" (NRSV). So the worldview that my grandmother, my father, and Bishop Mason have imparted to me has impacted my interpretation of the Great Commission.

Index of Subjects and Names

Index of Biblical References

EXTRA-BIBLICAL LITERATURE